Making
Motherhood
Work

CAITLYN COLLINS

———

Making Motherhood Work

How Women Manage Careers and Caregiving

PRINCETON UNIVERSITY PRESS

PRINCETON AND OXFORD

Published by Princeton University Press
41 William Street, Princeton, New Jersey 08540
6 Oxford Street, Woodstock, Oxfordshire OX20 1TR

press.princeton.edu

LCCN 2018944494
First paperback edition, with Discussion Questions, 2020
Paperback ISBN 9780691202402
Cloth ISBN 9780691178851

British Library Cataloging-in-Publication Data is available

Editorial: Meagan Levinson, Samantha Nader, and Jacqueline Delaney
Production Editorial: Natalie Baan
Text Design: Leslie Flis
Jacket/Cover Design: Emily Weigel
Production: Erin Suydam
Publicity: Julia Haav
Copyeditor: Lynn Worth

Jacket/Cover image © Getty Images

This book has been composed in Arno with Electra and Gotham display

Printed in the United States of America

To my mother, with all my love,
and the sincere hope that one day employers
will stop kicking trash cans across their offices when
women announce their pregnancies.

Contents

Preface

Your opponents would love you to believe that it's hopeless, that you have no power, that there's no reason to act,
that you can't win.

Hope is a gift you don't have to surrender, a power you
don't have to throw away.

Hope just means another world might be possible, not
promised, not guaranteed.

Together we are very powerful, and [. . .] yes, we can
change the world because we have many times before. We
need a litany, a rosary, a sutra, a mantra, a war chant of our
victories. The past is set in daylight, and it can become a
torch we can carry into the night that is the future.

—REBECCA SOLNIT, 2016 (EXCERPTS)

Let's be joyful warriors.

—KAMALA HARRIS, 2018

Alyson had always been a morning person. But the early hours assumed
greater meaning once she entered the professional world after college.
Nestled in the predawn darkness, Alyson savored her time moving slowly
at home, sipping coffee, watching the news, as if the world had yet to
wake up. The quiet was restorative albeit fleeting. For Alyson, these
morning rites were necessary preparation for the onslaught awaiting her
at work.

At work there wasn't time for coffee. In fact, coffee was discouraged. Alyson's boss advised her firmly not to drink anything at all. Restroom breaks were unwelcome in corporate sales and marketing. Lunch breaks were always with clients. So Alyson traversed high-stakes meetings, calls, and presentations at breakneck speed without interruption. Perfectly poised, ever-smiling, she found the need to be "on" all day exhilarating, but also exhausting.

In her early thirties, Alyson's morning rituals took on new significance once she married, gave birth to two daughters, and ascended the corporate ladder rung by hard-fought rung. Her need for rest became all the more pressing as downtime became more rare. She wasn't alone anymore for her predawn routines, though now she welcomed the company. Her older daughter, a toddler, arose and joined her each morning, wiggling sleepy-eyed into Alyson's lap as she applied her makeup sitting cross-legged in a long velvet robe at a low table. The *Today Show* with Katie Couric was always on in the background. It was dark outside, like before, quiet, peaceful, and intimate. This was Alyson's favorite part of the day. Before too long, her makeup routine was over and the day's rush began. She whisked her girls to daycare or into the hands of a nanny so she could get to work.

Alyson and her husband both worked long hours in jobs they loved. She cobbled together an impressive, frenetic, and ever-shifting network of caregivers for her daughters over the years. A team of babysitters, nannies, friends, neighbors, daycares, before- and after-school activities, sports, and summer camps kept her girls safe and busy until she arrived home. None of these solutions stuck for longer than a year. Some lasted only a few days or a week. Even then, babysitters fell ill and daycares closed for the day. The only remaining option was for Alyson to take her girls to work. They slept in red and yellow sleeping bags in the corner of her early boardroom meetings, much to her supervisors' dismay.

Alyson counseled her daughters from a young age about the importance of work for women and the obstacles they would likely face in their careers—especially if they decided to have kids. When her boss first learned that she was pregnant, he requisitioned Alyson's largest client markets, effectively demoting her and imposing a sizeable pay cut. Once she became a mother, Alyson endured colleagues' impatience when one of her kids ran a fever and she had to leave work unexpectedly. Vacations were a fiction. Although by day Alyson commanded roomfuls of men in suits, she felt frantic, overwhelmed, and inadequate—particularly after a nanny called in sick or a daycare worker admonished her for showing up late to retrieve her girls.

Alyson got divorced a few years later when her children were in elementary school, and she juggled work and single parenting for a time. Then she reached a breaking point and quit her job. She never returned to work full time, deciding instead to take a consulting position that paid far less and lacked benefits but gave her the flexibility to work from home, attend school events, and chaperone field trips. After "opting out" of an ambitious career, Alyson's goals centered on providing her daughters the loving presence of their mother, now that she had time to give. The cost, of course, was her own aspirations. In the years after, she often longed for the stability of that career ladder beneath her feet, and the recognition, pride, and sense of identity that often accompanied good jobs like hers. When two decades later Alyson tried to return to her career, employers considered her obsolete.

I offer this book by way of thanks to Alyson, my mother. To all mothers, really. It's with a sense of radical hope—an outlook I learned from her—that I believe a different, better world is possible: one that values the effort mothers devote to raising their children, too often at great personal sacrifice. Alyson deserved a world that was kinder, more egalitarian, and more just. And our family had it better than most. Poor mothers face predicaments that are far more dire.

The stories recounted in this book entreat us to forge a new path that more fairly and adequately supports women's caring labor, and encourages men to share equally in this labor at home. In the chapters that follow, I explore how middle-class working mothers manage careers and caregiving in Sweden, Germany, Italy, and the United States—four countries with very different social policies and cultures—in order to understand what they want and need to reduce their work-family conflict. We need a legion of "joyful warriors" to create the better, more loving future my mother and all women and families deserve.

Acknowledgments

No topic of conversation is at once more ordinary and more essential than the state of our work and family lives. We talk constantly about how things are going at home, what's new on the job. But it's rare to divulge to others the more intimate, messy parts of our lives and livelihoods—even to our closest friends and loved ones. Yet I find myself in the business of asking folks to sit down and share precisely these experiences with me, a total stranger. Remarkably, people agree, time and again. As a result, I get to share the stories of 135 women making motherhood work in its many incarnations—some heartening, some heartrending, often both. To these women: your insights are an extraordinary gift. Thank you.

Countless friends, acquaintances, and strangers extended their social networks on my behalf during fieldwork. I thank each of them for helping me find places to live, make friends, recruit participants, meet with local experts, and secure visiting researcher positions.

I am grateful beyond words to Christine Williams, whose tireless efforts and enthusiasm made this study a reality. From my early days as a graduate student at the University of Texas at Austin when you insisted that I should disagree with you more to recent animated discussions in this book's final stages, your mentoring means the world. You push me to be more critical and creative, to speak my mind, and to stand my ground. I'm fortunate to be your student, now and always.

My other dissertation committee members—Jennifer Glass, Cynthia Osborne, Becky Pettit, and Sharmila Rudrappa—were crucial in my intellectual development. Thank you for your wisdom and guidance. UT's Sociology Department is full of wonderful faculty who enriched my learning more than they could know: Ben Carrington, Shannon Cavanagh, Rob Crosnoe, Daniel Fridman, Gloria González-López, Ken-Hou

Lin, Tetyana Pudrovska, Kelly Raley, Mary Rose, Harel Shapira, and Debra Umberson.

Thanks, especially, to Javier Auyero. Your teaching and friendship made me a better writer and thinker. I often remind myself of your advice to suspend doubt, catch fire, and shine brightly—words for every academic to live by. I'm proud to have been a member of the Urban Ethnography Lab at UT. My thanks to those who shaped my thinking and writing about qualitative research by sharing their own works-in-progress and to those who commented on my proposals and drafts over the years. Ethnography Lab pioneers Nino Bariola (whose close reading of the book at a late stage was invaluable), Jacinto Cuvi, Jorge Derpic, Katherine Jensen, and Marcos Pérez were allies, confidantes, and good, true friends throughout.

Beyond UT, I appreciate fruitful conversations about this project with Irene Boeckmann, Liz Chiarello, Clayton Childress, Catherine Connell, Marianne Cooper, Sarah Damaske, Myra Marx Ferree, Elizabeth Hirsh, Michelle Janning, Erin Kelly, Sasha Killewald, Wendy Manning, Cynthia Miller-Idriss, Kumiko Nemoto, Shira Offer, David Pedulla, Aliya Rao, Liana Sayer, Jeremy Schulz, Pamela Stone, Esther Sullivan, and Wei-hsin Yu.

During my fieldwork, I served as a visiting researcher at the WZB (Berlin Social Science Center) in the Work and Care Research Group under Dr. Lena Hipp, in the Department of Political Science at Roma Tre University, at the Linnaeus Center for Social Policy and Family Dynamics in Europe (SPaDE) at Stockholm University, and at the Institute for Family-Focused Research and Policy Services (Familien-Forschung). European colleagues were ceaselessly kind and patient with my questions: Francesco Antonelli, Stephanie Bethmann, Leonhard Dobusch, Ann-Zofie Duvander, Torsten Engelage, Guðný Björk Eydal, Maren Haag, Lena Hipp, Nadiya Kelle, Mauro Migliavacca, Gerda Neyer, Debora Niermann, Rense Nieuwenhuis, Leopoldo Nuti, Livia Oláh, Lydia-Maria Ouart, Daniel Ritter, Tina Rostgaard, Erich Stutzer, and Elizabeth Thomson.

Caterina Biffis, Allan and Mimi Fallow (now my in-laws!), Kate King and Pedro Ivo, Anna Salvo, and Mario Schwarz put a roof over my head and served as local sounding boards during my fieldwork. Kate, my fiercely feminist friend, came to visit me in Germany, Italy, and Sweden and became a mother herself as I wrote this book.

Ann Lamott wrote once, "Almost all good writing begins with terrible first efforts." All writers know this, but not all writers have the good fortune of an exceptional team of minds to help coax unfortunate early drafts into something much better: Kate Averett, Kristine Kilanski, Megan Tobias Neely, and Katherine Sobering were steadfast supports in graduate school and remain so across three time zones.

I owe my gratitude to every faculty member of the Department of Sociology at Washington University in St. Louis: Tim Bartley, David Cunningham, Steve Fazzari, Cynthia Feliciano, Odis Johnson, Hedwig Lee, John Robinson, Jake Rosenfeld, Ariela Schachter, and Adia Harvey Wingfield. Adia, David, and Jake provided guidance about the publishing process based on experiences with their own stellar books. Koji Chavez and Patrick Denice kept me laughing daily. Candace Hall lent a knowing ear time and again. Thanks for your encouragement during the revision and publication process. I'm lucky to call you my colleagues. My students also motivate me daily to share what I learn in accessible, engaging ways. Undergraduate assistants Sydney Curtis, Rachel Hellman, and Ellie Zimmerman have been outstanding. I admire and appreciate the support of professors Marion Crain, Adrienne Davis, and Mary Ann Dzuback, who serve as role models at Washington University for what thriving academic careers as feminists can look like.

My editor, Meagan Levinson, at Princeton University Press responded with enthusiasm from the get-go and reminded me I had a story that mattered and that women wanted to hear. The end product is far better as a result of her discerning eye. PUP's all-star, all-woman team— Natalie Baan, Jacqueline Delaney, Julia Haav, Debra Liese, Samantha Nader, and Erin Suydam—worked seamlessly behind the scenes to shepherd this book into being. Feedback from reviewers at Princeton and Oxford University Press improved the book immeasurably. Allison Pugh, in particular, shared her linguistic talent and thoughtful reflections.

I received generous financial support for this research from the National Science Foundation (#1434863), American Association of University Women, European Union, German Academic Exchange Service (Deutscher Akademischer Austauschdienst), Swedish Council of America, Work and Family Researchers Network, Washington University in St. Louis, and the Department of Sociology, Center for Women's and Gender Studies, Urban Ethnography Lab, Center for European Studies, and College of Liberal Arts at the University of Texas at Austin.

There's no friend like a sister. Maggie dares me to be authentic in every endeavor and ensures that I never take myself or my work too seriously. And my dear friend Kate Nelsen has been by my side for eighteen years. Other abiding friendships buoy my spirits daily: Amy and Xander Barnes, Derek Burton, Rachel Ellis, Jeff and Jessica Graham, Jordan and Taylor Kuiper, Theo Martinucci, Ashley Mueller and Cheyne Sorensen, Caleb and Danielle Roca, Anna Romans, Gopi Shah and Jake Schuchman, Laura and Ryan Shock, Emily Titterton and Brian Keats, Catherine Thornton, Josefin Thorslund, and Angie, Chris, and Luca Toriggino. Chosen family is a thing, and you are mine.

My mom, Alyson, and my stepdad, Brock, taught me what a kind and loving home looks like. Though I wish you hadn't needed to, you sacrificed more than I can know to ensure that your four kids were happy, healthy, and able to pursue their wayward dreams. Parents like you shouldn't have to choose between your own aspirations and your kids'. But you did, and you chose ours. My grandmother, Martha Jane, the archetype of a 1950s suburban housewife and mother, made similar sacrifices that she's only just coming to terms with today, half a century later. This book implores us to give families the time and resources they need for all members to live the lives they want. Your child-rearing was herculean. Here's hoping that families one day get more support than you did. Thank you for all of it.

It may be poor advice to suggest that all graduate students adopt a dog, but really, I know of no better comfort. Flapjack kept me levelheaded through many months of writing, and years later, he remains a treasure on the tenure track.

And, finally, to Bennett. You encourage me to walk my talk every day by forging a fulfilling life both at work and at home—a task sometimes easier said than done. Thank you for coaxing me out of the office each evening for long walks and bike rides, homemade meals, and conversations that had nothing to do with sociology. You're the model of a feminist partner, and you'll make an awesome feminist dad. It's the honor of my life to walk this path with you. Thank you for crossing oceans every year to share this adventure with me. Here's to many more. I love you beyond belief.

Making
Motherhood
Work

———

CHAPTER 1

SOS

Let's face it: it's harder to be a working mother in the United States than in any other country in the developed world. The US has the least generous benefits, the lowest public commitment to caregiving, the greatest time squeeze on parents, the highest wage gap between employed men and women, and the highest maternal and child poverty rates. Alongside Papua New Guinea, it is one of two countries on the planet without federally mandated paid maternity leave. It is the only industrialized nation with no minimum standard for vacation and sick days. Most US companies don't offer any policies to support the caregiving responsibilities of their workers.[1]

It's no exaggeration to say that women's work-family conflict is a national crisis. Seventy percent of US mothers with children under age eighteen work outside the home. Most work full time.[2] Yet women still complete the lion's share of child-rearing and housework, which means that moms work a "second shift" after their regular workday ends.[3] Mothers are overwhelmed. Their partners know it. Their kids know it. So do their colleagues, employers, relatives, and friends. And the crisis transcends boundaries of race, class, region, and religion.

The great news is that it doesn't have to be this way. Alternatives to the seemingly intractable hardships that women with children face do exist. This book pushes the work-family debate across national borders to discuss policy solutions to mothers' overwhelm. I draw on wisdom gleaned from five years of conversations with 135 employed mothers in Sweden, Germany, Italy, and the United States to understand what they believe helps and hinders their work-family conflict. I identify what other countries are doing right—and wrong—in trying to resolve women's struggles.

Mothers' tribulations are central to this book. But this is not a chronicle of their despair. Their stories call us to action. Women's work-family conflict perpetually dominates the pages and airwaves of US media outlets. Each election cycle features heated debates about work-family supports. Yet folks in the States have seen little in the way of policy reform after elections end. The truth is that mothers in the US are drowning in stress. To be sure, moms with more resources can keep their heads a bit higher above the floodwaters than those with less capital to marshal in times of need. But no woman escapes the deluge entirely.

This begs the question: Why has the US done so little to support parents? The truth is, it's not an accident. And it's not the case everywhere in the world. Historians and sociologists teach us that the United States was founded on the ethos of individualism.[4] Today, the belief in personal responsibility is woven into the fabric of our country through our welfare state provisioning.[5] We can think of welfare states as "interventions by the state in civil society to alter social and market forces."[6] The US welfare state centers on the liberal belief that the market provides for citizens' welfare; the state should intervene only when the market fails. This free-market approach means that adults are encouraged to work and to find private solutions for child-rearing and housework.

The principle of personal responsibility is central to American society, and it underlies the country's social policies. The US is one of the few nations with no mention of the word "family" in its constitution.[7] Unlike most industrialized countries, it has no federal body dedicated specifically to family issues.[8] The country has no explicit national family policy. The federal government doesn't have any universal programs for work and family provisions, and it doesn't require employers to provide them. The limited policies available (mostly cash and in-kind transfer programs), what those in the US call welfare, are generally available only to the country's poorest.[9]

The message here is this: if you have a family, it's your job and yours alone to support it. Economist Nancy Folbre contends that US culture views having children as a lifestyle choice, much like having a pet. If you don't have the time or money to care for a pet, or a child, you shouldn't have one.[10] This line of reasoning meshes well with the tenets of individualism and principles of free-market capitalism.[11] But of course pets and children aren't the same. Children provide crucial benefits as future workers and taxpayers. We don't rely on pets to one day become our teachers, post office employees, doctors, and garbage collectors. Raising children well is in a country's collective best interest. And yet US society leaves parents, mostly mothers, on their own to accomplish this herculean goal that benefits everyone. Sociologists Michelle Budig and Paula England call this America's "free-rider problem."

The United States' privatized approach also exacerbates inequalities among workers. A few elite employers elect to offer helpful work-family policies, so only some privileged workers (typically highly educated, salaried employees) have access to these supports. The most vulnerable, oftentimes hourly workers—those most in need of support—are the least likely to have access to work-family benefits. Today, for instance, businesses offer paid family leave to just 14 percent of the civilian workforce—primarily white, male professional and managerial workers who are employed at large companies.[12] The highest income earners in the US are three and a half times more likely to have access to paid family leave than those with the lowest incomes.[13] Many millions of people in the US are forced to make do without work-family policy supports because their employers don't offer these benefits.[14] These days, Americans tend to believe work-family conflict is inevitable. And, following the discourse of personal responsibility, people in the US think women can resolve their stress—they just need to try a little harder to strike the balance so they can "have it all."

Mothers' work-family conflict is *not* an inevitable feature of contemporary life. And it's not the fault of women. Moms in the US are trying their best to resolve this conflict on their own. And it's easier for some than others, given the race and class inequalities that stratify society. But moms are at their wits' end. This privatized model is failing all women with children, women who numbered 85.4 million according to a 2012 US Census Bureau estimate.[15]

US senator Kamala Harris suggests that it's futile to brood in "depression and anger and anxiety" about the country's inequalities: "I'm done with that. I don't like that feeling, I don't think any of us do." Her suggestion? "We have to be joyful warriors."[16] Take up the gauntlet, Senator Harris argued: "I say we go in fighting with our chins up and our shoulders back, knowing that this is about fighting for the best of who we are."[17]

I couldn't agree more. We need to find a better way to organize work and family life. Can we envision a country in which *all* parents have access to the work-family policies they clearly need? What if we gave families a helping hand rather than collectively feeling resigned or pointing fingers at mothers? I'm optimistic. Folks in the United States are now thinking and talking about workplace supports for families. Work-family initiatives are front and center in the country's public debates, which were unlikely to make headlines at the turn of the twenty-first century. Now that politicians are talking about these issues, it's time to push them for real, lasting change.

But what would it look like to extend a helping hand to women and families? Rather than turning to firm-level solutions to work-family conflict, we can look to other countries for answers. The US doesn't need to start from scratch to envision a better, kinder, more just world. Different countries offer various roadmaps given their diverse histories of policy supports for employment and parenthood.[18] Policies like paid maternity leave have been available to the entire labor force in many European countries for decades. Some US scholars have pointed to Europe as a "gender-equality nirvana," often drawing policy "lessons from abroad" to try to improve women's status in the US.[19]

Surprisingly, there's been no systematic comparative study of *how women think about and experience work-family policies* to date. When pundits discuss European social policy on the evening news, rarely do audiences learn more than the basics about a policy's provisions. It's uncommon to hear more than soundbites from a handful of mothers, fathers, or policymakers. Sometimes those interested in expanding US work-family supports tend to idealize the offerings available in Europe and assume that they are uniform. There's a sense of yearning that, across the Atlantic at least, another world is possible. But we lack an understanding of how mothers in Europe perceive these policies in their day-to-day lives. Without these insights, how can we really learn from

European experiences? Transforming life for American women and families will take more than a sense of longing. It requires knowledge and insights gleaned straight from the source: we need European *and* American mothers in the conversation. Otherwise, policies intended to help moms may turn out to be idealistic, patronizing, and ineffective. This book shows what women themselves think they need to lead healthy, happy lives at work and at home.

All Western capitalist countries are facing the collision between new social and economic realities and traditional conceptions of gender relations in work and family life. The conventional breadwinner/homemaker model is now largely outdated, given that two-thirds of all mothers work for pay outside the home in the industrialized West today.[20] Different welfare states have responded with varying social and labor market policies to reconcile the modern puzzle of how to divide the responsibility for economic production and the social reproduction of child-rearing. Each arrangement creates a very different picture for mothers who work outside the home while raising children.

What are the day-to-day experiences of working mothers in countries that have offered very different policy solutions to work-family conflict and gender inequality? Such benefits include paid parental leave, affordable universal childcare and health care, part-time and flexible work schedules, vacation and sick day provisions, and cash allowances to parents, among others. In Germany, for instance, parental leave is offered for up to three years and used primarily by women, whereas in Sweden parental leave is largely gender neutral and more moderate in length. What lengths of leave do women prefer after having a baby? Part-time schedules are common in Germany, but less so in Italy and Sweden. How do women feel about part-time work in each context?

This book investigates how women in Europe and the US perceive and experience motherhood and employment in light of the policies available to them. I consider what we can learn from European countries in trying to resolve US mothers' work-family conflict. And since no nation is yet truly a gender-equality "nirvana," even the much-lauded Nordic countries, I reflect on what European countries may continue to learn from one another as they amend their policy provisions.

To understand what life is like under the main welfare state regimes of the industrialized West—divergent routes on the policy roadmap—I turned directly to mothers themselves to get their perspective on how motherhood works in different policy contexts.[21] Listening to women's voices, to what they have to say about their daily lives, their deeply personal struggles, and their opinions of what they need to be happier and healthier, is the best way to craft solutions to gendered social problems that seem intransigent. By gaining firsthand knowledge of how working mothers combine paid work with child-rearing in countries with diverse policy supports, I expose the promises and the limits of work-family policy for easing mothers' stress.

Work-family conflict is the product of public policies and cultural attitudes that must change if we are to improve the lives of mothers and their families. In other words, context matters. Moms don't work and raise their children in isolation, devoid or somehow outside of society, culture, history, and the political and legal structures they reside in day-to-day. Women with children inhabit what I call *lifeworlds of motherhood*—the distinctive social universe of individual experiences, interactions, organizations, and institutions shaping the employment and child-rearing possibilities that women can envision for themselves.[22] What mothers want and expect in their work and family lives is confined by their lifeworld—from the largest federal policies and dominant societal beliefs about women, men, families, and work, to the structure of jobs, to the minutiae of everyday dealings with partners, friends, relatives, children, and coworkers. I focus on mothers because in all industrialized nations, mothers have historically been the targets of work-family policies, they are still responsible for most housework and childcare, they report greater work-family conflict than men, and they use work-family policies more often than men.[23]

I argue that it's time to abandon the goal of *work-family balance*. Framing work-family conflict as a problem of imbalance is an overly individualized way to conceive of a nation of mothers engulfed in stress, and it doesn't take into account how institutions contribute to this stress. Instead, I issue a rallying cry for a movement centered on *work-family justice*. This change in phrasing matters because it *politicizes our understanding of mothers' stress and socializes the responsibility for solving it*. US society has long told moms that their work-family conflict is their fault and their problem to solve, which ignores the broader context of their lifeworld. Striving for balance is a highly personal, inadequate solution to a social problem that impacts every corner of society. Everyone needs care. What we need now is for society to value caregiving, as well as the people who provide that care.[24] And not just lip service about how great and important and honorable the labor of caregiving is: it means little as a country to praise families as the bedrock of the nation if we fail to reinforce these values with the material and financial supports that families need to care for one another. The rest of the industrialized world has already reached consensus on this. The US lags far behind.

Championing the cause of work-family justice requires approaching US society as a collective. To achieve *work-family justice* is to *create a system in which each member of society has the opportunity and power to fully participate in both paid work and family care*. The rhetoric of justice highlights the reality that this conflict is not the outcome of individual women's shortcomings or mismanaged commitments but rather the result of cultural attitudes and policies embedded in workplaces and systems of welfare provisioning. Indeed, work-family conflict, like all social problems, "doesn't reflect some unalterable law of nature; it reflects the existing social organization of power."[25] Put simply, mothers don't need balance. They need justice.

Sociologist Erik Olin Wright contends that, "While we live in a social world that generates harms, we also have the capacity to imagine alternative worlds where such harms are absent."[26] He calls these alternative worlds "real utopias"—viable, emancipatory alternatives to dominant institutions and social structures. In the right circumstances, Wright argues, utopian visions can become powerful collective ideas to motivate political movements. The movement for work-family justice is one such opportunity.

Across the countries where I conducted interviews, one desire remained constant among mothers. Women wanted to feel that they were able to combine paid employment and child-rearing in a way that seemed equitable and didn't disadvantage them at home or at work. Moms need the safety and confidence that come with social supports—at home, in their friendship groups, among their colleagues, with their supervisors, in their firms, and from the federal government. The pursuit of work-family justice means ensuring that every woman has access to support when she needs it, regardless of her income, education, race, or marital or immigration status. Men, too. These social policies are fundamentals, no-brainers. It's time for the United States to build a stronger safety net that meets the needs of *all* mothers, and, by extension, their families.

───

Let's start by considering what we already know about the role of the government in shaping gender relations. In the United States, opportunities in the public sphere appear gender-neutral. For instance, men and women can pursue any jobs they please. No one is legally barred from rising to the highest office in the US because of their gender. In these ways, the US is far ahead of the curve. One hundred countries still impose restrictions on the types of jobs in which women can work. Married women in seventeen nations are still obliged by law to obey their husbands. Thirty-one countries have laws that designate men as heads of household.[27]

Starting in childhood, we learn what appropriate gender behavior looks like as it relates to caregiving, housework, and paid labor. These messages rely on cultural beliefs and stereotypes about who women and men are, what they are good and bad at, and what they are capable of. The state itself is one key source of these messages: governments produce gendered subjects by the way they distribute responsibilities, entitlements, and protections to women and men.[28]

By implementing different types of work-family policies, states reflect and reinforce gender ideologies that are bound up in each state's specific history and culture.[29] These decisions are indicative of a state's "gender regime,"[30] normative beliefs about masculinity and femininity that reflect what is "right" and "proper" for women and men when it comes to paid work and unpaid caregiving.[31] Take maternity and paternity leave, for instance. Italy requires that women take five months' maternity leave surrounding childbirth at 80 percent pay. Until 2013, fathers had no mandatory paternity leave whatsoever. In 2013, the Italian government implemented a one-day compulsory paternity leave at 100 percent pay. They've since quadrupled it to four days. For Italian parents, the message is crystal clear about who "should" care for children.[32]

Laws are powerful symbols: they delineate a social consensus about what is right and wrong, which shapes people's moral judgments and actions.[33] Research by social psychologists demonstrates that majority opinion influences people's individual beliefs and behaviors.[34] For example, professors Catherine Albiston, Shelley Correll, and their colleagues found that implementing family-friendly laws and organizational policies like paid family leave for mothers and fathers can reduce longstanding gender biases in workplaces that disadvantage mothers.[35] Family leave policy signals to employees that caregiving is valued, which decreases stigma for those who typically provide this care. Work-family policies thus shape the way women and men act and are expected to act, and citizens learn to govern themselves in accordance with collective cultural beliefs.[36]

Given the government's role in shaping gender relations, some scholars suggest that Western welfare states can implement "women-friendly" policies to increase women's labor force participation and reduce gender inequalities.[37] At the same time, others argue that unintended consequences of these policies may create substantial trade-offs in reducing inequality—referred to as "welfare paradoxes"—that simply shuffle improvement and disadvantage around among citizens. In a 2006 study of twenty-two industrialized countries, Hadas Mandel and Moshe Semyonov found that, on the one hand, welfare states with progressive social policies enable more women to work, which we know boosts women's economic independence and strengthens their power at home and in society. Although this is heartening, the downside is that women tend to work in positions associated with lower pay and prestige.

Working women are underrepresented in managerial occupations and overrepresented in female-typed jobs such as teaching and nursing that pay less than other similarly skilled occupations.[38] In other words, the same policies that promote one dimension of gender equality seem to inhibit another dimension. Mandel and Semyonov's study highlights the potential drawbacks of seemingly forward-thinking social policies. Bear in mind, though, that welfare state interventions may be aimed at producing more equality among a country's citizens, but they may not. Other goals may take precedence, such as increasing a country's fertility or employment rate.

Work-family policies contain different assumptions about women's place in society and can aid or impede the larger project of gender equality depending on the context in which they are enacted, the cultural attitudes about women's employment, and the constellation of policies available in a given country.[39] Different policies thus tend to serve different purposes: subsidized childcare, for example, serves to encourage women's labor force participation, while long maternity leaves and sizeable cash allowances encourage mothers to commit themselves mainly to the home while raising young children.[40]

By exploring women's experiences with work-family policy in different countries that represent archetypal approaches to Western welfare provisioning, this book expands our understanding of how states use gendered strategies to govern populations, giving us greater insight into the relationship between the state and gender inequality. How women perceive, use, and resist the policies available to them can illuminate how states define and enforce ideologies about women's "proper" place at home and in the labor market. Although work-family conflict might seem like a personal, private difficulty, I highlight the profoundly political nature of these experiences. Mothers' difficulties working and raising children are part of a broader politics—a power struggle. If mothers' difficulties are political in origin, then surely part of the solution to their struggles must be political as well.

Because work-family policies are an important source of gendered messages for citizens that can inhibit or enhance gender inequality (or sometimes both), it's important that we understand the influence of these policies on mothers in their jobs and in their family lives. The past decade has seen a surge of quantitative research on cross-national work-family policy as countries strive to improve their fertility rates and women's rates of employment.[41] These studies show that work-family policies can be both a help and a hindrance to women. Policies like flex time, telecommuting, and reduced hours enhance mothers' engagement in paid work by giving them less incentive to leave work altogether. This labor force continuity is vital because it prevents the "downward spiral" that happens when women leave work due to family obligations.[42] Publicly funded or subsidized childcare, paid leave for parents of sick children, part-time work with full benefits, and paid maternity leave make it easier for women to stay employed in many countries.[43]

Sociologists Jerry Jacobs and Kathleen Gerson remind us, however, that many of these same policies "threaten to recreate earlier forms of gender inequality in a new form."[44] We know that mothers' employment tends to be lower in places with expansive child benefits and under systems of joint taxation in which married couples file their income as a single tax unit (particularly large benefits accrue for one-earner couples under joint taxation given the higher marginal tax rates for secondary earners, usually women).[45] When women take advantage of policies such as reduced hours and lengthy maternity leave, they are likely to increase their share of cleaning, cooking, laundry, and childcare in the home.[46] Work-family policy use may also result in less accrued employment experience, fewer working hours, discontinuities in career trajectories, and reduced wages, all of which can damage women's lifetime earnings and occupational attainment compared to men.[47]

Research across twenty Western countries shows that women who use accommodations like maternity leave are sometimes viewed as less invested in their jobs, and supervisors may be less willing to hire or promote them for positions that require extensive training or qualification periods or for high-status and managerial jobs. This in turn means women are less able to compete with men for these high-paying positions.[48] In another cross-national study of twenty-one industrialized countries, sociologists Becky Pettit and Jennifer Hook found that part-time work—a benefit used overwhelmingly by women—enhances women's labor force participation but also tends to reduce career mobility and widen the gender wage gap, lending further evidence to the welfare paradox argument noted earlier.[49] Other family-friendly policies like flexhours and home office accommodations mean that women put in less "face-time" in the workplace and are often considered to be on the "mommy track," which is problematic in working environments that seek devoted workers who are fully committed to the job.[50] These policies may thus be a double-edged sword depending on the context in which they are enacted and used by working mothers.

These international comparisons of work-family policies have given us a good understanding of the various policy structures as well as their outcomes.[51] However, this research is almost all survey- or census-based. It lacks the voices of working mothers, which means we are missing a crucial piece of the puzzle. We need an understanding of how policies are translated on the ground in mothers' lifeworlds. I will show that policies do not necessarily achieve their intended outcome because there is a mediation process. Mothers use, reject, grapple with, and bend policies in ways that lawmakers can't fully predict. I examine how working mothers configure their own lives in light of what they perceive as their options, and how these policies work as both constraints and opportunities.

Let's return to the US context again for a moment, where extensive interviews and ethnographic research have documented the untenable bind that working mothers feel today in trying to live up to impossibly high standards at work and at home.[52] Societal ideologies about motherhood draw on "cultural schemas"—the shared cultural models through which we see, understand, and evaluate our social reality. These schemas shape women's opinions and behaviors.[53] Mothers in the US face pressure to perform "intensive mothering"—that is, motherhood and marriage should be women's primary, all-absorbing commitment. This cultural ideal stipulates that women find meaning, creativity, and fulfillment in caring for a husband and children who are fragile and in need of a mother's loving care. Fathers are thought to lack the nurturing skills necessary to adequately care for a child.

For decades, this meant that women, and white women in particular, were expected to be stay-at-home mothers and housewives. However, African American and other racial/ethnic minority women were and are expected to work for pay as well as care for their families. The legacy of slavery in the US has meant that African American women have always worked outside the home.[54] Sociologist Dawn Dow found in interviews with African American middle- and upper-middle-class employed mothers that being a working mom was considered normal and natural. Staying home would be a deviation from society's cultural expectations.[55] The intensive mothering model, also referred to as the "family devotion schema,"[56] "concerted cultivation,"[57] or the "cult of domesticity,"[58] tends to privilege white, middle-class, heterosexual couples with children.[59]

The family devotion model competes with a second, equally persistent schema: that of work devotion.[60] Also called the "ideal worker" model,[61] this schema suggests that employees' primary emotional allegiance and time commitment should be to their jobs, which reward them with independence, status, and gratification. The belief of the ideal worker pervades modern workplaces, working systematically to advantage men and disadvantage women.[62]

The prevailing constraints of American workplaces conflict with those that prevail in American family life. Pamela Stone's study of the "opt out revolution" among elite, well-educated mothers demonstrated that the immense cultural pressures for mothers to enact an ideal worker role were so great and so deeply entrenched that women in the 1990s and 2000s left advanced careers in droves and blamed themselves rather than their employers for their seeming inability to adequately manage their work and family commitments.[63] Stone's research debunked the myth that women "choose" to leave their jobs. She argued that they are actually pushed out of the workplace as a result of inflexible policies, institutional barriers, and a system that punishes rather than rewards women for trying to balance their work and home lives.

Sociologist Mary Blair-Loy calls these tensions "competing devotions."[64] Women who are committed to their careers but take too much time away for their family are thought to violate the work devotion schema, while those who avoid or delegate their familial commitments violate the family devotion schema. This bind is the origin of work-family conflict for mothers. Poor women also face work-family conflict, but they are less able than middle- and upper-class women to marshal their resources or adapt their job schedules to address the "routine unpredictabilities" of work and family life.[65]

Although work-family conflict may appear to be a personal or individual predicament for women, Blair-Loy argues that it's in fact bound up in powerful moral and cultural understandings of what it means to be a good worker and a good mother, and what makes life worthwhile.[66] This clash of normative decisions takes a formidable toll on mothers. It shapes the gender division of labor at home and scheduling, corporate ideologies, and promotion patterns and evaluation standards at work.[67] But whether they decide to work or stay at home, both middle- and working-class women explain their decisions about employment through the lens of family. In fact, women of all social classes cast their job choices as doing what's best for their families.[68]

These studies have focused on women's voices to portray the difficulties that working mothers face. But they are specific to the United States. In recent decades, interview research with employed moms has been conducted around the world, and these studies suggest that life is no walk in the park for employed moms in any country.[69] But from the outside, life seems better and easier for moms in some places than in others. Or is it? It's hard to say because most research on the topic is siloed within countries. We need to compare and contrast women's perspectives *across* national borders. This comparison allows us to examine whether and how these cultural schemas of the ideal worker and intensive mothering play out in different policy landscapes. A cross-national comparison expands what we know about gender equality and work-family policy by investigating how working mothers' experiences vary significantly depending on context. I show how the work-family conflict described in the US literature is mitigated—or not—in countries with policies that reflect different notions of ideal workers and good mothers.

Cases of Study: Sweden, Germany, Italy, and the United States

Western industrialized countries fall into several categories of welfare state regimes according to shared principles of social welfare entitlement and homogenous outcomes. In this book, I explore the lives of women in four countries commonly used to exemplify these regimes: Sweden (social democratic), Germany (conservative), Italy (familialist), and the United States (liberal).[70]

Social democratic welfare states—including Sweden, Denmark, Norway, and Finland—are defined by the state taking full responsibility for citizen welfare regardless of fluctuations in the economy or in citizens' economic activity. Their federal governments provide universal benefits and override market principles to intervene on the behalf of citizens to promote equality. These measures buffer people from fiscal uncertainties and weaken the link between the market and life chances.

Conservative welfare states (seen in continental European countries like Germany, Austria, and France) believe the government, businesses, and other institutions all share the responsibility for citizen welfare. While they believe in the predominance of the market, they intervene on the behalf of citizens to shield them from some of the harmful aspects of overreliance on the market. A strong link exists between work position or family position and social entitlements. That is, social policy is generally tied to earnings and occupation. Families and communities are considered central providers of dependent care.[71]

Familialist welfare states like Italy, Spain, and Greece exhibit little state intervention in the welfare sphere. These states rely heavily on the informal market, particularly the extended family, to ensure citizens' wellbeing. Social protection systems are highly fragmented, and there is no specified net of minimum social protection, although some benefit levels are quite generous (such as old age pensions).

Liberal welfare states such as the US, Canada, and Australia organize social benefits to reflect and preserve the primacy of the market for ensuring citizens' well-being. Most entitlements are determined by need and are awarded only when the market fails. The provision of social support for families is privatized, and all adults are meant to participate fully in the market.

The policies offered in different welfare regimes are highly contested and change quickly.[72] The European Union (EU) has a goal of long-term integration and reconciliation of the diverse policy regimes across its member states. Different welfare regimes, through their work-family policy, promote different meanings of working motherhood. In-depth interviews illuminate how working mothers are interpellated into these systems of meaning: mothers understand their experiences of work-family conflict in and through their country's welfare state discourses.[73] These different meanings set limits on the policy reconciliation and integration currently sought by the EU.

Before delving into the stories of the mothers I spoke with, I want to zoom out briefly and paint a picture of the broad national trends regarding mothers' employment in each country. These macro-level patterns shape the micro-level experiences of the women I interviewed.[74] Employment rates for mothers differ widely across the four countries: As of 2014, 83.1 percent of mothers were employed in Sweden, compared to 69 percent in Germany, 55.2 percent in Italy, and 65.5 percent in the United States (see figure 1.1). Part-time work is far more prevalent in Germany than in the other three countries. Moms in the US are the least likely to work part time; only 12.4 percent of American mothers work a part-time schedule, while 53.1 percent work full time.

Mothers' labor force participation rates also vary depending on whether they have partners (see figure 1.2). In Sweden, single mothers' rates of employment are lower than those of partnered mothers (10.2 percentage points lower), while they are higher in Italy (11.4 percentage points higher). These differences suggest that single moms may have it easier in countries like Sweden than in Italy, where perhaps single mothers need to work to support their families.

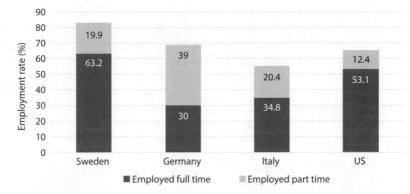

FIGURE 1.1. Employment rates for mothers (ages 15–64), with at least one child age 0–14, by full-time and part-time status, 2014. OECD 2016a; Statistics Sweden 2014. Part-time employment is defined as usual working hours of less than thirty hours per week in the main job, and full-time employment is thirty or more hours per week. Germany's data are from 2013 (the latest available). Maternal age range for Sweden is 15–74. Children's age ranges are 0–18 for Sweden and 0–17 for the US.

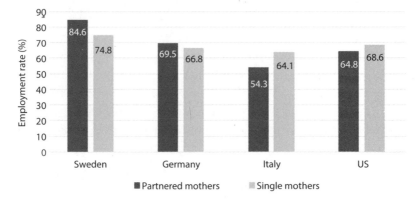

FIGURE 1.2. Employment rates for partnered and single mothers (ages 15–64) with at least one child age 0–14, 2014. OECD 2016b.

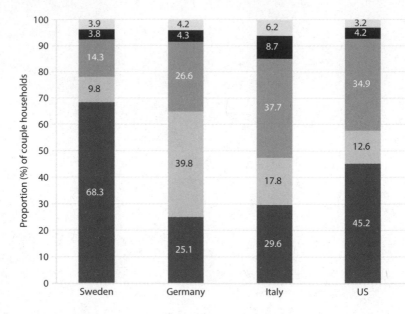

FIGURE 1.3. Patterns of employment in couple households with children ages 0–14, 2014. OECD 2016c. Data for Germany refer to 2013 (latest available). Data for the US include children ages 0–17.

For mothers living with partners, the patterns of employment within their households also differ from country to country (see figure 1.3). Households in which both adults work full time are far more common in Sweden (68.3 percent) and the US (45.2 percent) compared to Germany (25.1 percent) and Italy (29.6 percent). The "one-and-a-half earner" family model in which one partner works full time and the other works part time is most common in Germany (39.8 percent of couple households). That proportion is much smaller in the other three countries and the rarest in Sweden, where only about 10 percent of couples have one full-time worker and one who works part time. Italian and American families have the greatest proportion of households in which only one adult works—slightly over one-third of families in both countries. Only

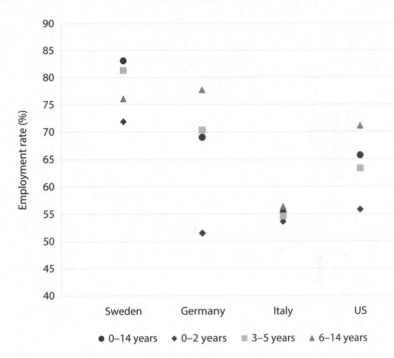

FIGURE 1.4. Employment rates for mothers by age of youngest child, 2014. OECD 2016a; Statistics Sweden 2014. For the US the age groups are 0–17, 0–2, 3–5, and 6–17.

one-quarter of German families and one-seventh of Swedish families have one breadwinner.

Their children's ages also affect mothers' rates of employment in these four countries (see figure 1.4). American and German mothers' employment tends to be affected the most, with the range of employment rates spanning from roughly 20 percent in these countries to less than 10 percent in Sweden and Italy. Employment rates are much lower for American and German mothers whose youngest child is age three or below, with only slightly more than half of mothers employed then.

Another important indicator of how well women with children are supported in the labor force is the gender pay gap. The difference in pay between women and men is much wider for mothers than for women without children in Germany and the US, and to a lesser extent in

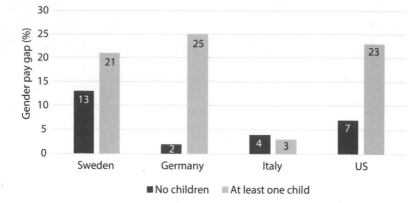

FIGURE 1.5. Gender pay gap by presence of children (women ages 25–44), 2012. OECD 2012b.

Sweden (see figure 1.5). In these countries the pay gap for women without children ranges from 2 to 13 percent, whereas the pay gap for mothers is 21 to 25 percent, indicating a large wage penalty for motherhood. Italy has virtually no motherhood penalty, only because so many women are excluded from the labor market altogether. Italy exhibits less occupational segregation and fewer glass ceiling effects because women with lower earnings are more likely to leave the labor market in that country than in many others.[75] Recall also that Italy has the lowest rate of maternal employment of the four countries, meaning that a narrower swath of mothers opt into the labor force in the first place.

Public spending on family benefits also differs drastically among the four countries (see figure 1.6). Sweden spends more than three times the amount the United States spends on family benefits, with Germany and Italy falling in between. Sweden spends 3.63 percent of its GDP on family benefits compared to 3.05 percent in Germany, 2.02 percent in Italy, and 1.19 percent in the United States. The types of benefits also differ. For instance, as a defamilialized welfare state, Sweden gives no tax breaks to families (instead prioritizing services and cash benefits), whereas the other three countries do provide family tax breaks.[76] Germany and Italy

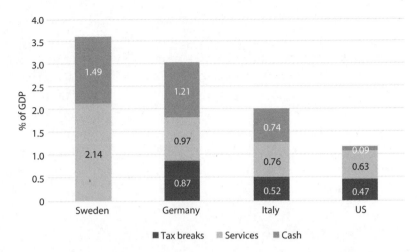

FIGURE 1.6. Public spending on family benefits in tax measures, services, and cash, in percentage of GDP, 2011. OECD 2014b. Note: Public support accounted here only concerns public support that is exclusively for families (e.g., child payments and allowances, parental leave benefits, and childcare support).

provide roughly equal proportions of tax breaks, services, and cash benefits to residents, while the US gives very little to families in the way of cash benefits.

Given these numbers, we could make claims about which country is best for working moms. But interpreting these statistics requires an understanding of *what these trends mean for working mothers on the ground in their daily lives.* Speaking to mothers themselves leads to insights we can't glean from statistics alone. Are high rates of mothers' labor force participation associated with increased or decreased work-family conflict? Does public childcare denote more or less gender equality in the eyes of working mothers? Is part-time work considered more stressful or beneficial than full-time work?

Cross-national research on work-family policy and gender and welfare states are at an impasse until we understand mothers' perceptions. American moms tend to marvel at the three-year parental leave entitlement in western Germany. Yet German mothers told me they generally despised this policy. They felt a great deal of stigma as working mothers. Some were called "career whores" to their faces. Swedish mothers expected their partners to share the responsibilities of housework and child-rearing, and they did, while most Italian women laughed at the idea, saying that their partners were incapable of helping out around the house because they were *mammoni*, immature mama's boys. American and Italian mothers often outsourced housekeeping as a way to resolve their work-family conflict, while mothers in Sweden and Germany said this practice was frowned upon—culturally, it was a sign of women's incompetence.

Studying Working Mothers

To understand women's experiences under different work-family policy regimes, I conducted in-depth interviews with 135 working moms. I was interested in what these women had to say and what this tells us about how they imagine and perceive their lifeworlds.[77] In-depth interviews allowed me to bring individual agency to conversations about work-family policy in Western countries, and to understand the interplay between the two. Women's perspectives should be central to any feminist endeavor to craft, advocate for (or against), and implement work-family policy as a force for positive social change.

I interviewed women in the capital cities of each country: Stockholm, Berlin, Rome, and Washington, DC. Because of its particular history, the case of Germany merited attention to cities in both the former East and western German regions. Reunification in 1990 brought together two different gender regimes—the male breadwinner and dual-earner models. During its forty years as a socialist welfare state, the former East Germany mandated full employment. After reunification, the East was required to adopt the conservative model of the West. The welfare framework in former East Germany today formally matches that of the conservative welfare regime, but it tends to have better provisions for workers and families because it maintains the cultural legacy and many of the social institutions supporting dual-earner families that existed under the German Democratic Republic (GDR), such as extensive housing developments and universal daycare. I therefore decided to interview women in Berlin in the former East and Stuttgart, Munich, and Heilbronn in the former West. I explore women's experiences in the two regions in chapters 3 and 4.

During our interviews, I asked women questions about navigating motherhood with a career, workplace interactions with supervisors and colleagues, work-family conflict, employment history and plans for the future, dividing family care with a partner, opinions about parenting, use and perceptions of various work-family policies, interpretations and understandings of their careers, families, successes and regrets, and general views on working mothers in each country.

For this book, I also draw on my firsthand observations of women in their homes, neighborhoods, and workplaces. I often spent time with their children, partners, relatives, neighbors, and colleagues. I stirred pots of pasta on the stove while mothers changed diapers. I drank wine with women at their favorite after-work bars. I washed soap out of a child's hair while the mother prepared dinner. I walked with mothers and their babies to pediatrician appointments. I ate cake and drank coffee in women's backyards with their friends. And I played in the sand with their children at the park.

I spent a summer in each international city for my fieldwork. These extended stints allowed me to participate in and observe the rhythms of daily life in the neighborhoods where I lived. I got to know families who lived in my apartment buildings and on my block—shopping at the corner grocery, riding the metro during rush hour, spending quiet afternoons in parks and playgrounds, and chatting with parents bringing their children to and from daycare. These firsthand observations provided helpful background for understanding the lifeworlds of my Swedish, German, and Italian interviewees. For example, when I asked a Swedish mother whether she had considered taking longer than one year of parental leave, she laughed and told me that her son would have no one to play with. Playgrounds were mostly deserted during the day since all children over age one were in daycare, "where children should be." Sure enough, I noticed only parents with newborns visited Stockholm's abundant playgrounds and parks during weekdays, but these places swelled with moms and dads accompanying young kids starting around 4 p.m. and all day on weekends.

For comparison purposes, I interviewed middle-class mothers. These women provide a conservative test of how employed moms perceive work-family conflict, because they are more likely to have the networks and means to help assuage feelings of stress or guilt, such as paying for quality childcare. Their experiences therefore constitute a best-case scenario or extreme case.[78] As sociologist Pamela Stone writes, if middle- and upper-class working mothers with social and financial capital and job stability have difficulties balancing work and family, these difficulties are akin to "the miners' canary—a frontline indication that something is seriously amiss."[79] Things are much, much harder for mothers with meager incomes, little formal education, unrewarding jobs, and unreliable or no transportation, and for people without legal residency or citizenship in the countries where they live.

Mothers' stories here are framed by racial, ethnic, and class privilege. They had greater access to sustainable employment and other resources that are often harder to obtain for working-class women and many women of color—those most in need of policy supports.[80] Ninety-eight of my 103 interviewees in Europe (all but five) were white and ethnically European. The women I spoke to in Washington, DC, were more racially and economically diverse than those I interviewed in Europe because language and sampling were smaller barriers to my recruitment efforts. Of the thirty-two women I interviewed in DC, nineteen identified as white and thirteen as racial or ethnic minorities.[81]

All women were employed when we met. They all had one or more children living at home. I interviewed middle-class women with a range of occupations, working hours, and family structures, which all impacted their abilities to manage work and family.[82] In Germany, Sweden, and Italy, I also interviewed several women living outside their countries of origin. Their perspectives are illuminating because they offer comparative insights into the country's cultural and political environment. I use their insights to help tease out variations in social norms and policy supports that may go unnoticed by women born and raised in each society. More information can be found in the methodological appendix.

This book does not include the voices of mothers who are low-income, unemployed, or have low levels of education; non-English-speaking mothers; stay-at-home mothers (whose labor force exit can be one extreme solution to work-family conflict); women without children (another solution to potential work-family conflict); and working fathers. These groups' experiences of work-family conflict are likely quite different. Cultural norms about parents' involvement in child-rearing and employment interact with work-family policies in different countries to produce a range of intended and unintended outcomes varying by race/ ethnicity, education level, socioeconomic class, and country of origin, among other factors.[83] Low-income mothers, for example, are likely to feel a lack of policy support more intensely than the women I interviewed because their options to resolve conflicts with private market solutions are more limited. Stay-at-home or unemployed mothers may feel more constrained in their options and less supported by public policies than working mothers do, because access to some work-family policies in these countries are contingent on employment. Studies with these populations are highly needed and merit attention in future research.

Moms in Sweden were the least conflicted and most content out of those I interviewed. I therefore begin with their stories. We then move successively through Germany, Italy, and finally the United States, where mothers were the most stressed and overwhelmed. This book helps readers understand that working mothers' desires and expectations regarding their jobs and family lives depend on where they live. The lifeworlds mothers inhabit are shaped by different norms about gender, parenting, and employment, and work-family policies are part of these larger cultural discourses. Overall, the most satisfied mothers I spoke with had extensive work-family policy supports and felt that prevailing cultural attitudes encouraged the combination of paid labor and caregiving for both mothers and fathers. The least satisfied mothers had to turn to market-based solutions to ameliorate their work-family conflicts, and they felt unsupported by their partners and the state in cultural environments that suggested child-rearing was women's responsibility.

Moms don't deserve to feel as if their lives are crumbling around them. No one does. Some mothers see insurmountable barriers to happier, more livable lives. And in this case, it's easy to feel hopeless—especially because these lifeworlds limit what women can even imagine as alternatives.[84]

This is where *radical hope* comes in. Hope has always been central to feminist movements and other collective efforts to improve people's lives. Renowned writer and activist Rebecca Solnit reminds us:

> For a time people liked to announce that feminism had failed, as though the project of overturning millennia of social arrangements should achieve its final victories in a few decades, or as though it had stopped. Feminism is just starting. [. . .] Things don't always change for the better, but they change, and we can play a role in that change if we act. Which is where hope comes in. [. . .] We write history with our feet and with our presence and our collective voice and vision.[85]

Let's respond to mothers' collective SOS with radical hope—the belief that our world can be different, better, and more just, if only we can envision "a future goodness that transcends the current ability to understand what it is."[86]

Radical hope may enable us to forge a stronger sense of collective responsibility. Recognizing our mutual interdependence might help transcend the tenacious creed that families are personal responsibilities and that raising children is women's domain—beliefs as American as apple pie. Like the countless many who came before us, let's choose the hard work of proceeding as joyful warriors in the movement for work-family justice. It's time to confront the wholly unnecessary difficulties facing too many women today as they work and care for their loved ones.

CHAPTER 2

Sweden

———

"IT IS EASY IN SWEDEN TO WORK AND HAVE KIDS."

Josefin is Swedish and has a master's degree in business administration. She works as a marketing manager forty hours a week in Stockholm, and she and her husband, Markus, have a three-year-old daughter and a two-month-old son. We met for our interview at a bustling café in Hornstull, a hip neighborhood teeming with young families on the western side of an island called Södermalm in central Stockholm. Her daughter was at childcare, but Josefin brought her infant son to our meeting. He slept most of the time in his stroller, waking occasionally to wave his arms, smile, and babble softly at us before his heavy eyelids closed and he teetered back into sleep. A half dozen or more mothers and fathers with strollers were seated around us meeting friends for coffee. They came and went over the course of our hour-long interview, replaced by other parents with infants and toddlers in tow.

Josefin took ten months of paid leave to be with her daughter and was in the middle of an eleven-month leave for her son when we met. Markus is a consultant and took eight months of leave when their daughter was born and planned to take the same with their son. Her responses typified the experiences of the working mothers I interviewed in Stockholm. When I asked Josefin whether any of the Swedish policies and benefits could be improved to make things better or easier for her or her family, she replied,

I really think we have really a great system. [...] I think, in general, it's very much accepted. It's in the culture that, you know, you need to be—either have flexible hours or you have to work reduced time for a couple of years when the kids are young. And that's in the policies as well, that you have the right to do that. So ... I think ... no, I think that we're pretty good.

I then asked Josefin whether she thought it was possible for women in Sweden to be successful workers and successful mothers at the same time. She answered without hesitation:

Yes, yeah. Absolutely. [...] Our whole system and all of our policies are based on the thought that you're supposed to be able to work as a woman, if you have a family. Then I think I see, you know, a lot of people who have been able to manage a family and a career.

When I conducted these interviews in 2013, the United Nations and the World Economic Forum ranked Sweden as the most gender-egalitarian nation in the world and first for women's economic opportunities. US researchers and media pundits often point to Sweden as the paragon of how women really can "have it all"—successful careers and family lives— thanks to Sweden's policy focus on gender neutrality, socialized child-care, and what sociologists call a "dual earner-carer" model for family life where women and men equally share in breadwinning and child-rearing.[1] Feminist scholars often hold up Scandinavian countries as confirmation that "governmental social policy is a productive act that can help overcome traditional gender roles and thus lead to increased justice in gender relations."[2] Sweden is also regularly used as the inspiration for other countries' social policy initiatives, and is frequently cited as the exemplar in cross-cultural studies of family regulation and gender equality.[3]

What policies attract this high level of praise from feminist scholars and produce high degrees of satisfaction among Swedish working mothers like Josefin? As the classic model of a social democratic welfare state, Sweden has a long history of intertwining family policy with gender equality policy and labor market policies. Since the 1970s the Swedish government has almost continuously reinforced a dual earner-carer model,[4] a stance supported by organized women's interests both within and outside political parties.[5] Its policies actively promote equality among citizens. Sweden conceives of family support and the task of child-rearing not as private issues, but as collective responsibilities. As a result, the Swedish government socializes the cost of child-rearing across society. In these policies, Sweden has enmeshed the aims of gender equality, the combination of work and family, and high employment rates.

Sweden's Work-Family Policy

Sweden is a Nordic country of ten million people in northern Europe bordered by Norway to the west, Finland to the east, and Denmark to the south. It has a prosperous economy and a large government sector. Sweden boasts very low poverty rates among children and single mothers thanks to its supportive policy infrastructure.[6] Astoundingly for some audiences, Swedes report high trust in their government and high satisfaction with their public institutions—including the Swedish Tax Agency (Skatteverket). In fact, the Swedish word for tax—*skatt*—also means treasure. Taxes don't have negative connotations for Swedes as they do elsewhere, even though the country is famous for its high rates of personal taxation.[7]

The country is more racially, ethnically, and religiously homogenous than the United States and among the most homogenous in Europe. Swedish economist Lars Jonung attributes the success of the Swedish welfare state to the fact that it is a "consensus society," one that is not deeply divided across political party lines. For instance, Swedes strongly agree that equality is a major goal in their society. The ability to work and support oneself is also considered a basic right.[8]

As in all countries, Swedish policies have shifted over the years as different political parties have held office and cultural attitudes have changed. But for the past several decades, the government has promoted gender equality as a cornerstone of Swedish society. Lawmakers are expected to be feminists: "For a Swedish politician to take an explicitly antifeminist position is considered politically incorrect."[9] The current administration has gone so far as to declare itself a "feminist government."[10]

The state explicitly uses work-family policy to further the goal of gender equality in the labor force and at home. The parental leave scheme is a clear example. Maternity leave has been available for many decades, but in 1974 it was replaced with a formally gender-neutral parental leave program (*föräldraledighet*), the first of its kind among Western welfare democracies to offer leave for fathers as well as mothers.[11] This legal change represented a powerful symbolic shift. Swedish sociologist Ann-Zofie Duvander suggests that the inclusion of fathers in parental leave policy signaled that parents should share the responsibility for paid work and child-rearing:

> Essentially this means that fathers should take a greater part of child responsibility by using more parental leave. This is related to children's rights to access to both parents. It is also related to gender equality in that fathers' leave facilitates women's return to and involvement in labour market work. The parental leave policy is thus related to the goals of increasing employment levels, gender equality and children's rights.[12]

Sweden is often regarded as an ideal model for parental leave policy. In 2018, Swedish parents were eligible for 480 days, or 16 months, of paid leave. This time is meant to be divided evenly, with eight months for each parent. Single parents receive all 480 days' leave. The government implemented a "use it or lose it" leave model in 1995 that reserved one month solely for each parent to encourage fathers even more explicitly to take leave. These months couldn't be transferred, so they were forfeited if either parent decided not to use them. In 2002, a second month was reserved for each parent, and in 2016, a third month was introduced— meaning each parent has an exclusive right to 90 out of the 480 leave days. Parents often refer to these leaves as "mommy months" and "daddy months." To put it differently, the Swedish government offers three months' paid leave solely for mothers, three months' paid leave solely for fathers, and ten months' paid leave to be shared between parents at their discretion. Today, some portion of this leave is used by virtually all mothers and nine in ten fathers.[13] Included in this time is women's specific right to seven weeks' leave before and seven weeks' leave after having a baby. The majority of women begin leave sometime in the month before giving birth. In Sweden, policies like parental leave apply to single parents and couples regardless of sexual orientation (though this hasn't always been the case[14]).

Parents can arrange their leave time any way they choose, but for heterosexual couples it's common for mothers to stay home for roughly the first nine months to one year of a child's life while they breast-feed, perhaps with a month of overlap with the father toward the end of their time at home (both parents can take leave simultaneously for up to a month during a child's first year, referred to as "double days"). As mothers wean their children off breast-feeding and return to work, fathers often stay home solo for the remainder of the leave before they also return to work. Children then begin public daycare, typically between ages one and two. Although the vast majority of Swedish fathers now take parental leave, it is still women who use most of the leave days. In 2012, men took about one-quarter of their families' parental leave time.[15]

Swedish law offers a lot of flexibility about the timing of when parents may use the available policies to be home with their children. Mothers and fathers can take parental leave any time until their child is eight years old, not just right after childbirth. Many parents save part of their leave to enable them to work part time, thereby extending the length of leave considerably. It's common for moms and dads to take some of their leave incrementally—for example, by going back to work three days a week and taking parental leave for the remaining two days of each week. Some families choose to have both parents work part time for a period, with the mother home with their child part of the week and the father the other part. Others use the time to extend summer vacations when their children are young. The length of leave therefore varies widely among parents because of its flexibility.[16]

This flexibility extends to leave for family members' illnesses. Parents get a "temporary parental benefit" (*tillfällig föräldrapenning*) to stay home with a sick child for up to 120 days a year until children turn twelve (remunerated at 80 percent of a parent's annual earnings, up to a limit).

These days can be used for a part or full workday. And for children with serious illnesses, there is no limit to the number of days a parent can take off work. Workers are also entitled to take paid sick leave when they fall ill. For those employed for at least one month, they get roughly 80 percent of their income for the first fourteen days of their illness. After fourteen days, the employer contacts the state, which works with the person's doctor to determine eligibility for extended sickness benefits. Unemployed or self-employed individuals receive a sickness benefit from the government.

Yet another aspect of Sweden's policy flexibility is the parents' right to reduce their working hours when children are young. Workers with children under age eight can choose to work a 75 percent schedule, or thirty hours a week, at any time (with a commensurate pay cut). Part-time work is therefore widespread among parents with young children (though less so for fathers than for mothers). As a result of these policies, women rarely leave the paid labor force when they start a family. Instead, many women choose to work "long part-time" weekly hours (over thirty hours a week) in the first couple of years of their child's life.[17]

Clear in these policies is the value placed on time away from work; this extends to vacation policy as well. Vacation time in Sweden is paid and plentiful. Workers are entitled to a minimum of twenty-five days each year. Some employees receive more as a result of union agreements. In fact, it's illegal in Sweden to negotiate a job contract without including vacation time. To take advantage of the long days of sunlight and higher temperatures that are ephemeral in Scandinavia, employees have the right to take at least four consecutive weeks off during the summer months of June to August. And if someone gets sick while on vacation, those days aren't counted against their vacation allowance.

The financial remuneration parents receive under Sweden's various work-family policies also tends to be quite generous. For example, parents are paid 80 percent of their previous earnings for the majority of parental leave. The Swedish Social Insurance Administration (Försäkringskassan) pays out the benefit, which has a maximum monthly income ceiling, meaning that wage replacement is capped for high earners. But as a result of collective bargaining agreements, many parents receive more than 80 percent of their pay while on leave from their employers to minimize their loss of income.[18] For instance, all state employees get an additional 10 percent of their income while on leave, on top of the 80 percent wage replacement rate the government provides. Unemployed parents without previous income receive a flat rate for their entire leave.

Sweden's self-proclaimed feminist government even put its money where its mouth was in order to strengthen the gender equality dimension of its leave policy. Between 2008 and 2016, it awarded a "gender equality bonus" (*jämställdhetsbonus*) to give mothers and fathers the incentive to split leave time more evenly (whether they were married or living together). Because Sweden still has a gender wage gap, women's lower earnings are often used to justify why mothers take the majority of leave. A family's income loss is usually larger when the father takes leave compared to when the mother does. So the bonus was meant to largely cover this loss (especially for low- and middle-income families). The bonus nearly eliminated the purely financial reasons why a mother might use most of the leave, thereby encouraging parents to divide the leave more equitably.[19] Swedes take pride in their country as a world leader in gender equality and parental leave policy.

Swedes are also proud of their public childcare system. Sweden consistently tops the charts of best early childhood education and care programs. Municipalities provide preschool and school-age childcare with a strong focus on education for all children ages one to twelve. Current debates about childcare in Sweden today center not on whether it is suitable for children to attend, but on when they should begin.[20] In 2014, roughly 50 percent of children ages zero to two attended daycare, as did 95 percent of children ages three to five.[21] Childcare workers are well educated; all Swedish childcare center staff are trained to work with children.[22] Childcare services are increasingly offered in the evenings and on weekends to accommodate parents who work during these times.

This childcare system is considered exemplary in part because of its affordability. For Swedish families, childcare costs are a fraction of those in other countries. The cost of care for parents is income-related up to a low ceiling, and the government sets a general maximum rate. Low-income families pay nothing at all for their children to attend daycare.

The maximum rate is 1,287 Swedish kronor per month (US$160). Parents' fees cover roughly 11 percent of the cost of childcare and the state pays the rest. The Swedish government spends more on subsidizing preschool services than it does on its defense budget.

In another effort to alleviate the costs of child-rearing, the government also gives parents a monthly "child allowance" (*barnbidrag*) for each child. Until children reach age sixteen, their parents receive this flat-rate benefit—currently 1,050 Swedish kronor (US$132)—per child per month. *Barnbidrag* was instituted in 1948 after concerns over a decade of declining birth rates. On top of the child allowance, if families have more than one child they also receive an "extra family supplement" (*flerbarnstillägg*) depending on the number of children they have.

Child-rearing isn't the only costly, time-intensive aspect of maintaining family life: basic housekeeping tasks are also necessary. In 2007, a tax deduction of 50 percent of the cost of household services was made available. This deduction had two goals. First, it aimed to create a private formal market for these services, which elevates the status of the workers who provide them. It also meant to assist families with two parents working full time. Covered services include cleaning, cooking, gardening, childcare at home, and help with children's homework, among others.

From 2008 to 2016, the government also provided financial benefits to parents who chose not to send their children to public daycare and instead wanted to extend their parental leave time. A law was passed in 2008 allowing municipalities to offer cash for childcare benefits. Called a "child home care allowance" (*vårdnadsbidrag*), this benefit amounted to a government payment of roughly US$400 a month, tax-exempt, for one parent to stay home with their preschool-age child. This legislation was touted as allowing more individual choice and pluralistic solutions for families. But the law was criticized for encouraging a continued traditional division of household labor and marginalizing mothers—particularly immigrant mothers—in the labor market.[23] Opposition called it a "housewife trap." The benefit was abolished in 2016.[24]

Taken together, these supports help explain the country's high fertility rate, women's labor force participation rates, which are nearly equal to men's, and low rate of childhood poverty.[25] Still, full gender equality has not been reached. The gender equity issues that concern Swedish policymakers today are the persistence of occupational sex segregation, women's greater use than men of reduced working hours after childbirth and longer parental leave, and the gender wage gap.[26]

To outsiders, Sweden's work-family policy offerings look fantastic on paper. Chelsea, an American mother living in DC whom we'll meet in chapter 6, told me wistfully, "I wish I lived in a country that had a year off for maternity leave. When I was pregnant with [my son], I was reading all that stuff, like, 'Why don't we live in Sweden?!'" But how do *Swedish women* feel about these policies? Are the policies perceived in the same glowing terms?

The Universality of Working Motherhood

Employed mothers in Sweden felt very little work-family conflict. Women believed they were highly supported by these policies and did not feel at all stigmatized for working outside the home while raising children. In fact, they considered being a working mother a universal experience. The women I interviewed were satisfied with their dual roles. They didn't express guilt or tension between their work and family responsibilities. Instead, women insisted that being a mother and having a job were compatible and complementary identities.

An indicator of this thorough integration of work and family life for Swedish women was the fact that several moms stopped me, seemed confused, or even laughed when I used the term "working mother." Lisa, a married Swedish mother of two who works as an urban planner, echoed a sentiment I heard often in Stockholm. We sat on her sunny backyard patio as the daylight stretched long into the evening. Lisa and I sipped on cucumber water and talked while her husband, Erik, played inside with their sons, whose laughter filtered out into the yard from time to time. Lisa looked at me with confusion when I referred to her as a working mother: "I don't think that expression exists in Swedish. [...] Because it's—I mean, it's—you can't be anything else [...] it's not like there's sort of a 'non-working mother.' Of course she [any mother] is working, I mean, what else would she do?" Lisa said with a laugh. "That's sort of an abnormality if you stayed home. I don't think I've met anyone that has been 'stay-at-home mothers.' [...] Everyone is working."

Swedish moms like Lisa seemed to struggle to put their thoughts into words when it came to the term "working mother" and to the question of whether they had ever considered being a stay-at-home mom. During interviews, comments on this topic were accompanied by stutters, pauses, furrowed and raised brows, pursed lips, and usually laughter and head-shaking at the thought of leaving paid work long term to raise kids.

Women's sense of confusion about the prospect of staying home aligns with countrywide statistics. According to the International Social Survey Programme's study Family and Changing Gender Roles, less than one-half of 1 percent of Swedish women reported being housewives in 2012. Only 3.1 percent of women and 9.3 percent of men believed that a man's job is to earn money while a woman's job is to look after the home and family. Similarly, a scant 8 percent of women thought mothers should stay at home when they have a child under school age. Less than 1 percent of Swedish women (0.8 percent) thought mothers should stay at home after children began school.[27]

I asked every woman I spoke with whether she had considered being a stay-at-home mother, and not one said yes. Camilla is Swedish; she and her husband, Elias, are both lawyers. They have two young children. We met at her spacious flat south of the city center while she was on maternity leave. Camilla was typical in her quick reply to my question: "No. No, I don't think there's an option. I don't know that anyone in our generation has ever thought that. No." She seemed adamant. We sat on the sofa in her living room—a space that looked like the home of two lawyers, and also a very typical Scandinavian-style home: white, sparse, and tidy. Camilla glanced down at her four-month-old son bouncing on her lap and then back up at me, explaining: "If someone would think that—if someone was planning that or if someone is a housewife I guess you would ask, 'Is she religious or is she very, very rich?' You know? It's very, very uncommon." I tried to press the issue a little further and asked Camilla whether she personally knew any women who stayed at home with their children. But I only got so far as "Do you know any-body who is a—" before she cut me off with a firm "No." She laughed and repeated: "No." "No?" I replied, surprised. "Everybody you know has a job?" Camilla nodded and said yes.

Even when pressed, only three of the twenty-five women I interviewed could think of any woman who was a stay-at-home mom in any of their social networks, however distant. These three women each knew someone whose partner worked in a very high-paying job, usually for an international company. Moreover, because Sweden is a highly secular country (only 5.6 percent of Swedes report being active members of a church organization[28]), Camilla's questioning whether a stay-at-home mom is religious is likely a reference to immigrants, who tend to be more religious and have lower levels of employment than native-born Swedish women.[29] Being a housewife was strange and unappealing to Camilla, whether for financial, religious, or cultural reasons—she seemed to think it was a life that few women would choose if given the option.

When I asked about the ubiquity of mothers working outside the home, my interviewees pointed explicitly to the country's policies and their interplay with cultural attitudes. Ida, who is Swedish, divorced, and works full time for a government agency, explained to me:

> They have built a system that makes it possible for women to work. So, I think it's a double situation, because since they want us to work they have arranged for it to be possible. So, of course, it's healthy. I think it would be more difficult, actually, to live in a country where it's not so proper for women to work, where you have to fight for going out, if you have the tradition of being a housewife [at] home with the kids, where you have no system whatsoever to—you have to have a private nanny or something, it would cost a fortune. [...] But, [here] it's a totally different system. They [the government] want me out [working], they give me the opportunity to do so.

Ida believed the Swedish government purposefully created a system that normalized and facilitated working motherhood in order to encourage women's labor force participation. She appreciated this arrangement. Ida told me, "I think we are raised in that way—it is possible to make a career as a woman, a real career, your own career." The median age for my

Swedish respondents was thirty-six, meaning that most were born in the mid-1970s. Ida was forty-four when we spoke, born in 1969. Those were times of substantial politicization around the issue of gender equality in Sweden both for women and for men. This wasn't always the case: until the early 1960s, attempts at reforming traditional gender roles in Sweden were considered women's issues. Women were the primary targets of Sweden's family and social policy programs in the 1940s and '50s. But the Swedish women's movement of the early 1960s caused a shift in the debate.[30] Gender equality in the labor market was central to this movement.[31] The Swedish government introduced individual taxation in 1971, expanded the number of preschools and childcare facilities, and actively recruited women—especially housewives—into traditionally male sectors of the labor force. Social policies like those described earlier were implemented to encourage men's involvement in family life, and the Swedish government considers men central to the project of gender equality—a goal that has remained front and center for Swedes since the 1960s.[32]

Swedish women talked at length about how their mothers, who were adults during the women's movement of the '60s, encouraged them to see motherhood and employment as compatible goals. In national surveys conducted in 2012, only 6.5 percent of Swedish women reported believing that a working mother cannot establish a relationship with her children that is as warm and secure as that of a mother who does not work.[33] In Sweden, women's rights and gender equality are part of the national discourse, the result of longstanding feminist and social democratic politics.[34] Today the vast majority of Swedes (81.4 percent) believe that equal rights for women and men are an essential characteristic of democracy.[35]

Ida also acknowledged that career aspirations were especially common for women with more education and for those living in urban areas: "If you live in the city, or if you go to the university to study, you want a career. And you want to combine family life with a career. And then you just do it. And you have the system, I think, to be able to make it." Ida acknowledged that women's choices and ambitions are shaped by *what they feel is possible*. In Sweden, being a working mother is the norm.

Women in Stockholm often drew comparisons between Sweden and other countries to explain why they were so satisfied with their infrastructure of support. Ida couldn't conceive of the expense of a private nanny for her children, which she had heard was necessary in countries without a publicly subsidized daycare system. Her two children attend a low-cost public daycare like virtually all Swedish children. Josefin, introduced at the start of the chapter, is a marketing manager with a two-month-old and a three-year-old. She contrasted Swedish policy to that of the United States and reflected,

> I think the whole system here in Sweden makes it possible just to be a working mother. I—I mean I've seen and heard about how things work in the US, for example, but other countries as well, and I don't think—I mean I can't imagine going back to work when he is this age, when my son is like two or three months. I—I couldn't do that. So, I know if I lived in the US I would probably choose to stop working, at least for some time. I know that would have been, you know, not beneficial for my career, my professional development. [...] I do want to work, I don't want to stay at home for, you know, ten years of my life to take care of my kids. I mean, I really think we have really a great system.

Josefin acknowledged that her ability to pursue a career while raising kids was shaped by public policy. Her hesitation and pauses when trying to imagine returning to work with a newborn suggest how inconceivable this notion was for her. The rest of the women I spoke with in Stockholm adamantly agreed.

Pamela Stone's research on the "opt-out revolution" in the US points to the same source of conflict that Josefin and other Swedish women identified: American mothers' decisions to leave their careers and stay home with children aren't a sign of traditionalism; instead they are pushed out of the workplace as a result of inflexible policies and institutional barriers.[36] Unlike the United States, Sweden has sought to eliminate stigma and marginalization for parents in the workplace. Moms in Stockholm made it clear that this policy context enabled and normalized the combination of motherhood with employment—so much so they couldn't envision the idea of staying at home to raise children long term.

Both Swedish moms and the Swedish government espoused the belief that adult women should work full time and raise children. Mothers' goals for themselves aligned with Sweden's stated political objectives: high fertility, high labor force participation, and gender equality. The women I spoke with tended to perceive the available work-family policies in positive terms. I got the sense from their comments that they believed the Swedish government was on their side and had their best interests in mind. The mothers I interviewed thought that the government and lawmakers echoed their own desires to work and raise children free of stress.

What about the reactions of women's colleagues and supervisors? I wondered whether the working mothers I interviewed in Stockholm also felt this sense of support in their day-to-day lifeworlds at work. Did work organizations reinforce the state-level support of dual earner-carer households and the mission of gender equality? The short answer was a resounding yes among my interviewees. Women told me their interactions with coworkers and bosses were consistently supportive. They insisted they never felt disadvantaged at work for being parents. Most told me they weren't concerned about announcing their pregnancy to their boss and coworkers, and didn't fear reprisals or other repercussions.

Elise is a journalist employed part time and a single mother of a one-year-old. She brought up the topic of gender equality within the first minute of our conversation at a leafy outdoor café in the neighborhood of Hornstull. After spending several hours across a picnic table from her, I would describe Elise as talkative and opinionated. Yet when I asked how her supervisor and peers responded when she told them she was having a baby, Elise didn't have much to say. She shrugged and replied with an unconcerned air: "They were all just happy for me. He [my boss] was like, 'Great,' you know? Everyone was happy for me, because [. . .] lots of people who are working have children, obviously. And, yeah, everyone just thought it was great. So, yeah. No problem at all." To clarify, I asked, "Because there were other people who had children there, women and men?" Elise looked at me quizzically, like I was hard of hearing, and replied, "Yeah, of course some people have children. They all have careers and children, and, you know, combine family life with a career, so there's nothing strange about it." Disclosing her pregnancy didn't seem to have worried Elise because it was commonplace in her office—we will see in later chapters whether mothers in other countries felt the same way.

I was surprised that women in Stockholm seemed nonchalant about announcing their pregnancies to colleagues. Despite my best efforts, I couldn't get people to elaborate. I'd grown up hearing my own mother regale our family with the story of her boss kicking a trash can across his office when she told him she was pregnant with me thirty-some years ago. At first, I thought their reticence was due to a problem with the sequence of my interview questions. A good researcher asks questions to elicit rich answers and encourages people to share in ways they often don't in everyday life. It typically takes time for people to warm up to interviewers, especially when discussing sensitive topics. So I organized my lines of inquiry such that earlier questions served as icebreakers, while more personal questions came later in the interview (see appendix B). Given my own memories, I had decided that the question about announcing one's pregnancy at work would be an opener. Surely all mothers would have a lot to say. But in Stockholm, this question fell flat. Like Elise, most women recounted some version of the reply, "It was no problem, everyone was happy for me."

Swedish women's terse explanations were a fascinating finding in and of themselves. Their brief answers weren't the result of my inability to elicit more nuanced responses. Rather, the topic wasn't a source of concern or drama for them. For this study, I had to break from my own preconceptions about employment and motherhood in order to understand women's lifeworlds from their perspectives. I couldn't assume announcing one's pregnancy was memorable for all mothers regardless of context.[37]

The few women who mentioned being slightly concerned about announcing their pregnancy were on temporary contracts and weren't sure how their leave would impact the timing of the remainder of their contract—though this wasn't a concern for all freelancers or temporary workers. In fact, Elise had a temporary contract at the time she announced her pregnancy. This consistency among women suggests that there is alignment between Swedish work organizations and the government on work-family compatibility.

The one woman who expressed meaningful concern about disclosing her pregnancy wasn't worried about herself; Maja worried about the well-being of her boss, colleagues, and customers in her absence while on leave. Maja is a Swedish engineer working for a small, private firm on a permanent contract. She said her primary worry was in knowing she would be "really missed when I was gone. So that was my main concern, how can I make this transition easy for them." She was one of two women I interviewed in Stockholm to report working over forty hours a week. Maja said employees in her office were expected to work overtime, but she had been honest with her boss when she was hired that she wanted to work no more than forty hours. Her unhappiness evident, Maja told me, "I'm not sure it's going to work out. I hope it will, because I really, really like this place." But this implicit assumption of long hours didn't make Maja hesitant to talk with colleagues about being a mother: "Oh, no, absolutely not," she replied quickly when I asked. She also received a substantial raise while on maternity leave, and she used both telecommuting and flexible working hours options after returning from leave.

Maja felt valued by her company and genuinely liked her job. Her sentiments are widely shared: 80 percent of women in Sweden report being satisfied with their jobs.[38] Rather than fearing for her livelihood or career prospects, Maja worried that her supervisor would have too much work in her absence, and that her customers would be dissatisfied. Although she was asked to put in long hours on par with my Italian and American respondents (which I discuss in chapters 5 and 6), Maja expected to be treated fairly and equally. Her experiences stand in contrast to what sociologist Allison Pugh calls the "one-way honor system" that defines US workplaces, in which employees believe they owe their companies hard work and devotion and expect little in return.[39]

Swedes don't reap the same economic rewards for overtime work as employees elsewhere do. Like the US, Sweden has a progressive income tax, meaning marginal tax rates rise with income. As I said earlier, the country is well known for its high rates of taxation. In 2015, the top marginal effective income tax rate in Sweden was 56.9 percent, which applied to all income over 1.5 times the national average. This means that Sweden's income tax system is relatively flat with a broad tax base. Most Swedes are taxed at high rates, not just high-income earners. Compare this to the United States, where the top marginal tax rate in 2015 was 46.3 percent (in other words, the top federal marginal tax rate plus the average of top state marginal tax rates), and it applied only to those whose salary was 8.5 times the national average income or higher, around US$400,000.[40] Sweden's high marginal income tax rates may work to discourage people from working overtime.[41] But high tax rates do not prevent Sweden from having a very successful economy. According to International Monetary Fund data on per capita GDP adjusted to purchasing power parity, Sweden ranked eighth in the group of thirty wealthy OECD countries in 2017.[42]

To put it simply, Swedes pay a lot in taxes, but they also get a lot for their money.[43] Income inequality is much lower in Sweden than in other OECD countries because income taxes and cash benefits play a big role in redistributing income.[44] Whereas working hours have increased in other OECD countries, they have stayed the same for roughly twenty years in Sweden; only 1 percent of employees work very long hours.[45] So in the Swedish context, career ambition and advancement aren't necessarily tied to extremely long work hours. Many of the Swedish women who met with me held high-status positions and still reported working a maximum of forty hours a week. The thirteen women represented in the 40–44 working hours a week column in figure 2.1 all worked forty hours a week. Two women were the exception (in the far right column): Maja the engineer and Susanne, an emergency room nurse, whom I discuss below.

Sweden also lacks the "insecurity culture" prevalent in the US.[46] The majority of Swedish workplaces today have collective bargaining agreements between unions and employers that regulate pay and working conditions. Unlike employees in the United States, where unionization has declined drastically in the past several decades,[47] nearly 70 percent of Swedish workers belong to a union. Ninety percent are covered by a

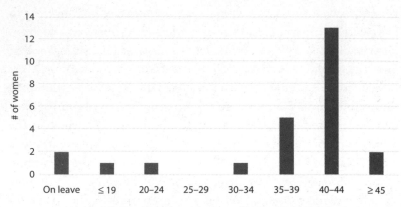

FIGURE 2.1. Weekly working hours for respondents in Stockholm, Sweden.

collective agreement of some sort.[48] Swedish moms generally expected to be supported in their family responsibilities by both their employers and the state.

As a result, women felt confident combining employment and motherhood because they believed their employers were willing to help them achieve this goal. I asked Elise whether she talked to other women at work before giving birth about what it would be like to manage her job and family responsibilities. She looked at me like I was a bit daft and replied:

> No, I didn't because, you know, everyone knows here that this system works really well. So, you don't really have to ask anyone for advice. It's like, you know, you can put your child in childcare when he or she is one year old and then you can continue with your career. It's like a fact, everyone knows it. So, it's not . . . yeah. But, yeah, of course I talked to them about other things, about pregnancy, about, you know, raising a child and stuff like that. But, not regarding to, you know, to work.

Elise indicated that she spoke with women colleagues about everyday child-rearing concerns, but not about the work side of the work-family equation. In her experience, the policies were clear and the system easily facilitated parenthood and work.

Mothers also told me they readily used work-family policies like maternity leave, flexible schedules, telecommuting, and vacation or sick days without fear of stigma—as did their peers and supervisors at work. Susanne, a Swedish emergency room nurse who works forty-five hours a week, told me: "A lot of my colleagues have children and they are home with them when they are sick, and that's never talked about or frowned upon." She said even her highest-ranking colleagues use the policies; a male neurosurgeon had recently taken lengthy parental leave after his son was born. This policy use by both colleagues and superiors created a comfortable work environment for mothers.

Employers seemed to be both supportive and unsurprised when they heard that multiple employees were expecting children around the same time. Johanna is a Finnish mother of two and works 37.5 hours a week for an advertising agency. She said her boss was a father himself, and expressed only joy when she announced her pregnancy right after two other women in the office did:

> He congratulated me. I think he was probably expecting it. [. . .]
> He has three kids himself. [. . .] Most of the people have children.
> Most of us are at the age of having kids who are about, like, starting
> school, or let's say between five to ten years old. [. . .] Which is
> good because then you have that understanding for it, because the
> general manager, he will go and pick up from kindergarten as well
> sometimes.

When a general manager leaves work to care for his young children like Johanna's boss did, this signals to employees that it is acceptable to use policies like flexible schedules, reduced working hours, and leave time. Stories like Johanna's indicate that policies on the books in Swedish workplaces are helpful especially because there's a *culture of support* around their use. If coworkers or employers were frustrated with parents' policy takeup in the office, none of the women I interviewed ever heard about it.

Sara said her workplace went even further to make explicit that family was a priority. Sara is Swedish and an educational administrator at a local university who works forty hours a week. She told me her office cleared out at 4 p.m. I asked whether she felt comfortable talking about family responsibilities at work, and Sara replied with a shrug, "Absolutely, yeah. [. . .] And we often say [in the office] that the family is the most important part in your life." She felt her office was "quite a humane place to work," and as a result it was an unusually comfortable environment: meetings were never scheduled late, all employees could work flexible schedules and telecommute, and they talked often and openly about children in the office.

Sara's comment implies that other workplaces may be less comfortable or humane. Women often mentioned that the public sector tended to be more accommodating of parents than the private sector, offering one possible explanation for the occupational sex segregation that characterizes Swedish firms—women work more often in public firms and men in private firms. This segregation is a topic of great debate and the target of several current initiatives. Maja, the engineer who worked long hours for a private company, said she previously worked for the government: "And that was really, really great for people having families." She told me the pace was slower there, and she earned compensatory time (*kompledighet*) she could take as paid vacation, which she didn't accrue at her current firm. Yet Maja told me she stayed with her private sector employer because "I think this job is really, really fun. I love it. It's much more fun, it's much more inspiring to me." Maja's insights into these differences, however, suggest that some mothers may be deterred from private sector employment in Sweden because it's considered less family-friendly.

The cultural integration of work and family life was further evidenced by Marie, a single mom and German foreign diplomat living in Stockholm who works thirty-nine hours a week. She was bewildered when she discovered that her Swedish office emptied out by mid-afternoon. Having grown up in Germany where drastically different working norms reigned (see chapter 4), Marie said this would never happen in her German office: "I think that's the way with typical Germans, you know? You stay a bit later to show you're a good worker. And in Sweden it's more like everybody goes at, like, 4:30, because everybody has to pick up their children from childcare. [. . .] I mean this I find quite fascinating here in Sweden. They're still efficient." Since Marie didn't grow up in Sweden, the idea that work adjusts for one's family needs was new and odd to her. She also seemed surprised that the shortened workday didn't impinge on productivity. Being accustomed to the German approach to working hours, Marie thought her colleagues left the office quite early. She felt uncomfortable doing the same because it might indicate she wasn't dedicated to her job.

In contrast, several of my Swedish interviewees who were accustomed to the Swedish approach to parenthood and employment experienced a lot of unexpected stress when working for *non*-Swedish employers. Sofia, a Swedish mother of a five-year-old, works forty hours a week as a mining business developer. She has a slight Scottish accent when she speaks in English, a remnant of her time spent studying abroad. We talked over snacks at a sidewalk café near her office building just north of the city center. The mining company she works for was recently purchased by an Australian firm. Even though she works in the same office in Stockholm, along with the rest of the Swedish employees, the new CEO and other executives are all Australian and unfamiliar with Swedish work culture (though they are required to abide by Swedish labor law). Policies like flexible hours are technically still available, but many employees have become wary of taking them. One day, Sofia was on a conference call with the CEO that ran late, and she told him she needed to leave to pick up her child from daycare. She said the CEO called her supervisor the next day, outraged at her behavior. Sofia reported that her supervisor, a Swedish man, instructed Sofia and the other employees to say in the future that they had another meeting to run to rather than tell the executives the truth about their family commitments. Sofia said many of her colleagues, both men and women, are unhappy with the new Australian management. They are inflexible and don't understand that families are a priority. Several of Sofia's colleagues have contacted their unions to complain and plan to leave the company.

Policy provisions for work-family reconciliation *and* supervisor support are crucial for moms. Sofia's account highlights the potential disconnect between a policy on the books and the cultural climate surrounding policy use in a given office. Having new, non-Swedish employers meant that Sofia and her colleagues were suddenly expected to profess a singular devotion to their jobs—a cultural schema that was novel for Swedish workers but both familiar and expected for the Australian firm. Sofia followed her supervisor's suggestion to simply lie about where she needed to be, and she reported that the Australian CEO seemed none the wiser.[49]

Sofia's story reminds us that the social organization of work takes many forms. It doesn't need to center around the ideal worker model for firms to succeed. Likewise, the social construction of motherhood in a Swedish context does not preclude the ability to be a good employee. Overall, the Swedish women I spoke with believed the gender bias associated with parenthood seems to have been overwhelmingly eliminated in their workplaces—whether they were employed at hospitals, schools, private firms, or government agencies. Mothers didn't feel pressured to outperform their colleagues by ignoring family responsibilities, working significant overtime hours, or being silent about their families while at work—even for those who worked in the private sector or in male-dominated occupations. Maja is the only woman who felt obliged to work long hours, but even she expressed no fear or stigma related to being a mother at work.

Even though laws exist at a federal level, it doesn't always mean they are implemented, used, or condoned in individual workplaces or by particular supervisors and colleagues. In Sweden's case, national dual earner-carer policies seem to be reinforced by work organizations that make women and men feel supported in their family responsibilities. I noted a remarkable consistency between the stated objectives of working moms, firms, and the state, at least from the perspectives of the middle-class women in this study.

Sofia's experience of an Australian company purchasing her firm exemplifies the importance of consistency within mothers' lifeworlds—from the broadest public policies down to everyday conversations during conference calls. Tensions arose from the misalignment of the Swedish state's work-family policies and job protections, the new employer's understanding of Sofia's workplace responsibilities, and Sofia's family commitments. This anecdote highlights the importance of synchrony across the institutional, organizational, interactional, and individual levels of mothers' lifeworlds.

"Good Parenting" and the Discourse of Gender Equality

I've suggested that the mothers I interviewed in Stockholm felt the federal government and its policies supported them well, as did their supervisors and colleagues. This begs the question: What about their partners at home? For those in heterosexual relationships (none of the women I spoke to in Sweden were partnered with women at the time), what did women expect from their boyfriends or husbands when it came to raising kids, earning a living, and doing housework?

Every Swedish woman I interviewed endorsed the principle of gender equality at home and in the workplace. The degree to which they succeeded in achieving this goal varied, but the belief was universal that men and women should participate equally in breadwinning and caregiving. This collective belief seems to be further evidence that working mothers' value systems aligned with the Swedish welfare state's goal of dual earner-carer families.

For all of the partnered Swedish women I met, having an egalitarian relationship and equal division of labor was central to being a good mother, echoing the prevailing cultural expectation and policy endorsement of gender equality. It was important to women that their kids felt equally connected to and reliant upon both parents. One Swedish mother, Kajsa, proudly recounted recent evidence of this success: her daughter Ebba had recently spent the night at a friend's house, and after a bad dream woke up calling out "Mom or Dad! Mom or Dad!" For Kajsa, Ebba's call for either parent signaled that she and her partner had succeeded at building equally close relationships with Ebba.

During each interview, I asked women what they thought it meant to be a good mother and a good father. All my interviewees responded to this question with similar answers, but in two different ways. One group gave short answers and looked at me curiously—mirroring the looks I received when I used the phrase "working mother" and when I asked Elise the journalist about announcing her pregnancy at work—as if it was silly or too obvious to even ask. Maja the engineer replied, "They should do the same things. They're both parents." When silence followed and it was clear that Maja wasn't going to elaborate, I asked, "So it doesn't occur to you, for example, that moms should do one thing and dads should do another? That to be a good mom or dad—" Maja interrupted me, shaking her head and frowning. "No. I don't think that men and women . . . they are parents. I think that's important. I don't think it's different things. Perhaps, I mean, from who you are and what you're good at, you should be a role model from that." As she responded Maja slowed her words and enunciated clearly, holding eye contact with me. It felt as if she thought I was being thickheaded because she had to explain something so simple to another woman and reply to a question with an obvious answer.

The second group of women gave more detailed explanations about the need for gender equality in parenting. They felt strongly that women shouldn't be the only parent cooking, doing laundry, and bathing their children—these tasks should have no connection to one parent over another because of their gender. For example, Lily is a Swedish geologist working roughly thirty-seven hours a week. She and her partner, Isak, have a three-year-old and a five-year-old. She was putting her two boys to bed when I arrived at their flat, nestled on an upper floor of a historic building in posh central Södermalm. After her sons settled in to sleep, Lily and I had an animated conversation at her cozy, dimly lit kitchen table late into the night. Lily told me that she and Isak worked diligently to ensure they divided household tasks equally. She had established this expectation with Isak from the very beginning:

> We talked about it on maybe the first date. Not really, but very early [*laughs*]. And that was—for me that was something I've always known, that I don't have sex with someone who—if I get pregnant you never know. They are supposed to be equal in that opinion. So, it's not been an issue. [. . .] We talked about it before we had kids. We had to be equal. And that was his opinion also—maybe

sometimes even more than I am [...] because his parents weren't that equal, so he felt that he had to make a big change. [...] To do that he really had to get to know them, the kids, much more than [his dad] got to know his kids.

Lily had made it clear to Isak that she expected to have an egalitarian relationship, and that one day, if and when they had children, they would play equal parenting roles. Indeed, Lily and Isak split their parental leave time down the middle after each of their sons was born. Lily is responsible for laundry. Isak cooks. She explained it wasn't always easy to maintain this equal division and recounted a recent dispute over how she felt that, slowly and unintentionally, she had started picking up around the house more every day. To address this problem, they came to an agreement that Isak would clean up the kitchen every night before bed. For now, she said, they were both pleased with this arrangement.

On the flipside, Lily explained that Isak takes care of their bicycle maintenance, and he recently chided her that she should learn how to repair her bike as well. Several other women mentioned that they and their partners try to hold one another accountable to their agreement to divide tasks equally. Camilla the lawyer declared, "I think it's important to share equal, you know? Both the fun parts and not the fun parts. The cleaning and cooking and everything." Maintaining equal responsibility at home was sometimes laborious. But equality seemed to matter a lot for these women and their partners, at least from women's points of view. They suggested that this equality was important not only for adults, but also for children.

The rhetoric women used to describe men's involvement with child-rearing was particularly striking to me. They didn't talk about men's "duty" or "obligation" as American moms tended to say, but rather talked about men's "right" to be equally involved in their children's lives. Camilla reflected on her own childhood; her mother worked full time in social welfare and her father worked night shifts as a firefighter and cared for her and her siblings during the day. When they were out in public with their dad, older women would make snide comments to him about his children—"Can't you see your child is cold?" for example—assuming he didn't know how to care for them. It was unusual during Camilla's parents' generation for fathers to be so involved in the daily care of their kids, but to Camilla, this behavior is completely normal and expected today. In a conversation about parental leave, Camilla said, "Our generation, I don't know any couple or friends where the dad won't stay home or doesn't wish to stay home. They see it as their right and all: 'Half the time is mine.' Kind of like that." Swedish sociologists have demonstrated that men's attitudes and behaviors about gender and parenting shifted *within a generation* of the state implementing social policies like "use it or lose it" parental leave that incentivized dads to be more involved at home. This shift is remarkable. The sense that fathers are *entitled* to time with their children helps normalize Swedish dads' participation in child-rearing and absolves women of full responsibility for this caring labor.

And what's more, this belief seemed to hold for fathers across the education, income, and occupational spectrums. Recall that nine in ten Swedish fathers take parental leave. Intrigued by men's purported interest in equal caregiving, which women referred to so often and so nonchalantly, I wanted to talk to men about it directly. I interviewed five fathers toward the end of my time in Stockholm, and they confirmed the women's accounts. Henrik, a bricklayer, told me, "A good man takes care of his child." He said it was important to split the parental leave time fifty-fifty in order to bond with his daughter and to learn to take care of her alone. Rickard, a daycare assistant, made similar comments; both he and his partner agreed he did more work around the house and in childcare than she did. Rickard split the parental leave days evenly with his partner: "It was never a question of doing it, it was kind of understood from the beginning that we were going to split . . . it's always been—as long as I've been thinking about it, it's been . . . it's been the only way I've seen . . . looked at it." Just like the women who seemed to consider me doltish for asking how they defined good mothers and fathers, Rickard struggled to explain the decision to divide parental leave evenly. His English was flawless, yet he had trouble articulating the reasons behind what to him was an obvious choice. It wasn't an issue of translation or a language barrier. Instead, his struggle demonstrates how deeply Swedish men have internalized the belief that they should participate equally in child-rearing.

Beliefs about gender equality and a father's right to spend time with his children shaped the way couples like Rickard and his wife decided to use benefits like parental leave. Sara, a Swedish mother of two working as an educational administrator forty hours a week, told me, "I think it is super important that parents split leave time equally. It is unfair if women take longer leave than men—this is selfish. This is controlling of women." I asked Sara how she and her husband, Hugo, divided their leave, and whether she had shared this view with him: "Yes, yes, because he thinks it was really important that he should be [using] parental leave as well. And it was kind of just natural that we divide it fifty-fifty." This rhetoric of rights, embedded in Sweden's welfare law, was echoed throughout the interviews. It is also reflected in national survey data: most Swedes think the ideal division of parental leave is an equal split between mothers and fathers. Among women, 70.4 percent believe this to be true, as do 69.8 percent of Swedish men. Less than 1 percent of women (0.6 percent) and 2.2 percent of men think the ideal scenario would be for mothers to take the entire leave and fathers none.[50]

Men's involvement in child-rearing was apparent day-to-day on the streets of Stockholm. They were out with their children, often with no mothers in sight. Elise, the journalist and single mom, reflected that it was entirely normal for fathers to use policies like leave time to complete the same caring labor that mothers have done historically, while mothers pursued advancement in their careers:

> It's quite funny because I think this is the part of the city, or the part of the country, where most dads take out paternity leave. And the situation here is like lots of men earn less money than their women here, which means that the women have top jobs and the men, they don't earn as much. So, they tend to stay home more with the children while the women go to work. So, they have kind of reversed roles here, which is very interesting, I think. We have this expression "latte mommas" or "latte moms," but it's like "latte

daddies" [*latte-pappor*] here. You know? They go to the café and they have a latte and see other daddies with their children and they hang out. If you go to like a playground here you will see lots of dads with their children. Yeah, it's quite an exotic view, I suppose, for some people.

Elise's comments suggest that fathers caring for their children not only has been normalized, but is expected. Elise said this extends beyond the "fun" parts of parenting like time at the playground to the more mundane tasks of changing diapers and doing dishes: "People are very equal here. There's nothing to even question, it's like, of course, you're equal. Of course, the father can change a nappy or he can do the dishes, or he can—there's nothing—nobody would find that strange in any way. I suppose in maybe smaller cities in Sweden, in maybe . . . I don't know."

The widespread expectation that fathers participate equally in all aspects of child-rearing seemed evident even to me around Stockholm. I often saw fathers grocery shopping, feeding, commuting, and playing with their children in public. I saw "latte dads" out on walks pushing strollers and spending time with their kids at playgrounds every day around the city.[51]

Although Swedish law is explicitly gender neutral and women emphasized continuously that mothers and fathers perform the same role in their children's lives, the cultural belief that a child deserves access to both parents seems to imply that mothers and fathers each provide something different to their children. If parents perform the same role in their children's lives, as mothers said repeatedly, then I wondered why the insistence on two-parent involvement is so dominant. Several mothers mentioned that some of their strengths and interests overlapped with their partner's, but that they also had different ones depending on their personality—which they said were unrelated to gender—and that their children benefited from engaging with them both for this reason.

To me, the Swedish government's offer of a gender equality bonus (*jämställdhetsbonus*) to families who shared parental leave equitably was closely tied to this idea of "good parenting." Was good parenting in fact egalitarian parenting in women's eyes? Did "good parents" in Stockholm split the leave evenly? I was curious whether women thought the benefit had any real influence on their families' decisions. Some moms indicated this was a nice perk but said it didn't influence their decision to share the leave down the middle; they had planned to split it evenly anyway. Susanne the ER nurse told me she and her partner divided the parental leave equally, so I asked whether they received the bonus. "Yeah, we got a bonus, a lot, a big bonus," she replied, "since we shared so equally the days. We got a big bonus, I think, I can't remember how much it was . . . 8,000 krs [roughly US$950], which I thought was really strange to get a bonus [*laughs*]."

"Did the bonus weigh into your choice to split the leave equally in the first place?" I asked, and she replied,

> No, definitely not. To me it's the right thing to do. It's a normal thing to do. So, I was a bit surprised [to receive it]. I mean in Sweden, it's to encourage people. [. . .] But, to me, it's just normal, definitely normal to share as equal as we could and share the responsibility as well. I mean, it's strange to me to not think it's normal. But, yeah, it was nice. We got money [*laughs*].

In contrast, other moms suggested that the bonus explicitly influenced their decision. Helena is Finnish, works forty hours a week as a governmental coordinator, and has two children, born five years apart. I asked how she and her husband, Jonas, decided the length of parental leave they would each take after their children were born. Helena explained that with her first child, when no bonus was available, she and Jonas played it by ear, determining who would take how much time as the child grew. After the bonus was instituted, however, she said they were more intentional in splitting the parental leave evenly to receive the largest bonus possible. Helena mentioned, "At least with my friends and colleagues, it's quite usual that you share those days of leave, you know, kind of 50/50, not necessarily exactly, but kind of. Or at least it's very usual that the father is at home during some time." In Helena's case, both the cultural norm among her friends of fathers taking parental leave and the availability of the gender equality bonus seem to have shaped her and Jonas's decision to divide the leave equally.

Susanne and Helena highlight the interplay between policy and culture in their discussion of dividing parental leave. Swedish culture idealizes people who incorporate equality into their family life, which tends to put pressure on people to live up to that ideal. This pervasive cultural norm is encouraged by Sweden's work-family policies like the gender equality bonus, but it's also a product of Swedish social organization and cultural values.

For the moms I spoke with, good parenting was indeed egalitarian parenting. Their explanations about what it meant to be "good parents" sounded to me as if they were deeply informed by feminism, though women rarely used this word explicitly.[52] The language of equality permeated women's discussions. For example, mothers said that good parents showed their children that men and women can have similar interests and participate in the same activities and occupations. Lisa, for example, is the Swedish urban planner whom I interviewed in her sunny backyard while her husband, Erik, played with their sons indoors. Lisa said that when she read bedtime stories to their one-year-old and three-year-old, she often switched the gender pronouns throughout the books so they would hear about men and women in all roles equally. She also used the gender-neutral pronoun *hen* for people and objects in these stories, rather than the gendered terms *han* and *hon* for "he" and "she." She explained that many of her friends also used this gender-neutral term as a political statement in teaching their children to disassociate certain roles with men and others with women. In spring 2015, two years after I conducted my interview with Lisa, Sweden made headlines in outlets like the *Washington Post* and National Public Radio when it added *hen* to the official dictionary for the Swedish language.

Lisa recounted another anecdote about waking up her three-year-old one morning to tell him that a repair person would be coming to the house to fix their refrigerator. She used the gender-neutral pronoun *hen* to describe the worker, and her son told her, "Girls don't do that job in real life, mom!" An hour later, a woman knocked on the door and greeted her son with a smile. He was surprised, and Lisa was thrilled that her son saw a woman repair technician. I saw this interest in gender neutrality reflected around me often during my time in Stockholm. For example, children tended to wear gender-neutral clothing colors. I spent an afternoon with another Finnish couple and their twins: their son wore an orange shirt with green pants, and their daughter wore a green, white, and blue striped shirt with brown pants and blue socks. It was rare that I was able to guess a child's gender by their clothing. This is a small example of how gender neutrality and the pro–gender equality discourse are embraced in Sweden.

Women's beliefs about gender equality explicitly guided their parenting philosophies. Women with sons often told me that they conscientiously raised them to respect girls and women. I asked Elise (the Swedish single mother and journalist) about her approach to parenting her small son and her hopes for him as an adult. Elise told me that she intended to teach her son about treating women with dignity and respect:

> God, I mean I've been thinking about that a lot, because, you know, the world is going to look so different when he's at that age, you know? . . . I'm trying to raise him to respect women. I mean, I think that's really important. And that he will—I will never tolerate, you know, him being macho or sexist or, you know, treat women in an unequal way. I mean, that's not acceptable at all [*laughs*]. And I think that's really important, as a single mother, to be strong. [. . .] I think especially if you're a single mother with a son you need to be strong and you need to show him that women are strong and that— you know, for him to respect women. And, of course, men too.

To Elise, being a strong female role model was central to being a good parent.

The women I spoke with in Stockholm were proud of Sweden's status as a world leader in gender equality and progressive work-family policy. At the same time, they recognized that things weren't perfectly equal yet between women and men. Challenges remain. Women were mindful that the government was working to eliminate Sweden's persistent gender wage gap (though it's much smaller than in other OECD countries, as I mentioned in the introduction), and bemoaned the reality that women tend to take longer parental leave and work part time after returning from leave more frequently than do men. Mothers seemed to embrace the goal of gender equality in their personal lives. During our interviews, mothers often connected their personal work and family decisions to these larger political goals of equality, working conscientiously in their own families to further the broader project of gender equality through their own personal choices about work schedules, policy use, career paths, choice in partners, and child-rearing techniques, among other arenas.

Another trait that mothers consistently named as central to raising their child well was teaching them independence. Ida, the divorced Swedish mother of two preteens, explained:

> I want [my kids] to be individuals. I want them to learn how to make their own decisions, how to make mistakes, actually, and how to learn to solve their conflicts and mistakes. I'll be a support. I think it's really important for the kids to have other adults in their lives, not to be dependent on mother and father, that there are other grown-ups that are other people for them.

Ida signaled that teaching her children individuality and problem-solving were crucial, as was exposing them to other adults who could provide a system of support outside the nuclear family. And Ida is not alone: seven out of ten Swedes consider independence an important quality for children to learn at home.[53]

The egalitarian parenting strategies deployed by these Swedish mothers are in some ways similar to those used by gay and lesbian parents in the United States. A study of American LGBT parents found that they resist the binary gender order and deconstruct gender stereotypes as a way to resist heteronormative child-rearing practices.[54] Similarly, Swedish mothers explained that their parenting practices bolstered a gender equality or neutrality paradigm that was widespread in Sweden.

Like Ida, my respondents unanimously voiced the opinion that children were healthy and well-rounded when they were socialized by a wide spectrum of people in a variety of environments—not just by their mothers at home, which they thought was harmful for both baby and mom. They implied that children are less healthy and well-rounded when raised by only one or a few people. They all agreed that daycare or pre-school (*dagis* or *förskola*) from a young age was crucial to a "good upbringing." In fact, the vast majority of Swedes, 82.5 percent, think government agencies should be the primary providers of childcare for children under school age. Only 10.4 percent believe family members should assume this role.[55] The mothers I interviewed often referenced the high standards for care workers, healthy food, time spent outdoors, and the pedagogical focus to explain why they had no sense of guilt for plac-ing their children in daycare full time and returning to work after pa-rental leave. They thought so highly of the childcare system that women told me it would be selfish to keep a child over age one at home, given the valuable experience of attending Swedish daycare.

The Swedish government actively works to disseminate information about Sweden's world-renowned early childhood education and care pro-grams. The official website of Sweden, sweden.se, is available in English, Arabic, Russian, and Chinese. On its Society page, it features articles in English called "Play Is Key in Preschool," "Sweden—Where Children Count," "Free Education from Age 6 to 19," "First Ban on Smacking Chil-dren," "From Preschool to University in Sweden," and "10 Things That Make Sweden Family-Friendly."[56] Of course, Swedes don't need a series of articles in English to explain the importance of quality child-rearing. But these articles aren't meant for Swedes. By publishing them in Eng-lish, perhaps the Swedish government is attempting to promote its part in providing a high standard of living for the country's children as a desirable model for other EU countries. The state sends a public message that it is not parents alone who are responsible for raising children. Women agreed with this during our interviews.

The women I interviewed expressed disdain for parents who overly meddle in and are obsessed with structuring their children's lives. Swedes have a name for these people—"curling parents" (*curlingförälder*). The term has a cultural parallel with the US idea of the "helicopter parent"—parents who flit about their child and over-involve themselves in their upbringing. The term "curling parent" is a playful but disapprov-ing reference to the sport of ice curling, suggesting that some parents hover over their children and frantically sweep away obstacles to smooth out their path in life. These parents aim to cushion the blows of reality and make their children's lives a bit easier. Elise, who wanted to be a strong female role model for her young son, explained:

> Have you heard of the curling mothers? Curling fathers? [...] It's a concept that means that if you help your child and you—how can I say? You don't let your child think for himself or herself, you don't let your child make mistakes on his own. Or you're there for the child all the time and support it and pamper it, you know the child gets really spoiled. [...] I'm not like that. [...] I think my job as a parent is to teach my child about life. It's both good and bad, it's sad and it's tragic. [...] I don't want to protect him too much from reality. [...] I think the two things that are most important to me to teach my child is independence and self-confidence. Yeah, that's really important, I think. I think that's the most essential thing.

Elise believed she would do herself and her son a disservice by sheltering him. Although as a single parent Elise is entitled to all 480 days of leave, she decided to put her son in daycare at age one after having used only part of this paid time off. She described her decision:

> I went back to work because I was bored just being at home. I also thought that my son needed to meet other children and to— yeah, because he was really bored with me as well, you know? He couldn't wait to [*laughs*] get out of the apartment and do other things. You know? Because he's very active—very, very active and very curious about the world. ... So I thought that I, both me and my son, needed to see other people, to see other environments and that's the main reason why I decided to put him in daycare at this young age.

Elise was able to use a period of paid leave to stay at home with her son and public daycare to return to work and provide a "healthy" environment in which her son could learn and grow. High-quality public childcare eliminates inequalities in access to care.[57] In Sweden daycare is considered an important tool to eliminate disparities in children's development and outcomes that stem from parents' own differences in education, income, and other resources.[58]

The Swedish government has facilitated this beneficial learning environment for every child in the country, from those living in the smallest far-flung towns to the largest cities, and from families with different migration, educational, and economic backgrounds.[59] The middle-class moms I interviewed believed childcare should be a universal experience for all children in Sweden—a discourse also promoted by the Swedish welfare state. The provision of high-quality public childcare more broadly has the effect of recognizing and valuing caring labor.

The Pressure of Intensive Parenting Norms

Although in general the Swedish moms I spoke with seemed quite content, their lifeworlds of motherhood weren't entirely free of stress. Many interviewees in Sweden seemed to feel quiet but steady pressure to perform a version of "intensive parenting" (a gender-neutral version of sociologist Sharon Hays's "intensive mothering"[60]) rooted in class privilege. The majority of the women I spoke with referenced the need to make home-cooked meals, enroll their child in the best daycare possible, ensure their children don't spend too much time in daycare, and spend plenty of time outdoors. When mothers did feel work-family conflict, they tended to blame these intensive parenting ideals.

For instance, women explained that picking children up "too late" from daycare was considered taboo. The German single mother Marie—who works thirty-nine hours a week, sometimes staying later than her colleagues in her Stockholm office that empties out at 4 p.m. daily—said her daughter's daycare workers had commented on the fact that her child was at times the last one to be picked up. "I'm not interested in telling them, 'Oh, I'm a stressed-out single mom,' you know? I cannot please everybody. If I decide to pick her up at 5:00, and if she's happy and she's well, then that's the most important thing. Please let me do whatever I want."

Norms about when "good parents" first use daycare and how many hours a day children are left in these facilities shaped mothers' decisions about when to return to work and how many hours to spend at their jobs. Although my respondents seemed universally happy with their children's daycare experience, parents didn't want their children to be in daycare "too long" in the afternoons. Those who were partnered worked hard to alternate their work schedules so one parent could pick the kids up in the afternoon, the earlier the better (many cited 3 p.m. as the ideal time even though daycare is open later). Johanna, the art director whose boss also often left early to pick up his three children, explained her own hesitation about long days at childcare:

> I think kindergarten is great. [...] It's a good place, but not for too many hours. I think that is a breaking point. [...] I mean, it's like us [grown-ups], if you had to be at work from 7:00 in the morning to 9:00 in the evening [*laughs*] it wouldn't be fun. It's too much. [...] I think the general view here is that kindergarten is a great place for your kids. [...] And, I mean most kids are OK with that, it's not like they're suffering or anything, but it's—I'm not sure if it's good when they are one year or two years old, three years old, they are still so, so, so small.

Johanna expressed the most hesitation about childcare for her young child among the mothers I interviewed. She and her husband, a management consultant, work hard to ensure that one of them picks up their daughter every day by 3 p.m. Also evident in Johanna's comments is the belief that children deserve balance in their lives, just like their parents.

Several women confessed to me that they felt a great deal of pressure to be perfect parents. Maja, the engineer, reflected:

> I'm trying not to get stressed out about all of the tips and all of the books and—a lot of books and a lot of pressure, I think [is] on parents these days . . . in Sweden and in Stockholm. I think it's a big deal [*laughs*]. [...] I'm trying not to feel it, but I know it's out

there. Like, you have to be the perfect mother, you have to pick your child up early from daycare at the same time that you're making your career and you're really good at your job and you have to cook well and you have to be a perfect partner and, you know, all of these bits and pieces that are not fitting together [*laughs*]. Unless you relax a bit.

When I asked Maja where she perceived this input was coming from to excel at work and at home simultaneously, she told me she honestly couldn't pinpoint a source other than herself:

> I don't have anyone telling me that I should do this or that. I think everyone believes we do a great job with [our daughter]. When I look at her she's a happy kid. We must be doing something right [*laughs*]. I don't think society expects that much of me. [...] But, I do, I'm afraid. [...] Combining—especially combining working life and a family life. And that's with the internal pressure. Because I think I'm going to do absolutely well enough for everyone around me. But, to convince myself of it, that's going to be the tricky part. And being a good parent, I think really if I'm calm and content then she's going to be too. So, that's what I'm trying to be [*laughs*]. And that's what maternity leave is really good for.

Maja held herself to high standards when it came to parenting. Even though all evidence suggested she was doing a great job and she felt well supported and admired by those around her, she didn't think she was doing a good enough job combining work and family. Perhaps this worry stemmed from the rhetoric that the combination of motherhood and employment should be seamless and harmonious for women in Sweden. When Maja experienced stress, she thought something must be wrong with her, since the system is famous for being arranged to help mothers succeed.

One Swedish woman thought working motherhood was so pervasive and the dual earner-carer system so deeply engrained in federal law as to exclude other choices for mothers who might be interested in staying at home. Ida, who deeply values Sweden's work-family policy infrastructure, is divorced. She makes a high income by Swedish standards and reports loving her forty-hour-a-week job for the government. Yet her frustration is palpable in her comments:

> They really want women out in the labor markets so they somehow make it impossible for just one person to work, with the mortgage rates, the rent for an apartment. Everything in Sweden is based on two people working. So, we don't have a system based on one [person] working. No one can afford it. You really don't have a choice. In that sense everyone says, "It's so good in Sweden," but you don't have a choice. You cannot stay at home, [unless] you have married someone who had a really, really, really high salary, then it might be possible, but they [lawmakers] built the system to give no choices, you have to work, both of you, in a sense. Then they give you daycare centers and benefits, but you don't give the people choices.... But, on the other hand it's not politically correct in some sense. A woman, a Swedish woman today who wants to stay at home with her kids is not seen with good eyes, I would say. I mean people would think she's weird and stupid, and perhaps she has a husband who is deciding this for her. They never think it's a free choice. And she's— you always look at those persons as something strange.

Ida acknowledges the system is based on the couple-centric assumption that a household has two earners, but her comments reject the dominant ideal of the dual-earning family. As a single mom, her family doesn't fit this model. Luckily, her high income means she is able to support herself and her two children. (She told me that even with the assistance the government provides for single parents, she couldn't afford to stop working for pay if she wanted to stay home entirely. Staying home would be impossible even if she were married to a high-income earner.)

As Ida explained, being a stay-at-home mother is considered abnormal in Sweden. Swedish journalist Peter Letmark tried to find a housewife to interview for a 2010 article about contemporary parenting. He had no luck: "Housewives are a near-extinct species in Sweden. And the few who still do exist don't really dare to go public with it."[61] In a recent national survey, only 3.6 percent of Swedish women said they strongly agreed with the statement that "a job is all right, but what most women really want is home and kids." Likewise, a meager 5.7 percent of women strongly agreed that "being a housewife is just as fulfilling as working for pay."[62] Ida is right that the Swedish welfare system and society generally expect all adults, including mothers, to engage in paid work. For the nation, mothers' employment increases economic growth and raises tax revenue. On an individual level, paid employment increases women's social benefits, personal fulfilment, and financial independence. So if a mother living in Sweden has any interest in staying home, this would be both financially difficult and culturally denigrated.

What's more, advertisers in Sweden don't even bother trying to target ads to housewives: they're considered a "nonexistent segment." Commercials from other countries are sometimes re-dubbed to remove references to housewives. As Swedish brand consultant Jonas Andersson explains, "You want to target working mothers."[63] It's tough not to romanticize or stigmatize housewives, argues feminist economist Nancy Folbre. "That's the way social norms work: They put pressure on people to conform." Working moms may feel a great deal of support in Sweden, but the flipside may be that women wanting to arrange their work and family lives differently find themselves outcasts. This may be one unintended consequence of Sweden's well-meaning social policies.[64]

The Swedish women like Ida whom I spoke with were well versed in their legal rights, as well as their intricacies and stipulations—an awareness scholars refer to as "legal consciousness."[65] Most women mentioned that they interacted with the Swedish Social Insurance Agency directly via a smartphone app, evidence of how easy it was to use their benefits.[66]

Although Swedish mothers were satisfied overall, they thought there was still room for improvement in the country's work-family policies. For example, several Swedish mothers said they were frustrated that the government paid only 80 percent of their wages during parental leave and when they had to miss work to care for a sick child. Others felt that daycare centers needed to expand their opening hours to accommodate the flexible economy. Although some twenty-four-hour daycare centers had opened in Stockholm for workers with unusual schedules, women believed more of these facilities should be available. One mother mentioned her frustration that parents lose the right to reduce their working hours when a child turns eight. She felt that preteen children needed to be closely supervised, and the government should develop a system for helping care for children of these ages. Another woman said the filing system to get paid for sick days was overly bureaucratic.

The vast majority of mothers reported that part of the reasoning behind their full-time work schedule was their knowledge that when women reduced their working hours legally to, say, 75 percent, they actually continued to work full time at 100 percent but weren't paid for all the hours. Still, others thought the public sector was more hospitable for parents than the private sector. Finally, although mothers all reported that barriers to their occupational success related to their parental status had been removed, several perceived that barriers remained because of their gender. The women I interviewed took the equality mandate very seriously. They trusted and expected the government to work toward the shared goal of gender equality. I got the sense generally that mothers were quite content with their day-to-day lives, but felt adamant that even more could be done to improve the lives of women in Sweden.

Overall, my Swedish respondents said they were satisfied with their ability to manage work and family commitments. They explained that they had a strong social safety net. They felt well-supported by Sweden's gender-egalitarian policies: the government supported their dual roles, and mothers expected and in fact felt entitled to this support. There seemed to be close alignment between Swedish cultural ideals, work-family policies, workplace cultures, partners' interests (at least according to my interviewees), and women's own perceptions of work and family life. This alignment is key to understanding the lack of work-family conflict among mothers in Stockholm.

I didn't sense that women were tugged in opposing directions by competing devotions to home and work (more about this in the chapters on mothers in western Germany, Italy, and the US). Intensive parenting norms caused working moms in Stockholm to feel stressed at times, but they didn't have a strong sense of guilt in the workplace. They didn't believe they were letting their employers down as mothers, or short-changing children at home by having a job. These women indicated it was inconsequential that they were a parent at work, and that they had a job while raising kids.

Women's lack of work-family conflict and sense of a just division between employment and motherhood seemed to stem from the fact that they conformed to the ideal woman citizen under the Swedish welfare state.[67] The middle-class mothers I spent time with benefited from their alignment with the government's political objectives for women. The government has paved the way for working mothers by removing the obstacles known to impede employment and parenting. Sweden's welfare state philosophies and policies were designed to support and encourage precisely this arrangement.

Women without children and mothers who don't work or don't want to work likely feel greater stress and stigma than my interviewees because the welfare state is not oriented to support their family models. Because I didn't interview these women, I can only conjecture about their experiences. But I imagine they feel marginalized in Swedish society. When I asked women specifically whether they had ever considered being a stay-at-home mother, they thought the prospect was rare and odd. Such women run counter to the prevailing cultural schema that women should have children and be employed. My interviewees didn't mention stay-at-home partners or parents without being prompted, because these are largely absent from Sweden's cultural discourses about the range of possibilities for family formations.

Single parents may also feel stigmatized given their divergence from the dual earner-carer family model. Sweden's work-family policies are universal for all parents, but as I mentioned, the state also offers supports specifically to aid single parents. As a result, unlike many other Western industrialized countries, Sweden has very low rates of single mother poverty.[68] The six single mothers I interviewed mentioned feeling lonely sometimes, and household finances also seemed to weigh on them more than my partnered Swedish respondents. But they didn't report feeling stigmatized. They said they were well supported and satisfied with the available policies. Nationwide surveys show that three in four

Swedes believe one parent can bring up a child as well as two parents together.[69] It's possible that their native-born status and employment gave the single mothers I spoke with a level of privilege unavailable to others, such as unemployed immigrant mothers.

Indeed, the well-being of lower-income immigrant mothers remains a central concern in Sweden, given that immigrants comprised 15 percent of Sweden's population in 2018. As in most countries, immigrants remain disadvantaged in the Swedish labor market, especially those who are mothers.[70] Their rate of labor force participation is far lower than that of native-born Swedish mothers, which may be a source of stigma. Although Sweden has the most welcoming asylum policies and takes in more refugees per capita than any other European country, integration is the subject of considerable debate and tension.[71]

My interviews with middle-class working mothers show that what women want and expect in Sweden when it comes to their work-family lives are heavily shaped by their social context. Swedish mothers fully expected to combine employment with raising children without stress or difficulty, and they wanted gender equality at home and at work. They expected their employers and the state to help support these goals, and indeed, the Swedish government and private firms—as well as Swedish cultural norms—are oriented toward these ideals. This belief and expectation of gender equality is central to women's ability to smoothly combine work and family in Sweden.

CHAPTER 3

Former East Germany

"I WOULDN'T KNOW HOW TO HANDLE
FORTY HOURS. . . . THAT'S NO LIFE."

Dorothea greeted me at the front door to her second-story flat with her nine-month-old daughter on her hip. She invited me through the entryway and across the hall, seating me at a two-person table in her small kitchen. We ate sliced pears and peaches while she breast-fed her daughter periodically throughout our conversation. Dorothea was born in East Berlin. Like the country itself at the time, the Berlin Dorothea knew was divided between the democratic West and the socialist East. Separating the city was an imposing swath of concrete twelve feet tall and twenty-seven miles long. The Berlin Wall symbolized the separation of not only two different states, but two radically different ways of life during the forty years when East Germany (that is, the German Democratic Republic or GDR) operated as an independent country in the aftermath of World War II (1949–1989). Although East and West Germany shared a language and cultural background, the GDR had its own economic and political systems—especially regarding women's participation in the labor market.[1]

The GDR's constitution guaranteed the "right and duty" to employment, so mothers like Dorothea's worked full time. Maternal employment was quasi-compulsory as part of the dual-worker family model.[2] This requirement was driven by economic need and the cultural ideology that everyone had to work for pay. East Germans felt moral pressure to work, and the scarcity of institutions to support the unemployed drew people into the labor force. Even so, women also maintained responsibility for the home. Socialist labor and family policies were pronatalist and sought to help women combine child-rearing with employment, promoting family and paid work as equally important for women but not for men. The GDR socialized the caring labor of child-rearing so all adults could work full time.[3] Young children like Dorothea entered state-run daycare facilities within a few months of birth. She attended daycare until age six, when she began primary school.

The family model in East Germany was nothing like West Germany's, where policies sought to preserve and facilitate a traditional family structure with a male breadwinner and female caregiver.[4] Dominant cultural ideologies in the West long presupposed that women took care of the home and perhaps secondarily worked part time once children entered school. The general assumption was that men and women had complementary, different but equal, gender roles.[5] This family structure was reinforced by laws in the West that discouraged full-time working motherhood: marginal income taxation, lengthy and rigid parental leave, short school days, and few public daycare facilities for young children (with short, inflexible opening hours) were long the standard.[6] Mothers' caring labor at home was further materially supported by up to three years' maternity leave from work (if they worked at all), and by public health care and pension systems that automatically granted insurance rights to an economically inactive wife of a working husband.

After mounting political unrest and massive antigovernment demonstrations, the Berlin Wall came down in 1989, making news headlines around the world. Dorothea was seven years old. After the two Germanies reunited, change was abrupt for those who had been living in seclusion behind the wall. West German institutions and policies were transferred to the East. This included support for the male breadwinner family model. Mothers in former East Berlin and across the former GDR were suddenly discouraged from working, especially when their children were young— the opposite message they'd received from the East German government under socialism.

Now age thirty-three, Dorothea has a master's degree and teaches German and English at a nearby school twenty-three hours a week. She explained to me that she loves her job and has never worked full time.

She envisions working in this position indefinitely. Her three-year-old was at daycare when we met, and Dorothea was home on parental leave with her younger daughter. She had taken one year of paid leave after each child was born, and her husband, Karl, took four and then three months' leave respectively from his job as a computer scientist. Dorothea is satisfied with the leave time available to her and never questioned that she would return to work:

> It was normal to see that my mom was working, not a stay-at-home mom. I went to [childcare] really early. I think when I was six or eight weeks old. And I thought, "Okay, one year is okay. I can take care of her basic needs and then I go off to work." […] [I'll be] breast-feeding and everything but other than that it would bore me out. So, I need to work again. I also want to earn money again for my pension and everything. I don't want to stay home for three years [the norm in western Germany]. And the other reason is that I think going to daycare early is better for the kids. […] I think, especially young kids, they totally benefit from other kids.

Dorothea mentioned how easy it was to find daycare in Berlin for her own children given the universal facilities left over from the GDR, which were still available to families twenty-five years later.

In light of the region's tumultuous history regarding women's roles, I asked Dorothea whether she felt any guilt about returning to work while her children were young. She replied, "I'm not guilty that I work. I think it's important to be a role model. And when they are older I want to work too. And for me [demonstrating] another world that a woman has is important. […] I want to imprint that on my daughters as well." Like the Swedish mothers I spoke with, Dorothea said she wanted to model a gender-egalitarian arrangement with Karl for their girls. She continued:

> I think it's more common for women in my environment to start working again. Maybe after one year or two years. Stay-at-home moms are not around that much [in Berlin]. But I wouldn't

judge them. If they say, "I want to stay at home for three years or more or longer," it's okay for them. They have good reasons to do that, and I couldn't do that personally, but it doesn't mean that other people can't.

On the one hand, she expressed frustration that women in Berlin who did work still lagged behind men in earnings and occupational attainment, and she wanted better for her children: "I hope for my daughters that they can have jobs where they can fulfill themselves, and where they can be successful without any hindrance. Without the glass ceiling. I hope in twenty years that life is going to be different." On the other hand, Dorothea pointed out the positive changes in men's involvement in family life. Karl had also grown up in East Germany, and both of them wanted more equality in their relationship than their parents had: "I found a partner who agrees to that." Of Karl's contribution, Dorothea said:

He not only [does] housework but [is] also taking care of the kids. And he also loves spending time with them, and I think that's a changing father role. [. . .] The parents of the child have an equally big role. He can't breast-feed but that's the only thing that he can't do. And I see a lot of fathers in my environment [. . .] and they are doing the same parenting style as we do. Some men are more at home taking care of the kids. [. . .] So that's really cool.

However, toward the end of our conversation in her kitchen, she reflected on the pressure she felt at times to live up to a traditional version of motherhood that still places the burden of child-rearing and domestic labor mostly on women:

I think the demand society has for moms, they are like, "Mom has to do everything perfectly. And when the kids are not well behaved, it's the mom's fault. When they have another problem it's the mom's fault." I try to distance myself from that or to reflect on the things that society wants from a mom. And you have to be perfect in any direction. Perfect homemaker, look great, and bring home-baked cookies to the kindergarten. I feel that pressure but I distance myself from it. "No, I'm working, I can't bake a cake."

Dorothea's reflections echoed much of what I heard from women in Berlin: they enjoyed their work and didn't want to stay home. They thought it was important for themselves and the broader project of gender equality that mothers engage in paid work, and it seemed to them that the majority of mothers in Berlin also worked—though they said they wouldn't criticize a mother for deciding to stay at home. They were eager to share things equally with their partners, and though fathers took a more active role in family life than in previous generations, they realized moms still tended to work fewer hours than dads and shoulder more responsibility for children. Most women I talked to in Berlin said a full-time schedule was unappealing. They told me they were content with the available parental leave, childcare options, and opportunity to work flexible and part-time schedules. They also perceived some pressure to live up to an idealized version of motherhood that required intensive time and attention. Overall, they reported having lifeworlds relatively free of work-family conflict.

Germany is an interesting case for a study of working mothers and work-family policy. Because of its unique history, it doesn't fit neatly into existing categories of welfare state regimes. Mothers in Berlin seemed wedged ideologically between the two neighboring welfare state models: the social democratic model to their north, and the conservative model that predominates to their south and west. Even twenty-five years after reunification, the working mothers I interviewed—some of whom grew up in former East Berlin and others in West Berlin—expressed attitudes shaped by the socialist legacy of the GDR. This legacy has much in common with the contemporary policy in social democratic welfare states like Sweden. Moms in Berlin were highly work-oriented, had easier access to childcare, talked openly about motherhood at work, and seemed to feel much more equality in their relationships with their partners than did their counterparts in western Germany. However, two-thirds of the mothers were less career-driven than my Stockholm respondents, worked fewer hours, and generally hadn't reached the level of gender equality in their division of labor at home as had women in Sweden. Yet moms in Berlin still reported experiencing more equality and more ardently espoused a rhetoric of dual earning and caring than American, western German, and Italian mothers. Geographically and politically, Berliners remain closer to their Scandinavian neighbors to the north than to their counterparts in western Germany.

Germany's Shifting Work-Family Policy

Former East Germany occupies the northeastern part of the country. As of 2014, roughly 16 percent of the country's population lived in this region (12.5 million people) and 64.6 million people lived in western Germany.[7] During its forty-year life span, the East German economic system was a well-oiled machine. It was centrally organized, and the state provided public transportation, subsidized food prices, and universal health care. Through their schools and daycare facilities, the government sought to teach children socialist principles like patriotism, good citizenship, and the importance of work.[8]

Social provisioning was especially generous for those who lived up to the state-endorsed life-course model for East German citizens: early marriage, full employment, and several children.[9] This model privileged heterosexual married couples. The state incentivized marriage and parenthood by controlling access to resources like housing, loans, and public holiday camps.[10] For instance, married couples could apply for an interest-free "marriage loan" intended to help buy furniture and household appliances. The loan was forgiven in increments with each child's birth. Working mothers with two or more children could take paid parental leave (*Babyjahr*), and those with three or more children received extra holidays and the right to reduce their working hours.[11]

Although the East German government touted a commitment to eliminating gender inequality in paid work, this goal was never fully realized. Under the GDR women lagged behind men in earnings, experienced occupational segregation, and were burdened with most of the domestic tasks, even into the 1980s and among younger cohorts of women.[12] The GDR was heavily criticized for being dictatorial, engaging in widespread censorship and political repression.[13] For the most part, people weren't permitted to travel outside the GDR, and there was little freedom of information. The government controlled the press, television, and radio stations. All public exhibitions of arts and culture were subject to censorship. Western publications were forbidden. Criticizing any aspect of the East German way of life or political regime was cause for investigation, surveillance, or arrest.[14]

Official reunification between East and West Germany in October 1990 meant the collision of two radically different welfare regimes: after 1990, East German institutions, policies, and dual-earner employment structures transformed rapidly once the West German government took over, converging toward the conservative male breadwinner welfare state model of the West. This model valued a traditional gender division of labor and discouraged mothers from working. Western Germany remained virtually unchanged after reunification.[15] Sociologist Elizabeth Rudd conducted interviews with former East Germans between 1993 and 1995 to understand how they experienced combining work and family under both East German and postsocialist conditions. She found that men and women agreed that after the transition to a conservative welfare state and capitalist economy, established patterns of employment and parenting were disrupted and work-family conflict increased dramatically.[16]

Like other EU countries, Germany today is required to meet mandates and legal directives established by the European Union and the United Nations to promote gender equality between women and men. As an EU member state, Germany follows gender mainstreaming guidelines, meaning the government has to consider the potential impact of any planned policy for both women and men before enacting legislation. These agreements have propelled the topics of work-family policy, gender equality, and antidiscrimination law to the forefront of current political debates.[17]

Reunified Germany has one set of work-family policies. Employed women may take maternity leave (*Mutterschutz*) for up to six weeks before childbirth and are required to stay home for eight weeks afterward, receiving full pay (*Mutterschaftsgeld*). Mothers' employers bear most of these costs, with a small part paid by mothers' health insurance. Self-employed and nonemployed women don't qualify for these benefits. Germany has no statutory requirement for paternity leave for men.

Couples may take up to twelve months of paid parental leave total (called *Elternzeit*, literally, "parents' time").[18] The financial compensation for this time is *Elterngeld*, or "parents' money." *Elterngeld* is paid at two-thirds of the couple's net earnings (with a ceiling of €1,800 monthly, roughly US$2,000). If both parents take at least two months of parental leave, they earn two extra months of paid leave for a total of fourteen months. The government implemented these "bonus" months to get men to take more parental leave, as Sweden had done years before. And as in Sweden, parents can take parental leave flexibly anytime up until the child is eight years old. Employers are legally required to keep a position open for a parent's eventual return to work (but not necessarily the same position) after parental leave. Parents who are temporarily out of work prior to their child's birth receive a flat-rate benefit of €300 per month (US$370). To supplement the cost of child-rearing, the German government also pays families a "children's allowance" (*Kindergeld*) of €184 per month (US$200) per child until the child is eighteen, or until age twenty-five if she or he is still in school.

Germany also has a robust childcare system—but not for kids of all ages. The catchall term for daycare centers available for children before they start primary school is *Kindertagesstätte*, or *Kita* for short. State-sponsored childcare has been available for decades across Germany for children ages three to six (called *Kindergarten*) before starting primary school. But unlike in former East Germany, daycare in western Germany for children younger than three (called *Kinderkrippen* or *créches*) has always been hard to come by. Parental leave entitlements were progressively expanded beginning in the 1980s and early 1990s to enable parents (again, mostly mothers) to stay at home in order to bridge the time between birth and *Kindergarten* at age three.[19] However, paid parental leave was shortened in 2007 to a maximum of twelve months.

As of August 2013, following decades of public debate, all children between age one and school entry age (usually six) are legally entitled to a space in a daycare facility under the new Child Support Act (*Kinder-förderungsgesetz*). However, German municipalities are mainly responsible for the provision of these new facilities (with funding by the federal government), and they aren't yet universal. This mandate requires an estimated 750,000 pre-kindergarten childcare slots, an expansion of roughly 35 to 40 percent per birth cohort.[20] In addition, the German school day typically ends between 12 and 1 p.m. for primary and secondary schoolers, and few childcare opportunities are available after this time. Full-day schools are becoming more widespread for older high school–age students across Germany, but they remain the exception.[21]

Despite these shortcomings in Germany's daycare provisioning, the country has substantial paid vacation. All full-time workers have a legal right to twenty-four days of fully paid vacation per year. Employees working less than full time get proportionally fewer days, depending on how much they work. Workers may take as many personal sick days as needed over the course of a year at full wages. All employees get ten days per year to tend to a sick child at 70 percent pay. All of these benefits extend to couples registered in same-sex partnerships and to parents who adopt children.

In addition to substantial vacation and sick day benefits, Germans also face a labor market in which many jobs are available as part-time positions across both white- and blue-collar job sectors. Currently 27 percent of all workers in Germany are part time.[22] Part-time work isn't associated with lower wages in Germany like it is in the US.[23]

Taken as a whole, the work-family policies offered in Germany today bear little resemblance to those of previous decades. Until as recently as 2006, the German government still encouraged a male breadwinner/female caregiver model of family life through its welfare provisioning. Since 2007, however, Germany has been evolving quickly toward an entirely different welfare model.[24] Its new "de-familialization" framework, also called "sustainable family policy" (*Nachhaltige Familienpolitik*), promotes mothers' continuous employment, invests heavily in early childhood education services rather than giving cash to families, and generally endorses a dual-earner ("adult worker") family model—a huge shift from the previous conservative welfare regime.

The planned and enacted legal measures bring German family policy much closer to a Scandinavian dual earner-carer model. The social policies implemented in Germany represent one of "the most radical series of changes in terms of policy goals […] in taking steps to promote the adult worker model family, accompanied by significant reform of and changes in policy instruments" compared to other EU countries.[25]

German work-family policies have therefore been in a state of flux in the second half of the twentieth century and at the start of the twenty-first. Competing political interests mean there is no consensus about the "best" work-family policy.[26] Disparate voices around the table—European Union mandates, feminist groups, conservative parties, progressive parties, and religious groups, among others—have all shaped the current policy landscape. As a result, institutional supports for working mothers remain contradictory. For example, although the government now explicitly encourages employment for women with young children, most primary schools remain open only part of the day regardless of federal laws encouraging them to expand their opening hours.

In an editorial lambasting the complexity of Germany's shifting family policy, the country's largest newspaper, *Spiegel*, wrote in 2013: "The web of benefits is so complex that even experts don't fully grasp it: There's a 'child supplement,' 'parental benefit,' an 'allowance for single parents,' a 'married person's supplement,' a 'sibling bonus,' 'orphan money' and 'child education supplement,' not to forget the 'child education supplementary supplement.'" Germany is clearly a nation in the midst of a major work-family policy overhaul.[27]

Despite the legal convergence between East Germany and West Germany since 1990, the socialist legacy of the former GDR is still evident in several institutional arenas. First, as Dorothea noted, far more public daycare centers for young children (ages 0–2) are available in former East Germany than in western Germany.[28] Second, the proportion of women who work outside the home remains higher in former East Germany than in western Germany, especially for mothers with young children.[29] Third, gender norms regarding the household division of labor are more egalitarian among women and men in the former East.[30] For instance, those living in the former GDR remain firm in their support of women's employment. They are more likely to agree with the belief that women's paid work is beneficial to families and that children do not suffer when their mothers work, compared to people in western Germany. Greater interaction between former East and western Germany since reunification has not weakened East Germans' egalitarian beliefs about mothers' employment. Sociologists Kristen Lee, Duane Alwin, and Paula Tufiş write, "Clearly, the state socialist provision of child care and preschool for children virtually removed the belief that women's working outside the home would harm their children."[31] These regional differences in beliefs about mothers' employment were also evident in my interviews.

Frieda, a teacher, recounted an anecdote that exemplifies the remaining difference in attitudes between former East and western Germany. Frieda and I met while she was on maternity leave with her first child. She grew up in western Germany, and on a recent visit home she told her grandmother that her one-year-old son would begin attending childcare in the coming weeks. Frieda's grandmother admonished her, saying it was way too early for a child to be away from his mother while she returned to work. The following week, Frieda was at a party in Berlin and mentioned offhandedly to an elderly woman her plans to begin public childcare soon. "You haven't started him there yet?" the woman scolded. "He should be there already!" Frieda said the latter experience made her thankful she lived in Berlin, where attitudes were more progressive toward moms interested in working while their children were young.

Compared to the rest of Germany, Berlin's population is both young (more than 40 percent of the population is under age thirty-five) and racially heterogeneous (with people from roughly 180 countries, representing about 30 percent of the population).[32] Like Sweden, Germany is struggling to integrate its substantial foreign-born refugee population, who have higher rates of unemployment and lower rates of education than native-born people.[33] My interviewees occupied a place of privilege in Berlin given their education, incomes, and occupations, as their families conformed closely with the welfare state ideal of dual-earning parents with children. Any difficulties they experienced are likely magnified several times over for mothers who occupy more marginalized positions in German society.

————

The women I interviewed in Berlin expressed a strong orientation to work, regardless of whether they were born and raised in East or West Berlin. Their views on employment echoed those of the moms I met in Stockholm: they explained that they benefited from working and their children benefited from daycare. Clara, who is German and works thirty hours a week as a political adviser, has two-year-old twins and was pregnant with her third child at the time of our interview. She told me, "I never questioned working [while having] children. That was always 100 percent clear to me." I asked whether she had considered quitting work altogether to be a stay-at-home mom, and she responded with laughter and shook her head with a vigorous "no":

> Never, no. I think it wouldn't be to anyone's benefit [*laughs*]. Including the twins' [*laughs*]. I think because we would just be really, really annoyed with each other. I mean, they are so much work and so much trouble. And I think they also like to be around other kids. I know this sounds like the things that mothers tell themselves [*laughs*]. When I stay at home with them for a day or two because the *Tagesmutter* [babysitter or nanny, literally, "day mother"] isn't around or she took a week off, then I really have to find ways to fill our days. [...] I just wouldn't be able to fill an entire year of 365 days [*laughs*]. And I actually really do think that being around kids is fun for them. That's why I'm looking forward to them going to the *Kita* [daycare] in September because there are more kids there and I think they are ready to dive into even more complete social life.

She acknowledged that this reasoning might seem like a justification for hiring the *Tagesmutter*—"the things that mothers tell themselves" to reduce feelings of guilt rooted in intensive mothering norms, which I discuss later in the chapter.[34]

Some women also justified their interest in working for pay by pointing to unhappy women acquaintances or relatives who didn't work. Junni, who is Danish and an urban planner working thirty hours a week, told me, "My mother definitely believes she had too little to do and that she was kind of an unhappy woman." She laughed when I asked if she had ever considered a similar path, replying, "I like working. I think it's a big part of my identity." Most mothers explained that they had worked hard to obtain an education; all but two held a bachelor's degree or higher. Eighteen had advanced degrees. For mothers living in Berlin with lower levels of education, who are disproportionately immigrant women, the incentive to work outside the home is likely lower.

Education is related not only to *how likely* mothers are to work for pay, but also people's opinions regarding the *consequences* of mothers' employment for young children. Across national contexts, people with higher levels of education tend to have more progressive gender attitudes. National survey data in Germany show that 44.3 percent of adults with less than a high school diploma (*Abitur*) believe a preschool child is likely to suffer if her or his mother goes to work. Only 16.8 percent of those with more than a high school diploma believe this to be true. These figures also vary between former East Germany and western Germany. In the former East, a scant 13.3 percent think preschool children suffer when mothers work, and more than double (32.1 percent) feel this way in western Germany. Similarly, 17.4 percent of people in the former East believe family members should mainly provide preschoolers' childcare, while nearly three times more people in western Germany (42.2 percent) believe that to be the case.[35]

The women I spoke with who were born in the GDR held the strongest beliefs about how normal it was for mothers to work outside the home. In keeping with the dictates of the socialist welfare state they were raised in, women said it was never a question that they would work as adults. As was standard practice at the time, they started childcare when they were eight weeks old in state-run *Kitas* and grew up with mothers and fathers who worked full time. The *Kitas* were central to East German life.[36] Twenty-five years after the fall of the Berlin Wall, many of these same *Kitas* are still in operation, referred to as *Ost Kitas* (Eastern day-cares), with some of the same employees working there today.

Adela grew up in the GDR. I interviewed her in the living room of her modern, airy flat in central Berlin. Adela's one-year-old son, Theo, greeted me at the door, tottering unsteadily on his chubby toddler legs but seemingly pleased with himself for motoring on his own. We met while Adela was on parental leave from her job as a secretary. Her partner Stefan, a dentist, was at work. Theo sat on her lap for most of our conversation, chattering in the way that babies do. Adela held his small feet, clad in soft, brown leather shoes, in her hands as she explained the governing pattern of work and family formation for her parents' generation:

> My mom was born in '52, I was born in '76. They needed everyone in the production work. It was really common to give your baby to the *Kinderkrippe* [childcare] at eight weeks old. The parents used to be very young, she [my mom] was twenty-one [when she gave birth the first time] like all of her friends. That was the common thing to do. You go to school, you do some sort of degree, then you marry right away, get children right away, up until [at] the age of twenty-five all the families were complete.

Adela's mother followed the state-endorsed life-course trajectory for women by combining employment and caregiving: she went to school, got married, gave birth at ages twenty-one and twenty-four, enrolled her children in daycare at eight weeks old, and then went back to work full time. The majority of East German women followed the same pathway through education, paid work, marriage, and childbearing.[37]

Women's inculcation with GDR ideology surfaced during interviews when they recounted their first experiences outside the GDR after the wall came down. Gerda—a mother of three separated from her partner and working full time in communications (though she aspires to teach yoga full time)—described her shock upon visiting the West for the first time when she was thirteen years old. She vividly recounted her elementary and middle school days in the GDR where students were required to wear uniforms and memorize and repeat chants about working hard and being neighborly and cooperative. She reflected at length about her assumption that "beyond the wall" everyone was unemployed, impoverished, and living on the streets—a message she heard constantly. After the wall came down in 1989, Gerda and her family traveled to Hamburg, a city in western Germany, for the first time. During our interview at her dining room table, Gerda's eyes were unfocused and cast away from me, as happens when one recalls an old memory. She described her astonishment that there were no homeless people on the street. Instead, she remembered Hamburg as being colorful, bright, and filled with advertisements. She felt overloaded with sensory stimulation after a lifetime in the comparatively more uniform world of the GDR, which she described several times as feeling gray.

The mothers I interviewed who were born under the socialist welfare regime thought it was inevitable that they would work while raising children, because this was the only model they had witnessed. This ideology shaped how women perceived employment: they believed it kept people from living on the streets like they were told happened to other Germans "beyond the wall." Even when the bubble burst after reunification and it became clear to these women that life could be lived another way, the deeply engrained cultural beliefs seemed to survive for many.

Most women I interviewed in Berlin said they wouldn't want to be stay-at-home mothers themselves, though they were quick to mention they wouldn't judge mothers who did. But two respondents were outliers in this regard, saying they had considered staying at home at least temporarily. Adela, whose toddler had greeted me at the door, worked twenty-eight hours a week as a secretary. She thought it might be less stressful to stay at home and search for a job she enjoyed more rather than trying to job hunt while working part time and caring for her home and son. Another mother, Irena, is Dutch and had been living in Berlin for several years. Her second child was due in three weeks, and her basketball-sized belly was prominent through her black t-shirt when we met in her third-floor flat in the central neighborhood of Kreuzberg. Although she was enthusiastically pursuing a career at the moment, she said she could imagine taking a period of time off to spend with her children before continuing work again. Both of these women still envisioned working after taking a short break from employment and didn't want to stay home indefinitely.

It seemed to me that a primary reason why mothers in Berlin wanted to work was because they were very satisfied with the available work-family policies. Mothers felt that the culture in Berlin was supportive of working mothers, and that they could take advantage of work-family policies to resolve conflicts between child-rearing and employment, making the transition to motherhood easier. Most worked a part-time schedule, used flexible hours and telecommuting options, took the full one year of available leave, enrolled their kids in the high-quality affordable childcare universally available to Berliners, and had partners who helped at home and used the policies themselves.

Several mothers discussed how helpful the various public supports were before and after giving birth. Soon-to-be mothers often took free or low-cost courses on topics like cloth diapering and breast-feeding, and after their babies were born they joined neighborhood support groups. In addition, all new mothers living in Germany are entitled to midwife home visits for postpartum care, fully paid for by the state's public insurance program.

Parents' centers can be found in every neighborhood around Berlin. These centers offer family support services and educational activities, with programs for everyone from babies to grandparents. I visited one such center, within a stone's throw of the old Stasi headquarters—a landmark several employees mentioned to me during my visit. I arrived shortly before a toddlers' music class began and drank a cup of strong black coffee with the center's director, watching parents file in. These parents, mostly moms but also a couple of dads, parked their strollers outside the door, removed their shoes, lifted their babies over a short gate, and entered a brightly lit room for the music class. I casually chatted with the supervisor and two more employees during the hour-long class to learn about the various course offerings and the sorts of families that frequented their center. The building was situated in a lower-middle-class neighborhood surrounded by tall, drab concrete GDR-era apartment buildings. The walls of the center displayed pastel-colored posters that were slightly dated and faded, picturing smiling babies and parents. The sound of tambourines and singing floated across the room, and parents eventually filed out chatting, intimate in their familiarity with one another. I wondered to myself how different life would be for parents in the US if they had this level of institutional support.

Given these sorts of provisions, it's not surprising that mothers were hard pressed when asked to brainstorm what they would like to see improved in the workplace or by the government. Three women wanted access to job shares, which are employment contracts in which two people split a full-time position. Several said daycare centers should employ more men and extend their opening hours. Some wanted women to be allowed to choose whether they took the eight weeks' paid maternity leave after childbirth that was currently mandatory.[38] One woman who worked in an office with rigid rules about clocking in and out suggested that a bit more flexibility would reduce her daily stress. Many mothers mentioned the outdated tax structure that still encouraged a male bread-winner/female part-time worker model. They advocated moving to the Scandinavian model of individualized taxation.

The European moms I interviewed in Berlin were satisfied but not overly so when discussing these work-family policies. They expected these supports. However, I also interviewed two American mothers living abroad during my time in Berlin, and they were both effusive in their gratitude for the work-family policies, widespread cultural acceptance of working motherhood, and universal childcare facilities. Erin works twenty hours a week as a scientist (a work schedule practically unheard of for women in the US, since very few white-collar jobs there allow part-time schedules). Nicole works in social media marketing and was the only woman I interviewed in Berlin to report working long hours, roughly fifty hours a week—similar to the hours mothers talked about in Washington, DC. Both Erin and Nicole said they did not plan to return to the US because they didn't want to lose the supports they enjoyed so much in Berlin. Silke, a German mother who had worked as an au pair in the US for several years, thought it must be hard to be pregnant in the States:

> People work until they basically pop. It's such an advantage to be able to take care of yourself and mentally prepare yourself and physi-cally prepare yourself. And I know in the last few weeks [of preg-nancy], at least the last four, it would've been really hard for me. I

mean, I couldn't even sit that long. And I don't know how—I mean, I guess you'd do it if you have to.

At a different point in our interview, I asked how many sick days she was allowed to take off from work, and Silke replied with incredulous laughter, shaking her head, "Just the word 'sick days' alone just is *crazy* to me! [*laughs*] Because there's no limit on sick days here. If you're sick, you're *sick*!" Silke also couldn't fathom not having parental leave time to breast-feed and recover from childbirth:

> It's such a luxury to know that I can take this time and that it's my choice whether I want to breast-feed or not without having to worry about how I'm going to do that when I go back to work. [. . .] The sheer physical stress of doing breast-feeding and not sleeping at night, I have no idea how people handle that when they're working. [. . .] It seems so—I mean, it's just so hard for me to get my head around that.

Silke had a hard time conceiving of the idea that a mother may not have the option to stay home after having a baby, as evident in her stuttering, halting speech patterns.

Nicole, the American mother, told me she laughed when she heard German moms complain about the child allowance (the *Kindergeld* benefit I explained earlier) being too small a sum, roughly US$200 a month: "I think it's very generous. [. . .] And I hear a lot of complaints, 'Oh, this is not enough.' And then I say, 'Okay, well I don't know of anywhere else where you get this. [. . .] This is *not* a given.' " German mothers felt entitled to these benefits, while Nicole knew these regular cash payments were exceptional for most US mothers. For Nicole, living as an American in Berlin afforded her this outsider's perspective. She reflected, "I'm so thankful for what you get here. I can't say that there is any sort of extra cherry on the top which I think I deserve or need. I feel like Germans sort of see it that way but I certainly feel like everything that they give you is pretty good." Nicole thought Germans should be more grateful for the policies they were afforded. Unlike the circumstances in the United States, these work-family policies are part of Berlin's culture: German mothers in Berlin expected support for their work and family responsibilities, whereas American mothers who were unaccustomed to these norms were thrilled to receive it.

Although these women differed in their appreciation of the available social supports, there was unanimous approval of the diversity of work-family models that seemed acceptable in Berlin. Unlike Stockholm mothers, the moms in Berlin all said they knew some women who were stay-at-home mothers, some who worked full time, and others who worked part time. They said it was also common for men to work reduced hours and to participate in child-rearing and housework alongside their partners. Women told me they believed single motherhood was commonplace in Berlin. The five single moms I spoke with there echoed this sentiment. They said they felt no stigma for raising a child alone, although these women all thought the government should increase benefits for single parents. These views indicated a cultural acceptance but lack of policy support for their families, and therefore a disconnect in these mothers' lifeworlds.

My respondents perceived Berlin as a place where the combination of work and family took many forms without judgment. As I mentioned earlier, Berlin touts itself as a city that celebrates diversity, and many respondents referenced the well-established LGBT and immigrant communities when describing what they liked about living there. I interviewed several non-German mothers living in Berlin who all said they were attracted to Berlin's heterogeneity compared to their home societies of Finland, Denmark, and Holland. While the mothers I interviewed seemed to embrace the fact that Berlin was a place where families could combine work and family in a number of different ways without facing criticism, most of the women I spoke with worked part time. Only five of twenty-five mothers worked forty or more hours a week.

It's possible that this finding may be influenced by what researchers call a selection bias: perhaps full-time working moms were less interested in carving out time to meet with me. But I think mothers' decisions to work part time reflect the peculiar historical legacy of Berlin, in particular its hybrid framework that has undergone several major shifts over the past half century. Part-time working mothers in Berlin embody both (1) the socialist and social democratic welfare state ideal that women work while raising children, and (2) the conservative welfare state ideal

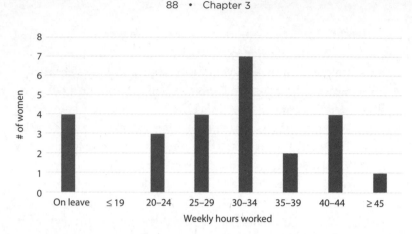

FIGURE 3.1. Weekly working hours for respondents in Berlin, Germany.

that women prioritize family over work. These mothers reflected these two ideals simultaneously—part-time work allowed them to prioritize both work and family. But unlike the research conducted with American mothers working part time who claim to enjoy the "best of both worlds" and actually do not,[39] my respondents in Berlin were well supported in their choice, although they acknowledged certain costs associated with working part time that I discuss below.

While many worked part time, women's total working hours were not uniform (as they were for the women I spoke to in Stockholm and most of those in Rome and Washington, DC). Figure 3.1 shows this wide dispersal. A full-time schedule in Germany is generally considered forty hours per week. Again, the only woman who worked more than forty-five hours a week was Nicole, an American mother living in Berlin.

Privileging Part-Time Working Motherhood and "Jobs," Not "Careers"

Women told me that working fewer than forty hours per week was central to their lack of work-family conflict. Clara, the German political adviser and mother of two-year-old twins, was in the last trimester of her pregnancy with her third child when we met at a street café in Prenzlauer Berg, a neighborhood north of central Berlin. It was a weekday afternoon, and Clara had just finished a coffee date down the street with a friend who was also pregnant. They said hello to me and then hugged one another goodbye, craning their heads and arms above their round bellies. With a wave, Clara's friend departed, lumbering slowly down the street. Clara and I sat down at a wooden table on the sidewalk patio. Clara has a master's degree, as does her partner, Torsten, who also works in politics. She told me they both love their jobs. Clara works thirty hours a week, and Torsten works twenty-five. Among the nineteen women I interviewed in Berlin who were partnered with men (one woman had recently separated from her wife and five more were single), it was common for their boyfriends and husbands to also work reduced hours, but Clara's was the only one who worked fewer hours than she did.

I asked Clara how they had decided upon their part-time schedules. She sipped her drink and replied with a shrug, "I think all my friends said that I was going to regret going back full time. And looking at it, I wouldn't know how to handle forty hours. I know a lot of women do, so it's stupid. Of course, I'd be able to handle it." I nodded. "But I leave the house at 7:30, take the kids to daycare, leave there at 8 and then work until 3:30. And so I'd have to work two more hours and I'd be home at, what? 6:30? And then my kids go to bed at 8. That's no life. And all of that at the expense of my husband who would have to take care of them by himself during the long hours of the afternoon," Clara laughed.

I asked whether Torsten's reduced work schedule was also by choice. "That's also by choice, yeah," Clara explained. "I mean, the job was advertised at twenty hours and then he increased after he started. And I think they'd be happy for him to increase further but we don't really see how that would fit into our family schedule." I wondered how they had come to this arrangement and asked, "Did you have an explicit conversation with your partner about how much you were going to work after the twins were born or was that something you decided on your own?" Clara said it was a joint decision:

> We definitely did because I basically had a free choice of how many hours I was going to do. And so, we definitely said that thirty hours

works well with our family schedule. And then when his job was advertised it was twenty hours. And we both said that this is really good for us. That working part time, both of us, was—especially going back into work after the kids are born—would be really good.

Clara had the most egalitarian relationship among the women I met in Berlin, including the equal sharing of parental leave. She continued, "It's also something we said we wouldn't change now even though we're going to do the classic parental leave model now with the kids, me staying at home for seven months and then him staying at home for seven months." With this schedule, Clara felt she was succeeding both at work and at home as a mother. As I mentioned, part-time workers don't experience wage penalties for working reduced hours as they do in the United States.[40] Clara acknowledged that her part-time schedule and satisfaction at work and at home were also enabled by the progressive workplace culture and her supportive boss, participatory husband, and prevalent daycare facilities. These supports seemed to facilitate Clara's contentment with employment and motherhood. She brought this up when I asked whether it was possible for women to be successful workers and successful mothers at the same time in Berlin: "I think I am," she laughed. "I think it depends on the employer as well. [. . .] I think I do have a very progressive work environment with really, really cool colleagues who understand most of my worries." She also explained that her "personal setup at home isn't quite the average setup [. . .] having a husband or partner who works less, earns less, takes care of the kids more, it's not so usual." She thought this might be uncommon in Berlin but was common among her own friends: "They mostly have relationships that are eye to eye or working on getting there."

Clara acknowledged that the long opening hours of Berlin's daycare facilities meant women had more options regarding their work schedules. She told me, "It's not necessarily a question of choice. I think that especially in the countryside, daycare facilities have really different [shorter] opening hours than in Berlin. It's much more common for women to stay at home for a longer period of time, to work less hours a week." These shorter daycare hours meant that women in more rural areas—especially in western Germany, as we'll see—often worked shorter part-time hours (e.g., twenty hours per week) since daycares closed earlier than in large cities. In Berlin, though, Clara felt well supported. "I think Berlin is pretty accommodating to a certain degree. I think in that sense with my 80 percent [schedule] I'm, again, very average of a middle-class working mom," she chuckled. Clara's comments exemplify how work-family policies, workplace environments, and cultural attitudes go hand in hand in supporting a life where part-time work in a highly satisfying job is possible as a mother with young children.

A handful of American mothers also reported using part-time schedules to reduce their work-family conflict.[41] I discuss in chapter 6 how many of my American respondents wanted to work reduced hours but didn't have this option. It's clear something different was happening for the women in my Berlin sample who worked part time.

The presence of extensive work-family policies and childcare facilities in Berlin suggests that families and caregiving are considered worthy of public support and investment. Unpaid carework is not devalued in this context. The widespread availability of part-time work also suggests adults are encouraged to combine parenthood and employment, reducing the overvaluation of paid work we see in liberal welfare states. Mothers' uptake of part-time schedules is normative in a conservative welfare state that privileges a male breadwinner/female part-time earner family model (sometimes called the "modernized breadwinner model"[42]). It's also normative in a socialist or social democratic welfare state for both men and women with small children to work part time. The majority of moms I spoke with in Berlin felt highly satisfied with their work and family lives not just because they had secured part-time work, but also because it was widely available, commonly used, and culturally accepted.

Women's ability to work part time, as well as their interest in reduced-hours schedules, were not limited to two-parent households. The six single mothers I interviewed also preferred part-time work. All worked between twenty and thirty-two hours a week. Although several expressed financial worries, working full time was not mentioned as an option to address these concerns. The German government has created a safety net for single moms. In Berlin, these women could maintain their households without working full time with the help of work-family policies. These single mothers referenced the utility of full-day childcare, support groups, public health care, and the right to reduce working hours after childbirth.

In Berlin, women told me that job advancement and a reasonable work schedule were not mutually exclusive. They thought they could work part time and still have satisfying professional lives. However, most did not aspire to high levels of career advancement with positions in the C-suite. Instead, they told me they wanted to work in jobs they liked with enough time left over in their days to be involved mothers. Although all the women I interviewed in Berlin wanted to work, several expressed to me that they weren't interested in "aiming for a high career," even among those with advanced degrees. Adela, the East German mother described earlier, had earned a master's degree in theater history but was currently employed as a secretary twenty-eight hours a week, a job she disliked and wanted to leave as soon as she found a position related to her training. But six months after she started work as a secretary, she got pregnant. I asked Adela about her career plans for the future, and she told me, "I've never been an ambitious person. You really have to know what you want and how to get it. You know the modern mantra, 'Work for it, fight for it, be it, every day, every hour.' That's not me."

Adela equated ambition with being an ideal worker. The prospect of fighting every hour of the day and embodying the work ("be it") to achieve her occupational goals didn't appeal to her. She paused and looked down at her toddler, Theo, sitting on her lap and continued:

> Maybe it's also my upbringing. When I went to school it was—you knew there was already a path laid out for you and you never really had to think about what you want to do and how you can get it. From the East German times, it was laid out because, you know, you do your ten-class education like everybody else [equivalent to a K–12 education in the US] and maybe if you're very smart you can do this college thing. [. . .] And then whatever you do, they need you, you get a job. You don't really have to think about when or where. I just

grew up with this thinking that, "Once I finish school, something will happen."

Growing up in East Germany, Adela hadn't spent much time reflecting on her future career. In the GDR, everyone graduated and got a job because everyone's labor was needed. She believed there was little reason and reward for career ambition in East Germany, and Adela attributed her lack of interest in a high-powered career to this upbringing.

Yet Adela had a graduate degree like her partner, Stefan, and she expressed a lack of interest in a career while he had his own dentistry practice. She said Stefan worked full time, brought home a considerable income, and expected her to maintain full responsibility for their home. This unequal division of household labor frustrated Adela a great deal, but she continued to care for Theo and do the housework. Adela's story sheds light on the process by which women are involved in the reproduction of gender inequalities. Her self-professed lack of ambition, part-time work schedule, and smaller income left her unhappily responsible for the domestic sphere, a responsibility she very much wanted to share. Adela's unhappiness didn't surprise me. Women's part-time work typically increases gender inequality in the division of labor at home.[43] But not always. The married couple Clara and Torsten, who had twins and were expecting their third child, both work part time. Clara told me they have an equal division of household labor. Part-time work for women is not inherently associated with gender inequality at home. Adela's and Clara's two very different experiences with part-time work and the division of domestic labor highlight how men's work schedules and contributions to the household shape the consequences of part-time work for women.[44]

Of course, women's comments about their partners' participation in family life and the division of work around the home may not necessarily reflect reality. It is possible men like Adela's partner do more around the house than mothers recognize. However, it matters that women *feel* that they do far more than their partners do. Whether or not this is actually true, it's a source of stress for women. Conversely, couples like Clara and Torsten may not actually divide all tasks equally at home, but what is significant is that Clara felt that it was equal.[45]

For some women, part-time schedules signaled their devotion to child-rearing above their careers. Patricia from western Germany was one such mother. We chatted for several hours at the old wooden dining table in her kitchen—a high-ceilinged room with large windows overlooking the central courtyard of her apartment building, nestled into a quiet side street in Prenzlauer Berg. Patricia said mothers were selfish to put their children in daycare at young ages. She is a writer married to an artist named Emil, and they have a ten- and thirteen-year-old. Patricia works from home roughly thirty hours per week, and more when she travels to promote her books. Patricia was unusually reflective in the way writers often are, pausing frequently to choose her words with care before articulating her thoughts. She is self-employed and never took any official parental leave. Patricia and Emil enrolled their children in daycare when they were three years old—much later than most parents in Berlin. She said that the only reason they decided to enroll their kids at all is because "they didn't have friends to play with because all the children are in the *Kita* until 4 or 5 o'clock." This suggests Patricia's family was in the minority in their decision to keep their children home for three years, a practice that was much more commonplace in western Germany where Patricia was raised. Most former East Germans do not believe that young children are harmed by mothers' employment.[46]

I asked Patricia what advice she would give to women who were working and about to become mothers, and she replied slowly:

> Maybe it's also old-fashioned but I think they can try to work and to have babies, but if they have to work in an office or something, they have to find someone who gives all this love and warmth to their children. If you can find one, it's okay. But if not, then I don't agree that it's a good choice. I think at first you have to think about the children and not about yourself. The life is so very long and I think the children … [for] ten years they need you very much and then … ten years more they don't need you so much. But if you will [live until age] eighty, you have sixty years by [yourself].

I clarified by asking, "So, you should make them a priority maybe for those ten or twenty years?" Patricia replied, "Yeah, if you can. But many women *have* to work and they have children, and it works of course. So, it's also a privilege to think about how you would like to make like this or that, or in this way or in that way. But I don't like this discussion about 'career,' I think."

Patricia believed that good mothers—ones who care for their children—put their children's well-being ahead of their job aspirations for the two decades it takes to raise them. She also acknowledged that her own opinion was rooted in class privilege; many women have no choice but to work to support their families or work in jobs in which a person cannot pause or pull back for a number of years and then return again. When Patricia said, "I don't like this discussion about 'career,'" I asked her to tell me what she meant. "I think our society is just: 'Only look at this career.' And that's not life." She explained, "This career, it's interesting if you are thinking about money but in Europe or in Germany we have all [these benefits] so money isn't our first problem. But living and life and love," she laughed, "*this* is our problem."

Patricia's husband, Emil, returned home at this point and entered the kitchen bearing a paper bag full of pastries. He arranged them on a plate and placed them on the table between Patricia and me. The three of us chatted for a few minutes between bites. Then Patricia and Emil exchanged a few words in German, and he drifted off to a different part of the flat. Patricia continued her previous train of thought:

> We all [do] this just to earn money and to have our big and wonderful career and I don't know if we are all happy at the end. [. . .] So, I don't want to make a law about this or say, "This is bad," or, "Women who try to work and to have children in the same moment are bad," or something. It's not my opinion. But sometimes I feel that many women trying to do this at the same time are not happy and they are very, very tired.

She paused and looked out the window before continuing, "I think people who are not healthy in the soul when they are adults, the problems were in their childhood. So, you have to think about it. You have to manage this childhood." She smiled and chuckled. "For me it's so strange that we are now in the moment where everybody is thinking about his own career and about the career of his children. Is this a way of living? I don't know."

Patricia's comments espouse the cultural ideology that good mothers "manage this childhood," a belief that conforms to a conservative welfare regime. She felt that focusing on a career prevented mothers from performing this caring labor.

Many moms in Berlin seemed to associate full-time work with lofty and even selfish career goals. They believed mothers should work, but not necessarily full time, as they still needed substantial time to dedicate to their children and home. Most of the women I interviewed seemed to take a "middle of the road" stance in their own lives, working in jobs they liked but usually not forty hours a week, and using benefits like telecommuting and flexible schedules, without a clear trajectory to advance in their jobs. Reduced hours seemed to allow the women I spoke with to live up to gendered ideas of being a "good mother" while also engaging in paid labor that carried benefits and lacked job penalties. I found myself wondering after conversations with women like Patricia whether they would be equally content with their job choices if I interviewed them fifteen years in the future, after their children were grown and out of the home. I hoped so. Mothers across Western industrialized countries interested in "on-ramping" back to full-time jobs after years spent working at a reduced schedule or out of the labor market altogether often find companies unwilling to accommodate them.[47]

Even though most women told me they didn't have explicit career ambitions, they acknowledged that it was difficult for mothers in Germany to advance in their careers. Several explained that although they didn't aim for a high-level position themselves, they felt strongly that in the interest of gender equality, women and men should occupy top positions in equal numbers. Dorothea, the East German teacher introduced earlier, explained:

> Maybe because of the old boys' network. And then you have to be extra "bitchy" as a woman. I don't know. I'm not at the top. I'm a

teacher [*laughs*]. We have flat hierarchies. It's kind of accepted that [to get to the top] she has to use her elbows and then she's not feminine enough. So, we have the [gender quotas]. But only for a certain part of the economy or for the companies. I hope for a fifty-fifty quota in all of the leading positions. I don't think that women work better or are better employers but for our society we need that— for our kids, that they see moms [are] a contributor to society as well. They are working, earning money and they are much more than just a mom. They can lead a party or a company as well. And I think it all depends on qualification of course. But even qualified women [*laughs*] don't get a chance to rise up.

Dorothea distanced herself from the goal of a leadership position by reminding me she was a teacher, and pointed out that women who were ambitious were looked down upon. To overcome these stereotypes, Germany had instituted gender quotas at some firms, which pleased her.[48] She thought some women should aim for these top positions, but she didn't include herself in this group. Embedded in Dorothea's comments is also the rhetoric that breadwinning is valued as a contribution to society, but she didn't say the same about caregiving. She thought it was important that mothers work so their kids saw them as something other than caregivers. This also implies that stay-at-home mothers don't contribute to society in the same way working mothers do. Dorothea believed women and mothers were capable of occupying top positions, but often weren't given the opportunity. I heard this sentiment often from my respondents in both former East and western Germany. If the prevailing discourse in Berlin is that mothers face substantial barriers to their occupational advancement, this likely hampers their interest in aspiring to top positions by shaping what they consider possible and desirable.

Following this logic, women often repeated to me that women and mothers are *capable* of getting to the top in their careers but aren't necessarily *interested* in doing so. Even the staunchest self-proclaimed feminists in Berlin repeated this refrain. Heike, for example, is from western Germany. She and her husband, Peter, have a four-year-old son, and she works thirty-five hours a week as a political organizer. Heike said she saw this pattern in her own life and among other working mothers she knew. She described growing up in a "socialist-minded household," and she now lives in a "commune-type setup" in the ethnically diverse, working-class neighborhood of Neukolln with friends in the flats near hers. They help care for one another's children. Heike and Peter consider themselves feminists. I met Peter briefly as I arrived and he departed from their flat with their son, Oskar, in a flurry of coats given the unexpected rainstorm. Heike and I sat at a tiny two-person table in her lime green kitchen with a row of coffee cups hanging from hooks on a shelf near our heads. She told me she had been the sole breadwinner for their family for several years while Peter cared for Oskar as a stay-at-home dad. Heike confessed that although she loved how progressive this arrangement was, she found the financial responsibility taxing and stressful. She reflected, "It's also about your idea of what is important. It's not just the question, 'Am I able to?' It's also the question, 'Will I do so?'"

Reaching for a few blueberries from a bowl between us, Heike ate them slowly, one by one. She explained that as the sole income earner, she "was feeling like a traditional father who is just bringing the income home and didn't want to have any stress with kids. If you are willing to have a [life-style] like that, it's probably much more easy to get to the top of your career." She thought it was possible for mothers to reach the pinnacle of their careers, but she said:

> I think there are not so many women who decide that they are will-
> ing to do so because they want to stay at home. And I think there
> are also a lot of men who want to have more time for their family.
> But for women, it's like if they want to stay home or want to have
> more time for the family, it's nothing they have to fight for because
> it's still normal. So, it's harder probably for men not to climb to
> the career top but stay home [instead].

Heike ultimately decided she wasn't interested in climbing a career lad-der. She explained that a person, man or woman, who wanted to advance needed to adopt the proper mindset and be comfortable with the life-style of a breadwinner who comes home exhausted every day. She guessed that few mothers in Berlin wanted this lifestyle. Mothers who chose not to work or worked part time were supported culturally because these were still viable, acceptable options for women with children. For fathers, though, Heike sensed this would be a more difficult choice given the cultural expectation that men are the family breadwinners. Heike's perceptions generally align with regional survey findings about mothers' and fathers' actual and desired working hours. In former East Germany, mothers with children up to age sixteen living at home worked an average of thirty-five hours a week in 2013. But their desired working time was two hours less, thirty-three hours weekly. Fathers worked an average of forty-three hours a week, but wanted to work thirty-nine hours a week, or four fewer hours.[49] Both mothers and fathers want to work less, but it remains the case that fathers both want to and do log more working hours than mothers, reflecting the persistence of the male breadwinner ideal.

Mothers who did have explicit career goals told me they felt varying degrees of stigma for these decisions. I interviewed seven women who weren't raised in Germany, and their outsider perspectives drew into sharp relief the cultural expectations about work and family for mothers in Berlin. Nicole is an American who grew up in Connecticut and had impressive plans for her career. But she believed her goals were rare among women in Germany. She thought it was typical for German mothers not to have high work aspirations. Nicole is married with a five-year-old daughter and helps manage the social media for a major corporation. Echoing earlier comments, she reflected, "I don't know too many moms who made it to the top. I think about this company [...] and there's a few women in top positions and they are not moms. [...] But I don't really see women being pushed in general."

Nicole is interested in starting her own company in a few years if she doesn't get promoted to management at her current firm. Her husband, Matthias, who is from western Germany, "is not very supportive of that. Because he thinks that's too risky." She reasoned, "It's just a very German thing. He thinks it's better to get the salary every month, and I'm making a good salary here, so he doesn't see the need to rock the boat." Nicole said Matthias valued job security and a stable salary over a leadership position for her. But Nicole would rather "rock the boat" and take a risk, she explained, if it meant more money, independence, and a better career. She thought that seeking a private solution to job mobility—like leaving a secure job with an uncertain career ladder to start one's own company—was distinctly un-German. But this was normal in the United States, where beliefs about labor and employment are steeped in the rhetoric of the American Dream: that there are economic opportunities for everyone, that individualism and self-reliance are paramount, and that hard work is rewarded.[50] Nicole's plan, while culturally denigrated from a German viewpoint, is logical when we understand her perspective as embedded in the American discourse that people achieve their goals by working long hours and solving the resulting work-family conflict on their own (a topic I expand upon in chapter 6). Hard work is a value that runs deep in American culture: long working hours and goals for occupational advancement are lauded. Fully two-thirds of Americans (66.4 percent) believe hard work is an important quality for children to learn, while only 17.9 percent of Germans believe this to be true.[51]

Nicole works much longer hours than most of my Berlin respondents, forty to sixty hours a week. She employs a housekeeper and a nanny for her five-year-old. To Nicole, hiring a nanny was an obvious remedy for the conflict between her long working hours and the shorter hours of her daughter's kindergarten class: "It's super necessary because the kindergarten doesn't stay open as late as you work." Outsourcing is a common solution for middle- and upper-class American mothers' work-family conflict, though it is unusual in Berlin. In Germany as a whole, fewer than one in ten people (8.9 percent) believe private childcare providers (nannies, babysitters, or private centers) should primarily provide daycare for children under school age. This figure is nearly three times higher for Americans (24.1 percent).[52]

Nicole received pushback for her long working hours and career ambitions from her father-in-law: "He thinks I'm trying to be president of the world. With my full-time job," she laughed. Surprised by this hyperbolic language, I asked, "What does he say to you?" She replied, "He says exactly that. I mean, there's no filter. He says exactly what he thinks. [...] His wife made him breakfast, lunch, and dinner every day, and he thinks the woman should be in the kitchen cleaning and cooking." She said she tended not to invite him to visit their home because he commented on it being too dirty due to her work schedule.

Her daughter's daycare workers would also "comment on my working." The facility managers requested a meeting with Nicole to tell her that "it's nicer when the mother comes and picks the child up once a week," reinforcing the discourse that good mothers don't work full time. Although daycares in Berlin accommodate parents' forty-hour-a-week work schedules, not all stay open long enough to assist parents who work fifty or sixty hours a week like Nicole often did. Her work choices didn't align with cultural expectations for mothers in Berlin.

The women I spoke with didn't seem to passively accept this stigma. Instead, they actively combated the negative stereotypes of being a mother with career goals. These women were vocal advocates for mothers in their personal and professional lives. Kristin, from Finland, was the most career-minded mother I met. She works forty hours a week as a nonprofit lobbyist and has two master's degrees. She is married and was pregnant with her fourth child when I interviewed her at her flat in an upscale neighborhood in central Berlin called Mitte. She told me:

> My story is extreme by German standards. I am ambitious with my work, and I love my work. I love the routines, and I like the social environment and the intellectual environment as well. Whenever I've been home for longer and even during the consulting phases I've noticed that I'm happier when I'm in an office-work environment and integrated somewhere. [...] Germans hate the word "career." [...] I get a lot of criticism because "career" is becoming a CEO, being a power freak. [...] If you ask any mom they'll say, "Oh, *I'm* not pursuing a career, I am happy just working. I don't want a career." It's purely negative if you ask anyone in the street. This kind of acts as a brake for many women. [...] It's not something they think about as kind of an investment in something that would progress across time.

Kristin unapologetically loved her job, but she sensed that her passion for working went against powerful German norms for women and families that cause women to curtail their ambitions. In her opinion, this decision damaged mothers' long-term career prospects and earnings. She mentioned that in countries like Finland, France, and the US, women don't shy away from the word "career" like German women tend to. She continued:

> That's been one of the biggest kind of taboos in Germany to say I'm a mom and I work full time and my partner works full time. That's something that most people don't understand. And I felt like I need to explain why it makes sense for some people who want to do it and that the children do not suffer from it.

Kristin told me that even some of her close friends suggested she cut back her hours and her ambitions once her fourth child was born:

> I get them daily. I mean from everybody. Especially from other moms who say, "Yeah, but now isn't it a good time to work less?" "And now you could transition to part time and stay in part time?" And there's just an expectation that the mothers are much more active in their children's life and do all the play dates and pick them up. So that's something that it was very important for me to kind of show that—or have those discussions and explain why I find full-time work valuable or why it's important for a career.

The overwhelming pressure to reduce her work schedule frustrated Kristin enormously. Every time women made disparaging comments, she felt the need to explain to them why a part-time job would damage her career development, and that children aren't harmed by their mothers working, a common cultural trope in Germany.

Kristin also explained that having a supportive husband is central to her ability to withstand and resist peer pressure and continue her career. She said her partner, Florian, is a more active parent than she is, and unlike her, Florian would love to be a stay-at-home parent. They work hard to model a "fifty-fifty" egalitarian division of labor for their children:

> And a lot of our friends commented on that. Also, when the kids were small they were amazed how well the children accepted the father as an alternative for the mom. It didn't make a difference. And

we had a lot of friends commenting that, especially when they were parents, that their kids were so mommy-fixated and that they found that wonderful that I could just leave and say, "Well, daddy is here now and I don't need to be here."

Frustrated at the pushback she received and the persistent barriers she witnessed, Kristin started a website where she posts interviews with parents and academics discussing employment and parenthood. I asked why she decided to start this project, and Kristin explained:

> We were some of the first in our circles to have children and I noticed a lot of people were successful, and then the women started dropping out or downscaled or started taking very unambitious jobs. And I thought that that's just not something that should be happening. That's really the kind of context that we need to change. Because at some point you end up in a part-time job that's not satisfying, doesn't pay, and women are frustrated, and then they have their third child and they drop out completely.

Kristin wanted to support mothers' decisions to continue working. She admitted this was her own political agenda to counter the pervasive traditional discourses she heard circulating among her acquaintances that pressured mothers to scale back or drop out of the labor force. In the same way that Patricia was critical of career-oriented mothers for selfishly taking time away from their children, Kristin pushed in the other direction and advocated to mothers that they consider their own well-being:

> I always try to encourage personal choice and just say, do what feels right and don't think about the financial incentives and the system and what others expect. I don't try to encourage people to do what I'm doing because there are so many different models that work and not everyone wants to work full time. But I try to encourage, especially women, to demand an equal footing to say, "Why should it be you who takes the full parental leave? Why not try to encourage your husband to take part of it?" Because it really practically does have consequences for transitioning back into work and just keeping a foot in the door.

Kristin tried to pose questions to the women she spoke with to encourage critical self-reflection about their choices at work and with their partners. She thought women were often too shortsighted in their work decisions and neglected to consider the long-term repercussions for their own financial independence and security.

Internalizing Discourses of Good Mothering and Feasible Work Schedules

Several mothers who wanted to advance in their careers said it simply wasn't possible to work full time while raising children. Even though they loved their work, they knew a part-time schedule would derail their career plans. Silke, who I mentioned previously worked as an au pair in the US, is an excellent example. She is a film producer from western Germany, and she and her partner, Arthur, have a fourteen-month-old son named Gabriel. They live in a renovated walk-up flat where we met before walking to a nearby park on a Monday morning. Silke pushed Gabriel in a stroller. His wide toddler smile mimicked the cartoon smiley face on his overalls. We passed through a short gate and entered an expansive playground surrounded by towering leafy trees, which shaded most of the giant wooden play structures, slides, and toy-filled sandboxes. Gabriel was crawling but not quite walking and played near our feet as we settled onto a park bench. Dozens of children, mothers, and fathers played around us. Silke mentioned that she and Gabriel came here almost daily. I was surprised at the number of parents at a playground with their children at 11 a.m. on a weekday. Parks and playgrounds like this one were dotted throughout Berlin, and felt central to public life. They were buzzing with people whenever I visited.

It was clear early in the interview that Silke loves her job. She works full time, and often into the evenings and on weekends, regularly traveling for shoots. I told her these long hours seemed unusual among the mothers I interviewed in Berlin, and she reflected, "I have a feeling that most people think full-time work isn't something you want to achieve. [. . .] I'm actually the only one where both me and my boyfriend are going to work full time. I don't know anyone else where both parents are working full time." She remembers being concerned when she found out she was pregnant because she knew that although part-time work was quite common in Berlin and the norm among her friends, it wouldn't be possible for her after childbirth, given the nature of her job and the film industry more broadly. She planned to return to work full time after maternity leave, but she seemed skeptical that this would work out:

> It's kind of my only option at the moment. They have agreed to let me leave at 4:00 twice a week. . . . I'm going to do it for a year and if it turns out to be impossible to balance it then I will have to reconsider and talk to them about whether I can go part time. But then that would probably mean that I couldn't do the same kind of things. I would probably do more administrative work and less project work, [which is] more interesting and I get paid better. It would be a different job. The career opportunities would be very limited if I went part time.

Silke's voice was steeped with apprehension and regret when weighing these options aloud. She realized she would be transitioning out of the work she enjoyed if she requested a different position with a part-time schedule. But Silke seemed resolved that full-time work as a mother would incite too much stress and guilt to be sustainable for long:

> I know it's going to be really stressful when I really do work full time and I don't have my boyfriend at home [on paternity leave]. . . . I'll probably feel guilty that Gabriel has to stay in the daycare place and that I don't have as much time as he would like and I would like. I'm also going to feel guilty at work because I don't have 300 percent. I have 100 percent. I have to split them up. So, I can't perform in all the departments equally and I'm never going to perform in any department to my full satisfaction probably. But I'm going have to make the best of that.

Before returning to work full time, Silke was already convinced that a full-time schedule was incompatible with being a good mother, and, conversely, that she couldn't fully succeed at work with the guilt she would experience. Given that none of her friends with children worked full time and there were no women with children working in her office, it becomes understandable why she might feel so torn. It's curious that Silke didn't know any full-time working moms: more than half of mothers work full time in former East Germany (55.7 percent), compared to only 25.2 percent of mothers in western Germany, where Silke was raised.[53] Although plenty of mothers work full-time schedules, especially in Berlin, these women don't seem to overlap with Silke's social networks. This suggests that women's perceptions of prevailing cultural norms may be more influenced by their social circles than by broader trends. Nonetheless, these cultural beliefs—whether empirically true or not—exert strong pressure over women like Silke.

Silke said her relatives and friends questioned her decision to work full time: "Most people are skeptical of our setup." I asked how people communicated their skepticism to her. She replied, "They don't judge me but they make me feel like that definitely is not something that they would do." She said a friend recently explained that she couldn't work full time because she would "miss too much of [her] son's development." Silke reflected, "I mean, it's implied. Obviously, no one wants to offend me. I think they do judge me but they don't say anything bad." However, her sister, a child psychologist living in western Germany, did tell her outright that it was unhealthy for a very young child to spend eight hours a day in daycare. She had tried this with her own son at eleven months and thought it wasn't good for him, but believed that he "flourished when he's in the daycare place less." Silke said despairingly, "It's good, it's important because obviously [my sister] has the experience and I'm happy to listen to her, but there's only so much I can do about a situation I can't change. I can only try it and if it fails, it fails."

Although Silke's friends in Berlin didn't openly chastise her for planning to work full time as a mother, she had internalized a sense of guilt stemming from the dominant discourse that good mothers work part time. Silke believed she would have to sacrifice her own career ambitions by working reduced hours to give Gabriel the time he needed once she returned to work.

Three mothers (Frieda, Lena, and Vera, all German) mentioned how they had ambitious career plans but changed course once they discovered they were pregnant or decided to have a second child. Frieda, whose western German grandmother chastised her for returning to work too early after her baby was born, seemed resigned to this change in plans. She found out she was pregnant while finishing her master's in business administration and then sought a job teaching business administration rather than working in the private sector, as she had planned. She saw teaching as a more "family-friendly" job choice.

Lena has a boss who on several occasions overtly teased her for her work ambitions, which incited considerable guilt. When we met, she was pregnant with her second child and working as a postdoctoral researcher in Munich, commuting six hours each way by train from Berlin every week. Living on the opposite side of the country from her husband and three-year-old for three or four days a week felt like an enormous sacrifice—in fact, nearly unbearable. Lena said she was exhausted and distraught at the prospect of continuing with this commute. Overwhelmed by this stress, she planned to use some of her upcoming year-long parental leave to look for jobs closer to home, even if it meant not using the skills she had gained during her doctoral studies.

The third mother, Vera, seethed with anger and remorse over her derailed career plans during our interview, but it was veiled behind an elaborate rationale for why she gave up a career to raise four children and enable her husband, Moritz, to build a flourishing career as a professor—a career path for which she had also trained and received a PhD. Vera got pregnant by surprise in the last few months of her doctoral program in economics and assumed she would finish the program quickly and move forward with her career like Moritz. While on maternity leave, she discovered she was pregnant again, this time with twins. Now with three children under eighteen months old, it took Vera an additional five years to earn her PhD, and then only after a great deal of effort and stress. At this point, she calculated the hours she needed for paid, private care for three small children and realized it would eat up her entire salary.

She explained at length that the *Kitas* weren't of high enough quality to leave her kids there. According to Vera, the facilities smelled bad, they had a poor teacher-to-child ratio, and her kids just didn't like them. Hiring a nanny would be cost prohibitive, and she felt that it wasn't the right choice for her family: "Why would I have children if I am just going to pay someone else to raise them? It didn't make any sense, so I decided to stay home." She worked part time as a lecturer for roughly ten years, during which she had a fourth child. When we met, she had recently begun a new job working twenty-five hours a week as an administrative research assistant. Vera and I spoke in the outdoor courtyard at her company shortly after lunchtime. Peering up at the walls surrounding us on all sides, she laughed bitterly, shaking her head. It started to rain on us, and Vera didn't appear to notice. She couldn't believe her predicament: she was deeply unhappy with Moritz, who she said was uninvolved in their family life, and resentful of her children for derailing her career. She disliked her job because it was beneath her abilities. For Frieda, Lena, and Vera, being a good mother meant sacrificing their career goals, lowering their ambitions, and working fewer hours.

Clearly not all was rosy for mothers in the workplace. Although most of the women I interviewed in Berlin said they were quite content with their bosses and colleagues, this wasn't the case for all the women I talked to. Three in particular—Erin, Clara, and Tine—recounted instances of workplace discrimination for being mothers. Two sought legal counsel and changed jobs. These women worked in diverse fields: Erin is American and a scientist, Clara is German and works in politics (recall that she and her husband, Torsten, have an egalitarian relationship and both work part time), and Tine works in publishing. All three are employed under fixed-term contracts, meaning their positions have a set term— with a specific end date, the completion of a specific task, or the occurrence of a specific event. These contracts can be renewed depending on the agreement with their employer.[54] Each of these women announced to their supervisors that they were pregnant and planned to take leave. Their bosses' reactions varied.

Erin, the American mother working twenty hours a week in a laboratory, avoided being fired by meeting her boss's mandates. As is the case in many families, her children got sick often. Erin's boss was angry that she had missed too much work. Although she worked only four hours a day, he required her to come in five days a week to complete her hours. She started going into work at dawn to ensure she completed her work while her husband watched their ailing children at home. Her boss reported being pleased at her "extra commitment," eventually renewing her contract, although she didn't receive a permanent one. Erin's anecdote shows the persistence of the ideal worker norm in the German workplace. It also demonstrates a disconnect between formal laws (i.e., one cannot be fired for taking sick days to care for one's children) and the reality of the day-to-day organizational working environment. This disconnect caused a great deal of stress for mothers like Erin.

Clara told me her contract wasn't renewed after she found out she was having twins. After a positive performance review, Clara's employers said they had every intention of renewing her contract. "Then this is probably a good moment to tell you that I am pregnant with twins," Clara had replied. She grimaced and met my eyes as she recounted the rest of the story: "And then after some weeks I was told that after all they weren't going to be able to give me a new contract [. . .] because of maternity leave and parental leave. But then they promised that after parental leave I could knock on their door again and then they [would] give me a contract." They never did. She sought legal counsel and was told she had waited too long to consider filing a lawsuit. With a shrug and a wave of her hand, Clara said she had moved on and found employment elsewhere after leave.

Tine used her leave as an opportunity to bring her three-month-old into the office to introduce her to her colleagues. Tine's boss had congratulated her and then mentioned, "I'd like you to think about staying at home because we have a difficult job situation here, and I am selling the publishing house." She was taken aback, though she says her boss was "very nice and friendly" when he told her. She learned that a male colleague who was also expecting a baby hadn't been asked to consider staying home. She consulted a lawyer and called her boss back, saying she would like to return to work. He replied, "You didn't understand me. That was not an option." Tine initiated the process of taking the company to court for this double standard, and ended up settling for eleven months' salary and lawyer's expenses.

These stories underline the damage wrought to women in the workplace by discrimination. In these scenarios, work organizations win out: companies get the ideal workers they seek, and men who tend to shoulder less responsibility for child-rearing tend to fill these positions.

Given former East Germany's recent history as a socialist welfare state that rejoined the conservative and now increasingly social democratic welfare state model of the West, one might think that working mothers would feel conflicted in the face of such dramatic changes in their lifeworlds. Cultural change on this scale is usually tumultuous. I think their relative satisfaction in the face of these shifts is explained by the fact that these women chose to pursue both of the goals that the German government desired: all three welfare state models encouraged women to bear children, and the socialist and social democratic welfare models also encouraged women to work in the paid labor force and maintain high employment levels (which were highest under the GDR). These women all had children and all worked. It's therefore unsurprising that my interviewees were satisfied with these available policies, which were implemented to support precisely their family model.

Yet most of the moms I talked to in Berlin had internalized the discourse that good mothers work part time. They didn't profess to want high-status careers. They were happy in their current positions, and they didn't feel that their families or jobs interfered with one another. These women were socialized in a cultural environment and policy context that inculcated in them a value system averse to full-time employment, which mothers conflated with career ambition. This discourse is part and parcel of the conservative welfare state model that idealizes a male breadwinner/female carer or part-time earner model of family life. This model shaped German work-family policy in post-reunification Berlin throughout the 1990s and early 2000s.

Most of the mothers I interviewed seemed to avoid work-family conflict by deciding not to pursue ambitious careers altogether, which seems to reflect both the socialist legacy that women work but also care for children, and the conservative model's mandate that women are responsible for the home. My respondents felt pressured to perform a certain type of motherhood that clashed with a lofty career trajectory, and most of my participants prioritized motherhood over a career as a result.

At the same time, I found clear evidence of resistance against these welfare state ideals among some moms in Berlin. Eight women held strong career ambitions and pursued jobs they enjoyed in spite of substantial pressure to reduce their hours, pick up their children earlier from daycare, take better care of their homes, and "take advantage" of the generous policies that would enable them to spend more time doing housework and childcare. Working full time and pursuing careers often came at substantial personal expense: these women enacted versions of motherhood and employment that ran counter to prevailing ideals for mothers. They experienced backlash at times from other mothers, their partners, and employers who disagreed with their choices, and some, like Silke, planned to reduce their working hours as a result.

The rhetoric these eight women espoused aligned with the discourses I heard among my Stockholm interviewees: that full-time employment and caregiving were compatible and complementary, and that men should participate equally in both spheres and be supported by the government in these endeavors. Only time will tell whether these women will feel less stigma for their decisions in years to come, as German work-family policy is moving quickly toward a Scandinavian welfare model of dual earning and caring.

CHAPTER 4

Western Germany

―――

"'YOU ARE A CAREER WHORE,' THEY SAY IN GERMANY."

Sonia is a journalist and has an eight-year-old boy and a ten-year-old girl. She recently earned a PhD and works twenty hours a week. Her husband, Nikolaus, also has a doctorate and works full time as an environmental scientist. We met outside Sonia's office building and conducted our interview over coffee while sitting at a picnic table on a warm summer afternoon. Sonia grew up in western Germany. Her mom stayed at home while her dad worked full time. Sonia's parents divorced when she was ten. Afterward, she recalled her mother returning to work as a secretary to support herself. Sonia remembers being the only child she knew whose mother worked for pay:

> She didn't want to work. She *had* to work to earn money. I was the only child with a working mother and so she had bad feelings. [...] She had no time with me and I was alone in the afternoon, and so it was very difficult for her to manage it because she always thought that she's a bad mother, you know. I don't know, in German, there exists the word *Rabenmutter*, like the mother of a raven. I think it doesn't exist in English.

I asked Sonia what a *Rabenmutter* was, and she explained, "A very bad mother. Like the ravens, they don't care for their children so it's like, yeah, the birds. The mother's a bad mother. And so, she felt like a *Rabenmutter*." Sonia reflected during our conversation on the lessons her mom taught her about what was "proper" for women once they had children of their own: "I learned from my mother that I have to stay at home, and it's better for the children. And the man has to work and the woman has to do the household and [take care of] the children."

Yet when Sonia gave birth to her two kids, she and Nikolaus had relocated to former East Germany for his job. As we learned in the last chapter, a completely different set of work-family norms prevailed there. Sonia reported being profoundly influenced by her new environment and "the different attitude of East German women. I was inspired by the working women there." She continued:

> We moved to East Germany and every pregnant woman around me, they said, "Oh, we'll start work after eight weeks," "I'll start work after three months." Everyone was working. So that was a decision for me, "OK, if so many women do work with small children, I will do the same." When I was pregnant I was sure that I will work after the birth.

Despite her mother's words of advice, Sonia took only eight weeks off for parental leave after each of her children was born. She told me she had no concerns about how she would handle her work and family commitments. Sonia explained feeling "quite confident" given the universal childcare system available for kids of all ages: "They have the old structure from the GDR, it's still alive." After they became parents, both she and Nikolaus went back to work part time (recall, this was a common household pattern in former East Germany) and put their children in a daycare facility that was open twelve hours a day, including holidays.

When her children were ages two and four, Nikolaus was offered a position back in western Germany, and they decided he would take it. Sonia planned to use this time after their move to complete a PhD, a goal she had wanted to pursue for years. The town they moved to, she mentioned with a chuckle, was "very typical West German." After moving back, Sonia recalled being rudely reminded of the comparative lack of infrastructure to support working families with young children, especially since she and Nikolaus had been so pleased with the supports in the former GDR:

The first day in kindergarten, I was [*laughs*] *really* shocked because it was totally different. "The [hours] are from 8:00 to 12:00, and during the school holidays it's closed, and your son is not allowed to come because he's not three years old. You have to wait until he's three years old." But I said, "He [already] went to the nursery!" "No, no, it's not possible." And so it was a bit [*laughs*]—a bit different.

Sonia tried to find a daycare facility that would admit her two-year-old and that had longer opening hours. The longest she found was five hours a day, from 9 a.m. to 2 p.m., yet this facility still declined her request. At this time in western Germany, it was rare for children under age three to attend daycare, and the municipality wasn't legally obliged to provide it (as I mentioned in the last chapter, the new Child Support Act [*Kinderförderungsgesetz*] meant that, as of 2013, all children over age one are now guaranteed a place in childcare). Sonia petitioned the mayor's office with a doctor's note saying her child wouldn't be harmed by being away from her because he had already been socialized into childcare in former East Germany. A meeting was convened, and the local governing body eventually approved her petition when her son was two years and nine months old, three months before he would have been able to start kindergarten anyway. But Sonia still didn't have a solution for her children after kindergarten finished midday.

Sonia finished her PhD and found a part-time job, which allowed her to care for her kids in the afternoons while Nikolaus continued to work full time. Because her youngest child was less than three years old, Sonia told me they actually would have netted more money as a household had she not worked and instead taken the parental leave paid by the government. The joint system of taxation penalizes dual-earner households. Indeed, the federal tax system explicitly discourages "secondary earners"—predominantly mothers—from working, in alignment with the conservative male breadwinner welfare model. She and Nikolaus had considered this, but they thought she had a good job and had invested so much time in her studies that "it would be a shame if you stay at home."

I asked Sonia how she and Nikolaus divided up household responsibilities. In her opinion, their relationship had been more egalitarian when they lived in former East Germany. Nikolaus had been able to participate more equally in caring for the children and helping around the house because they both worked part time. Yet after their move, their circumstances changed, and Sonia said with a frown,

> At the moment, it's very traditional because my husband has a full-time job and is working a lot, and often he has meetings all over Europe. So, I'm working 50 percent and I care for the children in the afternoons, and I do the cooking and everything, and so it's very traditional at the moment. So, yeah. It was better when the children were younger.

I asked how she felt about their arrangements now, and Sonia laughed. "It's not really good. But he earns the money, so I didn't find a job in which I could earn the same, so it's a financial decision." With disappointment in her voice, she told me they "stepped back to traditional roles" when they moved back to western Germany.

Sonia's children are now in elementary school. Toward the end of our interview I asked what she hoped her own children would do regarding work and family one day, and she replied, "I hope that they have more, like we had it in East Germany. It was very good for families, you know. It was easier to have a balance between children and working, so I would like to have all over Germany like there." On a positive note, Sonia also reflected on how she had witnessed changes to Germany's work-family policies since her kids were first born and as more moms entered the labor force: "But now times are changing. Last five years, there's a lot of new programs so now they [daycare facilities] take children up to two years and they have more hours, between six or seven hours per day. Now it's getting better [. . .] because now more women are working, and it's a process."

Germany, like other economically developed countries, is "involved in a process of 'unlearning' old policies [. . .] and learning new ones."[1] As I explained in the last chapter, the country has long exemplified a conservative welfare state and a "strong breadwinner state,"[2] evident in the stories Sonia recounted about growing up with a stay-at-home mother who ended up working outside the home only when a divorce compelled her to do so. Since the mid-2000s Germany has initiated a major shift toward a new defamilialization model called "sustainable family policy" (*Nachhaltige Familienpolitik*) that aims to be more gender egalitarian and family-friendly.[3]

Germany has a long history of intervention in family life. Combining work and family for women was explicitly discouraged for decades through policies that strengthened women's dependence upon a husband/breadwinner.[4] Until recently, as Sonia's story illustrates, little support was given for maternal employment in western Germany, with scant provision of childcare, short school days, and lengthy maternity leave. The punitive tax rates for second earners within families are still in place. Today, in contrast, the new logic of work-family policy, called a "sustainable," "social investment," or "increasing returns" model, is instrumentally driven by labor market demand, as I outlined previously.[5] This approach addresses the goals of reducing maternal and childhood poverty, enhancing fertility, and increasing women's labor force participation.

Countries like Germany care about national fertility rates because they need a stable population size. As of 2016, Germany's fertility rate stood at 1.6 births per woman of childbearing age, one of the lowest among OECD countries.[6] This figure is far below the rate of 2.1 needed to replace a country's aging workforce, generate enough tax revenue to keep the economy stable, and ultimately sustain a country's population. Germany's conservative welfare model intended to support fertility by enabling mothers to stay home with young children rather than work for pay. But this tactic proved ineffective in the face of new social and economic realities around the turn of the century.

Germany's new policies closely resemble a Scandinavian welfare model—for example, its new "use it or lose it" parental leave scheme encourages both mothers and fathers to take several months off after their children are born. In general, these new policies seek to support parents as workers in dual-earner families, promote mothers' continuous employment, get fathers more involved in caring for their kids, increase the availability of preschool facilities, and enhance early childhood education.[7] These are exactly the policies many scholars call for in the United States.[8]

Raven Mothers

Despite the rise in maternal employment and the presence of increasingly "family-friendly" and gender-egalitarian laws that Sonia noted, the western German women I interviewed sensed a lot of hostility directed toward them as working mothers. They reported feeling significant work-family conflict. Based on my interviews, it appears that a "good mother" in western Germany is considered one who (a) stops work when her child is born; (b) stays at home ideally for the early years of her child's life; and (c) works part time, if that, until her children are teenagers, and maybe until they leave the house altogether. According to my respondents, the dominant discourse in western Germany is that all children, but especially young children, are developmentally, psychologically, and emotionally harmed when their mothers are absent and working outside the home. This discourse differed from what women described to me in Berlin and Stockholm.

As Sonia mentioned, western Germans have a disparaging word for a woman who works while her kids are infants and toddlers: *Rabenmutter*, or raven mother. These women "leave their children in an empty nest while they fly away to pursue a career."[9] Anja, a mother of two who works as a personal care aide, explained: "Women are asked to work, to have a career. But if they have children and they work, it's—I don't know if in any other language there is a word like that—they are *Rabenmütter*. […] They are neglecting their children. They are no-good mothers."

My interviewees explained that calling someone a raven mother is an insult. It shames and embarrasses women, driving them to conform more closely to the culturally accepted definition of a good mother. In this way, the term "raven mother" acts as a disciplinary mechanism to police mothers' behavior. In her study of masculinity in American high schools, sociologist C. J. Pascoe showed how an epithet like the word "fag" shaped behavior because it was widely identifiable and pejorative.[10] Adolescent boys feared the term becoming permanently attached to them and tried to avoid it by adopting certain behavior seen as contrasting. Pascoe found that the high school boys policed each other with the epithet, but young men also policed themselves by performing hyper-masculinity and compulsive heterosexuality to prove they weren't "fags." Similarly for the German women I interviewed, the *Rabenmutter* was a well-known negative trope. Since the women I interviewed had to be employed as a condition of inclusion in the study, the raven mother discourse clearly wasn't a big enough deterrent to keep them from working. But this discourse had a profound effect on how these women viewed themselves, felt about their jobs, and made decisions about their work and families.

Many moms told me they were subjected to raven mother criticism by other women when they didn't take the full duration of maternity leave the German government provided at the time they gave birth. Ilona is a German university professor who works about forty hours a week. We met in her office, which overlooks a patio near the cafeteria where students clustered between classes, blue trays with plates of food and notebooks splayed before them. Ilona sat behind her desk and was animated throughout our conversation, gesturing often with her hands to emphasize her points. She and her husband, Leonhard, or Leo, have eight- and ten-year-old sons, and she said she was castigated for returning to work when they were young:

> It's culturally completely accepted that it's better to stay home as a mom, and it's completely culturally not accepted to go away [and work]. I experienced really many problems with other mothers. [...] Expressions like, "Do you really have to work?" "Do you think this is good for your children?" "Do you think that it's OK that they have to be in childcare for that long? Don't you see that they are not developed correctly?" "You are too competitive." [...] It's an open conflict.

Ilona felt stigmatized for working outside the home when she could have been on leave. The question "Do you really have to work?" implied that as a woman, she shouldn't work unless it was financially necessary for her family. She confronted the assumption that employment somehow damaged her children and meant that she was "too competitive," a stereotypically masculine trait. Having a job while raising young children made Ilona a raven mother.

These raven mother messages were sometimes covert, with gossip whispered on playgrounds or overheard around children's schools. Other times, though, mothers were confronted and told outright that they were raven mothers. Ilona described a specific incident:

> Something happened two months or so ago. I was talking to another mother from school about my son's school problems, and then she told me, "Yes, you know, I really had this feeling that your son is with your babysitter alone on the playground. And he can't go home to do his homework. Yes, Ilona, this is a problem. This is the problem of your son's weakness in school."

Ilona's eyes were brimming with tears when she quietly told me this story in her office. I asked how she responded. "I am always speechless. I am *always* speechless. I am always speechless. Then I cry for an hour at home and I have this feeling, 'Yes, you are an awful mother.' And one hour later it's OK, and then I can laugh. But yeah, it hurts. [...] They are very open."

Working mothers said they were criticized primarily by two sources: other women who were usually stay-at-home mothers, and people from older generations, often their own mothers or mothers-in-law. Julia, a German mother of two who works up to seventy hours a week as a teacher and music promoter, said stay-at-home moms criticized her. Maybe, she guessed, they disparaged her to make themselves feel better about their own decisions. As we sat in the courtyard of a popular local *Biergarten*, she frowned and looked out across the street toward the river that ambled through the town center.

Julia said she first confronted the *Rabenmutter* discourse when she enrolled her child in daycare and went back to work before the end of the allowable parental leave: "They think of you as a bad mother." She paused, then continued, "A mother has to stay home with their kids until they are like three or four years old and go to the kindergarten. And if they don't, and spend a lot of time at work, in Germany, they are called *Rabenmütter*." She made eye contact with me again and said, "You always have to justify yourself. [...] 'You cannot do this, you are selfish, you are a career whore,' they say in Germany."

Julia repeated that working mothers with young children were considered bad mothers "in Germany." She felt this was a national discourse, not an insult unique to her acquaintances or the town or region. Julia made the phrase sound pervasive, well-known—as normal a part of German culture as learning the national anthem. Julia also said she found it "very interesting" that it was other women who criticized her:

> They do make comments, you know. Especially the moms who are really staying at home. They're like, "Look at her, she's running late." And if your child is doing something wrong, it's like, "Oh, it's because she's not taking enough care. She's always at her job." You hear it from other women. You hear it in school. Because even in school, some teachers think the mothers should stay at home. [...] I think in these days it shouldn't be a question, but a lot of women, I think, justify their own staying at home, or their own problems. Anytime something goes wrong, it's like, "Well, yeah. It's because she's working so much."

Much like the high school boys who policed one another's masculinity in Pascoe's study to avoid being called "fag," women have a vested interest in identifying other women as bad mothers because it positions them in a better light. They come to represent proper femininity and good mothering. The threat of the raven mother epithet disciplined my respondents. Even Julia, who loves her work deeply, felt the need to justify to other women why she worked outside the home.

Women were also told by people of older generations that a woman's proper place is at home with her children, adhering to the traditional adage "Children, Kitchen, Church" (*Kinder, Küche, Kirche*) that several respondents mentioned with a laugh during interviews. They put pressure on mothers like Sandra to stop working. She is a married German mother of two, and works forty hours a week as an educational administrator. She recalled, "The older people in my neighborhood, they say, 'You can't work so much! Why don't you stay by your children?' And so, it's a question of a generation, I think. Yeah, the older generation can't imagine that it is positive also for the family that the mothers go working."

Andrea experienced tension with her in-laws throughout her children's adolescence because she worked long hours as a translator. Andrea is an American married to a German man. She said she could rarely confide in her in-laws when she felt tired or burned out: "Well, I couldn't actually share my experience because they'd say, 'Well, that's your fault. If you're so stressed out, then, you know, don't do that. Just quit.' So, I was rather isolated with that," she explained. "That's why I never complained." Andrea's in-laws argued that she was to blame for any difficulty she experienced in navigating between her work and family commitments because she elected to lead this incompatible lifestyle. This discourse induced considerable guilt and emotional anguish in mothers. Although Sandra's elderly neighbors and Andrea's in-laws criticized them, it isn't simply a matter of generation if women's peers also criticized them for being employed, as Ilona and Julia indicated. The discourse appears to resonate across generations.

Before I conducted interviews in western Germany, I naively thought I would hear lots of positive comments about how well supported women felt by the generous work-family policies available there. I began to appreciate quickly the enormous role culture plays in shaping mothers' lifeworlds. Culture interplays with policy in ways we may not expect. I was stunned to learn that women like Julia were called "career whores" to their faces. How did they respond to being called bad mothers who selfishly abandoned their children? I learned that women tended to respond in three ways. Some internalized the discourse and then espoused it themselves in reference to other mothers they knew. Another subset expressed ambivalence about their work and family lives. Finally, a number of women rejected the discourse and worked to define what "good mothering" meant to them.

Women occasionally expressed contradictory opinions about being a working mom and their views of other working moms. Even though they worked outside the home and said they enjoyed it, women sometimes used raven mother discourse themselves. These women sounded like a couple of my Berlin respondents: many elected to work part time and thought mothers who tried to reach the highest rungs in their career must not care about their children or be good parents. While a majority of these interviewees did not aspire to top positions, their judgments perpetuate a discourse in Germany that disadvantages mothers by opposing the realms of work and family. These moms escaped being labeled raven mothers by pointing to other mothers they believed were aligned more closely with that image, like those with full-time schedules and ambitions for career advancement.

Several women were critical of moms who didn't spend "enough time" with their children. Seven of the twenty-six women I interviewed spoke critically of mothers who saw their children "only in the evenings and on weekends." One comment I heard on several occasions was that women shouldn't have kids in the first place if they spent so little time with them. Tanja, a German actress and married mother of three, told me: "Not both parents can do a career. And a single mother can't do a career. [. . .] Because she's alone with the child. Why do you have the child? Then that's no family life. You have no time for it. [. . .] You can't throw them away," she explained with a sharp laugh. Tanja felt one parent in a couple had to scale back at work. And she believed single parents couldn't aspire for career advancement because it amounted to child abandonment. Her words align closely with the archetypal conservative welfare state discourse that families should consist of a breadwinner father and a homemaker or part-time working mother.

I asked another woman, Edith, why she worked twenty hours a week. Edith is German, married to a judge, and has a five-year-old and seven-year-old. Edith's own mother had trained as a pharmacist and stayed at home to raise Edith and her siblings. After they grew up and moved out, Edith's mother tried to find work as a pharmacist to no avail: "She stayed at home too long time," Edith admitted. "And this is where my anxiety [comes from]. If I stay too long at home, I won't get a job anymore." Edith holds a master's in civil engineering and works as an educational administrator, a job she enjoys. She wanted to keep her foot in the door so she didn't face the same dilemma her mother did later in life. So for Edith, a part-time schedule was a happy compromise. She explained:

Less hours was not possible. [. . .] And full time, I also want to have some time for my children. If I bring the children to the childcare in the morning and pick them up in the evening and I'm just having dinner and bring them to bed, I don't need children [*laughs*].

Edith's interview was memorable because we got wrapped up in our conversation and ended up talking in her office a lot longer than anticipated. She had mentioned before the interview that she needed to leave by 4 p.m. to pick up her children. I glanced at my watch much later on and pointed out with alarm that we had run over. Edith jumped out of her chair at the realization in a panic and apologized profusely for cutting our chat short. She grabbed her coat and purse off a hook on the back of the door, ushered me out into the hallway, and dashed toward the staircase, coat and purse flailing haphazardly from her elbow. I stood and watched her as she disappeared, feeling sorry for making her late. I remember thinking this was exactly the sort of stress Edith likely wanted to avoid by working part time. Forgetting about one's children is something only raven mothers do, and this had just happened to Edith, who clearly prioritized her children.

Tanja's and Edith's comments suggest that it's impossible to dedicate oneself to both a career and one's children. If a mother does choose to pursue a career, that implies that she chose work over her own children, making her a bad mother. The women laughed when making these comments, perhaps to soften these harsh judgments of other working mothers—judgments they nonetheless believed to be true.

Mothers also invoked the raven mother discourse when they expressed skepticism about enrolling their kids in public daycare. Unlike mothers in Stockholm and Berlin, some thought children couldn't receive adequate care in these facilities, and believed moms should be responsible for the direct care of very young children. Demand continues to exceed supply for childcare spaces for those under age three in western Germany. Angela, a divorced psychologist, entrusts her children to her in-laws rather than a daycare: "I think it's just knowing that you've got people there to look after your children, that they're being well cared for and not just being dumped in some place where nobody's looking after them."

Anja, a German mother of a two-year-old and five-year-old, explained that she didn't place her kids in childcare because she loved them. Anja was home on leave when we spoke and weighed her options aloud with me regarding her work schedule and childcare arrangements in the coming months: "I think I will start with half time, in a half-time job, because

I have two kids. OK, it's possible to put them into a kindergarten from 9 to 5 […] but I have kids. At least at the very beginning, I want to have a half-time job."

"And why is that?" I asked her. "So you can spend time with them or—"

Anja interjected, "Yeah, of course. Yeah. I *love* them. […] For me it's very important that they know they have a family and not just someone who puts them into bed, and in the morning brings them into institutional surroundings." She implied that moms who work full time don't love their children, and that these children might not know they have a loving family if they spend time in "institutional surroundings." For Anja, it seems that loving her children was justification enough for needing to work part time and keeping them out of childcare.

Heidi is a German mother who works seven or so hours a week as a fitness trainer. She and her husband, Philipp, have a one-year-old named Mia, and Heidi was pregnant with their second child when we spoke. She believed it was a mother's responsibility to properly socialize her young child: "That's one of the reasons that I don't want to put Mia in […] childcare, yes. Because I want to give her a lot of my way of living, as long as possible. When she is three years old, OK, then the others are in her life, but now I think I want to give her my and my husband's way of living." Heidi furrowed her brows and looked up at the canopy of trees high above the sandbox where we were perched while Mia played a few steps away. She explained, "I don't know [the word] *Werte* [in English]—we say *Werte* [values]." Heidi met my gaze again and clarified that only blood relatives could properly socialize Mia with the right values: "Only grandma and grandpa, OK. But we have no babysitting girl or something like that, or au pair, or what else." Heidi's tone made it sound like even the idea of hiring a babysitter was outrageous.

For decades, the German government supported and perpetuated this aspect of the raven mother discourse through its welfare provisioning. The state ensured a place in a daycare or kindergarten for every German child ages three to six, but not for those under age three. The state also provided three years of leave until very recently. The German government believed it was best for mothers to stay home and care for young children, so its policies explicitly encouraged this family model. Heidi's comments also explain why so few of the moms I spoke to in western Germany hired babysitters or nannies: outsourcing this caring labor was another sign of a bad mother.

Consider for a moment how profoundly damaging this discourse is for working mothers' sense of self—mothers work because they enjoy their jobs or their families need their income, or both. When the prevailing cultural attitude is that women fail their children simply by virtue of being employed, even the most independent-minded mothers are bound to feel a great deal of guilt, anguish, and upset—or, at the very least, social stigma.

———

The vast majority of the women I interviewed vacillated between espousing and rejecting the raven mother discourse at different points. They tended toward feelings of ambivalence as a result of the mixed messages they received about how to manage their work and family lives.[11] The German state and employers encourage women to work by offering work-family reconciliation policies, which suggests that it's acceptable to work as a mother. At the same time, mothers also perceive messages from the government, stay-at-home moms, teachers, and older people that being a good mother means staying at home, especially when their children are small. The dizzying conflict between these messages means that women often feel drawn in opposite directions. Julia, the woman who was called a "career whore," illustrated this feeling:

> You are in a bit of emotional conflict because everyone is saying, "That's wrong. You have to stay home with your kids." Sometimes it's like you take over these concerns. [...] When I work, I still try to take care of my family, so where does it leave you? Do you have any time for yourself? And is it good for your kids? That's mainly the question in Germany. And you take this over, you know. If

anything goes wrong, you think, "Maybe I should have stayed home a little bit more." "Maybe I should work less." So, you are always in kind of a conflict between the thing your culture is trying to tell you, and the thing you want to achieve. At the job, it's like, "Sorry I cannot do this job, because, you know, I'm a mom." And at home, it's like, "Sorry folks, I have to work tomorrow and I cannot come to your school concert." So, it's more the emotional conflict, I guess.

Julia loves her job and her children but said she felt debilitating emotional conflict. Her voice rose in pitch and she spoke quickly when trying to describe this sense of failing at home and at work, the words tumbling over each other, interrupted only by deep breaths. With seeming anguish, she told me she felt like she constantly disappointed both her children and her employer as a result of her duties to the other. Julia recognized she "takes over these concerns" and they influence the way she sees herself as a mother and a worker.

Julia poignantly summed up the pressures on working mothers in western Germany: "You are always in kind of a conflict between the thing your culture is trying to tell you and the thing you want to achieve." As I'll describe in chapter 6, while the American mothers I interviewed blamed themselves for their work-family conflict, Julia and the other western German women I spoke with seemed to understand these tensions were rooted in conflicting cultural norms.

Ambivalence was embedded in the comments of all the mothers I interviewed. It is impossible for women to grow up, live in, and raise their families in western Germany without being deeply influenced by the raven mother discourse.

And yet, some women did try to denounce the claim that they were raven mothers. Several mothers told me they knew they shouldn't feel guilty for pursuing careers. Instead, they emphasized that it was healthy for children to be widely socialized, and that good mothering was determined by the quality and not the quantity of time spent with children. Birgit, a married German mother of two who works as a government adviser thirty hours a week, summarized this perspective well:

I think it's very important to spend quality time with your children. Because many people think, "Oh, now that the child is at the kindergarten eight hours a day, then you are not a good parent, maybe." But if the time I have then with the children in the evening and the weekends—if I do something really nice, that we have nice experiences together, that's important. [...] I can't be 100 percent with them a day but I think that it wouldn't be good for them either, if I look at [my daughter], who learns so much at the kindergarten, and she enjoys it so much there. And she has her friends there, and she sometimes gets angry when she can't go there on a Saturday morning. So, I don't feel bad about that at all. I think I'd feel bad if I put her in front of the television in the evening when she comes home.

Others argued that a good mother is someone who is happy and confident, which comes from having a well-balanced work and home life that enables her to focus on her kids without stress or distraction.

Several women said it would be detrimental for children to have a stay-at-home mother. Silvia, a German mother of two who is married and works roughly fifty hours a week as a computer science professor, explained:

I don't see why women should stop working when they got children, you know. And a lot of Germans think that way. I don't think it's better for little children to be at home with their mother. I don't think that's the right social environment to develop ideally. How could it be? You know, if we had large clans or something like that, then it makes sense for one person to stay at home with all the kids. But one or two little children with one woman in a little apartment is just not the ideal development environment if you ask me.

Silvia pointed to countries like France, where it was normal for children to enroll in daycare and mothers to work. The fact that this was the prevailing ideal for good mothers elsewhere seemed to give her confidence in her belief, even if it ran counter to dominant German norms: "If you look over to France, they actually have a lot better childcare system," Silvia explained. "This idea of 'children have to be with their mother,' they don't have [that idea]. And that really makes a difference. They have the idea that [. . .] you're acting irresponsibly if you don't give your children to childcare because there they get socialized into the society in a proper way."

Although nationally representative survey data show that western Germans report significantly more positive attitudes toward women's employment over the past two decades,[12] the middle-class mothers I interviewed still felt criticized by their peers for not living up to the cultural ideal of a "good mother" if they worked outside the home while their children were small. Despite the expansion of public support for maternal employment alongside policies that aim to facilitate this employment, my interviews indicate this support has not translated into more perceived respect in the day-to-day lives of working moms. Women still thought they needed to dedicate all their time and energy to their kids and believed this unrealistic ideal had negative consequences for them in their home lives and on the job.

Sociologists refer to this phenomenon as a cultural lag.[13] There is often a delay that occurs between the implementation of progressive policy, or any kind of substantial change in the material conditions of a place, and the subsequent evolution of cultural attitudes. Mothers' guilt and stress can be explained in part by this cultural lag in western Germany. The government enacted progressive, gender-egalitarian work-family policy reform in a traditional cultural environment where beliefs about gender tend to be resistant to change. Cultural transformation tends to happen more slowly than changes to material conditions such as policy reforms. This period of incongruence may be inevitable. Nevertheless, these tenacious, outdated beliefs about gender, employment, and motherhood create a great deal of stress for working mothers.

Problems at Home

Women described a number of difficulties in their domestic lives when they used the available work-family policies to spend more time at home with their children. For example, women were entitled to take between one and three years of leave after giving birth. The moms I interviewed enjoyed their jobs; they seemed to value the ability to take paid leave while knowing they had job security. However, as I mentioned in chapter 3, because German mothers tended to expect this time and job protection, these benefits were considered unremarkable. The problem arose when women felt pressured to stay at home longer than they wanted and felt that using this leave time damaged their standing at work.

Some mothers, like Erika, seemed desperate to return to their jobs. She is a German single mother and a high school math and physics teacher who took the three years of leave available when she gave birth. Erika described feeling disconnected, lonely, and bored throughout her leave:

> I'm not very good with children, I think. I want to get ahead with things—learn things. And to just be forced to do nothing, this was terrible. I always told my sister the first three years was like living in a daze. You are not yourself; you don't have time for yourself. You are just like a machine.... It was just so boring and I felt all my brains you know, like not able to think anymore.

Erika didn't enjoy her leave and seemed to resent the expectation that she had to devote all her time and energy toward her child. These feelings spurred her to question her abilities. She told me she had never considered going back to work before the three years of leave were up because, as bad as she felt at home, the reproach she would face if she did return to work was a worse fate to her. She told me she was a better, more capable parent after she started teaching again.

Edith, the German educational administrator who had to run out of our meeting to pick up her kids, explained that she enjoyed her maternity and parental leave for a time, but found it untenable after one year following both pregnancies: "When I stayed at home for two years, in the end, I was very unhappy. And if you are unhappy, you can't listen to the children. You don't want to play with them." I asked Edith when she felt ready to return to work. "After one year, I want to come out to meet other people, don't talk about children. Talking to grown-ups," she laughed. Like Erika, Edith believed she was a better parent when she worked. The lack of adult talk and disproportionate time spent on domestic tasks made her stir-crazy. Many of my interviewees discussed the lack of stimulation, challenge, and fulfillment they felt while on parental leave.

Although the ascendant discourse about good mothering suggested that caring for children is a woman's most laudable task, mothers like Julia told me they paradoxically felt unappreciated at home and valued in the workplace:

> I thought maybe I [was] going to stay [on leave] for two years [. . .] and after one year, I called up my boss, and said, "I'm back! I need to come back as quickly as possible." I missed working actually. I missed doing something for which I was able to take the credits, you know. It's like being respected for something—not like caring for kids or something, because nobody respects you for doing that. But I missed the things [at work], I can achieve something you know, you're a part of society. Because when you stay at home with a kid you're kind of like out of it. [. . .] Separated from everything.

These statements echo sociologist Arlie Hochschild's findings that many workers find the gratification, praise, and support they need at work instead of at home.[14] In western Germany, stay-at-home mothers may feel gratified in their decision not to work because of the raven mother discourse and governmental supports for nonemployed mothers. But the moms I spoke with explained that although Germany may have political and cultural supports for mothers' caregiving activities at home, that didn't mean this support necessarily translated into women actually feeling valued, respected, or acknowledged for their caregiving.

There's likely a class dimension at play here for the women I spoke with. Most moms in my study were privileged. Most had the skills necessary to work in white-collar positions that afforded them validation and challenges. The opposite is sometimes the case for low-income women: low-wage workers do not necessarily gain as much value or recognition from their jobs as higher-wage workers do. Kathryn Edin and Maria Kefalas found in their study of low-income American mothers that they couldn't rely on their jobs as a source of motivation and respect. Instead, women turned to motherhood to "bring validation, purpose, companionship, and order to their often chaotic lives."[15] Raising children became the avenue through which these poor women demonstrated their maturity, competence, and self-worth: "Motherhood offers young women with limited options a valid role and a meaningful set of challenges."[16] In that sense, for many low-income mothers, policy entitlements like lengthy parental leave may feel more like an opportunity to gain much-needed validation for being mothers than an obligation. Other studies have found that even in the US, working-class women may gain a sense of competence, self-worth, and social connectedness from their jobs that they don't get from housework.[17]

My interviewees, ranging from a retail cashier to an architect, emphasized that the personal rewards they enjoyed for working outside the home were qualitatively different from those they received from the unpaid work of caring for their young children at home. For this reason, they wanted to both work outside the home for pay and raise their children. I heard this same sentiment among women in all countries where I conducted interviews.

Each mother's interpretation of how much time she wanted to spend at home after childbirth was different in western Germany. Erika and Julia could likely have returned to work quite soon after childbirth and been satisfied, while Edith was content at home for one year. The problem for mothers like Erika, Julia, and Edith arose when they felt *obligated* to remain at home longer than they'd like. Lengthy paid leave reinforces traditional cultural ideologies about good mothering, which may not be in mothers' best interests.

For those interested in gender equality in the domestic sphere, Germany's long-standing parental leave policies also have troubling implications for the household division of labor between women and men. My interviewees indicated that taking long periods of leave reinforced a traditional arrangement with their husbands. Mothers ended up shouldering most of the burden of housework. This was the case for Ilona, whose eyes welled with tears when she recounted another mom scolding her for working and leaving her son with a babysitter. She and her husband Leo are both professors, and they have two sons. When I asked how she and Leo divided up family and household responsibilities after their children were born, she laughed and said, "After birth, everything changed." She explained that they were together for a long time before having children and were emphatic about being equal partners. They divided all housework and chores evenly. She and Leo had separate bank accounts and separate bedrooms in addition to their shared room, kept their own last names, and alternated paying for meals at restaurants. Ilona took the legal minimum of two months' leave when she had her boys, and Leo didn't take any official parental leave. During and after her short maternity leave, though, Ilona told me, "We have a completely developed role system. I'm the one who's doing everything. I am the one who's cooking, washing clothes, buying clothes, buying shoes. He's the one who's doing the money, the house, the cars." She explained that both she and Leo noticed the drastic change when she went on leave, and neither liked the new system, but they have no idea how it developed or why it persists.

Most of these women living in western Germany described an unbalanced division of labor in their homes after they took parental leave. Compared to their partners, they did more of the laundry, cooked more of the meals, cleaned a larger proportion of the house, did more of the grocery shopping, and completed more of the caring tasks for their children during and after their leave. These women were aggravated by what they perceived as a backward slide from a more egalitarian relationship to a more conventional arrangement.

I didn't see fathers out alone in public with their children very often in western Germany like I did in Stockholm and Berlin (and in Rome, which I describe in the next chapter). Public parks, metros, and playgrounds were usually populated by mothers alone with children, or both mothers and fathers together with children. It was rare to see fathers alone in these spaces. As of 2012, the available twelve months' paid leave is formally gender neutral: it can be split evenly between partners, with an extra two months available if the leave is shared between parents. At the time of my interviews, according to women, this rarely happened.

Of the moms I spoke with, four were single and twenty-two were partnered with men. Of the twenty-two women with boyfriends or husbands, only six told me their partners took any leave time of consequence after their children were born. One woman told me she shared the leave days equally with her spouse. One father took four months, three took two months, and one took six weeks' leave away from work. In two cases, the men were unemployed when their child was born and therefore received the flat-rate benefit of €300 monthly (US$370) available for parents who aren't working at the time they request leave. Sixteen women told me their partners took no official parental leave whatsoever.

Birgit was the only western German woman I interviewed who split the leave down the middle with her partner. She was one of the moms who emphasized the importance of quality over quantity of time with children and who believed that daycare was a great source of socialization for kids. Birgit works as a government adviser, and she and her husband, Max, have a two-year-old and a six-month-old. Birgit was on leave with their youngest child when I visited their flat in a charming residential pocket of downtown Stuttgart. Birgit told me she and Max were adamant about having an egalitarian partnership. They divided childcare responsibilities and household chores evenly and rotated who picked up and dropped off their daughter, Corinna, from daycare, which was a twenty-minute walk from their home. On Max's days, he rode his bicycle and brought Corinna home in a seat attached to the back.

I saw this firsthand later that afternoon while Birgit and I sat with two of her friends enjoying hearty slices of homemade cake and coffee in their backyard. Max entered cheerfully through a side gate with Corinna on board his bike. She squealed in delight when she saw there were visitors, and then again when she spied the cake. We spent the next couple of hours together enjoying the sunshine and one another's company. I loved seeing Birgit and Max interact with their children, since Birgit and I had just had a long conversation about their equal division of labor, which started from the get-go with their sharing of parental leave. Birgit explained the logic that some couples used to justify their unequal division of leave time and reduced working hours:

You could also split up seven months the man, seven months the woman. Here in reality, unfortunately, most people split it up twelve months the mother, and two months the father. Unfortunately, many fathers don't even take the two months because they say, "Yeah, it's a really good thing [for fathers to take leave] but in *my* job, of course, that's not possible that I stay at home because I'm a project leader. I would have to give away my project if I do that."

Moms suggested that greater deference is paid to men's jobs over women's, although both careers can suffer from extended leaves. Since women were so heavily criticized for returning to work "too early," it was logical for them to shoulder the weight of maintaining their households because they stayed home longer than their boyfriends and husbands, who returned to work quickly after their children were born, if they took any leave at all. Women didn't seem especially angry with or resentful of their *partners* for this imbalance, but they were generally disappointed with the *situation* in which they found themselves over time. Because Germany's conservative welfare state and prevailing cultural attitudes explicitly encouraged a male breadwinner family model, mothers seemed to find their partners' comparative lack of involvement normal in their lifeworlds.

Some mothers did explain, though, that working for pay was important because it demonstrated to their partners that men needed to share in the childcare and housework. Annette warned that women could get stuck with these tasks if they stayed at home too long after giving birth. She and her husband, Martin, have an eight-year-old son and are both computer scientists. She teaches the subject as a college professor. I asked Annette during our interview in her office what advice she would give to employed women about having children. She laughed and replied immediately, "Well, try to get the right partner to do it!" I laughed too, and asked, "The right partner?" Annette nodded and explained:

I guess it's just important to let him know that that's the way it's going to be: that you're going back to work [after childbirth] and that this means he has to take some responsibility as well. [...] Because, I guess, as soon as you stay at home, you get all the cleaning and washing and cooking and all that stuff. [...] Because then you force your partner to take over part of the responsibility for part of the child. And also [the] responsibility for household things.

For Annette, declining to use all the available parental leave benefit was a strategy to create more equality in her household. In this way, mothers like Annette rejected the conservative welfare state's dictate that mothers should be primarily responsible for the home. It's possible that it was easier for Annette than some other women to refute this directive and ask Martin to share in child-rearing because they had the same level of education in the same subject. Being equal in this regard, it seemed obvious to Annette that they should share domestic tasks equally. Not all women have similar equity in their relationships. Some mothers may feel more constrained in their ability to call for more involvement from their partners.

Should policies incentivize mothers to stay at home? The German government offers a number of financial benefits to families to support their efforts in raising children. The state pays families "children's money" (*Kindergeld*) to defray the costs of child-rearing regardless of parents' work status, and "parents' money" or "parental allowance" (*Elterngeld*), which funds their parental leave and is based on their previous average net income. *Elterngeld* is meant to be a wage replacement, so it is only awarded if a parent takes time off from their job after childbirth. For parents who take the leave but weren't working before having a child, they get the flat-rate benefit for *Elterngeld* that I mentioned earlier.

The highly contentious "childcare benefit" (*Betreuungsgeld*), which was only available between 2013 and 2015, was a popular topic of conversation at the time of my fieldwork. Germany's two main Christian democratic conservative parties (the CDU and CSU) had pushed through a controversial bill that gave stay-at-home parents (usually mothers) financial compensation because they didn't use public daycare. This cash allowance explicitly encouraged the primary caregiver, almost always a woman, to stay at home. Advocates in favor of *Betreuungsgeld* likened the scenario to charging people to build a road that they won't ever drive on: some families didn't want to pay into a public system they didn't use.

Critics worried that this money disincentivized low-income mothers from working, especially immigrant mothers, and would mean that immigrant children would be slower to integrate into German society.[18]

At a time when Germany was investing many millions of euros into expanding public childcare for children up to age three, some research-ers thought the new policy was counterproductive.[19] Economist Marit Rønsen evaluated a similar bill in Norway and found that it had a large negative effect on women's labor supply.[20] My respondents also didn't like the principle behind *Betreuungsgeld*. While some women acknowl-edged the money could be useful to families, several thought that it encouraged mothers to stay out of the labor market too long, which ultimately disadvantaged them in the workplace.

Nadine, a German professor who works forty-five hours a week and has a three-year-old with her cohabiting partner, Fredrik, explained that in western Germany these incentives were referred to colloquially as *Herdprämie*, or "stove premium"—the government paid women to stay in the kitchen: "You should know about in Germany, we have the so-called *Herdprämie* [stove premium]," she laughed. "That's not the tech-nical term. [. . .] And I think that was the worst decision ever!" I asked her why she felt that way, and Nadine explained, "[Because] the people tend to stay at home this time, and for me, one year out of a job is too long. I don't understand why they put that in place. Of course, it's comfortable [. . .] and you are out of the game after a year. And the state has given an incentive to you that you do that. And that's something I don't really un-derstand," she told me, shaking her head. "It is backwards."

Besides their sense that the childcare benefit was in fact a "stove pre-mium," women were angry that the parental allowance (*Elterngeld*) could leave women who decide to work after the mandatory two months' maternity leave following childbirth financially worse off than if they remained at home and took parental leave. Nadine lamented:

> But the *Elterngeld*, I didn't get it because I was back at work then, and I didn't get a lot more [money] at work. So, I was working, pay-ing for [our portion of] the childcare, paying for the commuting, but didn't get the money from the state when I would have stayed at home. I would have had *more* money not working. And that's counterproductive, in my perspective. [. . .] It was less money than if I would have stayed at home.

Research across OECD countries has found that cash allowances depress women's labor force participation, while subsidies for childcare increase it.[21] The women I spoke with felt strongly that increasing the availability of high-quality affordable childcare would be more effective at helping them manage their work and family commitments than giving them cash allowances that seem to encourage women to stay home with their young ones. In late July 2015, the German High Court declared *Betreuungsgeld* unconstitutional, and the benefit ended.

Marginalization at Work

While most of the women I talked to in Stockholm and Berlin were comfortable as mothers at work, women in western Germany often recounted to me instances of gender bias while on the job. Their experiences tended to be more similar to those of mothers in Rome and Washington, DC, than to their closest neighbors'. Sometimes supervisors and colleagues expressed hostility, lack of support, and discrimination, which made mothers' work lives difficult. Though many regulations are in place to protect mothers on the job in Germany, it's likely that coworkers and bosses still felt comfortable exhibiting bias toward working mothers because of the dominant cultural belief that women are less capable than men at work.

The women I interviewed did not report that bosses were angry that they had children. Employers affirmed that women should be mothers, but believed mothers were worse employees and sometimes deserved to be fired. When I asked Birgit about telling her boss she was pregnant, she laughed and said, "He has very bad social competency so he said, 'OK. Um, why? How old are you? Oh, thirty-two. Yeah, then it's time. You should hurry up. But one thing I can tell you: then you will lose your contract here, that's clear.'" The law does not offer protection for employees who do contract-based work as it does for other workers. With little social grace, Birgit's boss made it clear that someone with a child was unwelcome at the company. This discriminatory behavior is rooted in the idea that women are categorically less capable workers because of their family commitments.[22]

Sandra, the educational administrator whose elderly neighbors chastised her for not staying home with her kids, recognized a double standard for expectations regarding men's and women's work-family commitments. She thought fathers were praised at their jobs for taking care of their children, whereas people looked down on mothers. I asked Sandra what the workplace could do to make it easier for mothers to manage work and family:

> I think it must be more popular to say that you have kids. […] I thought it was very funny because as a man, you often can do it easier because everybody said, "Oh, what a good man, looking about his kids!" And for women, it's often more of a feeling [as] I said to you before, "She's a mom, it's a problem." […] I think nobody will say it directly to you, but it's sometimes a little bit the feeling. [At my old job] it's not the things they say to you, but sometimes you hear it when they talk about others: "Ah, she always must stay at home with her kid." And when you hear this, you always have the feeling, "What they are talking about me when I am not here?"

Because Sandra overheard coworkers complaining about mothers who changed their work schedules, she worried that they badmouthed her in her absence. This bias against mothers in the workplace seemed to be a constant, underlying source of worry for the employed moms I spoke with. They sensed that German workplaces expected employees to commit themselves as ideal workers on the job.

Simply being a mother was reason enough for women to feel marginalized at work, but using the work-family policies that were legally available to them sometimes incited punishment on the job. In particular, some western German mothers thought using maternity or parental leave and job protection policies in fact damaged their standing at work. Ilona is one example. Prior to becoming a professor, she was a director for a multimedia company. But soon after she announced her pregnancy, she found out that the CEO was plotting to fire her. She described the announcement as a "nightmare":

I had to tell him, "I'm sorry. I'm pregnant." [...] They expected someone who was working twenty-four hours. And our culture in Germany says something completely different when you become pregnant. It says that you *stay home* from the day on. That's the German idea of someone who gets pregnant. They leave the company and they don't want to work. They want to stay with the kids, and this was not my idea when I got the baby. Or when I got pregnant. I thought, "I really want to work, I love my work. It's going to be very interesting. I'm going to manage the baby. I'm going to take it with me to my job in a cradle. I'm going to manage. This will not be a problem."

Although Ilona demonstrated her intention of living up to the ideal worker image at her highly demanding job by taking only the required two months' leave, her boss secretly consulted with a lawyer to find a legal loophole so she could be fired. An office secretary informed Ilona of this plan. When she angrily confronted her supervisor, he implored her "to understand us." He explained that Ilona was of little use to the company now, and was a financial drain given the legal mandates that the company subsidize her leave and keep her job secured.

Ilona's boss explicitly invoked maternity leave and job security policies meant to protect working mothers not only to make her feel guilty for getting pregnant, but to threaten her livelihood. This event incited her to quit. She eventually sought a position in academia, which she considered more welcoming to working moms, albeit with half the salary. Not all mothers have the option to quit their jobs if they experience discrimination at work—many have far fewer alternatives. And even if they do quit, women find it difficult to get hired if they show up to job interviews visibly pregnant.[23] The fact that this treatment happened to even a highly educated woman like Ilona doesn't bode well for mothers who have fewer resources at their disposal.

Julia's boss was also unhappy when she disclosed her pregnancy:

They put on a lot of stress and make you feel guilty sometimes because it's like, "We have to pay for you although you cannot work, and now we have to pay two people [you and the temporary employee] for the same job because of all these regulations." And it sometimes makes you feel a bit bad, even if it's not meant like that.

Remember that women have a legal right to job security, maternity leave, and parental leave. As I mentioned in chapter 3, the fourteen weeks' maternity leave is primarily funded by employers; Ilona and Julia said bosses sometimes expressed frustration because of the cost (only a small proportion is paid by mothers' health insurance). The moms I interviewed thought it was unfair that women *must* take eight weeks' maternity leave following childbirth while there is no similar statutory requirement for men, since these two months are justified as protecting mothers' health. So whatever resentment employers feel over these leave expenditures gets channeled to mothers but not fathers at work.[24] Over time, this bodes poorly for women employees.

Besides the financial burden, Julia indicated that some supervisors expressed annoyance at having to accommodate mothers' absences or find, hire, and train a temporary replacement: "Actually, I was the one taking care of it because they didn't know anything about like, 'What shall we do now?' [. . .] I proposed a plan and I got a replacement and I told my replacement how to do my job." Supervisors' displeasure often gets displaced onto women in a kind of "you created the problem, so it's your job to solve it" mentality—particularly because German men still use much less parental leave time overall than do women. Employers' anger at women for becoming pregnant was especially apparent in the experiences of the women who were the first to become mothers in their departments, and sometimes their entire companies.

When they realized they were expecting, mothers-to-be often worked especially hard to show they were capable, dedicated workers. Birgit believed that her boss may have seen maternity leave as a useful way to rid the workplace of "incapable" pregnant women and mothers of young children:

I heard from a colleague when I was pregnant again [. . .] that [my boss] said, "Frau Mezger is not so capable anymore now that she is pregnant." And that is a thing that irritated me a lot because I didn't miss work a single day because of my pregnancy. […] I think sometimes he thought, "These women with their problems and their children. Why don't they just stay at home for three years? Then they wouldn't make me so much problems." […] I think he thinks it's a little bit irritating that he has so many women there getting pregnant all the time.

Birgit's impressions from her boss' behavior and the conversation repeated to her by the office receptionist shaped her understanding of how she was viewed at work. This theme of overcompensation came up frequently among the western German women who met with me. They tried to counter prejudice and discrimination spurred when they took leave by demonstrating their proficiency at work. Mothers tried to embody the ideal worker and show that they were fully devoted to their jobs.[25]

In addition to employers' irritation about mothers' leave, several women said they thought employers sometimes interpreted mothers' decisions to work part time as a lack of interest, commitment, or ability. This is problematic because more than half the women I spoke with in western Germany worked fewer than thirty hours per week (two of these women were on maternity leave at the time of our interview; see figure 4.1), and three more worked longer part-time hours, between thirty and thirty-four hours weekly. Working part time seemed to be a tactic to deter raven mother criticism and alleviate work-family conflict.

Simone, a German researcher who works forty-one hours a week and has a one-year-old, thought that women's part-time schedules factored into supervisors' decisions about whom to recruit and mentor along the career ladder:

I think when you are in part time, they interpret this in terms of, "She does not want to develop further. She is not committed enough." […] I think the tendency is that when you step into the world of part-time jobs, that might be decisive for your future development. […] I don't think it's right. I'm not supporting these ideas that are dominant as it seems to me in personal recruitment […] where the decisions are taken about whom to foster and whom to put aside.

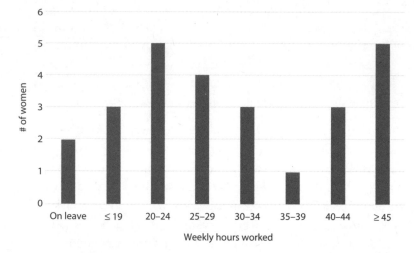

FIGURE 4.1. Weekly working hours for respondents in Munich, Stuttgart, and Heilbronn, Germany.

Simone's observation highlights another way women can be disadvantaged at work compared to men: women may be more likely to be overlooked or dropped by supervisors because their reduced hours are interpreted as a woman's primary devotion being to her children rather than to her job. Unlike men who are fathers, women who are mothers are presumed to be encumbered by family and unavailable to commit themselves fully to work. In other words, being a mother is viewed as incompatible with being an ideal worker.

Several moms explained their decision to work full time by pointing to the disadvantages they saw for women with part-time schedules. Both Ilona and Annette are professors working forty to forty-five hours a week. They recognize that part-time work hinders women's job prospects, leads them to do more housework, and highlights women's status as mothers and less desirable job candidates in the eyes of employers.[26] They adamantly encourage their women students to maintain their labor continuity and not reduce their hours, even though they admit that taking advantage of these policies could be appealing.

Adelheid, a married German mother working thirty hours a week in communications, was grateful that her boss let her have a flexible schedule. She was able to choose her own working hours and to change those hours after she gave birth to her daughter. However, she acknowledged regretfully that while a flexible schedule enabled her to spend more time with her two-year-old, it hurt her career in the long run:

> You have to expect less from work and from the position you can get, and from the salary you can get. […] It wasn't clear to me that it takes such a long time altogether [to raise children]—around fifteen or sixteen years that I have to work part time until I could change to full time again. But in my case, it's far too late then, because then, I'm fifty-five. Then I have to be happy if I can stay in this agency with all these young people, and that they don't ask me to sit downstairs in the cellar where nobody can see me because I'm an old woman. It's really like that. So, it's over. It sounds horrible but that's the truth. It's over.

What may appear to be a helpful workplace policy, like the ability to reduce one's working hours, may cause negative repercussions in the workplace for mothers when they are used in an unsupportive environment.

Although the conservative welfare state policy model is formally changing, its vestiges remain. Because German policy, culture, and workplaces all assume that women work for supplemental income, women and especially mothers are marginalized. Using the policies available to them signals that they won't prioritize their jobs and perform as ideal workers.

Mothers' Responses to Work-Family Conflict

I was alarmed at mothers' stories of workplace stigma and discrimination. How, I wondered, did women manage not to burn out from the stress? These middle-class mothers in western Germany faced a singular ideal of what it meant to be a good mother. Their coping tactics therefore operated within this limited cultural definition: what women considered possible solutions in their lifeworlds were *confined to options that allowed them to preserve self-identities as good mothers.*

To reduce work-family conflict, avoid the raven mother slur, and escape marginalization at work, mothers primarily used two strategies: (1) scaling back their own work ambitions, primarily by working part time, and (2) downplaying their family status at work. But both these tactics are ultimately oppressive to women. They perpetuate the status quo and contribute to gender inequality.

Despite the regions' different histories, interview participants in both former East and western Germany commonly worked part time after their parental leave. Edith's story, which I introduced earlier, captures this well: she has a master's in engineering but works twenty hours weekly as an educational administrator and dashed out of our interview when we ran late. She explained to me during our conversation in her office that mothers who work long hours cannot be good parents. She was careful to note, though, that she thought neither mothers nor fathers can do a good job at home if they strive for high status at work. I asked, "Is it possible for women who are mothers to get to the very top in their careers?" She paused for a moment, lips pursed and brows furrowed in thought, then answered with a slow nod:

> Yes, I think it is possible. But in this case, I think you are not really present in family as a mother. Such as men who are in the top positions, they are not really present in the family. When I ask my boss, "Where are you going for holiday?" And he says, "I don't know, my woman organized it." He has no time to do it, and it's normal. For men in top positions, they don't know what's going on in their family. And for mothers to come to the top positions, I think it's possible, but they need someone who cares about the family because they won't. [...] They could do it, but they are not present as mother in the family.

I asked Edith to clarify whether she thought mothers at the pinnacle of their careers could also be successful parents. She replied without pausing, "No. I don't think so. And also, I also think you can't be a successful man and a successful dad. Because to be a successful mother or dad, you need time." She explained, "Your brain [has] to be also in the family. You can't stay at home during dinner and talking to the children and, at the same time, you are thinking about your job. The children will notice it."

Edith thought it was possible for mothers to achieve high-status positions, but they wouldn't be good mothers if they did. She had internalized and reinterpreted the raven mother discourse: she believed both women and men are poor parents if they "leave the nest" to pursue career advancement, especially those who work full time. In her view, it's impossible for parents with full-time jobs to be present enough for their families. This view seemed to shape Edith's own decisions about work and family: she was overqualified for her job given her education, but her part-time schedule allowed her to fulfill her definition of a "good mother"—one who could focus primarily on her children. Edith confirmed my sense that her desire to be a good mother overrode her career aspirations when she revealed that she had begun a PhD program several years prior, but withdrew after realizing she was pregnant:

> Civil engineering is not comfortable to being a mother because you should do it as a full-time job. [...] I was specialized in hydraulic engineering and [...] you have to drive along all the country and you have to stay for two days there and for two days in another town, so it's not for me. That's not comfortable. When I began to study I didn't think about how I can combine it with having a family. For me it's not compatible. Maybe for some other mothers it can be, but for me not.

In Edith's view, she wasn't implicated as a raven mother. Her career sacrifices helped mark her as a "good mother."

Other women also saw the tenuous balance between work and family as a zero-sum game: a parent has a certain number of hours in the day, and a good mother simply can't work full time. Stefanie, a married mother of a two-year-old who was very pregnant with a second child when we met, job-shares her position as a business unit controller and works eighteen hours a week. She is German and had worked as an au pair abroad when she was younger. Stefanie witnessed what she considered the challenging household dynamics of a high-flying dual-career couple, knowing she never wanted this for herself:

> When you work full time, when do you see your child? I have a friend in Switzerland [...] and she has a nanny for thirteen hours a day. And I thought, "Hm, why does she have two kids? For what?" I was an au pair in France once. I was the thirteenth au pair in this family and the mom did work from 8 to 8, and the dad from 9 to 7. So, I thought, "Why do they have three kids? For the weekend? You have a daycare from 7 to 9 every day?" Both were very successful, sure, but why did they have three kids? I don't know. For me, it's not possible. But it is, sure. [...] I think you should spend some time from Monday to Friday with your kids! [*laughs*] Not only on Saturday and Sunday.

The raven mother discourse embedded in German culture made some people like Edith and Stefanie critical of mothers who dedicated "too much time" to their jobs, even if they themselves were working moms. It seemed unimaginable to some that a woman could be dedicated to her job *and* to her family. Stefanie couldn't understand why anyone would choose to have kids if the children spent most of their weekdays with hired caregivers. This perspective contrasts strongly with that of my Italian and American interviewees, who frequently adopted this model of family life with the help of paid babysitters and nannies.

The wide availability of part-time work in white-collar occupational settings helps explain why mothers in western Germany can more easily embrace this definition of good motherhood than mothers in Italy or the United States: highly educated women in Germany can often find white-collar jobs, like being a business unit controller, that are part time. This isn't always the case, though. Edith told me she searched for a part-time engineering job after her leave with no luck: "I looked but I knew before that there won't be anything." So she took the part-time administrative role. Working fewer hours and aiming lower on the career ladder (even if these jobs are less satisfying) help define good mothering in the western German context. Part-time work schedules seemed to be a crucial strategy for working moms in western Germany to manage work-family conflict and cultural opprobrium. Accounts like Stefanie's and Edith's help us begin to appreciate the gendered repercussions that ripple through the German labor market when mothers frequently adopt this strategy and fathers do not.

Another tactic mothers used to try and reduce stigma at work was to consciously avoid discussing their children in the office. Adelheid is the woman who worried that she would be asked to sit in the cellar at her communications job. She worked hard to downplay her status as a mother. Adelheid's company had quite a few women who were mothers, and her boss was firmly in support of them. Despite their numbers, she still believed that mothers were viewed as less capable than other employees:

> We don't talk about children. [...] We want to be part of this agency and we work there, and we want to do a good job. And if we talked about our children all the time, everybody will always say, "Ah, the mothers. We have just the mothers." I have a quite high position there, and I can't have this image as a mother all the time because I'm quite hard and quite tough. So, it's not going together. We don't do that.

In spite of the substantial presence of mothers, Adelheid acknowledged that motherhood and expertise at work were considered incompatible. Implicit in her comment that she is "quite hard and quite tough" is the cultural belief that mothers are soft and weak, traits considered undesirable in the workplace. Therefore, Adelheid minimized any mention of being a mother to prove to colleagues that she possessed the masculine traits of someone who deserved an elite role, and certainly not someone who belonged in the cellar. The fact that she sometimes worked full time—living up to the standard of the ideal worker—and sometimes worked part time meant she had to overcompensate for using this benefit.

While policies like telecommuting were available to many of the women I interviewed, not all used them because they thought there were consequences for putting in less face-time at work. Women worried about being put on the "mommy track." Birgit had a home office but rarely used it because she feared that coworkers would think she wasn't devoted to her job, even though she worked thirty hours a week:

> I didn't use it so much because for me [...] I felt more comfortable most often to go to the actual [office] because there I have my colleagues around—I can go for a coffee with them, I can be more "seen." Because it can be a problem if you work part time and then, three of these days, you sit at home, then maybe people feel like, "Uh, is she really working? Is she really there?"

Similarly, Sonia, the journalist and mother of two whose story opened this chapter, realized only after starting a flexible schedule that her time in the office rarely overlapped with her supervisor's. He scheduled meetings when she had already gone home for the day and couldn't attend, which she worried sent the message to her colleagues that she was disengaged and unavailable.

Despite mothers' hard work, commitment, and enthusiasm for their jobs, the presence of legal mandates and work-family policies don't necessarily advantage them in the workplace. Women reported feeling marked as inferior at work for being a mother and therefore felt ambivalent about work-family policy: it was potentially fraught with trouble for them on the job.

———

Although today's legal framework in Germany encourages women to work and have children, and relies on their labor in the paid workforce and at home, the working mothers I interviewed in western Germany felt devalued and criticized in both spheres. On the one hand, these women felt stigmatized for their family status at work: mothers' policy use highlighted their inability to enact an ideal worker identity that demanded full commitment without pause or respite—a model that continues to be associated with men. On the other hand, moms also felt stigmatized for being employed outside the home while raising young children. Returning to their jobs and shortening their leave incurred the "raven mother" slur. The women I spoke with expressed little desire to stay at home for years on end and great interest in working for pay, yet working mothers also described barriers to their occupational advancement despite and sometimes because of the work-family policies in place.

The cultural assumption remains that tending to children is women's work. When women used the available social policies to spend more time child-rearing, it came with consequences. The women I met with explained how their marriages slid from an egalitarian to a more traditional dynamic once they took parental leave. Women appreciated having flexible hours or a home office, but realized they had very little face-time with their boss as a result. Moms often took advantage of the right to reduce their working hours after parental leave, and later learned that their supervisors saw them as less capable and less dedicated to their jobs. Some mothers decided to take longer leave instead of returning to work because the cash allowance matched their normal salary.

For these reasons, the women I interviewed in western Germany were frustrated that they were unable to harmonize their careers with their domestic commitments using the policies available to them—even with more recent policies that seem more progressive in supporting mothers' work and family responsibilities. Policies like lengthy leaves and part-time work schedules may come across as "woman friendly" to outsiders like me at the outset of this project, but these women's stories make clear that using them can have real, negative consequences in mothers' day-to-day lives. Mothers seemed conflicted because cultural beliefs hadn't yet caught up with Germany's new laws. Their stress is evidence of the cultural lag between policy implementation and attitudinal change.

Women were unhappy with the state's available laws and their ability to use them without fear of stigma. Their dissatisfaction stems from the German state's enforcement through its legal structure of a gender regime that is pro-mother, but not yet pro-equality. Although German work-family policies seem to be mostly forging ahead toward a more social democratic model of gender equality and dual earner-carer families, this shift hasn't created consistent positive changes in the daily lives of the working mothers I spoke to. My interviews suggest these large shifts in the policy landscape leave working mothers on unstable ground. Although motherhood and employment are ostensibly compatible in this new model (as the EU, feminist groups, and progressive political parties have pushed for), it is clear this policy change hasn't trickled down into consistent, widespread acceptance and support of women's work and family commitments in western Germany's cultural landscape.[27]

In addition, when competing political factions with divergent goals all have an influence on a nation's work-family policy, the resulting inconsistencies in laws create uncertain terrain in working mothers' lifeworlds. For example, Germany's decision to provide paid parental leave for a maximum of twelve months is meant to encourage a swift on-ramp back to paid employment for new moms compared to the old three-year standard, yet the state simultaneously offered stay-at-home parents a monthly stipend (*Betreunngsgeld,* or *Herdprämie,* "stove premium") that interviewees perceived as encouraging women to stay in the kitchen. Public outcry helps explain why this policy was overturned in 2015. Additionally, the dearth of childcare for kids under age three continues to make it difficult for mothers to return to work.

The women I interviewed suggested that the prevailing definition of a good mother in western Germany is one who stops work after childbirth, stays home for up to several years, and then works part time, if at all. All the women I spoke with felt considerable guilt and work-family conflict in sensing that they didn't live up to this ideal. This definition of motherhood disadvantages all mothers who engage in paid work, and it privileges stay-at-home mothers who embody the conservative welfare state ideal. Progressive policies alone won't solve the dilemmas of the mothers I interviewed. Women in Germany need less rigid gender expectations and more expansive cultural support for a variety of options for combining motherhood and employment—as well as policies that support this wider array of choices.

CHAPTER 5

Italy

"NOBODY HELPS ME. IT IS VERY
DIFFICULT IN ITALY."

Elena greeted me at the door to her flat in an upscale neighborhood bordering St. Peter's Square and Vatican City. She had just arrived home from work, and after opening the door she retreated quickly to the kitchen where she was boiling water for her daughter's pasta dinner. Upon entering, I was met with the shy stare of her three-year-old daughter, Anna. She sat in a tall bucket of soapy water on the floor of the shower stall in their bathroom, clutching a plastic Cinderella doll in one hand. Elena asked distractedly if I wouldn't mind washing the soap out of Anna's hair so we could get her out of her bath and into her pajamas. I agreed and helped Anna finish her bath, and then Elena joined us, lifting her out of the bucket and into a fluffy, hooded towel.

Elena is a marketing manager for an international finance company. She typically works ten-hour days, arriving home around 8:30 every evening. She employs a full-time housekeeper and nanny named Oksana, who is a single mother from the Ukraine. Anna attended daycare during the day, and Oksana picked her up and brought her home, caring for her until Elena arrived. Francesco, Elena's husband, was out of town with his brother in southern Italy when I visited. He is a software engineer and works rotating shifts: one day from 7 a.m. to 3 p.m., the next day 3 p.m. to 11 p.m., the next 11 p.m. to 7 a.m., and then he has two days off. This means his schedule changes every week.

Elena said she felt exhausted at the end of her long workdays. But during our visit, she seemed full of energy to me, flitting from the kitchen to the bathroom to Anna's room and back again, finishing Anna's dinner and carrying her plate to a small table in Anna's bedroom. Anna ate her pasta and watched television while her mother and I perched on the bed and talked. Her room was cluttered with dolls and princess toys. A child-sized play kitchen sat to the right of the television.

Elena was direct, talkative, and eager to be interviewed. After Anna was settled, Elena dove into a monologue about her life as a working mother, and she didn't stop talking for two hours. I wrote in my field notes afterward that she seemed like a faucet that couldn't be turned off.

Elena grew up in a small village in southern Italy. She said her parents sacrificed a lot to ensure she and her three sisters wanted for nothing and could attend the country's best universities. She moved to Rome to study and work. When we met, Elena expressed ambivalence about her current job, describing it as a "golden prison." She worked fifty or so hours a week in middle management, had a good salary, and was well respected and liked within her company. But Elena felt middle management was a rat race. She had frequent performance reviews and needed to score higher than the other marketing managers internationally to move up the ranks. She was exhausted and wanted more time at home, but she said that wasn't an option in this firm.

Elena believed it would help enormously if she could telecommute more often. She compared the norms in various offices of her multinational firm: while telecommuting was so normal in the UK branch that employees had to schedule their desk space, it remained uncommon in the Italian branch. In addition to the lack of flexibility at work, she also couldn't rely on family to help with her daughter. Her parents still live in southern Italy, so they can't help care for Anna, and Francesco's parents have passed away. This lack of help from their parents felt like a great hardship for Elena.

She told me she was responsible for organizing every detail of their family's life: groceries, bills, vacations, doctor appointments, Oksana's schedule, and so on. She thought Francesco had no idea what went into running their home. Elena hated that she spent what felt like so little time with her daughter. While Elena had relieved her substantial work-family conflict by hiring Oksana, she felt the Italian government didn't provide the support families needed, and she repeatedly expressed great frustration about this.

Elena's story is typical of the Italian mothers I interviewed in Rome. She was well educated and enjoyed her job, but experienced a great deal of stress between her work and family commitments. In addition to her paid work, she was primarily responsible for the domestic sphere. Francesco helped care for their daughter, but he didn't help with chores or cleaning up around their flat. Elena was expected to show single-minded dedication to her job and conform to the ideal worker model at her company. She believed her family life suffered deeply as a result. She felt pushed to her wits' end every day, and outsourced much of the caring labor necessary to keep her household functioning by hiring Oksana as a full-time domestic worker.

Elena's work-family conflict is not surprising given the policies of the Italian welfare state and cultural norms surrounding gender, families, and employment. Italy follows a familialist welfare state model.[1] This means it is family-oriented, it has a weak welfare state, and its social protection system is fragmented. Health care is universally available, and some benefits are offered to help families, but generally the state doesn't intervene heavily in the private sphere. The dominance of the traditional breadwinner/homemaker ideal, heavily reinforced by the Catholic Church, means that women are expected to provide the caring labor and manage domestic life.[2]

Italy's Work-Family Policy

Italy is a country of sixty million people in southern Europe. Understanding mothers' experiences requires some context about the country's history, labor market, and economy in the face of recent demographic shifts. First, consider the power of the Catholic Church in Italy. Catholicism was the official state religion until 1984. The Church helped maintain the centrality of the family in Italian life, as well as traditional gender roles at home. "Family" here, culturally and legally, means extended family, not just the nuclear household. So unlike the social democratic dual-earner welfare model (as we saw in Sweden) or the conservative male breadwinner welfare model (as in Germany), Italy's welfare state is what sociologist Manuela Naldini describes as a "family/kinship solidarity" model. Public resources are channeled to men as breadwinners to support not only a spouse and children, but also an extended network of economically dependent relatives.[3]

This model helps explain, in part, why Italy's labor market is highly dualistic.[4] Even as Italian families and the economy have changed dramatically in recent decades,[5] discrepancies in social benefits persist among workers—mostly determined by gender, age, and migration status. Gaining access to the Italian welfare state's *cittadella del garantismo* (citadel of guarantees), as political scientist Maurizio Ferrera famously called it, requires securing a standard employment contract. "Standard workers" typically work full time on permanent contracts, with good wages linked to seniority and expansive labor protections. These benefits were secured in large part by unions' collective bargaining efforts in the mid-twentieth century. Standard workers tend to be older and native-born men, employed mostly in the public sector and medium-large firms. These jobs are more widely available in the center and north of Italy than the south.[6] Getting a job with a standard contract is harder for women, immigrants, and younger people. Those in peripheral, temporary, or informal employment face greater job instability and wage inequalities, with far fewer social protections. These jobs are common in small, privately owned firms that have greater managerial discretion and in Italy's substantial informal economy. Entrepreneurs receive the same meager level of social benefits and protections as these workers.

Given their class privilege and education, the majority of women I interviewed had standard contracts—though not all, as we'll see. Because women are presumed to rely on men for economic support, when women do seek employment, it's often found in peripheral/temporary or informal work—a hardship my respondents discussed at length. Across all three employment sectors, families still rely on women's unpaid carework at home. This has dramatic consequences for Italy, "namely the underdevelopment of the market for services, a lack of job opportunities for women and a correspondingly low female employment rate."[7]

The Church no longer maintains quite the same hold over Italian society, but gendered family obligations and intergenerational solidarity remain strong and the welfare state familialistic. Italy has among the lowest levels of public support for families with children in Europe.[8] It offers weak individual entitlements and few public services for care, while social policies provide ample support to pensioners and workers with permanent contracts.[9] In fact, the government spends the highest proportion of GDP on old-age and survivors' pensions of any OECD country (14 percent in 2010), and spends among the least on work-family policies as a percentage of GDP (1.4 percent).[10]

Although Italy's old-age pension system underwent a series of reforms starting in the 1990s that made it more sustainable and less costly, these resources haven't been redirected toward solving new welfare dilemmas arising in recent decades associated with three major demographic shifts: rapid population aging, declining fertility, and increasing female employment.[11] These shifts are interrelated. A striking 21.4 percent of the population was age sixty-five or older in 2016, meaning Italy had the largest proportion of elderly citizens in all of Europe.[12] What's more, Italy at one point had the highest fertility rate in Europe; now it has among the lowest, stagnating around 1.34 births per woman since the mid- to late 2000s.[13] Demographers ominously refer to this as "lowest-low fertility."[14] Like other advanced industrialized societies, Italy has also witnessed a dramatic increase in women's labor force participation. Recall from the introduction that today 55.2 percent of mothers in Italy work outside the home. Although this figure is far higher than half a century ago, Italy still ranks near the bottom for women's labor force participation across OECD countries, where the average maternal employment rate is 66.2 percent.[15] Central and southern Italy are troubled by lower rates of employment and fertility, childcare availability, and educational attainment than the northern region.[16]

Taken together, these sea changes have strained Italy's traditional welfare state configuration of limited social services coupled with informal care within the family.[17] Families increasingly need childcare and eldercare at the same time that family members—particularly women family members—are less able to provide this care.[18] Italian families thus find

themselves in a bind: "Traditional male breadwinner families are insti-
tutionally supported but no longer economically feasible, while dual-
earner families are the most economically viable yet are not institution-
ally supported."[19] Gender, employment, and family relations have
become highly charged public issues recently, but Italian policies to
support work-family reconciliation remain marginal, stagnant, and varied between regions. The increasing demand for care services in Italy has
not been addressed with new social policies (in contrast to other countries with similar needs like Germany and France, and even other southern European countries like Spain) due to the interplay of severe financial
constraints, inefficient state operations, and weak regulation of the labor
market and migration flows.[20]

Magnifying these dilemmas is the fact that Italy carries some of the
largest debt of all European countries except for Greece. Economic crises
in recent years have been used to justify sharp cuts in all sectors of public
expenditure: already meager national funding for social policies was cut
by 70 percent. Policymakers have generally prioritized the defense of existing (old-age) provisions rather than spending money in new areas such
as support for mothers and young children.[21] This tactic perpetuates traditional gender roles and the familialist welfare state. Without broader
public childcare provisions, mothers struggle to work outside the home.

Political change in Italy around these issues has been slow historically
because challenges to Italian law were seen as challenges to the Church
and its relationship with the state.[22] And although women's movements
arose as elsewhere following World War II, the historical absence of a
sustained, organized women's movement in the years since then also
helps explain why little conversation has surfaced in the public arena
about more work-family supports, such as family allowances.[23] However,
the mid- to late 2010s saw a resurgence of activist organizing around
women's education and employment, abortion rights, sexual violence,
and reproductive health, indicating a groundswell may be afoot.[24]

Italy's history contrasts strongly with that of its neighbors to the north.
Scandinavian countries started developing their care policies in the
1960s and 1970s during a time of welfare expansion, high rates of employment, and relatively greater wealth.[25] This approach bolstered the dual

earner-carer model explained in chapter 2. While these countries have "gone public" and greatly expanded public funding for and regulation of childcare and eldercare services, Italian policies have instead stalled and care has "gone private."[26] Neither women nor social movement organizations have pressed in a sustained way for policy reform. Instead, they have allowed and supported the development of an unregulated care market that is deeply racialized, gendered, and classed. In addition to grandparents and other kin, informal low-wage care workers remain a primary source of support for Italian children—topics I'll discuss at length later in this chapter.

This is not to say that Italian working mothers receive no state support. Mothers are required to take five months of maternity leave (*Indennità di maternità*) at 80 percent pay, which is funded by the National Institute for Social Security (Istituto Nazionale Previdenza Sociale, or INPS) and financed by contributions from both employers and employees (the rate depends on the job sector and type of employment contract). This time is normally divided up as two months pre-childbirth and three months post-childbirth, or one month before and four months after, provided that a woman receives a doctor's note that this will not harm her health.

A new law passed in 2013 gives fathers one day of mandatory paid paternity leave (*Indennità di paternità*)—time designated solely for the father—compared to the five months that mothers are required to take. Men are compensated at 100 percent pay for the one-day leave. Prior to 2013, there was no designated paternity leave whatsoever. In 2016, this provision was doubled to two days at full pay, and it doubled again to four days in 2018. Fathers are required to take these four days within the first five months of birth and while the mother is also home on paid maternity leave. Dads may get three additional days of paid leave if the mom agrees to subtract them from her leave.[27]

Parents are each entitled to six months of parental leave (for women, this can be used after their maternity leave) at 30 percent pay (*Congedo Parentale*). Parental leave is an individual and nontransferable entitlement funded by the INPS, and families can take ten months total. This leave time is flexible, and parents can use it at their discretion until their child is eight. If the dad takes at least three months' leave, the family gets an additional month for a total of eleven months' leave. Same-sex couples lag far behind heterosexual couples in legal rights, familial and otherwise. Italy passed a law in 2016 recognizing civil unions between same-sex couples, but although same-sex couples are now legally eligible for parental leave, their ability to use it remains unclear. The couple may not adopt children, and if one partner has biological children, the other is not allowed to adopt them.[28]

To promote women's return to work after maternity leave, a new law was passed in 2013 that gives mothers who choose to go back to work after maternity leave (without taking subsequent parental leave, meaning that they return to work three to four months after giving birth) a voucher equivalent to US$400 a month to pay a babysitter or daycare facility for a maximum of six months.[29]

In addition to paid parental leave, the Italian government offers a children's allowance for families. But unlike Sweden's and Germany's child allowance systems that award money to all parents after welcoming a child home, Italy's child allowance is awarded only to the lowest-income families on a means-tested basis. In other words, it's not a universal benefit.

Employment protections apply primarily to workers with permanent contracts, and legally prohibit workplace discrimination on the basis of sex, marital status, family responsibilities, and pregnancy. Workers have the right to return from leave to the same position. Employees (again, those with permanent contracts) on maternity, paternity, or parental leave are legally protected from dismissal while on leave. However, widespread reports have surfaced of workers in Italy being forced to sign *licenziamento in bianco* (undated resignation letters) upon hiring, which are used at employers' convenience to dismiss workers if they become pregnant, experience a long-term illness, or have family responsibilities that impinge on work.[30] A 2012 investigative report by a leading Italian newspaper estimated that approximately two million women workers were affected by this practice.[31] The report prompted new legislation that requires the labor inspectorate to validate any resignation by a pregnant woman or a worker with a child under age three.

Nursing moms who work at least six hours a day are entitled to two paid one-hour breaks daily, until their child is one year old, to pump breast milk or breast-feed. This effectively means that women are paid for a full workday but actually arrive at work later or leave earlier each day for a six-hour workday. Fathers are also entitled to these daily reductions of working hours when they are raising their children alone, or when the mother is unemployed or seriously ill. Those who work less than six hours a day are entitled to a single one-hour nursing break. However, part-time work is rare in Italy for women or men. In fact, part-time jobs are practically unheard of in the country's formal sector.[32]

After parental leave, Italian moms and dads returning to work find it difficult to enroll children under age three in public daycare facilities. About 29 percent of children under age three participate in formal childcare. Once kids reach age three, public daycare is nearly universally available. Ninety-eight percent of children ages three to five attend *Scuola dell'Infanzia* (nursery school or prekindergarten). Public childcare in Italy is highly regulated and has a reputation for high quality, much like that in northern European countries.[33] However, public childcare is rarely offered outside of school hours; only 6 percent of children ages six to eleven use these services in Italy. Formal childcare expansion in recent years has been decentralized (as in Germany; see chapter 3), and the northern and central regions have far more services available to families than in the south.[34] Given the shortage of formal care options, as I mentioned and as we'll see, Italian parents generally turn to informal care—grandparents, other women relatives, and low-paid caregivers—for children under age three and for those over age three after school hours.[35]

"No one helps me"

Italian working moms were *stressed*. Several were even brought to tears during our conversations. A primary source of their stress was a sense of economic uncertainty. This topic arose early and often in all my interviews in Rome. Women told me they had always expected to work, both because they wanted to and because they believed their families needed their incomes. They often repeated the refrain, "Even if I didn't want to work, I would have to. Families in Rome need two incomes. This city is very expensive." The three single mothers I spoke with felt it was an acute hardship to support their children on one income.

Of the women I spoke to, two had graduated high school but received no additional formal schooling, ten had bachelor's degrees, and fifteen held advanced degrees.[36] These women represent only a minority of women in Italy. In 2016, 20 percent of Italian women ages twenty-five to sixty-four had a college education, compared to 40 percent of women on average across OECD countries.[37] Yet despite the fact that all the women who spoke with me were well educated and employed, they all lamented their financial insecurity. Many had friends who were unemployed, and the women told me that the troubles of the Italian economy loomed large in their minds. The moms I interviewed in Rome were much more privileged than most. Their concerns are likely magnified many times over for mothers with lower levels of education and for those working in the informal economy.

In 2014, nine in 10 Italians (91.6 percent) considered the national economy of Italy "rather bad" or "very bad."[38] Benedetta, an Italian single mother working 38.5 hours a week as an event organizer at a local hospital, agreed. We met outside of MACRO Testaccio, one of Rome's beautiful contemporary art museums, where her nine-year-old daughter, Vittoria, was scheduled to take violin lessons. They arrived a few minutes late, speeding into the parking lot, and both leapt out of the car. Vittoria grabbed her violin case, and Benedetta shooed her toward class with a frantic wave of her hands. Benedetta went to park her car, and then we walked to a busy nearby farmers' market and drank fresh-squeezed orange juice at a table in the hot summer sun while we chatted. Benedetta explained early in the interview that she was unsatisfied and bored with her job at the hospital since her days were spent mostly doing administrative tasks. I asked whether she had considered changing jobs. She replied:

Yes. But now in this historical moment in Italy, it looks like I have a privilege. Because I have a fixed job, a fixed contract. To leave that before having something . . . [*long pause*]. There are lots of people my same age that are looking for a job, or they have contracts that aren't fixed. And the hospital [where I work now] cannot fire me. If they fire me, they have to pay me.

Benedetta explained she would never leave her current job unless she first secured another one with a permanent contract, which was difficult to come by. She said she couldn't afford any period of joblessness with Vittoria to support on her own. She felt privileged to have *any* secure job, even if she didn't like it and it didn't pay much: working just shy of forty hours weekly earned her about €25,000 (US$27,000) a year.

The mothers I interviewed believed they had limited job prospects, either to advance in their current position or to move to different jobs. This uncertain labor market weighed heavily on my respondents, especially those who were older. I interviewed Costanza, a forty-nine-year-old Italian woman with three children. She has a high school diploma and worked as a flight attendant until she and many thousands of other airline employees were laid off. Her severance would last her another year, but she felt pressured to find another job quickly.

Costanza and I met at a neighborhood café within walking distance of my flat. She fussed nervously with her coffee cup throughout our conversation and alternated between leaning back against a low-slung vintage sofa and sitting up straight, perching on the edge of the seat and leaning toward me. Costanza worried that her marketable skills were outdated. She said companies preferred to hire younger workers who cost less money. She lamented, "In Italy it's very, very hard because 50 percent of young people can't find jobs—girls and boys twenty to thirty years old. It's impossible that I find a job."

"It must be really difficult," I replied quietly.

Costanza interrupted me and said firmly, "It's *impossible*. It's not hard, it's *impossible*. It's impossible." Costanza's repeated insistence suggested she had no faith that she could find work after her severance money ran out. Although her perception of the youth unemployment rate was exaggerated (hovering around 35 to 40 percent rather than 50 percent[39]),

Costanza felt her prospects were worse than those of people younger than herself.

Women believed the jobs of their parents' era had more security and benefits, while their generation suffered the consequences of the double recession coupled with the growing portion of elderly citizens drawing on the pension system with fewer people paying into it. Carla is Italian and a self-employed tour guide. She said her mother didn't understand that times had changed for her generation. Carla and her peers were living with a great deal of insecurity and little support:

> Sometimes I don't think she's very aware of the fact that things have changed. She always says, "But you work too much. Work less. [...] In the summer, you work a lot. You should spend the summer at home with the children." But I can't. Because if I spent three months at home, there is no money. She doesn't understand that.

Carla seemed both wistful for what she saw as the more leisurely lifestyle her mother enjoyed and irritated with how out of touch her mom was with contemporary realities in Italy. "Now most of the jobs are not like the ones where there were a lot of rights. Rights are getting less and less," she complained, meaning that Italians today receive fewer and fewer benefits from the government. Carla was frustrated that she would never accrue the sort of savings her mom did as a teacher with a government salary: "She has that money—money that probably I will never have or maybe I will have when I will be very old. She retired when she was fifty-eight. Now this is not possible anymore. [...] We know that many of us will have to work until when we are seventy." All this instability made Carla feel the need for self-reliance. Her generation had fewer rights, greater stress, and less support from the state. Carla spoke as if her generation was resigned and preparing for the worst on its own.

Italian mothers also felt stress and guilt about being unable to to provide an intensive level of care like their own mothers did. Thérèse is French but has lived in Rome for many years because her husband, Gianluca, is Italian and stationed there as a journalist. She explained her sense that Italian women were held to extremely high cultural standards for what it meant to be good mothers, which usually meant not working. The attention of highly involved mothers used to be distributed among several children when families were still large. But now women often have only one child and work long hours for pay. Thérèse explained:

> They feel guilty because of the social pressure. Because in Italy women passed from the system in which there used to be only mothers home with lots of kids into a system in which they are working mothers with one kid, on which they exert a huge pressure, because it's one or two sometimes, but very often, just one kid. And so, they want to be the perfect mother because they used to have mothers who didn't work, only took care of children, and passed down the same thing. So, then a mother is completely adapted to the earlier situation [in which she was raised with a stay-at-home mom]. So, they always feel guilty in some way because they cannot be the same mother as their mother used to be, obviously.

This sense of guilt permeated the responses of Italian mothers: the majority said they had to work full time (see figure 5.1) and therefore struggled to provide the intensive mothering they believed their children needed, and that their own mothers had been able to provide because they stayed at home. These women didn't report wishing they could be housewives like many of their mothers. Like women in Sweden and

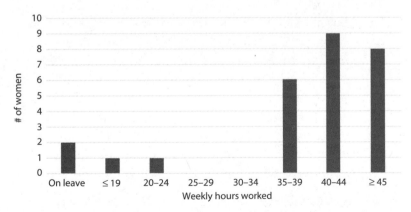

FIGURE 5.1. Weekly working hours for respondents in Rome, Italy.

Germany, they all said they valued working for pay. But Italian moms wished they felt less guilt, stress, and work-family conflict.

Italian mothers often brought up Italy's low fertility rate as evidence of desperate times for their country. Carla the tour guide worried, "The birth rate now is really low. Italy that was once the country with the greatest birth rate is now the one with the lowest birth rate." Some believed their financial uncertainty prevented them from having another child, especially those with temporary employment contracts lacking job security. Viviana, a married Italian biology researcher with a PhD, works forty hours a week for a university under a temporary contract. She has an eight-year-old son, and she and her husband, Piero, wanted another child but decided against it; her job was too unstable, and she received few benefits as a temporary employee. For instance, Viviana received only €2,000 (US$2,200) for all four months of her maternity leave.

Temporary contracts posed a major problem for women interested in becoming mothers, and for those who already had children. In Italy, 25 percent of women ages fifteen to thirty-four are employed on temporary contracts—fully one-quarter of young women. Yet, as we learned, most short-term jobs lack the policy supports that come with permanent contracts, like job security, paid vacation and sick days, and the right to a reduced schedule. In their lifeworlds, women saw temporary contracts and unemployment as major impediments to having children. Carla explained:

> The problem is because of the lack of work. Some ladies my age cannot afford having children because they are not independent. No money, no family. And that's why now most of the families in Italy, maybe they have one daughter or one son or only one child. But not because they don't want them, but most of the times because they wait until they have independence, but the independence [comes] very late and there is a time when unfortunately it's too late. This is the situation for some of the people I know. [...] No help from the government.

The moms I talked to tended to want financial stability before becoming parents.[40] For many, this period came too late in life. Because of health care expenses, daycare costs, and difficulties for those who couldn't rely on grandparents for support, the moms I met believed that many Italians ended up forgoing childbearing altogether. In their article "I Would If I Could," Italian scholars Francesca Modena and Fabio Sabatini confirm this sentiment. Italian women's employment instability does indeed discourage couples' aspirations to have kids. When women in Italy are unemployed or precariously employed, couples are far less likely to plan to have children.[41]

Money worries weren't the only source of stress and work-family conflict for women in Rome. Italian mothers were unwavering in expressing disappointment at their government's sources of support. This stands in stark contrast to Swedish mothers, who were unfailing in their approval of the available work-family policies. The majority of Italian moms I spoke with said the state provided them *no benefits whatsoever*. When I asked Carla how the government helped her as a working mother, she told me, "I don't get any money from anybody. Not one single euro. Nothing."

I said, "No money at all?"

Carla replied, "At all. Nothing."

"Even though you do pay taxes?" I pressed.

"I pay a lot of taxes, yes. I always regularly pay taxes since I started working, starting in the year 2000. So, it's now fourteen years I've been paying taxes regularly and nothing [*laughs*]." Implied in Carla's comments is a sense of injustice and wrongdoing: she has paid into a system for years and feels she has received nothing in return.

Two interview questions often elicited laughter from my Italian interviewees, as they did from Carla. These were: What sorts of benefits do you receive from your workplace and from the government? Is there anything that your workplace or the government could do that would help you as a working mother? Here are a few responses I heard:

BENEDETTA: About social benefits, zero. Less than zero.
Nobody helps me [*laughs*].
COSTANZA: [*laughs*] There is no help from nobody, and there is
always a problem.

GIORDANA: Well obviously the government could do a lot [*laughs*]. It could do a lot.

ADRIANA: Zero, nothing, no [*laughs*]. You get nothing.

Yet, I learned the following during conversations with the same women: Benedetta took paid maternity leave, enrolled her daughter in public daycare, and had a standard contract at the hospital. Costanza was collecting monthly unemployment checks when we spoke. She had given birth to both her kids in public hospitals and taken paid maternity leave each time. Giordana also took paid leave with her two children and then exercised her legal right to reduce her working hours for several months after returning from leave so she could continue to breast-feed. Her kids began public daycare at eight months and thirteen months old (which is difficult to come by).[42] Giordana worked a flexible schedule and received twenty-eight days' paid vacation a year, and her family relied primarily on the public health care system. Adriana's two daughters attended a public high school: "Both my girls went to the school where popes have come from, Nobel Prize winners have come from, for free." Seeming suddenly self-conscious, Adriana quickly added, "I can't say the government didn't do anything, that's not fair. What we paid for were books."

Despite most women's insistence on receiving "no support," all twenty-seven women I interviewed relied heavily on the available work-family policies. For instance, every mother took paid maternity leave, with the exception of two who were self-employed and ineligible (these two, however, used public childcare and health care). Women didn't consider these "benefits." They mentioned them offhandedly as rights and entitlements much like mothers in Germany did, though women in both regions of Germany mentioned these benefits when I asked about governmental supports. My interviews seemed to be opportunities for Italian mothers to vent their frustrations with the lack of support they perceived. Several women did mention that public education was one of the best social provisions the government provided. For the most part, though, women felt like circumstances for working mothers were worst in Italy. Their frustration aligns well with national data: 85.9 percent of Italians report distrust in their national government.[43]

Women thought that the Italian state didn't support working moms, and that they personally received little to nothing in the way of help. What confused me during interviews is that these women *did* have quite a few work-family policy supports, albeit imperfect ones, as we'll see. At times, I had to prod Italian women to name *any* of the supports they had—like paid maternity and parental leave, substantial paid vacation and sick days, heavily subsidized public childcare, job security during pregnancy and following childbirth, and universal health care. To a US audience, these supports likely seem generous. But Italian mothers' indignation differed from my American interviewees, who often responded with silence, blank looks, and puzzlement when I asked them the same questions about government support (see chapter 6). The women I spoke with in Washington, DC, hadn't spent much time considering how the US government could better support them, while Italian mothers were vocal about the sorts of supports they felt entitled to but didn't feel they received. When I told women in Rome where else I had conducted research, most countered immediately, "Things are the worst here, right?" or "Women there have it really good, not like here in Italy!"

Italian working moms unanimously agreed that their government did far less for them than countries outside of Mediterranean Europe did for families there. Claudia, an Italian banking analyst who works fifty hours a week, emphasized repeatedly, "Italy is not built for children." She cited the fact that there were no diaper changing tables in public restrooms and no good parks in Rome. She had recently traveled to a remote Swiss village, and she noticed changing tables for babies there. Several other moms pointed to the physical infrastructure of the city to demonstrate how families were unsupported: the sidewalks weren't wide enough for strollers, underground metro stations often lacked elevators or ramps for strollers or wheelchairs, apartment buildings often didn't have elevators, and so on. As a familialist welfare state, the country's focus on family seemed at odds with the lack of support for them. The paradox here is that, as we'll see, because families are central to Italian society, the government doesn't assume full responsibility for their well-being. Italian discourse espouses the value of family, but Italy's policies do not.

This awareness of the supports available for working mothers else-where fueled anger in these Italian women. After explaining a series of difficulties she had in getting her prenatal checkups at a public hospital, Carla reflected:

> It's typical. When you're Italian, you know, you think it's normal. Unfortunately, yes, sometimes you feel very angry. And we know that in other countries it's much better. We are surrounded by countries where things are better. For example, Germany. We know that families who have children have some help. Here, there is nothing [*laughs*]. We know. We unfortunately know because if we didn't know we would be, "Oh well, that's the reality." But unfortunately, we know. And now we feel even more angry because we know we are in Europe and so it should be kind of the same for all the European citizens. But there are big differences, I know, between Italy and Germany or Sweden or northern Europe.

My interviewees were aware that the European Union had set targets for gender equality, women's employment, and the support of families for all member countries.[44] They lamented that Italy lagged behind in meeting these goals. Cross-national survey data reiterate this sense. In 2014, over three-quarters of all Italians (77 percent) said the quality of life in their country was "rather bad" or "very bad." In contrast, only 7 percent of western Germans, 14.7 percent of former East Germans, and 9.1 percent of Swedes reported feeling this way about the quality of life where they lived.[45]

These statistics are telling given that cultural exposure shapes peoples' expectations in life. Sociologist Mary Blair-Loy explains this well: "Cultural schemas shape our action in part by defining what is possible or reasonable. People are able to seriously imagine an alternative to something [. . .] only if they come into contact with alternative cultural models. These alternatives provide new ideological resources [. . .] new ways of thinking about marriage and motherhood."[46] For Italian mothers, their exposure to the alternative cultural models present in neighboring countries like Germany gave them new frameworks to think about the relationship among the welfare state, mothers, and families. Italian mothers therefore found it reasonable to expect that they should be supported better by the state.

At the same time, though, mothers were skeptical about change. They felt the Italian government would never improve its work-family policies. This sense of impossibility seemed embedded in an Italian discourse of state ineptitude that my respondents drew upon often in our conversations. Mothers' resignation seemed to deter them from demanding more from the state or organizing for change. As I'll discuss in chapter 6, American mothers also seemed resigned to the fact that the government would never provide work-family supports. But moms in the US also lacked alternative cultural models with which to compare their experiences and thus expected nothing from the government. Carla said about Italians: "Unfortunately we know [about alternatives]. And now we feel even more angry." Italian mothers did in fact seem very angry to me.

For these women, many of the work-family policies in Italy were helpful in theory but not in practice, ultimately causing them a great deal of stress. Luisa is an Italian professor married to another academic, Domenico (Nico for short). Their son, Giovanni, is nine years old. In discussing Italy's work-family provisions, Luisa said she and Nico grappled at length over the years with "a big ideological struggle." They believed strongly in the public system of education, health care, and childcare. Giovanni attends a public school, but Luisa admitted he would probably get a better education in a more elite private school. They tried to use public health care but at times found themselves making doctor's appointments with private physicians because they didn't want to wait so long to see a specialist. Mothers with the extra income to seek out help in the private sector often did so, an option not available to Italian mothers without these resources.

The discourse of frustration I heard among my interviewees centered on three areas where governmental provisions "on the books" did not equate to the real-life support they wanted or needed: (1) public childcare and school, (2) job protections, and (3) health care. Italian women were unhappy with the availability and opening hours of public daycares and schools. These facilities are, in theory, universally available to children ages three to five and children age six and older, respectively.

All the mothers I met enrolled their children in public daycare at some point before they started primary school. Yet sometimes it took months on a waiting list before children were admitted. Once enrolled, many centers and schools closed down for long winter and summer vacations. Some had opening hours that were too short or inflexible, leaving a gap of several hours between when they closed and when mothers left work. I heard a similar complaint from western German and American mothers too. Benedetta, the Italian single mother whose daughter attended a violin lesson while we spoke, explained to me with laughter:

> Look, now it's summer. School is closed for three months. But I have one month of holiday. I have to pay, every week, 110 euros for summer school. Do they [the government] help me? No. Holiday is impossible. The mom is working and nobody can care for [my daughter]. They should think about helping you a little bit. Everybody here has grandparents taking care, but me, for example, I don't have that. No. The government relies on that.

Benedetta thought that the government *knew* about this shortcoming in care provisions and relied on the informal care of grandparents to fill the gap. Benedetta's parents had both passed away. Without this help, she was obliged to pay US$120 each week for summer school while she worked. She explained that she couldn't afford summer school so she paid with credit cards: "I live on debt. This is the reality." Benedetta complained about the high cost of childcare necessary outside school hours, saying the government didn't help her at all. In reality, childcare is heavily subsidized. The government actually helped her a lot, but Italian mothers didn't recognize subsidized childcare as help.

Besides the insufficient provisions for public childcare and schooling, women were also frustrated by the inadequacy of job protections for mothers. Some felt formal legal protections surrounding pregnancy and childbirth didn't always prevent women from being pushed out of their jobs. This often had the effect of making mothers work especially hard to show that they were committed to their firms, often to their families' detriment.[47] For instance, Antonia is Italian, married, has a two-year-old, and works as a customer relations assistant. She recently witnessed a woman receptionist get fired for taking too many sick days to stay with her children. Knowing it was illegal to fire her for that reason, her employers found a loophole: they claimed their small company no longer needed a receptionist. Antonia kept this experience in mind when she worked, and tried not to use her sick days or vacation days, even though they were legal entitlements. Costanza, the unemployed flight attendant, told me that not everyone in her office was forced to leave the company; employees without children kept their jobs. All three women who were pregnant at the time were fired, as were two men who had taken parental leave.

Government organizations meant to protect women's rights at work weren't always reliable either. Luisa works as a professor for a university under a famous left-leaning intellectual. When she showed up to a meeting with her pregnant belly visible for the first time, her supervisor was outraged to see she was pregnant. Luisa described her boss yelling at her in a room full of people. She filed a complaint against him with a government agency, but she said nothing ever came of it.

Perhaps the most telling example of the disconnect between Italy's available supports and mothers' ability to actually take advantage of them was Carla's experience trying to get a medical exam during her pregnancy. She explained, "For the health care in Italy, in theory we don't pay anything. It's true, but there are also long waiting lists. [. . .] The reality is that you cannot wait most of the time. Most of the time even if you need some surgery you need it now, you need it in two months, you cannot wait one year." Public health care is available to everyone in Italy regardless of citizenship, employment, or immigration status. The tax-funded Servizio Sanitario Nazionale (National Health Service), or SSN, guarantees the universal provision of comprehensive care. However, the Italian health care system is widely considered inefficient and poorly organized.[48] Pregnant mothers like Carla should be able to receive all the required prenatal checkups and tests for free through the public system. Older women like Carla, who is forty-two, are supposed to get priority for appointments because their pregnancies are considered "high risk." Yet when she called to book an amniocentesis at a public hospital, she was told that an appointment was available in eleven months. When she pointed out the obvious—that she would no longer be pregnant at that time—the operator said to her, "Oh, that's right. Let me check: OK. Ten months." I must have registered a look of shock on my face because Carla smiled and nodded, explaining:

> I thought, "But this operator must be young." And I tried again and again and again and I found out that that is the reality. Eleven months, ten months. Maybe the best result was ten months. And I told them, "Listen, why do you tell me that? You know it's not possible." And they said, "Well, we are operators. We must tell you the truth. This is what we find in the computer."

When I asked Carla if Rome had a shortage of doctors, she replied, "I think there are many providers, so it's strange that there is this long waiting list. In Italy, many things are not clear." She chuckled. "This is also very Italian." Carla ended up going to a military hospital since her partner worked for the military. Although this option was technically only available to wives of service members, she lied about her relationship status (she and her partner were not married), and she got her amniocentesis done for free. Carla pointed out that this exam at a private hospital would cost more than €1,000, and as a result, many pregnant women simply couldn't afford it and therefore went without prenatal exams.

Most mothers didn't speculate much during our interviews about why the Italian system seemed so broken to them. Bewildered but resigned to its disrepair, mothers seemed to have internalized the discourse that the "dysfunctional" Italian government was complicated, inexplicable, and inevitable.

One woman blamed immigrants for the system's dysfunction. Adriana, age sixty, was the oldest woman I interviewed in Rome. Her younger twenty-four-year-old daughter still lived at home with her—a common phenomenon in Italy—so she qualified for an interview and I thought she would have an interesting, if different, perspective than the younger mothers I had met in Rome. She reflected on the higher-quality health care of decades past in Italy:

> Thirty years ago, even, the medical system worked better because people were more caring, and people were more present. We didn't

have—I know it's a bad thing to say—but we didn't have so much immigration. Now in the hospitals you will find most of eastern Europe, you will find most of Africa, you will find—they are all getting the free benefits paid by us. So, the typical middle-class Italian is kind of pissed.

I clarified, "They're angry about how many people are here illegally?" and Adriana replied, "About how many people are here, and how many people we are paying for because our taxes keep increasing because it's just never enough. So yes, the Italian middle class is tired of—I can't say they are racist—but if they could be they probably would be," she admitted with a laugh. "Now you can have ten children here and be from eastern Europe and everything can be paid for."

Adriana believed the Italian system had deteriorated over the past several decades because of the arrival of immigrants who unrightfully took advantage of their public health care. She knew this explanation was problematic ("I know it's a bad thing to say") and tried to distance herself from racist Italians (using "they") while espousing her belief. Adriana isn't alone in this view: widespread political conflicts and cultural tensions have long surrounded the issues of immigration, ethnic minorities, and asylum seekers across Europe, particularly since the refugee crisis that escalated in 2015.[49] Tellingly, Adriana employed an undocumented immigrant as a housekeeper to improve her own work-family conflict, yet blamed immigrants for the broken health care system.

Italian women were outraged not only by the perceived unreliability of the Italian government, but also by Italian fathers. Mothers tended to feel that they were erratic sources of support. Some shrugged it off, while it seemed to make other women livid. Either way, the caring labor of running a household remained the domain of women.

Italian moms were irritated that the upkeep of their homes largely fell on their shoulders even though most worked for pay as much as their partners. All the women I met expressed that they'd like to have a more equal division of labor, but none of the women I spoke with thought they had this arrangement in their families. Many explained that Italian dads often cooked for the family and played with and looked after their children, but these tasks align with ideals of Italian masculinity.[50] As in Berlin and Stockholm, I often saw Italian fathers out in public with their children. Fathers carried them, kissed their cheeks, held their hands, and stroked their hair—behaviors that seemed to fit comfortably with their masculine style.[51]

Yet according to a majority of women I interviewed, their partners didn't contribute to the daily running of their households, although a few described their partners as wanting to participate equally and mostly succeeding. I say "mostly" because these mothers still tended to organize the family's schedules, book doctor's appointments and babysitters, and complete the mundane activities that often go less recognized in households.[52] No one described arrangements like those I heard from Swedish respondents and a fair number in Berlin. Mothers with more equal arrangements recognized that their families were unique. Florentina, an Italian mother with a six-year-old who works forty hours a week as a manager in the travel industry, has perhaps the closest to an egalitarian relationship. She expressed abundant gratitude that she found an Italian partner interested in equality, stating several times during the interview that he was "one of a kind."

Other moms said their partners were interested in helping equally but didn't actually share equal responsibility. Women described men who tried to help around the house, but cleaned the dishes after dinner only once in a while, or did the laundry on occasion but not regularly. They gave baths and read bedtime stories to their children sometimes, but didn't rotate routinely with their partner. This sort of participation by dads seemed to help moms, certainly, but they couldn't rely on it. This meant that mothers shouldered most of the responsibility themselves. Many asked grandmothers to help, or hired housekeepers and babysitters to fill in as needed.

Mothers with what they described as well-meaning partners reacted in two ways. A few were profoundly disappointed and surprised by this unequal participation at home. These respondents held strongly egalitarian views themselves, and thought they had picked partners who felt the same way. The lack of equality was usually heightened after they had children. Two mothers seemed especially resentful when their children noticed their fathers' lack of involvement. Luisa said she and Nico, both professors, often worked on their computers, and she would occasionally pause to clean, cook, or check on their son, Giovanni. One day Giovanni asked, "Is the work you do the *exact same* as dad's, or is it a bit less?" Luisa said he noticed his parents' unequal division of labor in the home and thought this translated into her career being less important than his dad's.

Another Italian professor, Luciana, gestured for me to stand up from her dining table where we were talking and led me to a corkboard hanging outside her kitchen. Pointing to several drawings her children had made, she narrated them to me aloud: her kids didn't feature their dad anywhere in their drawings because, she suggested, the children rarely see him. The two illustrations showed the children and mother clustered around the dining table, but the father was absent. Luciana's voice was firm, angry, and quiet when she showed me these drawings, eyes narrowed and mouth set in a thin line. We looked at these images for a few moments in silence before we walked back to the dining room, Luciana shaking her head.

Another group of women with well-meaning partners recounted this intermittent involvement in much lighter terms, often with laughter, eye rolling, and smiles. These women seemed unsurprised and accepting of spouses who professed an interest in an equal division of labor with little follow-through. I got this same response of laughter and shoulder-shrugging from moms whose partners never expressed an interest in equality at home. These women drew on cultural tropes about Italian men being immature *mammoni*, "mama's boys," to explain this disconnect between their hopes and realities. Carla, the tour guide, told me:

> Italian men always feel very young [*laughs*]. [...] We call them *mammoni*. Maybe in other countries they are already men but here they are still considered boys until they are forty or forty-two or forty-three. [...] They don't like to have responsibilities, they talk about football, they want to go to the disco. [...] They are very pampered and spoiled. And in Italy this is really true.

Carla's explanation made me laugh out loud. She grinned and continued, "My previous [partners] were from other countries like Sweden, England, Poland. But no Italians for this reason," she said with an emphatic shake of her head. "Usually in some northern European countries it works differently. They are much more independent. I like them," she chuckled, raising her eyebrows.

Bianca also laughed when recalling a memory of when she first started dating her now-husband, Tommaso. In her living room, she whispered as if confiding to a friend that he had lived alone in a flat in Rome and his mother cleaned his entire flat whenever she visited. Mothers used this *mammoni* adage often. Researchers link this cultural trope to the lengthy transition to adulthood in Italy and the persistence of deeply traditional gender roles in family life.[53] Fathers may also be invested in perpetuating the *mammoni* stereotype because it spares them from domestic responsibility.

Conceiving of their boyfriends and husbands as incapable mama's boys seemed to prevent women from asking more of them. For the moms I interviewed, who mostly worked full time, it was a lot of work to manage the majority of the household responsibilities alone. Maybe it was easier for women to label their partners *mammoni* than face the reality that men chose not to help even though they were capable of doing so. The extent to which these women recognized their partners' lack of involvement as a source of stress and work-family conflict in their lifeworlds varied—but the majority were unsurprised by and accepting of the unequal division of labor. Instead of asking their partners to do more, they asked grandmothers and hired babysitters, nannies, and housekeepers to share their workload. Instead of blaming men for their work-family conflict, most Italian working mothers blamed the state.

Ideal Worker Norms

Although more and more Italian women are employed outside the home,[54] workplaces still adhere to a traditional breadwinner model. It was clear in conversations with moms in Rome that they were expected to embody the ideal worker norm by being single-mindedly committed to their jobs. Bianca was one of two women I spoke with who had managed to secure part-time work. She is married, an Italian mother of three, and works twenty hours a week as a secretary. I asked Bianca whether anything during her workday changed once she became a mother. She replied hastily,

> No, no. Absolutely no. I am very responsible at work. So, if I decide I need to work, I need to be there physically and mentally. So, if I had to do overtime I try to organize myself with my husband, and with this girl I told you before that sometimes helps me. And so absolutely no.

For Bianca, changing anything about her workday would suggest she was not "very responsible at work." When she was at her office, she forced herself to be fully present without the distraction of outside tasks. If family-related tasks did arise, she asked her husband, Tommaso, or a baby-sitter to fill in so she could work without interruption. Bianca's part-time schedule seemed to be the only family accommodation she secured at work—and it was one many women in Rome wanted but couldn't obtain. Unlike women in Stockholm and Berlin who enjoyed and expected flexibility at work, these benefits seemed more like a rare luxury for moms in Rome.

Women felt that being a good mother, which meant prioritizing one's children, clashed with pursuing a highly successful career trajectory, even though many of the women I interviewed were on such trajectories themselves. I asked Thérèse (the French mother living in Rome) whether she thought mothers in Italy could advance to the top in their careers. She replied firmly,

> No. Definitely not. Because for that work has to be your priority. So, they [mothers] can do it, they can succeed in doing it, but in my opinion, doing a lot of sacrifice with respect to family life in that case. And the price to pay is very high. It's always very difficult because the assumption is always that you are first a mother. But you cannot have your kids as a priority and be also excellent in your job, which means that you could also have access to a very high position. This is the common opinion.

To achieve top positions, Thérèse thought women would need to sacrifice family time in order to dedicate themselves entirely to work. She also felt mothers would always be seen first as mothers and second as employees. To overcome this hurdle, women had to pay a high price to show their dedication to their careers and move up the ladder. Thérèse herself decided to leave her position at a law firm and begin consulting so she could have more control over her schedule and working hours.

Most women felt great tension between the need to demonstrate their dedication to work and their resulting inability to be the sort of mother they wanted to be for their children. This emotional conflict was gut-wrenching for these moms, especially those who worked long hours. Seventeen of the twenty-seven women I interviewed in Rome worked at least forty hours a week. Of these, four worked fifty to fifty-five hours and three worked sixty hours weekly. Fabiana, who is Italian and works sixty hours a week, has a managerial position for a branch of a transnational corporation. As we talked over lunch at a restaurant in the heart of Rome's business district, I asked her how she would define what it is to be a good mother. Her eyes welled up with tears, and she took a few moments to regain her composure. Fabiana recounted an anecdote about her six-year-old son asking her why she worked such long hours and was away from home so much of the time. This recollection made Fabiana even more upset. This story helps reveal the emotional consequences for mothers who try to live up to the ideal worker model and consequently feel like they are failing their children.

Donetta, an Italian professor, is a prime example of a woman forced to make great sacrifices to keep her high-status job. Before having children, she spent several years moving between temporary positions across Italy, living long-distance from her husband. She finally landed a permanent contract at a university in Rome. She knew once she secured this position she wanted to have children, but her adviser warned her against it:

> After I got my PhD [...] I had been told not to get pregnant. Otherwise my career was through. [My adviser] said that, "If

I have to count on someone, I'd rather count on someone that is always free [available]. [...] If I had to compare the free time that you will have, you and a man, I would take the man, definitely."

Donetta said her boss made clear that having children would derail her career. He was angry when he found out that she was pregnant, and asked her to keep working once she was officially on the mandated prenatal maternity leave. She also knew if she didn't keep working up until childbirth, other professors would try to steal her courses. Donetta said that at her employer's request, she administered exams to her students forty-eight hours before she gave birth, although she was legally required to stay home for one month before childbirth.

After she had her baby, Donetta's colleagues and boss refused to allow her to leave meetings to go home and take her legally entitled breast-feeding time: "So at work you don't even mention your family. This is how I got used to it. [...] You are pretending you don't have anything to do at home." Since it became clear they wouldn't allow her to go home to breast-feed, Donetta hired a second nanny to come to the university and stay in her office with her infant without anyone's knowledge so she could breast-feed between classes and meetings. She asked the nanny to turn on the radio if the baby started crying so her colleagues nearby wouldn't suspect anything. Many Italian mothers don't have the resources for this solution. Less economically advantaged women often leave the labor market altogether.

The flextime, home offices, and part-time schedules enjoyed by my respondents in Stockholm and Berlin were a rarity for my Italian inter-viewees. Only four mothers told me they had regular access to these policies. One worked for a nonprofit and the other three worked for international corporations. All four reported less work-family conflict than the rest of the Italian mothers I spoke to.

Women who didn't have these work-family policies at their jobs re-ported wanting them badly. Several mothers mentioned they would be happy with a part-time schedule to better manage their work and family responsibilities. However, these women indicated that part-time work was impossible in their companies, as was working from home. Putting in face-time seemed to matter a great deal in Italian workplaces. Florentina, who works in the travel industry in a management role, said her job could easily be done from home, but this was forbidden. She knew her company expected its employees to be available around the clock. They gave iPads to all employees for Christmas, but she realized after bringing hers home that it came preloaded with her work telephone number and email address. These "gifts" were really tools to make employees work more.

The few mothers who were allowed some degree of flexibility in their work schedule expressed a great deal of gratitude, but they earned this flexibility by enacting an ideal worker persona in the office. Giordana, who works in finance and told me the government "could do a lot" to help her, said:

> I'm quite free. Thank God I've got good bosses that allow me to do whatever. If I have to go to school for a meeting or for a drama show or whatever, I'm free to do more or less what I want. I have to organize my day. I have to organize myself. I'm usually here. I haven't had a sick day since two or three years. So, I'm quite responsible. They know I'm responsible.

For Giordana, always being in the office, organizing herself well, and never taking a sick day meant that her supervisors rewarded her with a flexible schedule. This was a gift rather than a right. This rhetoric of gratitude and overwork mimicked that of women in Washington, DC.

In work environments that stress the importance of full dedication to one's job, using flexible policies signals unreliability and a lack of commitment.[55] Although the Italian welfare state idealizes the family, businesses haven't accommodated the reality that most workers have outside responsibilities. The state assumes that families find private solutions to their caregiving needs, especially for very young children. And indeed, mothers in Rome universally perceived that the Italian welfare system was broken beyond repair, so they turned to highly individualized solutions to improve their work-family lives and make them feel a little less chaotic.

Mothers' Responses to Work-Family Conflict and the "Broken System"

Italian moms found a panoply of ways to reduce their stress. Some tactics were used by only a few of the women I spoke with, while others were adopted by practically all of them. I discussed earlier how wealthier mothers turned to private daycares, schools, and hospitals. Several became entrepreneurs or consultants. Others switched after having a baby from the private to public sector, where work was considered more secure and flexible but generally provided less pay and fewer opportunities for growth. Several told me they even considered transferring to international branches of their firms in countries with better work-family policies. All of these approaches are made possible by a level of class privilege that is not available to all mothers. But the vast majority of Italian working moms I interviewed turned to three sources for help. They "worked the system," outsourced some caring labor to grandparents, particularly grandmothers, and outsourced other responsibilities to housekeepers, babysitters, and nannies.

Women pointed to a loophole mothers could use to squeeze more from the government: fully paid sick leave during and after pregnancy. Mothers reported that it was extraordinarily easy to get a note from a doctor saying that a woman was ill during pregnancy and required bed rest until childbirth. It was also possible to get a note saying a mother had postpartum depression. These doctors' letters enabled women to leave work at full pay with job security while at home. Mothers were of two minds about this scheme.

Some argued that there were so few public benefits for working moms that all pregnant women should try to take advantage of this policy, whether they were actually ill or not. Benedetta, the single mom, explained without hesitation:

> If I would be pregnant now, I would go to the doctor and have them tell me that I have a risky pregnancy and stay home all the time again. [...] If I can stay home for eight months because I have a risky pregnancy, I would do that, yes. They pay me while I am at

home. [...] Even if I am super correct at work—I have never said I am sick when I am not. I am very strict in these things. But in this case, I would exploit this one thing if I could.

She understood that it was an "abuse" of the system for mothers to stay home when they weren't ill—she didn't abuse her regular sick days when she wasn't sick. But in the case of motherhood, she said she would feel no remorse in taking "the only good thing that the system offers." Several women thought the five months' maternity leave was too short, so they saw this illness leave as a smart way to get a bit more time off from work.

Several women who had normal pregnancies told me they had no interest in getting a note to stay home before giving birth but were pressured to do so by their doctors. Mariela—who is American, works as an accountant in Rome, and is married to an Italian man, Lucio—recalled her doctor imploring her, "You work such long hours; why don't you let me write you a note and you can just stay home?" Mariela enjoyed her job and had to explain adamantly that she didn't want to stay home. Mariela told me there is a "strong discourse of rights in Italy—people feel entitled to everything." She reflected at length about her observations of colleagues who worked the system to their benefit over the years she worked in Rome. She noticed other women taking advantage of their sick leave, getting doctors' notes, and abusing the firm's telecommuting and flextime policies. Some women like Mariela thought women who weren't ill should stop abusing the system, because she felt it hurt women as a group in the long run.

The abuse of sick leave was especially troubling to women who actually became ill during their pregnancies, like Valeria, who was confined to seven months' bed rest before giving birth. She and I sat on a café patio near the Borghese Gardens in northern Rome on a warm, sunny morning. Valeria is Italian, married, and a director of marketing. She seemed agitated, fast-talking and direct, like someone accustomed to juggling too many balls in the air at once. She thought the legal protections were important for women who were truly unwell. But she was irritated that some women took advantage of the benefit, and she explained emphatically, frowning, "It's too easy to get a certificate that says you're not well and [women can] stay at home for the entire period [of their pregnancy]. And there are too many women unfortunately that use this to stay at home who are not sick. I know many of them. And I think this is a problem for women." She kept gathering her chin-length hair into a ponytail and then pulling it out a few minutes later, only to retie it again.

She continued, "What happens is that when you are in a company, and you're [considering] hiring a woman and she's in the maternity period for [her] age, you think twice [about hiring her] because you know that from one day to another she can go on maternity leave." No one ever verified whether women were actually home resting:

> If there is a certificate that says you cannot work, you can even go to the Bahamas, no problem. And I know people that do that. They go on vacation, they do whatever they want. And I think this is wrong. I think it abuses the system. [. . .] There are many people who have used that, and this, of course, makes it difficult for women, especially young women, to be hired at a company.

Even though Valeria herself benefited from this policy, the widespread abuse of sick leave made her hesitate before hiring women around child-bearing age. This felt like a tragedy because she wanted to hire and promote women into positions of leadership—Valeria was often the only woman manager in meetings at the international firm where she worked. She reflected on this tension with concern in her voice: "I am a woman. I am a mother. And when I am hiring, you know, it's like, 'Okay, let's hope that she doesn't get pregnant.' You think about it because you cannot do anything. This, of course, creates a bad effect because nobody wants women in the office." For those who abuse the leave, "You know that you are basically untouchable. You're completely safe. [. . .] This is a part of the Italian law that I actually don't think is right."

Some Italian mothers seemed to "abuse" the state because the state "abused" them. Women worked the system as a gendered strategy to reduce their stress and sense of helplessness. This coping tool is very much connected to a primary source of work-family conflict that mothers reported: the inept, corrupt state. Working the system was a mechanism of mothers' resistance as well as their oppression.

While several women "worked the system" to reduce their conflict, a far more common tactic to reduce stress in their lifeworlds was to recruit the help of family to care for children. About half of the women I spoke to in Rome had relatives living nearby, sometimes on the same street or in the same building. Some even shared a home with them. Mothers relied heavily on these kin networks, primarily grandmothers, who were essential in helping alleviate their work-family conflict. Unlike in my other field sites, in Rome this dynamic seemed quite common and, in fact, central to everyday life. As I said, Italians exhibit strong intergenerational solidarity and a sense of familial obligation.[56] Relatives of different generations live together longer than anywhere else in Europe, and family members often care for young children and elderly relatives.[57] Grandparents care for grandchildren more often in Italy than in Germany or Sweden. One study found that grandparents are ten times more likely to be involved in the almost daily care of grandchildren in Italy and Greece than they are in the northern European countries of Denmark and the Netherlands. Of Italian grandparents who report any grandchild care, 50 percent act as full-time caregivers.[58] The share of mothers who relied primarily on grandparents for childcare in Sweden, Germany, and Italy varied substantially by region within each country; mothers in more conservative areas were more inclined to use grandparents rather than formal daycare centers as the main source of childcare.[59]

Children and young adults also tend to live with their parents much longer in Italy than in other OECD countries. Recall that the unemployment rate for those age fifteen to twenty-four has fluctuated between 35 and 40 percent since 2010.[60] According to the Italian Institute of Statistics, 92.4 percent of men and 85.7 percent of women ages twenty to twenty-four lived with their nuclear families in 2009. For twenty-five- to twenty-nine-year-olds, seven in ten men and five in ten women still lived at home.[61] In general, prolonged co-residence is typical in Italy because children are expected to leave their parents' home after they finish their education, find stable jobs, and get married.[62] Researchers point to the fact that Italy has few public policies aimed at youth independence, and both housing policy and the Italian housing market are oriented toward home ownership. Yet the ongoing economic crisis in Italy means that standard, full-time employment with sufficient income to accrue the savings necessary to buy a home is in short supply.[63] The support parents give to their grown children residing at home engenders the strong intergenerational obligations that are central to the operation of the familialist welfare state.[64]

Women whose parents or in-laws lived nearby described few concerns related to childcare when they found out they were pregnant; they knew they could rely upon nearby relatives. Grandmothers often cared for infants, picked children up from school, and fed them meals. Despite their daily presence, we spent remarkably little time discussing grandmothers' assistance or what sorts of tasks they helped with. Perhaps because this carework was so deeply engrained and commonplace in Italy, it seemed unremarkable to the moms I met. One woman told me a story of going out to dinner at a restaurant with her toddler and her in-laws, and the grandmother saw a high chair for the first time. Confused, she said, "But that's what grandparents are for." I was fascinated to realize that this intergenerational carework means different things to different people and can be shaped by cultural context. Several women who relied on the help of their own mothers or mothers-in-law didn't mention them immediately when I asked how they managed their work and family responsibilities. I had to ask explicitly, and women responded with some version of, "Oh, right. Yes, we have a lot of help from the grandparents."

Grandmothers' help, in particular, was so fundamental to how mothers thought of their families that the prospect of child-rearing without them felt overwhelming. Bianca (the Italian secretary and mother of three who works part time) explained she was really worried about how to care for a newborn before having her first child. Her mother and grandmother both passed away while she was pregnant. Bianca's grandmother had lived with her throughout her childhood: "She was the one who cooked, she was one who did everything. She was very, very important." Unlike the majority of American mothers I interviewed who assumed they would raise their children without relatives' support, the assumption of intergenerational support was so central to Italian mothers that women felt devastated without it. In Germany and Sweden, mothers told me that grandparents often helped out if they lived close by, but this was only the case for about one-third of the women I spoke to.

A few Italian mothers said their parents or in-laws were reluctant or unwilling to help out because they were involved in their own careers. It's rare for older people to work in Italy: the retirement age is historically one of the lowest among OECD countries, though the state has recently raised it, apparently to reflect the increase in life expectancy.[65] In 2012, the age of retirement was sixty-two years. It has increased incrementally since then, and as of 2018, retirement age was sixty-six years, seven months.[66] Women expressed great disappointment when their parents or in-laws lived nearby but weren't interested in helping care for grandchildren while the parents worked. Santina, for example, is an international consultant. Her mother-in-law, who is French, lives one hundred yards from their house on the same street. As we sat in her living room, Santina pointed over her right shoulder absentmindedly to indicate the direction of her mother-in-law's flat. "We never see her," she laughed. "She's seventy-five, she's still working. [. . .] When she found out that I was going to return to work she asked me, 'How are you going to do it with [your daughter]? [. . .] Don't count on me.'" Santina's smile faded, the laughter left her voice, and she said with sadness that her partner was "as disappointed as I am. [. . .] It's how she is. We cannot change her."

This grandmother's lack of interest ran counter to the predominant cultural expectation that grandparents want to and assume they will care for their grandchildren if they live close by. Santina had internalized this discourse. It shaped her expectations about what child-rearing would be like in her lifeworld one day. And now that she had a child of her own, Santina was disappointed by her mother-in-law's lukewarm attitude toward babysitting.

Santina's case aside, because grandmothers so often take over domestic carework in Italy, employers often assume that women like my interviewees are free to work longer hours. Rosanna, an Italian professor, told her department chair she couldn't attend a meeting because she needed to pick up her child. He replied, "Don't you have a mom to raise your sons?" Rosanna told me how irritated she felt that her boss assumed it was a grandmother's job to care for her children if she pursued a career.

Grandparents' care for children does impact women's labor force participation in Italy: a 2012 study found that grandparents' help with childcare in Italy had a positive, statistically significant effect on women's labor supply, especially for mothers with low levels of education in northern and central Italy.[67]

Women without relatives nearby, or whose parents had passed away, explained at length the difficulty of raising children without their in-laws' help. Half of the Italian mothers in my sample had migrated to Rome and away from their families for work. Recall that both of Benedetta's parents died two years before our interview. She said it felt like everyone else in Rome had the help of grandparents, which she desperately needed as a single mom. I asked Benedetta whether she thought it was possible to be both a successful mother and a successful worker. She replied:

> I think it's all a question of money. I think if you have money you can provide things to your children. You can pay a babysitter, so maybe that can help. [...] I think it's all a question of how you can find a substitute for you. Maybe it's possible if you are rich. I mean, in my case, maybe if my mom would be alive she would be a good substitute. But she is not.

Mothers in Italy seemed to believe strongly that their job advancement, work-family life, and ability to be good mothers were dependent on having a grandmother to care for their children, or on financial resources they could use to outsource this care as "a substitute for you."

Even for those women with grandparents close by and willing to care for children, I learned that the help of grandmothers and paid babysitters or nannies weren't mutually exclusive in the Italian context. My middle-class participants often used both forms of outsourcing to meet their families' needs.

The availability of low-cost immigrant labor combined with the scarcity of public services has created a large and poorly regulated market for immigrant workers.[68] These low-cost market solutions have lessened the political pressure for public intervention with regard to both service provision and financial support for working mothers.[69] Researchers call this transition as moving from a familial model of care to a "migrant in the family" model of care.[70]

This phenomenon hasn't developed in coordinated market economies like Scandinavia; these countries have highly regulated and protected labor markets that prevent the creation of a low-cost private market, which pushes the issue of care onto the political agenda.[71] Social democratic welfare states also lessen the likelihood that families will rely on migrant domestic workers because they have a universal benefit system with large-scale institutional support for mothers and families[72]—something Italy lacks.

Although recent EU expansion has allowed care workers to migrate from eastern Europe to Italy and work legally, labor market deregulation in the 2000s has facilitated the irregular employment of immigrant women.[73] A 2009 study by Italy's Institute for Economic and Social Research (Istituto di Ricerche Economiche e Sociali) found that half of domestic workers, three-quarters of babysitters, and half of care assistants had no job contract.[74] This informal labor market participation inhibits the political, civil, and social incorporation of these immigrant workers into their host societies, which further guarantees a ready supply of low-wage labor.[75]

All the Italian mothers I interviewed except one employed housekeepers, babysitters, or nannies. These domestic workers were from Ethiopia, the Philippines, Ecuador, Portugal, Italy, Sweden, and eastern Europe, among other places. The mothers I interviewed often employed a housekeeper and one or two babysitters or nannies simultaneously to care for their home and kids. Some respondents had helpers once or twice a week, but many had daily full-time assistance. Because women are still primarily responsible for housework and childcare in Italy, my interviewees skirted their gender disadvantage by relying on their class privilege to outsource some of their responsibilities.

A few women mentioned this outsourced help offhandedly to me, but many didn't bring it up when I asked how they managed their work-family conflict. Some failed to mention this help even when our interviews took place in respondents' homes while housekeepers cleaned in the same room as us. In two instances, I had to inquire, "It looks like you have a housekeeper. Can you tell me about her?" Women forgot to mention this source of support in the same way that they did grandmothers' help—it was so normalized and deeply engrained that some respondents rendered this labor invisible until I asked about it.

It was also puzzling to me that so many women talked at length about how they got "no help from anyone," as I highlighted earlier, yet so many got substantial assistance from grandmothers or paid domestic workers and from the government. The widespread discourse among these women that "working mothers get no help" concealed the help they did get. For example, Bianca mentioned that her boss let her work part time in her secretary job after she returned from maternity leave, and she hired a babysitter, an older Italian woman named Gina who lived next door in their apartment building, from 9 a.m. to 7 p.m. on the days she worked: "I could count on her. She was a big help." It seemed clear to me that Bianca valued Gina and acknowledged that Gina's labor enabled her to continue working once her third child was born.

Two minutes later in our conversation, I asked Bianca whether she thought Italian mothers could get to the top of their careers. She replied, "Of course you have to have a lot of help, but you can do it. [. . .] To be on the top, the very top you need somebody present in your home all day long. Because being at this level means you need to be available at any time. So, you need to have a presence, a fixed presence in your life." Bianca explained that she'd never wanted paid help herself: "I like my independence and I don't like somebody else in my house. I've been doing this for years with my independence. Done it all by myself." While it is true that Bianca never employed a babysitter full time, she received extra help two days a week. Again, the rhetoric that Italians get no help from anyone seems so rooted in mothers' lifeworlds that it obfuscates their dependence on low-wage workers like Gina to lessen their work-family conflict. Invisibilizing the labor of these caregivers perpetuates the cultural expectation that mothers are solely responsible for household labor.

However, women considered hired helpers a necessity. They were among the last things women were willing to forgo when money was tight. Benedetta, the single mother who funded summer camps with credit cards, still paid a woman to clean her house: "It sounds stupid, but I really need it. In my house [growing up] there was always a cleaning lady. I don't buy fresh flowers anymore, for example, but I will always have a cleaning lady." Benedetta couldn't imagine life without a housekeeper. Mariela, the American accountant, told me she paid her full-time nanny and housekeeper €12,000 a year (US$13,500). Her friends told her that seemed expensive, but Mariela told me it felt well worth it.

Mothers also employed domestic workers to solve conflicts with their boyfriends and husbands about the division of labor at home. Some women wanted their partners to help out more, and when they refused, they decided to hire domestic workers to lessen their own workload and even perhaps curb future resentment. This was the case for Roberta. She and her husband, Eric, are American. Roberta works for an international company, and Eric is self-employed. Roberta told me their two-year-old son, Jordan, went to private daycare full time across the street from her office (where she worked forty hours a week), but she also had an Ethiopian nanny/housekeeper. After Jordan was born, she often argued with Eric about tasks around the house. He asked her to work less and suggested Roberta tell her company she couldn't go on work trips once she became a mother. This didn't go over well. Roberta got angry and told Eric her job was equally important. He should take equal care of their son. Although she said it took Eric a long time to come around, he now helps out a lot more—and they still employ their housekeeper. Roberta said she paid "all my money" to her, but she couldn't picture it any other way because it greatly reduced her stress.

Only one woman I met didn't employ a housekeeper or caregiver. Viviana, the research scientist with a temporary contract, told me she had a "moral hesitation" about hiring someone to clean up her family's mess or care for her son, Alessandro. Her parents also lived in Rome and were highly involved, regularly caring for Alessandro, so she said she didn't need a paid babysitter. Viviana also admitted with a laugh that she didn't mind if her house was a bit messy.

While Viviana's decision not to hire helpers went against prevailing cultural norms in Rome, Oriana's story helps expose the underlying cultural discourses about employment, motherhood, and outsourcing that shape Italian mothers' desires and expectations. Oriana, who is Swedish and lives in Rome, believed her satisfaction with her job and family life was actually better than that of her Swedish friends who had strong policy supports. She attributed this to the fact that it was culturally acceptable in Italy to "delegate." Oriana works fifty-five hours a week. Her two children were often sick when they were young, so she and her husband, Massimo, who is Italian, decided to hire an au pair rather than pull their kids in and out of daycare and take days off work:

> In that sense, I think it worked better than for my friends in Sweden, because I have a lot of friends in Sweden who had kids around the same time, and they were going crazy trying to cope with sick kids and work. And if they had sort of a career job, it was hard. It was hard to deal with, not so much the maternity leave, but the coping with them being sick, having to be absent all the time, because in Sweden people don't have babysitters.

I asked Oriana, "No one has an au pair living with them?" She shook her head no quickly, as if to indicate the unthinkability of the idea: "No. So, I think despite the fantastic advantages they have, they were more stressed out than I was, because I was able to delegate more." I wondered whether Oriana's ability to delegate more in Rome was related to her finances or to the cultural acceptability of hiring domestic workers in Italy. I followed up: "And were you able to do that because you can hire one relatively inexpensively here compared to in Sweden? Or it's also just part of the cultural—" and Oriana interjected:

> I think it's part of the cultural norm. In Sweden people would not normally have live-in anything. [. . .] Having a live-in babysitter is really something they can't imagine. [. . .] Sweden has been, I mean it's changing a bit now, it's a very profoundly social democratic country. Having something that resembles a servant is really not

nice. People wouldn't even have help with cleaning, where here if you can afford it, you do.

Oriana thought Swedes have historically opposed the idea of domestic workers. She watched her Swedish friends struggle when their children were sick, while she outsourced this work to an au pair and continued in her job uninterrupted. In Italy, no one would judge her for it.

This isn't to say that Oriana felt completely free of guilt as a working mother. Curiously, she explained how her feelings of maternal guilt stemmed from pressures from her upbringing in Sweden, not from pressures in Italy. She felt better able to perform an idealized version of Italian motherhood since it was conventional for middle-class moms to outsource some tasks. She explained that the Swedish ideal of motherhood required a woman to do everything herself, which induced guilt:

> From what I've seen I think most mothers, especially working mothers, always feel guilty, it's just part of the thing. You always think, "Oh, I should have been able to pick them up from school every day." "I should have been baking homemade bread." And, "Why didn't I sew their carnival costumes?" You always, always, always feel guilty about something.
>
> But, I think—I always went for sort of the "good enough" kind of parenting. I scaled down on my ambitions after having cooked all of their baby food on my own on Sunday evenings and freezing little ice cubes with homemade stuff. I scaled down a little bit on ambitions and tried to take shortcuts sometimes. Just focusing on what I saw was more important to them, which was being together. And they didn't care if I baked homemade bread, that was just—that's just a motherly myth, they could care less. [. . .] In Sweden, there is a lot of mythology around, not only mothers, but maybe mothers and fathers, in general. You're really supposed to cope with everything, and clean your own house and bake your own bread and grow your own carrots, and build the bookcase, and paint the ceiling. [. . .]
>
> But, I think you will find that more among Swedish women than here. Here people are happier to just do whatever works, you know?

It's not such a big deal. [...] The Italian momma thing—there was a big rebellion against that. And now I find Italian women my age not even being able to iron a shirt, you know? Which would be totally unacceptable in Sweden.

According to Oriana, guilt is inevitable in mothers' lifeworlds. But she felt much more guilt in Sweden than in Italy because in Sweden, parents in general (not just mothers) believed everything at home should be homemade, natural, healthy, and crafted with one's own hands. In Italy, outsourcing was so normal that wealthier Italian mothers didn't even know how to complete some routine tasks typically associated with homemaking. Not knowing how to iron didn't make Italian women question their abilities as mothers. As long as children were healthy and cared for, even if it was by domestic caregivers, my participants considered themselves good moms.

This definition of good motherhood for middle-class working mothers in Italy was made possible by the availability of the low-paid labor of mostly immigrant women. Without this labor pool of readily available workers to complete the portions of housework and childcare that Italian mothers didn't want to or couldn't complete, my respondents couldn't engage in their own paid work or continue to think of themselves as good mothers—since having a clean home and well-cared-for children did matter to them. By obscuring this outsourced labor, mothers contribute to the unequal division of household responsibilities that assigns this burden to women, and to race and class inequalities among women.

The Italian mothers I met felt a great deal of work-family conflict. They sensed their situation was likely the worst among European mothers. In their eyes, Italy's troubled economy and the state's ineptitude in providing adequate work-family policy supports contributed greatly to their stress. They felt they truly received *no* help at all from the government. For my respondents, the available work-family policies were helpful in theory but not in practice—even though many readily used policies that were in fact central to managing their work and family commitments, like public childcare and paid maternity and parental leave.

Most of the mothers I interviewed in Rome said that with the exception of some cooking and childcare, their partners didn't contribute substantially to maintaining their families day-to-day, meaning that this work largely fell to women. At the same time, mothers were expected to live up to a masculine ideal worker model at their jobs. This spurred a great deal of guilt and stress for working moms.

A variety of gendered, raced, and classed social policies, workplace structures, norms, and discourses enabled Italian mothers' strategies to ease their work-family conflict. Women used three main tactics. First, they worked the system by taking advantage of loopholes in paid illness leave surrounding pregnancy and childbirth to take extra time off from work at full pay. In doing so, moms ironically did what they accused the Italian state of doing. Perhaps this coping tool is part of a perceived culture of deceit or corruption: Italians think everyone is working the system, so some mothers felt they should take advantage when they could.

Second, mothers relied on the help of kin networks, primarily grandmothers, to step in and care for children. Outsourcing care to grandmothers reifies women's role in domestic labor, but postpones it a generation. Several women said they hoped to live near their grown children one day so they could help care for their grandchildren. This solution doesn't ameliorate gender inequalities with regard to women's disproportionate responsibility for the domestic sphere.

Third, mothers hired low-wage, primarily immigrant workers to clean their homes and care for their kids while they went to work. Women often relied on grandmothers and hired housekeepers and caregivers to cobble together the help they felt they needed. But Italian mothers tended to overlook this labor, which only reinforced the societal view that household labor is solely women's responsibility—a mother's either to carry out personally or to outsource to another woman. While mothers with less education and lower incomes may also be able to rely on grandmothers' help, employing domestic workers is likely a cost-prohibitive solution for many working mothers.

Interestingly, the Italian ideal of motherhood seemed to allow mothers to outsource caregiving labor without calling into question their maternal abilities. This delegation of responsibilities did not mark women as bad mothers as it did in western Germany or Sweden. This outsourcing tactic displaced mothers' work-family conflict onto low-income, racial/ethnic minority immigrant women who often lived apart from their own families, or whose children lived close by but had to be cared for by others while their mothers worked in the homes of more affluent families in Rome. Moreover, their work often went unrecognized as Italian mothers maintained their self-definitions as good mothers.

For the most part, the women I interviewed didn't expect their male partners to play an equal role in domestic work like the men in Stockholm did. Instead, many turned to longstanding tropes about Italian masculinity to excuse men's lack of involvement in maintaining their household, which absolved men of these responsibilities and reproduced inequalities for mothers.

As part of the EU, Italian mothers regularly drew comparisons between their experiences and what they had heard about work-family policies in other EU states. However, their belief that the state was irreparably broken meant they never demanded better from the government. Like women in western Germany and the US who experienced substantial work-family conflict, Italian mothers did not engage in feminist activism to try to secure more government support or increase men's involvement at home.

Working the system and outsourcing to grandmothers and paid domestic workers are coping strategies that reinforce and reflect prevailing social arrangements. Mothers' abilities to address problems in their lives are confined to the options that are both socially acceptable and available in Italy.

CHAPTER 6

The United States

"WE CAN'T FIGURE OUT HOW TO DO IT
ALL AT THE SAME TIME."

Samantha is a lawyer at a Virginia firm located on a wide street lined with stately office complexes just across the Potomac River from Washington, DC. She and her husband, John, have a five-year-old son and ten-month-old daughter named Taylor and Candace. John works for the federal government. I interviewed Samantha in a windowless conference room in her office building, a high-security facility with fluorescent lighting and sterile white walls where employees spoke in hushed voices. She closed the door before we began. Samantha had worked as a teacher before waking up one day with the realization that she was "taking no risks." So she decided to attend law school and then pursued a career in private practice. After several years working at this firm, Samantha found out she was pregnant. She panicked: "I worked very hard to ensure that nothing was different as a result of being pregnant and that I was taking on the same workload and sometimes more, trying to prove that I was as available, as accessible, as committed."

In Samantha's opinion, her law firm wasn't family friendly or amenable to employees with outside responsibilities that detracted from their job commitment. She recalled:

> You could have children, but the general expectation was, if you made that choice, you needed to have a plan for someone else to care for them. [. . .] And fully committed meant that you were

available at all hours whenever anything was needed. There weren't boundaries. And this, ironically, was a firm that I joined because they billed themselves as a "lifestyle firm," as a firm that was supportive of families. Folks were supposed to be able to coach their kids' t-ball teams.

It became clear to Samantha that women could have children only so long as they didn't take time away from work to care for them. "Was this message explicit?" I asked. She said:

> Whether it was said in so many words or not, the message was perceived loud and clear. [...] I was thinking very much about having a second child, and thinking about the realities of how that would work. And looking back at the young go-getter female associates who had been in our office and in our practice, most had survived having one child, and those who went on to have a second child for one reason or another usually weren't at the firm six months later.

Samantha's firm asked her to start working from home nine weeks into her leave. She took four months off after giving birth to Taylor, cobbling together short-term disability leave with sick days and vacation days she had stockpiled. She went unpaid for the last month.

Taylor was born by C-section, and Samantha was "still knitting back together" when she started taking conference calls and working while her son slept. After her leave ended, she returned to the office. "I didn't do any sort of gradual ramp-up. When I went back, I went back. I came back full force into the busiest time of our calendar year." At this point in our interview, Samantha burst into tears. We paused for a few minutes while she closed her eyes and caught her breath, dabbing quickly at her cheeks with a tissue.

Samantha saw Taylor only in the mornings before he went to full-time daycare and on the weekends, although she worked a half day on Saturdays. Her husband picked Taylor up, fed and bathed him, and put him to bed each night. She returned home after Taylor was asleep. Samantha reflected softly:

Before I had children, the message that I received was, "I am woman, hear me roar. You can do everything. [. . .] You can be at the top if you put your mind to it. [. . .] You are awesome." . . . Load of crap. I *am* awesome, and I *can't* do everything. [. . .] If I keep all the balls in the air, I'm broken. What's going to fail is my health. While I was doing all of that, I was also suffering debilitating migraines. [. . .] I've talked to so many friends in a similar position . . . and we can't figure out how to do it all at the same time.

Samantha sobbed. Averting her eyes, with her hand over her mouth and tears streaming down her cheeks, she told me about an incident when Taylor was six months old. She had come home from work at 10 p.m. and had what she described as an emotional breakdown. She hadn't seen her infant in a month. Something had to change. John calmly tried to discuss how to make her life feel a little less insane.

Samantha explained their three tactics. First, she transferred to an in-house counsel position at a less prestigious firm that demanded fewer hours. She got pregnant with their second child after starting this job. Samantha's manager tried to convince her to not take *any* leave after giving birth. In fact, they "got into a bit of a tussle parsing weeks." But again, she and John built up their savings so she could take twelve weeks' unpaid leave under the federal Family and Medical Leave Act—this with no guarantee her position would be waiting for her when she returned.[1] Fortunately for Samantha, it was.

Second, she learned to be more efficient at work. "I get more done in a workday than most of my colleagues who are in a similar situation do in a day and a half," she said with a smile. Third, she bought a product online called the Freemie, a hands-free breast pump with breast milk collection cups that fit into a bra. At her cubicle, she showed me how she attached the pump to herself under a poncho while seated at her desk so she could pump breast milk and not waste time walking to and from her firm's lactation room (an extremely rare accommodation in American workplaces, as I discuss later). Because the lactation room available to her was a twelve-minute walk each way, she would have spent about ninety minutes of her workday traveling to and from the room. Samantha tried this briefly, but it got old fast. The Freemie was her time-saving solution. She laughed and told me, "Yeah, I'm pumpin' at my desk! I don't have time for this. I've got to go home and take care of people." She currently works roughly forty-five hours a week.

Samantha exemplifies how Americans individualize social problems. Her solutions are textbook examples of how American mothers approach their work-family conflict: changing jobs, becoming more efficient, and buying a Freemie are all individual strategies that approach child-rearing as a private responsibility and work-family conflict as a personal problem.

The United States is an outlier among Western industrialized countries for its lack of support for working mothers.[2] Its liberal welfare state approach means there is no federal mandate that individual employers provide supportive policies to working families with dependent care responsibilities. Without an explicit national family policy, what remains is a set of patchwork policies from employers that are weakly institutionalized and subject to employers' discretion.[3]

Because the state generally doesn't offer supports for care, people have to turn to the market to purchase this care. As in Italy, middle-class women who pay for nannies and housekeepers come to rely on other women's low wages to enable their own paid labor. Sociologists Jane Collins and Victoria Mayer remind us that, "Simply put, this is a case where the 'haves' doing well depends on the 'have-nots' having less."[4] Low-income mothers often lack the job security, living wages, and access to policies (e.g., maternity leave, health care, vacation and sick days) that would help reconcile the tensions between their own work and family commitments. The government does offer some assistance to very poor families, but it requires that mothers exchange certain civil rights for cash assistance. And in no state is this aid enough to pull poor families out of poverty. The United States' free-market approach leaves women, especially working-class and racial/ethnic minority women, in the worst straits.[5]

Moms like Samantha are far better off than most. Advanced degrees, marriages, and stable, well-paying jobs work together as a safety net to help some women when they falter. Samantha is also white. She hasn't had to contend with the lifelong set of cumulative disadvantages that constrain the lifeworlds of women of color.[6] Despite all this, the truth is that every working mom in the US is in dire straits. The outlook for some is less dismal than others, but the picture isn't pretty for anyone. Here's the thing, though. Life *can* be better for mothers.

The United States' Work-Family Policy

The US has no national work-family policy to support caregiving, no universal health care, no universal social insurance entitlement, no guaranteed income, no paid parental leave, no universal childcare, and no minimum standard for vacation and sick days.[7] Cities and states can elect to offer more generous supports than those offered at the federal level, but this means only workers in larger, wealthier, more progressive locales benefit from them. For instance, only four states currently offer paid parental leave—California, New Jersey, New York, and Rhode Island.[8]

The one federal leave policy is the 1993 Family and Medical Leave Act (FMLA) that Samantha used after having her second child. This policy gives eligible employees up to twelve weeks of unpaid, job-protected leave to care for a new or recently adopted child, to care for a seriously ill family member, or to recover from a personal illness. FMLA applies only to businesses with over fifty employees, and workers must have worked for at least twelve months and a minimum of 1,250 hours to qualify. Workers are guaranteed *a* job upon return, but not necessarily *their* job. Given these stipulations, only about 62 percent of Americans work for a covered employer and are eligible for these benefits.[9] White-collar workers tend to have greater access to this provision than low-wage workers. What's more, not many workers can actually afford to use FMLA and take a break from work without pay. As I outlined in the book's introduction, high-income earners are over three times as likely to have access to paid family leave than low-income workers in the United States.[10]

The US has no universal childcare for children of any age. The limited childcare provisions the federal government offers are means-tested for the poorest citizens. Low-income parents must be involved in work or a work-related activity, such as training, to receive childcare subsidies through the Child Care Development Fund.[11] Without governmental support for care, families are required to find private solutions to child-care. Those families that turn to the market find vast differences in the quality and cost of care. Until as recently as 2013, no national regulations governed quality of service, staffing, or health codes for daycare facilities, resulting in a wide range of care services.[12] Individual states were responsible for setting and enforcing minimum health and safety standards, such as the mandates for working smoke detectors, locked cabinets for dangerous substances, staff-child ratios, and a minimum age for caregivers. Many programs are exempt from any regulation or licensing requirements, such as those that care for a small number of children, those run by religious groups, part-day programs, and school-based preschool or after-school programs. Guidelines for nutrition, exercise, media use, and developmentally appropriate activities vary widely from state to state.[13] The lack of regulations in standards for childcare in the United States means that wealthier families are able to provide safer, higher-quality environments for their children compared to lower-income families. Again, common wisdom among virtually all researchers is that investing in children early in their lives through strong education and care programs has enormous payoffs throughout adolescence and adulthood.[14]

Work-family policies like paid family leave, childcare assistance, schedule flexibility, and telecommuting are typically available to workers with greater market power. These tend to be men, those employed at large firms, and high-income professionals.[15] Employed mothers are less likely to have access to family accommodations than fathers[16] and are more likely to receive financial penalties for using them.[17] The consensus among work-family researchers who investigate these phenomena is that the United States' free-market approach to social provisioning has failed.[18] We see evidence of this failure in high rates of maternal and childhood poverty, high rates of worker turnover, intermittent maternal employment, worker frustrations, and time squeezes.[19]

The failure of the US approach to work-family policy is reflected in happiness statistics. Parents report lower levels of happiness than non-parents across Western industrialized countries. But the difference in happiness between adults with and without children is reduced in countries that offer more assistance and resources to families than in countries that provide less support. In a 2016 study of twenty-two OECD countries, sociologists Jennifer Glass, Robin Simon, and Matthew Andersson found that the US has the largest subjective well-being penalty for parenthood, with the largest "happiness gap" between parents and nonparents.[20] In other words, the low-support context in the US means that parenting is particularly taxing and stressful compared to countries with greater work-family policy supports.

Polling data show that Americans today are increasingly supportive of work-family policy, including paid family leave, universal preschool education, and stronger laws regarding fair wages and working hours.[21] Younger workers also show more interest in work-family policy and less willingness to sacrifice personal and family time for work.[22] But this interest hasn't yet translated into federal policy change.

"I'm doing everything subpar"

"There are a lot of days where you feel like you are simultaneously a terrible professional and a terrible mother," Kelsey confided. We sat at her large dining room table covered with documents, with her laptop, cell phone, headphones, and notepad spread out between us. Kelsey was telecommuting for the day so she could carve out time for an interview. A white married mother, Kelsey works roughly fifty-five hours a week in business management. Kelsey and her husband, Ryan, have a one-year-old named Rosie who was at daycare when we met in her high-ceilinged row house in Ballston, an upscale suburb of DC. Kelsey told me she often felt like a failure: "You're like, 'I'm doing everything subpar. Nothing is going well.'" American moms like Kelsey said they felt enormous guilt and tension between their work and family roles, similar to my western German and Italian interviewees. But whereas western Germans blamed outdated cultural norms and Italians blamed the government for their problems, the vast majority of the Americans blamed themselves for not "balancing" or "managing" their responsibilities. Kelsey made the conscious decision to lower her high standards once she had a child. I asked her if she thought it was possible for American mothers to get to the top in their careers. She said:

In general, yes, but [...] you still have to negotiate a lot of the hurdles that may not necessarily be [set] by the industry or the business or other people's expectations, but they're hurdles you've set. Because you probably are a feeling person who has had a child. You don't want to miss every football game or every piano recital or even every bedtime. I hate missing bedtime. If I can figure out a way to even have a flight that leaves at 9 p.m. to go where I need to go to make bedtime, I'll do it. It's just understanding that there's gonna have to be a give and take, and that's OK. You don't feel like you have to be perfect in every way.

Kelsey believed that mothers put hurdles in their own way—they held expectations of themselves as parents that hindered their career advancement. She said these self-imposed hurdles are logical for any parent who wants to participate in their children's daily lives. In Kelsey's estimation, the problem wasn't the hurdles themselves, but figuring out how to clear them easily. Her solution was to "figure out a way" and "do it" herself, even if it meant working a full day, coming home to tend to her child and tuck her into bed, and then dashing off to the airport to catch a red-eye flight. Reminding herself that she didn't "have to be perfect in every way" implies Kelsey felt pressure to achieve perfection.

When US moms experienced work-family conflict and stress, they often thought it was their fault. Tiana is African American, has a bachelor's degree in public health, and worked for a time as a community health worker. But she felt she didn't get to see her daughter enough, and she took an administrative job working thirty-five hours a week at lower pay in order to have a better schedule. Tiana didn't blame her stress on her long, taxing work hours, but on herself for choosing the wrong career path:

I think I just picked the wrong major. [...] I really should have ended up as a nurse, because I would have been happy working in the hospital, in the doctor's office, doing that kind of stuff. I just always make the wrong decisions. I don't know what's wrong with me. I was just thinking practically.

Tiana believed her work-family conflict was due to her own poor decision-making. She solved her conflict by changing jobs—a common solution for many of the American women with whom I spoke.[23]

Many mothers felt guilty that the nature of their jobs, which they often loved, at times meant they had to sacrifice too much for their children—and their children lost out. Rather than critique their long hours, demanding employers, or lack of workplace supports, women tended to be upset with themselves. Lauren is a white ER doctor who works around forty-five hours a week. She has three children (ages one, three, and five), and her husband, Ken, is a stay-at-home dad. She cried during our interview as she recounted a health scare she had at work. A fluid splashed in her eyes while she was treating an HIV-positive patient, and the infectious diseases specialist at her hospital told her to stop breast-feeding her youngest that day. "I cried myself to sleep for, like, two weeks. I felt so awful about it." To Lauren, this incident "was such a representation of the sacrifices that I was making, that I was forcing them to make. That was really hard for me." Lauren faced a difficult trade-off: she got to keep working, but she had to stop breast-feeding—to her child's detriment, she thought. Her baby's switch from breast milk to formula felt like a heartbreaking loss.

With tears in her eyes, seated across from me at a two-top restaurant table, Lauren reflected, "In the end, I think the benefits of me working obviously outweigh the negatives. But when that balance shifts, it's really hard." Lauren's exposure to HIV at work and subsequent need to stop nursing made her feel extremely guilty and anxious about what she was asking her children to risk and sacrifice for her to have a job she was passionate about. Lauren admitted there were times when it felt like her job wasn't worth the hardships her family had to undergo. Although she wanted to serve as a role model for what women can achieve, she wondered whether she was being selfish and putting her children in harm's way.

I asked Lauren whether anything had changed in the ER to try and improve safety, and she explained tactics she herself adopted: wearing eye protection and standing near the door in case someone tried to attack her. Unlike Swedish and German mothers who are guaranteed a year's parental leave and usually stop breast-feeding before returning to work, Lauren had to return to work while she was still nursing, thus potentially exposing her child to the illnesses she treated in the emergency room. Yet Lauren only discussed what *she* could do differently to prevent another dangerous incident. She didn't ask for safer accommodations and instead took on the work of staying safe on her own as a mom. Lauren felt she hadn't protected herself (and therefore her infant) from the incident with the HIV-positive patient. She blamed herself, so she tried her best to implement steps to ensure it didn't happen again.

In addition to the sort of acute workplace concerns like Lauren's, women felt guilty about the mundane, everyday aspects of their jobs too. The moms I spoke to told me they worried that their busy work schedules and long hours detracted from being good mothers. Allie, who is married, white, and a writer working roughly fifty hours a week, explained:

> I have such mixed feelings about that. I miss my kids a lot now that I'm here [in this job]. And I also commute an hour each way. Sometimes that turns into an hour and a half each way with traffic. And if I'm in here nine hours, sometimes ten lately, I feel like I don't see my kids much. I feel like my husband is closer to my kids in some ways now than I am. And that's hard as a mom to be dealing with that. [. . .] But I do miss being able to be home with them. But I took this job.

Allie felt torn between her time-intensive job and her interest in being an involved and present mother. Her regret that her husband spent more time with their children is logical given that intensive parenting is typically reserved for moms in the US.[24] Allie didn't question her employer's decision to require such long hours and shouldered responsibility for this decision herself: "I took this job." Figure 6.1 shows that most women I interviewed worked more than forty-five hours a week. These working moms felt an extraordinary amount of guilt about their inability to achieve "work-family balance," usually blaming themselves for this conflict.

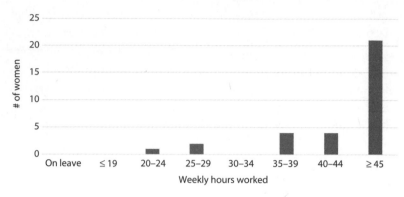

FIGURE 6.1. Weekly working hours for respondents in Washington, DC.

"I'm so lucky"

The American mothers I interviewed expected to be fully responsible for managing their households, children, and jobs on their own. Unlike their European counterparts, they generally expressed little confidence that their partners, workplaces, or the state would step up to help ease the stress and difficulties they experienced every day. When mothers received help of any sort—including when they earned it or paid for it—they used vocabulary like "being very lucky" or "feeling privileged." Kelsey said, "I've felt very lucky. [...] I did not know [maternity leave] was such a game-changer until I started talking with other friends of mine who [...] were now having to take three months unpaid, because they got, like, a two-week maternity leave." Kelsey worked for a corporation famous for its family-friendly policies and took four months' leave at full pay, acknowledging how rare this was. The more advantaged women told me they felt lucky to have work-family accommodations at their companies, whether formal or informal. I'll delve more into the quagmire of maternity leave like Kelsey's later in this chapter.

For the most part, German, Swedish, and Italian mothers didn't use this language of "luck." In fact, I heard the opposite: as I discussed in previous chapters, European working mothers invoked the discourse of rights and entitlements to work-family policy. These discourses never came up during my US interviews, and only a small handful mentioned the state as having a role in promoting "work-family balance." For most, the government stood outside women's lifeworlds as a source of possible help. When I asked whether the government could do anything to support working mothers better, Allie, the writer and mother of two, said, "That's a good question. I hadn't really thought about it before. I'd love to be home when [my kids] got home. To change the work schedule. But that's like turning around the *Titanic*." Allie found it implausible that her work hours might change to accommodate her family; in contrast, women in Stockholm and Berlin expected these accommodations.

Moms in DC were also grateful for understanding, supportive bosses. Usually this "generosity" manifested for women as informal flexible scheduling. Imani is a Hispanic/African American property manager for an office building. She has a demanding forty-five-hour-a-week work schedule and a two-hour daily commute each way—four hours a day in the car. In fact, we struggled to find time to meet because Imani's schedule was so challenging. Eventually her husband agreed to pick up their kids so she could stay late after work to meet me at her office. She let traffic die down as we talked before driving home. Imani told me her family can't afford to live closer to her work:

> You can imagine, my job is insane. I was so stressed it was making me sick. [...] I asked if I could work from home twice a week. That would take a huge load off. Not having to commute [...] would make it easier for me. Otherwise I felt like the pressure of it was—I don't know how to explain it. The pressure of it was—I was a key component to the big chain. [...] It pushed me healthwise to the limit. [...] The goal is to be here at 7:30, but that never happens. It's too unpredictable. And luckily, my boss, our company, this building, it's very flexible. [...] It's a blessing. It's amazing. It's the first time in my career when I feel like I'm at a place where I know what I'm doing, I can handle things, and it doesn't feel so super-overwhelming. It does get overwhelming sometimes.

Imani's ability to telecommute two days a week and adjust her start time made her job feel less overwhelming and helped ease her stress. Rather than feeling frustrated at her employer for the intense pressure and long working hours, Imani was grateful for the flexibility.

US interviewees also felt lucky when their bosses had children themselves and "got it." One mother said, "I'm lucky in the sense that at the time my boss in California had four kids of his own and he was a very good father, so he gave me a lot of flexibility." Another explained, "We're lucky that it's a nonprofit and that lots of people in the organization higher up have kids. Almost everybody on the executive team has kids. They all get it."

Women who had an office space in which to pump breast milk were effusive in their gratitude for it, knowing that this privacy was atypical. Chelsea, a white woman working forty-five hours a week in sales management for a transnational firm, said,

> I pump twice during the day. And I am so lucky about pumping. I am at a level in my company where I actually have my own office. At least for the time being, because we are moving to [a new space that is] open office, collaborative. It really saves money and whatever. So, I am dreading the day I lose my office.

Employers are required by law to provide the space and time for pumping. The rhetoric of gratitude obscures what is actually a *legal right* for mothers in the United States. I explore later whether the legal entitlement to pump at work was borne out for my interviewees.

Mothers also expressed gratitude if they liked their children's daycare. Many had personal experience or knew friends who detested the facility where their kids spent their days, which caused moms guilt and stress. Ashley, who has two daughters and is a white married mother working as a secretary, explained, "I'm sure there are below-average daycares, but [...] I have had great luck. Both her daycare providers are very kind people who just view the kids as extensions of their immediate family."

The lack of federal work-family policies in the US tends to exacerbate race and class inequalities among mothers. American moms may use the discourse of luck and privilege to sidestep the guilt associated with the knowledge that they have access to work-family policies (e.g., maternity leave, flexible schedules) or support (e.g., relatives, housekeepers, nannies) that help ease their conflict when other mothers do not, especially in a cultural environment that emphasizes personal responsibility. Mothers who had these benefits didn't express that they deserved or expected them as European mothers did. The rhetoric of luck seems to be the women's attempts at acknowledging their own privilege given systemic US inequalities: some women—white, wealthier women—have greater access to this assistance than others—racial/ethnic minority, lower-income women—as a result of racism and classism.

This rhetoric also reaffirms the mothers' sense that these are privileges and not rights—demonstrating their inculcation of a broader system that doesn't offer these policies or supports universally.[25] Mothers embodied the ideal of personal responsibility: they believed their work-family conflict was their own problem to solve. American women did not expect to have understanding bosses, supportive families, or accommodating jobs.

Sources of American Mothers' Work-Family Conflict

Moms in DC felt agonizing work-family conflict, and it seemed to come at them from all sides. The way they spoke, they seemed to me awash in stress, struggling to stay afloat in an unrelenting storm. The cause of their stress, though, was tough for women to pinpoint. As an outsider hearing their stories, which seemed defined by nearly constant struggle, I wondered, What's a person to do? Blame the whole ocean?

In unpacking their stories, I found that moms faced both normative and material sources of work-family conflict. Mothers felt caught between the competing devotions of ideal worker norms and intensive mothering norms.[26] Unsurprisingly, they also felt stressed because of the unequal gender division of labor in their homes and the United States' weak safety net.

These women felt pressured to live up to a set of pervasive norms that glorified workers who were single-mindedly committed to their jobs. Similar to Italian and western German moms, women often worried about announcing their pregnancies to employers. Makayla is an African American nonprofit public relations executive working forty hours a week. She and her husband, William, have two children. When Makayla first discovered she was pregnant, she told me, she believed her boss would be unhappy at the news:

> I work in PR, so I knew how to frame it [*laughs*]. I did a little research on how you tell your bosses that you are expecting. I went in and said, "I have fantastic news." You can't be disappointed when you go in telling people how they must feel about it. So, I walked in and said, "I have fantastic news! I'm pregnant! I'm gonna have a baby!" [...] It worked, like magic. My boss, a man, he was supportive. I'd been at the organization a long time.

Makayla's spin on her pregnancy seemed to work. She also indicated that she had earned her boss's trust with her long tenure at the firm. Moms like Makayla reported feeling relieved and grateful for bosses who didn't get angry at them when they announced their pregnancies.

And it turns out that Makayla isn't the only woman who has felt the need to devise a strategy. *Forbes*, the *Washington Post*, and *New York Magazine* have all run stories in the past few years with some variation of the title, "So you're pregnant. How do you tell your boss?"[27] Mothers generally don't feel their pregnancies will be supported, which suggests that motherhood is perceived negatively at work. Stories wouldn't appear in top news outlets if it wasn't a source of worry for women.

Moms were expected to be dedicated to their jobs regardless of any family emergencies, even during their pregnancies. Mary is a white attorney who works fifty-five hours a week. She is also a single mother "by choice."[28] Her twins were born prematurely at twenty-eight weeks. They spent two months in the hospital, and she petitioned HR to let her work from their hospital room so she didn't use up her short maternity leave: "[W]e talked about it, and he let me work. [...] It allowed me to stretch my maternity hours a lot longer. That was really nice, that I had that flexibility." This is more evidence of American women's low expectations of their employers. Any leave time at all felt like a luxury to these moms. Mary explained that the mother of the child in the room next door was a Hispanic housekeeper who worked nights. She took the bus to and from the hospital, and had no choice but to leave her infant alone there for long stints. This mother couldn't ask to work remotely, and she had no leave available to her. Mary thought that, in contrast with this other mother, she was extremely fortunate because she could work remotely. Mary didn't seem to question whether new mothers should be required to work at all while their newborns were ill in the hospital.

Disrupting work for childbirth was a big concern for the women I interviewed in DC. American moms who were allowed to take maternity leave or were given some flexibility after having a baby often explained that they owed it to their employers to work right up until childbirth and to dive back in when they returned. Some worried that the timing of their childbirth would be problematic for their employers, so they worked hard to "make up" for any time off as soon as they returned to their jobs. And others worked hard literally up until childbirth, like Chelsea. She told me she was "a little worried" when she found out she was pregnant for the first time. She organized a major event for a top client that took place two weeks before her due date. Chelsea went into labor seventy-two hours after the event ended. She went to the hospital with contractions and felt obliged to work from her hospital bed as she started labor—"I was on my BlackBerry the whole time"—because she worried that her junior colleague who would fill in for her during her leave couldn't do the work alone. Recall that in Italy and Germany, mothers are *required* to leave work four to six weeks before childbirth. This isn't an option in the US.

Some mothers felt the need to continually earn this support or repay employers by working harder and longer, as was the case for Italian mothers (see chapter 5). Yasmine is a single Lebanese mother who has a flexible schedule: "It is the flexibility, mainly, that made me stay here. This is why I like to put in more hours of work, because I want to pay back for that flexibility." As I mentioned, sociologist Allison Pugh calls this the "one-way honor system" between employers and employees in the US: workers feel loyalty to employers, but expect very little in return.[29]

Mothers told me they were sometimes expected to be available to their employers at a moment's notice, even right after maternity leave. Robin, who is white, married, and a psychologist working at a prison roughly forty-eight hours a week, occasionally had to drop everything to go to the prison when she was off-duty. After having to stop breast-feeding her fourteen-week-old to return to work at 9 p.m. one night, she recalled thinking, "I can't live like this. This can't be my own existence on their clock anymore because I have someone else's clock that matters to me." Robin explained that she also had to travel for work, often last minute, which was a great source of work-family conflict (a comment other mothers echoed): "Why is travel so important?" she asked. "Why does it have to be me? It's like it's a test. You have to jump through hoops." Robin remembered aloud,

I was in my office one afternoon, and they know I have a family. None of them do, so they can do whatever. But they decided they wanted me for an event the following morning in another state, and I had to run. There was no way I was gonna get a flight out if I didn't physically run. I came home, I ended up with four pairs of shoes and no pantyhose because I packed so frantically. [. . .] I was a mess. But they needed me there. I thought, "Thank God Andrew could cover." I stopped by the preschool. [My daughter] was napping, and I just gave her a kiss, because I was not leaving without seeing her. And then hopped in the cab and off I went. I arranged the flight on the phone.

Robin thought it was unnecessary to be asked to drop everything and literally sprint for a flight. She thought these requests were really about performing a sort of all-consuming allegiance to her job, even though she knew it was irrational.

The sense that workers needed to be ever-present also made women feel like their workday never ended. Whereas flexible schedules could make life easier for women, they could also enable this culture of constant work for mothers. Still, mothers expressed gratitude for the benefit. Chelsea the sales manager called this constant blending of work and family "the swirl":

I think my big key here is I have an awesome, awesome, understanding, flexible boss who takes advantage of things herself and just kind of trusts me to do my job. We always talk about the swirl. That's what we call it. Like when you're a working mom, there is no hard line between work and home. So, you swirl from one to the other, it's all swirled together. You get online at seven in the morning and you send a couple of emails that have to get out, and then you're making breakfast, and you drop the kids off and maybe at lunch you either go for a run yourself or run to the grocery store because you have no other time to do it. But then after you put them to bed, you're back online.

It all bleeds into each other. All the time. I'm sending work emails and then I'll jump over really quick to Amazon and order more diapers because that's what I need to do and it popped into my head. There is no guilt for doing it that way because—you know, it's good and bad. It means I can easily work from 8 to 10 at night a lot, but it allows me to do what I need to do and see them as much as I can.

Chelsea said her understanding boss, flexible working hours, and ability to work from home early in the morning and late at night made her feel less stressed. Yet she expressed ambivalence about this arrangement, saying she didn't feel "guilt for doing it that way" but also admitting that "it's good and bad." She implied that perhaps this setup worked best for her children and household. But Chelsea also signaled that this scenario caused her to have "no hard line between work and home." She seemed to sacrifice her own sense of balance, time, and boundaries for the sake of her job and her family—in alignment with dominant ideals about the self-sacrificing mother. So in addition to feeling that they needed to demonstrate an all-absorbing commitment to their employers, moms like Chelsea also felt pressured to live up to extraordinarily high expectations at home as mothers.

Sociologist Mary Blair-Loy found in her study of American mothers working as finance executives that they tend to feel caught between feelings of work and family devotion.[30] In the same vein, the women I interviewed believed their employment made it difficult to be the devoted mothers they wanted to be. Susan's comments exemplify the intensity of this conflict. She is Puerto Rican, a mother of nine-year-old twins, and a senior-level manager in the banking sector who works between fifty and fifty-five hours each week. Susan called this tension "mommy guilt":

> For me, mommy guilt is the constant trade-offs and being sure that you're making the right decisions. I've told people, for a woman, nothing undermines your innate self-confidence as much as the moment you become a mother, because from that day on, you are constantly aware of the fact that you're not just responsible for yourself any more. Every choice you make, every act you portray, you are shaping this life. Therefore, you second-guess yourself all the time. [...] And it gets easier over time, but [...] it's crippling.

She implied that every move a mother makes shapes her child. Not only are moms responsible for their children's development in general, but even the smallest, most inadvertent parenting choices affect who their kids become. Susan told me it took "nine years of tears" to stop feeling guilty all the time. The guilt finally abated when she rearranged her schedule in order to attend an event at her children's after-school daycare, and she saw that they were fine even though she worked full time. For the first time, Susan perceived her daughters as resilient.

Blair-Loy finds this is a common tactic among career-committed mothers in the US: they craft a definition of children as autonomous and resilient, preserving their understanding of themselves as good mothers. I heard this same definition among women in Sweden, who also mostly worked full time. My interviewees in Germany and Italy held a different cultural definition of childhood, one that Blair-Loy calls "family-committed." Family-committed mothers "define their children as fragile and needful of their attentive care,"[31] a definition that prompts German mothers to work part time and Italian mothers to outsource childcare to grandmothers and paid careworkers.

Although my Swedish and US participants saw children as highly capable, their opinions diverged when it came to who they thought should raise children. American women largely believed child-rearing was a family's personal responsibility—they didn't expect help. Swedes' views aligned with the social democratic welfare state model: they believed everyone has a responsibility to ensure that children are raised well.[32]

Cross-national survey data about cultural attitudes make these differences clear. For example, 57.3 percent of people in the US think that primarily family members should provide childcare to children under school age. Only 5 percent of Swedes agree. Three-quarters of Americans believe that families themselves should cover the costs of childcare for children under school age, compared to one-quarter of Swedes.[33]

Americans tended to talk about the importance of "family members" raising children and caring for the home, but this really meant mothers. The majority of my participants believed in dividing childcare and housework equally with their partners in theory, but few achieved this goal in their day-to-day lives. Most women in DC explained to me why an equal division of labor wasn't possible in their own homes. Some mothers said that their husbands' work schedules prevented them from helping much. Ashley is a white mother with daughters ages eight and three, whom we met earlier. She works twenty-five hours a week as a secretary and is married to James, a police officer who works 2 p.m. to 11 p.m. five days a week:

> This has offended him, but a couple of my mom friends have said, "It's like you're temporarily a single parent." In some ways I am, but I have the emotional support of a second person to talk to, so I'm really not a single parent. But when it comes to Girl Scouts and soccer practice and showers at night, that's all me. He's just not around. [...] That's the biggest flaw in our whole relationship. We have this little window of time to download information between each other. We leave a lot of notes for each other. He comes home at 11:30 and I'm usually asleep. I'll talk to him for ten or fifteen minutes and then I've got to go back to bed.

Ashley was responsible for virtually all of the housework and childcare. I asked her whether she and James divided tasks differently around the house before having children. "Not so much," she said. This didn't come as a surprise to her. "I knew from the moment we had talked about getting married that this was how it was going to be. He was never going to be the guy who was around a lot and very involved." She thought James became a more involved parent once their children reached toddler age and beyond: "He's especially good once they can talk. When he's home, he will take them on walks or give me a break. But I always knew that the general day-in, day-out tasks were gonna be mine. [...] I'm the oldest of five kids, so I'm already used to doing all that. I didn't mind. This way I get to do it my way." Ashley said she didn't expect anything different and justified this vastly different workload by explaining that she liked getting to parent and care for their home herself.

Most women told me their husbands would participate with a specific housework or childcare task if the wives asked them and explained how to do it. Some mothers said they didn't mind having to ask for this help because they were more aware of what needed to be done than their husbands were, which is logical in a culture in which women are socialized to assume responsibility for these arenas. Others were irritated that they had to ask, feeling exhausted by the added burden of constantly speaking up and requesting help. Some said they felt it was easier just to do it themselves.

A few mothers drew on gendered understandings of women's and men's parenting abilities to explain why they did more of the caring labor than their partners. I heard these explanations often during my conversations with women in Germany, Italy, and the US, but not in Sweden, where parenting discourse was gender-neutral. Ruth, whose husband, Gunnar, is Swedish, hinted at the fallacy of this explanation for men's incapacity to help out at home: "He does his own laundry. My friends are like, 'That's incredible.' [...] I don't know what it is about having a penis that makes you not able to do laundry." The women I spoke to thought that their partners were willing to help out at home, but they said the issue was that they literally didn't know how to—it wasn't in their genes, or at the very least, they weren't socialized to know how to complete basic household tasks.

Some women said they decided to "train" or "teach" their husbands to help out more as a method of self-preservation. Makayla, the nonprofit executive whose husband, William, had a high-ranking government job, explained:

It is normally *me* asking and he says yes. It's not common that he will just *do*. I've been training my husband on certain things, so he's now been officially trained that Mom does not do dinner on Fridays and Saturdays. [...] Little things like that where even I am learning for myself to self-preserve and not do things.

She tested out this new approach by not arranging everything at home before she took an international business trip, leaving it to William to manage the household. "I got home from London and I opened the refrigerator and there was, like, an echo," she told me, shaking her head in what seemed like frustration and a tinge of embarrassment. "There was nothing in the refrigerator, no milk, no bread, nothing." Facing a giant snowstorm that was projected to shut down the city the next morning, Makayla explained, "At 8:00 in the morning—literally the day after I got back from London—I jumped in my car, I drove to the grocery store and got us basic provisions to get through the snow day." Men's clumsy lack of awareness was a common trope I heard among American women. Interesting, too, is Makayla's phrasing that William had been "trained that Mom does not do dinner"—maybe implying a sense that she had to parent her husband at times.

Whereas Italian women described Italian men as being immature, lazy, and self-involved, American women tended to say men were poorly trained, as Makayla indicated. Both groups of moms thought their partners had no idea what it takes to run a household. It fell to women to continually ask their partners and try to teach them to help out regularly. Women laughed often during our interviews about men's perpetual inability to help in even small ways, but their laughter was accompanied by shaking heads, raised eyebrows, shrugged shoulders, rolling eyes, and pursed lips. These nonverbal cues signaled an underlying annoyance and resentment toward their spouses.

Even when moms worked hard to teach their husbands to contribute, men's efforts seemed lackluster. Knowing that most of these women's husbands held high-paying jobs in Washington, DC, it is puzzling that these men who were clearly successful at work couldn't succeed in helping their wives feel less stressed by helping at home. Sociologist Francine Deutsch calls this disconnect *learned helplessness*.[34] These men may assume that if they don't follow through on household tasks, especially those involving kids, it's likely that their female partners will complete the task instead. When men fumble, women are likely to solve the problem. When women fumble, fixing the issue is also on them. Because keeping a nice home and taking good care of one's children is central to the American understanding of good mothering, it makes sense that these moms were unwilling to simply let these tasks—like laundry, changing diapers, helping children with homework, and scheduling doctor appointments—fall by the wayside.

While twenty-five American mothers I talked to couldn't routinely rely on their partners' help, seven of the thirty-two described greatly reduced work-family conflict because their partners *did* participate actively in child-rearing and housework. I noticed this trend in families in which husbands' jobs were more flexible than their wives' (Robin); both parents identified as feminists or worked to have an egalitarian relationship (Kelsey, Layla, Talia, and Rachel, who was married to a woman); the father was a stay-at-home dad (Lauren); or the father was from a country where it was normal for dads to be equally involved at home, as was the case for Ruth's Swedish husband, Gunnar. As in Sweden, it often took substantial effort to try to achieve equality at home, but in the US, this planning tended to fall to mothers even in the most equal households.

American mothers experienced a weak public safety net—the collection of services provided by the state that gives citizens social supports to try and prevent hardship and improve people's quality of life. Some of the frustrations I heard from moms in DC were particular to large metropolitan cities. For instance, women like Imani often had long commuting times and the cost of living was higher than elsewhere in the country. But the majority of women's frustrations stemmed from issues common to all American working families.

One of the most significant challenges is the lack of paid maternity leave, which hugely shapes mothers' lifeworlds. The women I spoke with wove together sick days, vacation days, short-term disability leave, unpaid time off, and, for some, paid time off in order to leave work after their children were born. Admittedly, I often felt confused and over-whelmed when mothers recounted exactly how they scraped together time away from work after giving birth—a feeling I rarely had in inter-views with moms in Europe. Here is Gail (who is Asian, married, and a librarian with two children), explaining her two maternity leaves:

> For both of them I took six weeks completely off and then I did another six weeks—well actually, with my first one I did a six-week transition time back, so it was part time three days in the office, two days out. And with my second child, I ended up quitting that job and then starting a new job, so I got an extra—those extra six weeks in between. And then with my new job, I worked out that I would be three days in the office. That was just, sort of—they approached me and said, "We want to hire you," and I said, "Oh, great," but I wasn't sure that I wanted to go back to work after having my sec-ond one, and so they said, "Well, what would it take?" and I liter-ally said, "I want to work three days in the office and I want this much money." And they were like, "Fine." And I said, "OK, I guess I'm working for you, then."

Gail's explanation took well under a minute, and of the bunch, I'd describe this as a fairly straightforward account. I still struggled to follow answers like these and asked for clarification in nearly every interview. Gail's de-scription also underscores just how central maternity leave and schedule flexibility are to mothers' employment decisions.

All in all, I surmised that most women in my sample took between six weeks and four months off work after childbirth, depending on what they were allowed and could afford. One mother quit and took ten months off because her children were gravely ill. Several took only a few days off before returning to work. A few women who could afford it quit work altogether because they had no access to maternity leave, and they found new jobs when they were ready to return several months to a year later. Several lower-income mothers also quit their jobs when they had chil-dren because they had no leave and no daycare solution. The key differ-ence is that these less advantaged women had little savings and greater difficulty finding work again. The decision to leave work and remain unemployed for a period was detrimental to their job prospects, putting them in a precarious position when it came to supporting their families.

A number of moms hoarded their vacation and sick days (which varied between five and fifteen days annually) for several years knowing they would get no paid maternity leave when they decided to have children. Of course, this means women have to work nonstop through their pregnancies, and then after they return to work, new moms are unable to take a paid day off when they find themselves or their children ill, or to enjoy a day of rest or vacation. Women repeatedly told me they used their "vacation" days for children's dentist and doctor appointments, back-to-school meetings, parent-teacher conferences, and so on. Women who worked part time, in temporary positions, or as freelancers and entrepreneurs received no paid vacation or sick days, so saving these days wasn't an option. Some mothers even went into the red, borrowing from their future paid days off to stay home with their infants—a labor practice called time banking. Chelsea, the sales manager who felt she lived in "the swirl," will need to work for two full weeks above her normal working hours, eighty hours total, to get back to zero on her paid time off this year. This tactic is out of the question for the majority of American workers, who lack the job security and occupational prestige to take this additional time.

When discussing their short maternity leave and life with young children, moms in DC talked constantly about sleep.[35] Women said things like, "I was kind of like a zombie," "I was in hell for three months," "I didn't sleep for five years," and, "It was exhausting. I remember getting home [from work] and just falling asleep." The European mothers I talked to also described being tired when their children were infants, but their exhaustion occurred while they were on paid leave. Unlike Americans, European mothers reported overcoming their most acute exhaustion before returning to work. US moms told me they felt drained, wiped out. They were also sad to have missed key milestones with their children, they felt punished at work, they were unable to take paid vacation or sick days, and some reported being forced to quit their jobs.[36]

Once women returned to work, their challenges continued. I spent an enormous portion of my interviews talking about mothers' difficulties breast-feeding and pumping at work. Section 7 of the Fair Labor Standards Act (FLSA) requires employers to provide "reasonable break time for an employee to express breast milk for her nursing child for 1 year after the child's birth each time such employee has need to express the milk." Employers are also required to provide "a place, other than a bathroom, that is shielded from view and free from intrusion from coworkers and the public, which may be used by an employee to express breast milk."

Women told me they wanted to breast-feed for a few months up to a year, but most returned to work one to four months after giving birth. Pumping at work usually wasn't an issue for the European moms I interviewed, who had between five months and three years off work through their leave systems. The European participants hardly ever mentioned pumping breast milk because they weaned their children while on leave before returning to work. Breast-feeding was emotionally fraught for US mothers. Some women cried when talking about it. The intensity and moral weight with which they discussed their own decisions makes sense because the practice of breast-feeding is connected to gendered ideals of good mothering.[37]

Mothers felt enormous apprehension about pumping in the workplace—worrying about when, where, and how often to pump, and around whom. Women with access to a room at work that was designed for this purpose were effusive in their gratitude for it. Mothers considered a lactation room a "luxury." Mackenzie, who works at an international financial institution where I interviewed her, told me:

> It's beautiful. I can take you down there. It's really nice. It's a separate room with a lock key entry. [...] It has lockers, it has I think four individual rooms with curtains, and each of them has a commercial-grade pump in it—those are the ones where you can share safely. [...] It has a fridge and a microwave and a sink. It's a good situation. [...] They [the company] make it as easy as it could possibly be. [...] You hear a lot of people down there on their computers or their phones.

Mackenzie gave me a tour of the lactation room. Women employees had a fridge designated just for breast milk, separate from where employees kept their bagged lunches.

Just to reiterate, the supports Mackenzie was so grateful for included a room with a curtain, a pump that's safe to share, and a fridge in which to keep her breast milk. This to me is further evidence of the very low expectations of US mothers. Yet this is much more than the vast majority of American mothers receive at work. The law stipulates only that a space and "reasonable time" be provided for pumping breast milk.

Even for the most privileged participants, pumping at work often proved difficult. Using the lactation room could be so inconvenient and time-intensive that women opted for different solutions (like Samantha's use of the Freemie). Sometimes the designated places made mothers feel uncomfortable or were unsanitary and inadequate. Women told me they pumped in supply closets, storage rooms, handicapped bathroom stalls, rooms with windows, and their cars. Under these circumstances, mothers usually stopped breast-feeding earlier than they'd hoped.

Women also had uncomfortable experiences with male colleagues and supervisors who didn't understand exactly what pumping breast milk entailed. Men's lack of knowledge required additional emotional labor[38] when women found themselves in the awkward position of having to maintain a professional persona while explaining pumping to men, or insisting that men not enter their office while they were pumping. The mothers I interviewed were embarrassed at the prospect of colleagues and employers seeing them breast-feed.

Some bosses refused to provide privacy for breast-feeding mothers, occasionally with disastrous consequences. Robin, who works at a prison, was denied a request to install a lock on her office door (a converted prison cell) and decided to pump anyway. After an inmate walked in on her, a lock was installed.

Mothers' desire to pump in a clean space and unwillingness to pump in restrooms sometimes damaged their standing at work. Gloria, a Hispanic sales director who works 37.5 hours a week, told her boss she was unable to travel for work trips around the country while breast-feeding.

So she was instructed to give away her accounts to other colleagues and build a client base back up from scratch.

Breast-feeding in the US clashes with contemporary employment practices and the architecture of most American workplaces. The difficulties women experienced trying to pump at work highlight how gender inequality is built into the structure of work organizations.[39] Modern careers are not organized to be conducive to motherhood. The lack of alignment in mothers' lifeworlds among federal policies, work organizations, and working mothers' needs and desires causes tremendous problems for women.

When women did return to work after childbirth, many struggled without access to benefits like flexible schedules, reduced working hours, or the ability to work from home on occasion. Many US mothers told me they'd be thrilled to have a bit more flexibility in their work hours, to telecommute every once in a while, or to work fewer hours a week. However, the majority of women in DC told me that this flexibility wasn't an option. The rigidity of work schedules and long hours caused a great deal of work-family conflict. By comparison, remember that Swedish parents have the legal right to reduce their normal working hours by up to 25 percent until their child turns eight. In Italy, mothers returning from parental leave were legally entitled to work two fewer hours per day to facilitate breast-feeding. In Germany, white-collar jobs are often available part time.

Again, most mothers didn't mention their desire for more flexibility as something that could be made available through federal work-family policy. When I brought it up, interviewees thought this policy intervention would be wonderful, but all felt it was unrealistic—even those who were unusually knowledgeable about American public policy. Talia was the most well-informed of my participants about the lack of work-family policies in the US compared to other countries. She and her husband, Michael, sounded like the most egalitarian, feminist couple among the women I spoke with in Washington, DC. She had just returned from maternity leave with their four-month-old daughter, Naomi, and said wistfully with a sarcastic laugh that she wished everyone could work part time: "I definitely think that decreasing the length of the workweek would be a primary place I would start for thinking about how to make work life better in America. For parents and for nonparents.... People are working way too many hours." Even Talia, who knew a lot about American and European work-family policy, thought it would be unrealistic to increase the availability of part-time work in the US. Only three of the mothers I interviewed were able to work part time (Ashley, Jill, and Layla).

Those who were permitted to show up later, leave earlier, or work from home invoked the gratitude discourse when describing this benefit. Imani, the property manager with the four-hour daily commute, explained,

> What's really been awesome is, my boss has been super-flexible. [...] It's a privilege, not a given. It's very informal, and I try really hard to respect that privilege, because I don't want to lose it, because I'm the one with that flexibility and I'd like to be able to use it if I absolutely need it. [...] I like to bring myself in to work. I like being where I'm supposed to be.

Some mothers with these benefits stayed at their companies even if they could find higher-paying or more enjoyable jobs elsewhere, because the benefits were so central to improving their work-family lives. Chelsea, as we will see, turned down the same major promotion twice because she valued her flexibility at work so much—even if she still lived in "the swirl."

Others experienced job penalties for using these flexible policies at work. Jill, a white elementary school teacher and single mother, struggled with depression and was in the midst of a messy divorce when her daughter was one year old. She had been working full time but couldn't take the stress any longer, so she approached a colleague who had also recently had a child. They devised a job-sharing plan where they would both work part time, splitting one full-time teaching position. The principal reluctantly approved it but said, "This year, no births"—meaning the school couldn't handle more pregnant teachers. It was the second time in fourteen years anyone had been allowed to job-share with reduced hours. Jill loved this reduced schedule: "It allowed me to breathe and play with [my daughter]. It's been good."

Later in our conversation, Jill mentioned off handedly, "I probably won't even have a job there this fall." She could tell I was surprised to hear this. "That's the other thing. As a part-time employee, your contract is year to year. That's the other thing I gave up."

Shocked, I replied, "Oh! Your job security went out the window?"

Jill replied with a sad smile, "I don't have any."

Jill traded job security for a part-time schedule so she could keep her head above water during her divorce proceedings. Hers is a heartrending example of how mothers often have to trade off employment benefits when life throws them curve balls. Overall, mothers tended to feel that the structure and culture of overwork in the United States was inexorable, and they believed it was up to them to adapt their own behaviors to solve their work-family conflict.

This burden is carried almost entirely by women, in part because paternity leave, paid or otherwise, is rare in the US. For the twenty-four women I interviewed whose partners were men (one interviewee, Rachel, identified as a lesbian; her wife's name is Danielle), most of their partners took off work only a few days or a week after their children were born. These fathers all worked full time. None took official paternity leave; mothers said it wasn't offered at any of their partners' workplaces. Others took two or three weeks off using sick days and vacation days. Kelsey's and Janet's husbands took the longest leaves, taking six weeks and twelve weeks off, respectively. Most mothers were home alone with their infants within days of childbirth.

Survey data from the US Department of Labor show that nine in ten fathers take some time off work for the birth or adoption of a child, but these are very short leaves. Seventy percent take ten days or less. In 2015 only 13 percent of men who took leave received pay for any portion of the time away from work, compared with 21 percent for mothers.[40]

Although I asked every mom I interviewed in DC whether her partner took any leave, we spent remarkably little time on the subject. Gail, whose explanation of her two maternity leaves confused me, is Asian and was born and raised in Canada. She is married to Patrick, and they have two children, ages ten and twelve. Gail works over fifty hours a week as a school librarian. I interviewed her in their formal living room while

Patrick and their kids hung out in the adjacent kitchen at the back of the house.

I asked Gail, "Did your husband take any time off work when both the kids were born?"

She paused and cast her eyes above my head, thinking hard. "I don't think so. Maybe a week."

Given the lengthy accounting of her own maternity leave a few minutes prior, I followed up, "But no official paid paternity leave?"

"No," Gail replied. "I think he probably took a week or half days or something. When my daughter was born, we had asked my mom to come help out for a bit, so she was here."

I wanted to make sure I understood correctly since Gail was being vague. "So he might have taken off work a bit for a week or so, and then he went back to his full-time schedule?"

Gail nodded, "Mm-hmm," her mouth in a firm line. I heard these brief responses often from American and Italian mothers. My sense was that paternity leave was a foreign concept to US mothers; they had heard of it, but it simply didn't register on their radar as a possibility for their families, as it did with mothers in former East Germany and especially in Sweden.

Mothers seem to have internalized a gendered version of the liberal discourse of personal responsibility—not that *families* are responsible for their own well-being, but that *mothers* are responsible for their families' well-being. When I asked what sorts of policies could help support them better, two of the thirty-two mothers mentioned that paid paternity leave would help reduce their work-family conflict and enhance equality with their partners. Michelle wished her husband, Christopher, could take a year off work to fully experience the labor involved in caring for their two young children, which she did alone. Talia, the white married mother who had what seemed to be the most gender-egalitarian relationship of any mothers I interviewed in DC, works about forty-five hours a week as an editor. She thought that a "longer" paternity leave of eight weeks would give fathers the practical incentive to learn parenting skills that they wouldn't bother to learn if they were home for only two weeks. Talia saw leave as a tool to motivate fathers to participate in the care of their children, which would ease mothers' burdens. Recall that in Sweden the goal both in welfare law and among parents themselves is for fathers to take half the parental leave time—seven months.

For many women, the return to work brings with it the challenge of finding safe, affordable, and high-quality childcare. All my American interviewees reported difficulties doing so. We spent more time discussing childcare than any other topic during my US interviews. Those who found safe, high-quality care credited luck for securing this care. No women found what I would consider affordable care; all discussed at length the expense of childcare. Some reported that it used up to two-thirds of their income, in some cases costing tens of thousands of dollars a year for one child. It was even more expensive for mothers with more than one child. In contrast, the maximum *monthly* cost for a child in Sweden is around US$160 (US$1,900 a year) for even the wealthiest families, with successively lower costs for more children. This yearly maximum is not meant to exceed 3 percent of a Swedish family's net income. Swedish families pay roughly 9 percent of the costs of childcare. German families pay 14 percent, while Italians pay, at most, 18 percent of the costs for kids under three to attend childcare; it is free for those ages three to six. These governments subsidize the rest through taxes.[41]

Ideals of "good motherhood" were embedded in mothers' discussions of childcare in all the countries where I conducted research, but American mothers' comments belied an anxiety that Europeans lacked. In Europe, mothers were concerned with the affordability and quality of childcare, and we also spent substantial time on this topic. But in Germany, Sweden, and Italy public daycare is provided by municipalities and is both heavily subsidized and regulated. These countries also have national standards for caregivers and facilities that the US does not, which meant that the moms I interviewed in Europe didn't mention any worry about their children's physical safety while at daycare—something that greatly concerned American mothers.

For those who could afford it, paying for expensive, high-quality childcare helped assure mothers that their children didn't suffer for their decision to work. This expenditure assuaged mothers' sense of guilt to a degree (though none seemed free of it), and thereby lessened one source of work-family conflict. Many women described knowing that the daycare facilities where their children spent their time were of questionable quality, but they couldn't afford different solutions.

US mothers also seemed distressed because no one daycare solution was reliable. These arrangements often shifted without warning. A daycare run informally out of someone's home could close, a babysitter or nanny could start school or move away, or relatives who agreed to help could suddenly fall ill. Even when women secured space in daycares that they liked and trusted, the inflexible opening and closing hours were a major source of stress. Some, like Makayla's children's daycare center, charged up to $10 a minute for late pick-ups. She told me "it's like white knuckles trying to get there on time." Makayla, again, is middle class. For a mother earning minimum wage, which was US$9.50 an hour in DC in 2015, the penalty for a ten-minute delay at a center like this would cost a mother more than a full day's paycheck.[42] It's small wonder why low-income mothers experience employment disruptions after having children more often than do middle-class mothers.

Without a universal system, childcare difficulties are inevitable. Families, and primarily the women in them, find individual solutions for their children's daycare needs, which vary significantly in their levels of safety, cost, and convenience. The lack of universal daycare fuels class inequalities not just for mothers, but also for children.[43] Women's childcare experiences and solutions depended on their level of economic advantage: mothers who had the most financial resources available to dedicate to childcare unsurprisingly tended to be the happiest with the solutions they found. Still, most American women didn't mention a public daycare system as a potential source of support for their families. All interviewees expressed profound stress and frustration about their difficulties finding childcare, but only a few mentioned socializing daycare as a helpful policy solution. One mother, Michelle, did express indignation with the cultural assumption that children are parents' responsibility alone. She was the woman who wished her husband, Christopher, could spend a year at home to appreciate just how much work it is to maintain a household:

Here in America we say, "You shouldn't have children if you can't afford it." That's just like, what do we value in the society? Having nurturing parents and their children to make good citizens down the road? If a child is sick, being understanding of that, supporting that, not having to think of the financial implications is huge. I know parents who will take their [sick] kids to the daycare, because it's like, "I have to get to work." Aren't they running a fever? You shouldn't have to make that choice. They should support us more in our country.

This more structural understanding of work-family conflict was a rarity among my American interviewees, but not for those in Sweden, Germany, and Italy. External assistance in ameliorating their work-family conflict seemed to sit outside most American mothers' lifeworlds, even when it came to childcare.

Another worry that consumed mothers day in and day out, year after year while their children were growing up was the lack of guaranteed paid sick leave. Some mothers had access to paid sick days through their employers, while others who worked as temps, freelancers, or part-time employees didn't receive any paid days off work for illness. Moms in DC often went to work sick themselves or sent their children to school sick because they ran out of paid sick days, or they couldn't afford to or weren't allowed to take an unpaid day off, risking penalties or job loss if they did. We spent a lot of time during interviews talking about the catastrophe of a sick child for mothers at work.[44] Mothers' carefully laid plans for childcare, commuting time, and work schedules unraveled when children fell ill.

The US is also the only OECD country without guaranteed paid sick days. The country's labor laws don't require employers to provide short-term paid sick days or longer-term paid sick leave, and they do not protect workers from being fired if they miss work as a result of illness.[45] Several states—including Arizona, California, Connecticut, Maryland, Massachusetts, Oregon, Rhode Island, Vermont, and Washington—have legislation that allows eligible workers some amount of paid time off for illness. However, the laws vary widely and have a lot of exemptions.[46] As of February 2018, eighteen cities and counties had passed paid sick days statutes, most recently Austin, Texas.

On top of worries about sick leave, mothers talked frequently about their paid time off (PTO). Many would forgo time off during certain parts of the year and work overtime to have enough days saved up to take a week-long vacation with their families or to stay at home during the workdays in the recess between Christmas and New Year's. The US is the only economically developed country in the world that doesn't guarantee workers paid vacation or paid holidays. The availability of paid days off is distributed unevenly among workers: only 50 percent of low-wage workers (the bottom quartile of earners) receive any paid vacation, compared to 90 percent of high-wage workers (the top quartile of earners).[47] The average worker in the private sector receives ten days a year. In comparison (as I've outlined), Swedes receive a minimum of twenty-five days of paid vacation, Germans receive twenty (with nine to thirteen additional paid holidays, depending on which state they reside in), and Italians receive twenty (alongside ten paid holidays).

A few women suggested more paid vacation or sick days when I asked what could be changed to reduce their work-family conflict, but each one followed this statement with a bitter laugh. This seems to be more evidence that US mothers usually think of workplace policies as unchallengeable.

Generally speaking, the American moms I interviewed seemed frazzled, tired, and overwhelmed with stress. They stood apart from all the women I interviewed in Europe in this regard. The sources of work-family conflict I've detailed in this chapter help explain this difference. Although working mothers in Europe also faced prevailing norms about employment and parenting that caused them to feel stress and guilt, they had more material sources of work-family support than American mothers, even if this support varied in usefulness and was sometimes far from perfect (as in Italy). It is this *confluence of both normative and material sources of work-family conflict* that makes American mothers' difficulties particularly acute.

Mothers' Responses
to Work-Family Conflict

To minimize their overpowering work-family conflict, some mothers tried to change their work lives. Several of the women I spoke with told me they "leaned out," found part-time work, or switched jobs.

During our conversations several moms referenced Sheryl Sandberg's bestselling book *Lean In*. Sandberg's book argues that women don't advance in their careers in part because they unintentionally hold themselves back at work. Sandberg suggests that women should "lean in" and "sit at the table," seek challenges, take risks, and pursue their goals in order to find professional achievement and personal fulfillment. Some felt *Lean In* spoke to them profoundly while others were more skeptical. One called it "total crap." Some women adopted the term into their lexicon and used it to explain their own work-family decisions. Chelsea said she was currently "leaning out" at work. She has a prestigious position in sales management, but turned down the same major promotion (to a C-suite position) twice because it required substantial travel and less flexibility. The promotion was attractive, but Chelsea declined it. She said:

> I can't do that. I just can't do that right now. My husband thought I was a little crazy for passing on it because he's like, "If the CEO wants you to work for him . . ." I was like, I just—I can't do it. I'm going to stick with my current job because I have the flexibility that I need.

Chelsea is primarily responsible for their household and children and thought this promotion was incompatible with her domestic commitments. So, while Chelsea didn't "lean out" entirely by quitting work, especially since she secured the flexible schedule she wanted, she declined opportunities to "lean in" further: "I need to be leaning more to the family side right now and just maintaining the work side. I can't lean into the work."

Mothers also discussed the need to "lean out" at certain points over their career trajectory in order to accommodate their families. Gloria, the advertising sales director who had to give away her clients during maternity leave and explain pumping breast milk to her boss, used this approach herself: "You have to pick when you lean in and when to lean back." Gloria chose to lean back from work during her thirties to make sure she could have children and spend time with them once she did. She now has a three-year-old and five-year-old and works 37.5 hours a week. She plans to lean back in and work longer hours when her children are a few years older, when she said they'll rely on her less.

Chelsea's and Gloria's explanations for leaning out are rooted in the American cultural ideal of good mothering: they couldn't dedicate themselves fully to work while their children were small. They also wanted to spend more time with their kids. For mothers who leaned out, some criticized those who remained "all in" at work, indicating that their children suffered. Gloria criticized moms who worked long hours, like lawyers. She positioned herself as someone who made sacrifices for her children's sake: she decided to forgo law school so she could pick up her children from daycare, conforming to intensive mothering ideals. Leaning out is a gendered tactic mothers used to reduce their own work-family conflict and affirm to themselves that they were good mothers. For some moms, this also involved becoming active agents in the shaming of other mothers who made different decisions.

I mentioned earlier in this chapter that part-time work was hard to come by for the women I talked with, though many wanted it. Only three moms worked part-time schedules, but they told me their reduced hours were central to achieving a greater sense of ease in their work and family lives. Layla is an Arab married mother with a two-year-old and was expecting her second child. She now works as a consultant twenty-five hours a week after being fired from her previous job while pregnant. Layla settled a discrimination lawsuit out of court and decided to work for herself as a political consultant so she could have a part-time schedule. The other two women did not work in prestigious occupations. They work in heavily female-dominated jobs: Jill is a third-grade teacher with a job-sharing arrangement and Ashley is a secretary. These three women told me they felt lucky and grateful to work part time. However, their part-time jobs offered limited benefits, unlike in Germany (see chapters 3 and 4).

In her study of elite women in the finance industry mentioned earlier, Mary Blair-Loy described the women who managed to secure part-time schedules as mavericks "trying to imaginatively redefine what is possible."[48] None of the women I interviewed working in white-collar and professional occupations said it would be possible to negotiate a part-time schedule. Perhaps the resources necessary to secure reduced hours at work are more available to the high-income women Blair-Loy interviewed, and are less available to the largely middle-class women I spoke to for this book. It's also possible that the sense of impossibility prevented mothers from trying to secure part-time accommodations.

Two other women were able to negotiate part-time schedules temporarily when transitioning back from maternity leave before returning to full-time work, and they described it as "the best of both worlds."[49] Talia reflected, "While I was working part time I just kept saying, 'This is the life.' I wish we could all work part time. It's such a more humane approach to work life, period. Not just for parents. I think we are all really overworked." Allie did the same, especially because one of her twins had health problems; she said she would advise women to try out part-time work if they could after becoming mothers. Allie implied this strategy helped her keep her foot in the door and allowed her to maintain a professional identity that gave her validation and satisfaction. Since maternity leave in the United States tends to be quite short, both Talia and Allie found it helpful to work part time for a period after transitioning back. The mothers who worked part time explained their decisions similarly to the German mothers I interviewed, who seemed better able to conform to their country's ideal of a good mother with a part-time schedule (see chapters 3 and 4).

The US by and large lacks the political, cultural, and organizational support for part-time employment in white-collar occupations. In contrast, part-time work is widespread in low-paying retail and service work. But, again, these jobs come without the benefits, job security, or protections that are available in countries like Germany. Many Americans who are employed part time would prefer to work full time but are given no choice. Thus, women at the middle of the income distribution (like those I interviewed) or at the top often want part-time hours but most can't have them, while women at the bottom of this hierarchy (concentrated in retail and service jobs) want full-time hours but cannot have them. Sociologists Jerry Jacobs and Kathleen Gerson refer to this disparity as the "time divide."[50] As we saw, in a place like Berlin policy and cultural supports for a wider range of employment models— alongside support for the unemployed and mandatory overtime compensation—can help remove this form of inequality. Mothers in the United States don't have this range of options.

Many of my interview participants changed jobs in order to gain access to work-family benefits or stayed in jobs they might otherwise have left because they needed the policies available there. Sometimes women traded one handful of benefits for others when they changed jobs: usually less pay but more flexibility. Changing jobs to secure better policies seemed to eliminate some but not all of mothers' work-family conflict, suggesting that policies alone are not a panacea for working mothers' struggles. Many less privileged American mothers don't have the option to switch companies to secure better work-family benefits. It comes as no surprise that the mothers working in the most prestigious jobs among those I interviewed tended to have the most—and most generous—work-family policies available to them. Regardless of their economic advantage, all the women explained having to devise a set of makeshift solutions to turn to when the going got rough—which, it turns out, was often.

Given the lack of a national public safety net of work-family policy supports, the women I met in Washington, DC, described creating their own private safety nets to reduce their daily stress.[51] These social and financial safety nets helped catch mothers when they stumbled— whether they fell ill, lost a job, felt alone, needed someone to pick up a sick child from daycare when they couldn't leave work, or unexpectedly found themselves single parents.

Mothers spoke often about their desire to be in touch with relatives, friends, and other working mothers to lessen the feelings of isolation they sometimes felt. The five single mothers I interviewed felt particularly lonely and overwhelmed. They relied on family members and friends to support them day-to-day. One of these single moms, Mary, was much higher income, and she also relied on her parents to help with her twins. She explained how she had joined a "single mothers by choice" group. "Choice moms" are single women who decide to have children through adoption or conception using donor sperm. Mary explained to me that she used this term to prevent people from constantly asking about her husband, which she found irritating and exhausting. The term "single mother by choice" also has race and class connotations. Given the discourse of personal responsibility and the centrality of individualism in the US, it may unconsciously serve as a distancing tactic from the stereotype of poor single mothers who are thought to irresponsibly have children out of wedlock or by accident. Using the phrase "choice moms" indicates that their childbearing and family model are intentional.

Several women told me they had started a working mothers' support group in their neighborhood or workplace. Natalia started a group called the Mommy Mafia that ballooned to two hundred members. She said mothers were comforted by talking openly about sensitive and often painful parenting topics like trying to have another child. They also discussed parenting approaches and ways to reduce work-family conflict. These conversations seemed to make participants feel more informed about their own decisions and therefore like better mothers. Susan was the only woman, only mother, and only person of color in her high rank at work. Having told me it took "nine years of tears" to stop feeling guilty as a working mom, Susan decided to start a support group in her office after years spent researching the available policies and managing her work-family conflict alone. She said she learned the hard way that going it alone was impossible: "You should have some kind of support network there. This is why I started that group. Find the other working moms. [. . .] Sometimes I look back now and I'm not really sure how I didn't totally break down sometimes. [. . .] It became a mission for me, and it has been ever since then."

Susan argued that no one could understand the plight of working moms unless they were one—not even working dads. She was the youngest senior staff member by at least twenty-five years and started informally meeting with other moms in her office to "have lunch and support each other." The support group was such a success that her workplace formalized it. Moms in Europe never mentioned starting their own grass-roots support groups. I suspect Italy's strong familialist culture meant that women had ample interpersonal support. In Germany and Sweden, these groups are widely institutionalized at the municipal, state, and sometimes federal levels and are often run as public entities.

In addition to weaving together a social safety net of other working moms they could rely on, women told me they felt responsible for creating a family financial safety net. Given the rise in families' economic insecurity and shrinking national safety nets over the past several decades, sociologist Marianne Cooper found in her 2014 study of American families that regardless of their position along the socioeconomic spectrum, all families feel anxious about finances.[52] Cooper learned that mothers tend to be the "designated worriers" about their families' financial security. I found this to be true for the mothers I interviewed as well, another aspect of the uneven division of household labor described earlier.

During our conversations American mothers talked about money far more often than the moms in Europe did. They worried about the high cost of childcare and health insurance, and the higher earners told me they worried about saving for retirement and their children's college. While some European mothers also complained about the cost of childcare and health care, these were heavily subsidized in Germany, Sweden, and Italy, and college in these countries is free or low cost. Single mothers in all four countries mentioned financial worries more often than partnered women did. But federal governments provide financial safety nets for citizens and single mothers in Europe (though these vary widely) that are largely unavailable in the United States. Many American mothers reported that their employment decisions were tied to achieving financial security. They explained that they had in their mind a certain level of financial security that was necessary to provide a "good childhood."

Mothers who were better off financially outsourced some of their childcare and housework to help ease their workload, often to women who were immigrants, racial/ethnic minorities, or both. While Italian mothers also relied on outsourcing care and cleaning, American mothers were notably effusive in their gratitude for this help. Michelle, the white, married mother of two who works remotely as an engineer thirty-five hours a week, employed an African American nanny named Jessica. I got the chance to meet her when I showed up for our interview on a particularly cold weekday morning. After inviting me inside her home, Michelle waved me to follow her into the kitchen where Jessica was zipping up the two-year-old's coat while talking softly to the six-month-old girl waiting in a baby carrier by her feet. Michelle introduced me to Jessica and we shook hands. Michelle said they were just leaving for the park. Her gaze darting back and forth between Jessica and me like she was watching a fast-paced tennis match, she explained that Jessica was a student, and that I was also a student who wanted to learn about her work-family balance. She smiled at Jessica, laughing and saying she was their family's "lifesaver." Michelle thanked her and confirmed when they would be returning, and then Jessica ushered the two children out the door. This experience contrasted sharply with those I had in Italy, where mothers didn't acknowledge the presence of domestic workers or introduce me to them. Michelle seemed eager to show Jessica and me how much she appreciated and valued her caring labor. Because US culture prides itself on a model of equality regardless of race, gender, or class, she may have been uncomfortable with the display of privilege and unequal race and class dynamics in this relationship, and was eager to compensate by performing gratitude that the Italian mothers felt no need for.

Several mothers told me they worked hard to squeeze the cost of domestic workers like Jessica into their budgets. My participants explained that they were making a financial sacrifice in favor of greatly reduced stress. Mothers who employed domestic workers explained to me with wide eyes and raised shoulders, shaking their heads, that they literally didn't know how they would manage to keep their household functioning without this help. American mothers paid childcare facilities, nannies, and housekeepers to try and resolve their work-family conflict. As I mentioned earlier, the more privileged women I spoke to were able to work outside the home because they relied on the caring labor of much lower-paid women workers.[53]

Mothers also tried to resolve their work-family conflicts by changing their own outlook or their approach to juggling work and family responsibilities. This solution implies that the source of mothers' work-family conflict in their lifeworlds is not the structure of the workplace, oppressive cultural norms, or gender inequality, but mothers themselves. I observed three tactics that moms used to shift their own perspectives.

First, mothers tried to educate themselves about parenting and work-family conflict. US mothers often thought they hadn't yet adopted the right parenting approach, weren't spending enough or the right kind of time with their children, or weren't knowledgeable enough about their needs. As a result, American moms often consulted books, articles, Facebook and blog posts, podcasts, and classes about parenting and work-family conflict to try and resolve these dilemmas. Although European mothers mentioned these resources occasionally, American moms talked about them more often and in greater detail. They seemed to spend a fair amount of time reading about, listening to, and attending classes on these topics. Enrolling in courses and reading parenting books made mothers feel that they were working to fulfill their duties and improve their abilities as mothers, which they believed had the twofold benefit of alleviating their stress and helping their children.

Middle- and upper-class American moms often turn to expert advice to inform their child-rearing decisions.[54] But this expert advice is fraught. Sociologist Orit Avishai argues that complying with these mothering standards requires immense time, energy, and self-discipline.[55] For my interviewees, doing motherhood right meant performing a professionalized version of motherhood that involved continual research. Their partners didn't do this work, according to moms in our conversations. I asked women in DC how they defined good mothering, and on several occasions they replied by saying, "I read this really interesting article about this," and then explained the article's take on good parenting without giving me their personal definition, as if the article's explanation stood in for theirs.

For Makayla and her husband, William, their impatience and exhaustion with their three-year-old's stubbornness led them to sign up for a "parenting boot camp" at their friend's recommendation. This class reminded them that their son Jamal was, in her words, "no different from any other kid," affirming that nothing was wrong with him and that they simply needed to refine their approach. Makayla's voice changed when she started discussing their new approach to disciplining Jamal, almost as if she had memorized a pamphlet from the course on this topic and was repeating it to me when I asked her what it meant to be a good mother. Avishai calls this invisible labor of staying up-to-date on expert advice a "contemporary mothering project [...] [and] a burden of mothering in late capitalist America."[56] Trying to become better parents—ones who were more organized, more calm, better at multitasking and dealing with temper tantrums, and so forth—was one more way mothers took responsibility for solving their work-family conflict by themselves, whether by reading, listening to podcasts, or taking classes.

Second, American mothers talked constantly about their efforts to improve their efficiency and organization as a way to reduce stress. Mary, the attorney and white single mother of twins, said: "I'm very grateful, even if I occasionally get stressed out. But it's such an inefficient state of being to be stressed out. [...] It's usually something that can be resolved with a little bit of extra work. It's not an unsolvable problem." Mary implied that she could choose to resolve it on her own if she just applied herself.

Women explained that they were continually refining a system for managing what felt like a hectic, packed schedule. Imani, the Hispanic/African American mother with the four-hour daily commute as a property manager, reflected with exasperation, "One of my goals for this year, hello!"—she threw her hands up in frustration—"ten years later, almost eleven, is to try to get to a place where we can organize and come up with a little bit of a better system." Imani explained, "I think we could stop flying by the seat of our pants. That's what I feel like our life has been like." She rolled her eyes, shaking her head, and continued:

> Very hectic. [...] I wish I could tell you that I cooked all the meals on Sunday, and on Monday and Tuesday we had this and that. That's also a very idealist way I would love to live, but on Saturday and Sunday I'm exhausted. And not to mention, my son has sports, and my daughter's getting ready to have activities. That's going to blow

our world up. We have to have a schedule of some sort. [...] We decided that for spring break we wouldn't go anywhere this year, and that we would focus on trying to get our house in a functional, organized manner so that we can have a slightly better life.

Imani expressed a common refrain: if she could create a good schedule, or reorganize her house, or plan out their weekly meals, or reduce her commute, or carve out an extra hour in her day, her life would feel less chaotic. I heard some iteration of this thinking from every American mother I interviewed, whether she worked full time or part time, whether she had an understanding boss or not, whether she worked from home or had a long commute. Mothers held high standards for what they felt they should be able to accomplish in a given day or week; many thought meals should be planned out and children should participate in several after-school activities, for example.[57] Regardless of their circumstances, all the mothers I interviewed seemed to think that one key to better work-life "balance" lay in working harder to squeeze more time out of their days.

US interviewees had the sense that good mothers were hyperorganized, and yet no one in my sample felt they met this high standard. Makayla explained,

Figuring out a way to do better planning for yourself, not only time for you to have for yourself, but also, I don't do as good of a job as I know that I should in terms of planning out meals, planning out trips to go shopping. Organization is gonna be your best friend. [...] Organizing for you so that you're not constantly—you're never catching up, you're always busy. [...] I feel like I'm constantly busy.

My field notes from Washington, DC, are full of references to time: Stressed. Busy. Exhausted. Rushed. Out of time. American mothers talked obsessively about time: not enough time, how to get more time, how to carve out time, how to squeeze in time. In a field note from DC I wrote: "These are extremely capable, hard-working women, and they can't make it work. It's too much. These are superheroes barely staying afloat."

Mothers' explanations of their approaches to balancing their work and family commitments made me feel physically anxious while listening to them. I got the sense that one small and unexpected change to their schedules (a nanny arriving ten minutes late, a traffic jam on the way to work, etc.) would cause their carefully laid plans to crumble and throw their day into chaos.

One way mothers increased their efficiency and reduced their stress was to find technological solutions to the tasks that ate up their time. European mothers rarely mentioned technology. I discussed Samantha's discovery of the Freemie (the hands-free breast pump) in the introduction to this chapter. Wealthier mothers used grocery delivery services, online shopping, housekeeper and babysitter finding services, smartphone apps, and shared calendars to manage their family's complex schedules and to-do lists. Chelsea breast-fed her son during our interview on her living room couch with one arm and showed me an app on her phone that tracked her son's breast-feeding schedule with the other hand. This was far easier than keeping a notebook, she explained. US mothers often answered calls, emails, and texts during our interviews, or stopped to open an app and type something into their phones before they forgot it.

The third way mothers tried to resolve their work-family conflict was to redefine what it meant to succeed, which often entailed lowering their expectations for themselves, their careers, and their family lives. Chelsea said she felt much less stressed once she decided she could accept doing an A or B job rather than an A+ job at work. Ashley, one of the few mothers who secured part-time work as a secretary, explained:

> They talk about mommy track type jobs. I think in a way, that's not a bad thing. You can't do it all, at least that first year or two. [...] Working and mothering were first, and everything else just went way down. I think in some ways cutting back your hours, cutting back your ambitions temporarily is not such a bad thing. [...] The only way you can have it all, something's got to give somewhere.

Ashley thought she couldn't work full time and still be the sort of mother she wanted, so she switched jobs and justified to herself that the mommy track is "not a bad thing" because "you can't do it all." She said, "This sounds so small-minded, but I think you have to scale back your ideas of what success means." But Ashley expressed some ambivalence about this decision:

> Here in DC, I've taken myself out of that circle, but there's a large group of very accomplished women, and it can give you an inferiority complex if you choose. [. . .] You can feel like, "What have I accomplished?" And they have kids, too. [. . .] Making cocktail small talk sometimes can be real ego-puncturing.

As she spoke, I felt an underlying sense of dissatisfaction from Ashley. She seemed to feel uncertain about this approach even though she had chosen it herself.

Moms admitted feeling guilty and even lowered their voices to a whisper when explaining their sense that elite career advancement was incompatible with good mothering. Scaling back and redefining success was their way of adhering to ideologies of intensive mothering. Janet, a white banker who is married and works forty-five hours a week, occupied a prestigious position at her firm. But she explained that it was only possible because she climbed the career ladder, then got married, and then adopted a child when she couldn't have one of her own. Her son was four years old when we spoke—I saw photos of him once she ushered me through the glass lobby of her office building and up into her well-appointed office. These large photos filled the wall by her desk. I asked whether mothers could advance to the top of their careers, and Janet paused and whispered, "I don't know. Honestly, I feel guilty, and I don't work very hard at this point. It takes a unique woman to be able to rise to the very top and still have a work-life balance, where you still see your child enough." I asked, "What are the qualities of a woman who is capable of doing that?" She paused again, clearly hesitant, and answered, "I don't know if it's possible. [. . .] It might not exist, and it might not be someone I would like. And that's mean of me to say of other women, but at some point, you have to choose your full-force-ahead career or your family."

Evident in Janet's comments (and Gloria's earlier) is the "mommy wars" discourse that good mothers can't advance to the top of the career ladder because they wouldn't be able to see their children enough. In this regard, American mothers sounded like the German women I interviewed who worried about being called raven mothers. Yet most German women who criticized the "go-getter" moms had sought part-time work, which is much more widely available in Germany than in the United States.

Even women I interviewed who held high-status positions, like Chelsea and Janet, thought scaling back was important in order to reduce their work-family conflict. The ER doctor Lauren confessed similarly, "You can't expect to be perfect in everything. Something's got to give. [. . .] I have lowered my expectations for both [*laughs*] to make it manageable for myself. That doesn't mean that I'm not feeling badly about one or the other at various times." This sense of inevitable disappointment was palpable for most of the moms I talked with. Moms felt resigned to the fact that they would never feel guilt-free about both their jobs and their family life at the same time. This sentiment echoed western German and Italian mothers' comments, though scaling back for German mothers meant working part time. Both ideal worker and intensive mothering norms require such high levels of commitment and energy that it's logical that mothers never feel they've succeeded in both realms. Mothers always thought they had fallen short.

I felt low as I left Washington, DC, when my fieldwork came to an end. After hearing heartbreaking story after heartbreaking story, I was drained and pessimistic. Witnessing a sliver of the stress American mothers endured in their day-to-day lives wore me down and, honestly, made me feel apprehensive.

Women in DC believed it was their own fault that they couldn't manage their feelings of guilt and work-family conflict. They created intricate webs of support for their families and an array of creative solutions to meet their needs, but mothers still felt pulled to their wits' end each day. And the mothers I spoke with were the ones who still worked for pay outside the home. When faced with the impossibility of juggling competing demands at home and work, many American mothers of all social classes simply quit, though with very different consequences depending on their socioeconomic status.[58]

The US was the last country in which I conducted interviews. I had spent the four previous summers speaking with German, Swedish, and Italian mothers about their work-family conflict. I learned that mothers everywhere experience stress and hardship. But the differences in policy supports were laid bare to me in meeting women face-to-face in these different field sites and seeing such drastically different options available to them to combine paid work with motherhood. American mothers had strikingly little in the way of support, *but they didn't realize it.* They took personal responsibility for problems that European mothers recognized as having external causes.

At the end of my interviews with European mothers, they often asked me what it was like in the US for working moms, and their jaws dropped as I began to explain the lack of policy provisions. Similarly, American women sometimes inquired when our interviews had finished about the policies available in Europe. I felt myself hesitating to tell them about Sweden's year-long leave paid at 80 percent of women's salaries, the universally available, full-day childcare open for all children in the former East Germany, or Italian women's right to return to the same position after their paid leave. I felt bad giving women concrete examples of how far behind the US is in supporting mothers and families—mostly because I thought it would only make them feel worse. But I told mothers anyway, and my explanations were usually met with looks of vague surprise, but mostly resignation. I could have been talking about policies on another planet, given how little it seemed to impact them.

From the perspectives of American mothers, shouldering the load for their work-family conflict was inevitable, even if mothers in other countries had more support. Like Allie said, simply altering work hours "would be like turning around the *Titanic.*" It felt like an impossibility to the women I interviewed, and I understand why. They worked doggedly to remedy their own struggles and felt grateful for even small amounts of help. In the United States, the family continues to operate as a gendered institution that privatizes social costs that are conceptualized in other nations as public responsibilities.[59]

The liberal welfare state is perpetuated through the discourse that mothers' work-family conflict is both their own fault and their own problem to solve. This discourse of personal responsibility disguises the social and structural causes of mothers' difficulties in trying to work for pay while raising children. And it exacts high economic, emotional, and physical costs on working mothers.

CHAPTER 7

Politicizing Mothers' Work-Family Conflict

"It is easy in Sweden to work and have kids."

—JOSEFIN, SWEDEN

"I wouldn't know how to handle forty hours. . . . That's no life."

—CLARA, FORMER EAST GERMANY

"'You are a career whore,' they say in Germany."

—JULIA, WESTERN GERMANY

"Nobody helps me. It is very difficult in Italy."

—CARLA, ITALY

"We can't figure out how to do it all at the same time."

—SAMANTHA, UNITED STATES

Working mothers around the world have vastly different experiences of work and family. Josefin, a Swedish mother, lives in one of the most gender-equal countries in the world and feels very satisfied with her ability to both work and have a family. Clara, living in former East Germany, expresses the legacy of the GDR's socialist era and believes it is normal for mothers to work outside the home, but thinks part-time employment is ideal. In western Germany, with its long history of stay-at-home mothers, Julia experiences cultural stigma for working while her children are young. She constantly feels guilty and stressed as a result. In Italy, a nation famous for its strong family ties, Carla is unhappy at the lack of help she feels she receives from unreliable male partners and a corrupt government. Samantha lives in the US, which has the most family-hostile public policy of any Western country. She burst into tears during our interview, admitting that she was stretched to the breaking point every day and felt she could barely keep it together on her own.

This book highlights the everyday experiences of middle-class working mothers in Western industrialized countries with different work-family policy supports. Research suggests that American social policy is failing, and argues that we look to Europe for alternative models.[1] I've done that, and this book is the result. After spending five years talking to 135 working moms in Sweden, Germany, Italy, and the US, here's what I've learned.

What working mothers want and expect when it comes to their work and family lives depends on their social context (see table 7.1). Social policies alone do not account for the problems of employed women with children. The larger social context, including beliefs about gender equality, employment, and motherhood, are all critical factors for understanding and resolving the conflicts these mothers experience.

In Sweden, working mothers wanted full gender equality and expected to seamlessly combine paid work and child-rearing. Mothers also expected the government to support them in these endeavors, and that's precisely what the Swedish state, its work-family policy, and the country's cultural ideals about work and motherhood do.

In former East Germany, mothers generally felt little work-family conflict and readily used the available policies, but few aimed to advance to "high careers." Those who did felt they were looked down upon for it, and penalized in the workplace.

In western Germany, mothers did not expect gender equality. They wanted to work while raising children without being made to feel guilty for it. These women were frustrated by their inability to use the available

TABLE 7.1. Mothers' perceptions of work-family conflict

	Least conflict				Most conflict
	Sweden	E Germany	W Germany	Italy	US
Substantial work-family conflict?			✓	✓	✓
Unsupported by available policies?			✓	✓	N/A (didn't expect support)
Stigmatized for taking leave?			✓	✓	✓
Stigmatized for pursuing career?		✓	✓		
Stigmatized for motherhood at work?		A few	✓	✓	✓
Pressured to be ideal worker?		A few	✓	✓	✓
Pressured to be ideal mother?	✓	✓	✓	✓	✓
Mostly responsible for household?		✓	✓	✓	✓

work-family policies without being stigmatized. They badly wanted outdated cultural ideals about women's roles to catch up with the times.

Italian middle-class mothers felt substantial conflict between employment and motherhood, although they expected to combine both roles. They experienced pressure to live up to ideal worker norms while relying on family and paid caregivers and housekeepers to bridge the gaps.

US mothers wanted and expected to work and raise families simultaneously. But it didn't occur to them that anyone might help them achieve these goals, least of all the government. They felt a great deal of work-family conflict, but thought it was their job alone to manage it.

When mothers find that their expectations are not met, they blame different sources depending on where they live. The majority of mothers in Berlin blamed career ambitions, while the few who had explicit career goals blamed outdated cultural ideals. These ambitious women were similar to mothers in western Germany who also felt frustrated with traditional cultural beliefs about gender. Italian mothers blamed the government for its lack of support. And Americans largely blamed themselves. These beliefs are the embodiment of prevailing discourses about work and family that the women I spoke with themselves carry and express. In Sweden, the government takes an active role to ensure that both women and men are equally responsible for breadwinning and caregiving. In former East Germany, women are expected to work while maintaining the home with increasing help from their partners, while in western Germany, women are expected primarily to take care of the home while men supply the bulk of the family income. In Italy, middle-class mothers are expected to use the fragmented policies to both work outside the home and retain responsibility for family life—especially in Rome, where the cost of living is comparatively high. In the US, mothers are expected to "do it all"—to work for pay outside the home just like their partners, but also to complete the housework and childcare without the help of the government.

The solutions working mothers employ to reduce their work-family conflict are also highly dependent on their social context. Table 7.2 outlines these tactics. Mothers in all field sites used the policies available to them, but those in western Germany, Italy, and the United States usually did so with the fear that their policy use would incur stigma at work. As a result, these women usually downplayed their family status on the job as one method to reduce work-family conflict.

Mothers in western and former East Germany tended to scale back on paid work, made possible by part-time jobs that were widely available (without wage penalties) and culturally accepted for women. A few mothers I interviewed in Italy and the US found part-time work, but these jobs were rarer and usually lacked benefits. Full-time work was the norm for the women I spoke with in Stockholm, Rome, and Washington, DC.

Middle-class Italian and American mothers turned to outsourcing to reduce their workload at home. They hired housekeepers, babysitters, and nannies, while Italian mothers were the only ones among those I

250 · Chapter 7

TABLE 7.2. Mothers' solutions to work-family conflict

	Least conflict				Most conflict
	Sweden	E Germany	W Germany	Italy	US
Use available policies	✓	✓	✓ (w/ some fear)	✓ (w/ some fear)	✓ (w/ some fear)
Scale back on paid work		✓	✓	A few	A few
Downplay family status at work			✓	✓	✓
Outsource to grandmothers				✓	
Outsource to domestic workers				✓	✓
"Work the system"				✓	
Increase organization/ efficiency					✓
Redefine success/ lower expectations		✓	✓		✓

interviewed who relied heavily on the help of grandmothers. My Italian interviewees whose older relatives (usually mothers and mothers-in-law) were unavailable or unwilling to help care for their children reported great upset. Most of the Italian moms I met relied on and combined all these outsourced forms of labor to care for their children and maintain their homes. Employing domestic workers was frowned upon for mothers in Sweden, former East Germany, and western Germany. Mothers in these places didn't report turning to this solution to alleviate work-family conflict (though some had considered it, or used it sparingly).

Some Italian moms took advantage of illness leave surrounding child-birth to get more time off of work. In a system universally considered corrupt, some mothers felt this tactic was a reasonable response.

Although all the women I spoke with discussed having less time and more need for organization in their everyday lives once they became mothers, only American interviewees talked at great length and in great detail about the array of organizational solutions they adopted to be more efficient. This unique solution to work-family conflict seems tied to my American respondents' distinctive levels of reported exhaustion and stress, and to their constant discussion of time, which I didn't hear during my European interviews.

Former East German, western German, and American participants said they felt better when they lowered their expectations and redefined what it meant to be successful at work and as mothers. For German mothers, this went hand in hand with working part time. American mothers usually didn't have this option, so they tried to hold themselves to lower standards in their careers and around their homes. In their words, this meant striving for "90 to 100 percent at work and at home" instead of 120 percent in both. On the other hand, Swedish and Italian middle-class mothers wanted and expected to advance in their careers while raising children. Swedish moms felt that the government facilitated these dual goals, while Italian mothers believed the government failed in this regard. But Italian mothers didn't seem to alter their ambitions at work.

Mothers' desires and expectations for "work-family balance" and their explanations and solutions for work-family conflict are confined by their lifeworlds: the particular set of personal experiences, interactions, organizations, and institutions that shape the possibilities women can imagine for themselves when it comes to raising children and working for pay. Mothers' lifeworlds are defined by the gendered, raced, and classed repertoires made available through their countries' cultural schemas and welfare state policies. Mothers opted for solutions that maintained their own self-definitions as good mothers without attracting cultural opprobrium. For instance, working part time or hiring domestic workers aren't typical solutions for the Swedish women I talked to, while working part time was expected for Germans and employing domestic workers was commonplace for all the middle-class Italians and more privileged American moms.

None of these women believed gender equality had been reached in their respective societies. However, not one mother suggested it was time for a women's movement to demand more from men, employers, and the government to help resolve their work-family conflict. In Sweden, Germany, and Italy, there was consensus among the women I spoke with that the government should do more to support them. Yet their grievances didn't translate into collective action. Some moms in Berlin and Washington, DC, did seem to see the benefit of women's collective action: several told me they turned to other working moms and joined support groups to relieve their stress. Swedish women mentioned the strength and importance of collective bargaining and unionization in securing existing labor rights historically in Sweden, but these weren't topics of discussion in the other places where I interviewed mothers.

All the mothers in this study were relatively privileged—"canaries in a coal mine," as Pamela Stone called them. They represent a best-case scenario when it comes to managing work-family conflict. Most were highly educated and privileged by their social class, race, and citizenship status. Most conformed to their welfare state's ideal woman citizen and the cultural ideal mother. Yet conforming to these ideals came with varying costs for moms across these countries. Swedish mothers felt their goals for themselves and those of their government aligned closely. Most of my former East German participants worked part time and also felt content with their work-family lives, but those who strived for careers and worked full time felt criticized for it. The moms I spoke with in western Germany, Italy, and the United States felt pulled between competing norms and felt a great deal of stress and work-family conflict, although they also largely conformed to the ideals dominant in their respective countries. Because Italy's and the United States' welfare states do not reward women for conforming to idealized models of mother-workers with policy supports like Sweden's and Germany's do (with universal childcare, substantial paid parental leave, etc.), Italian and American mothers felt compelled to seek private solutions to their predicaments, such as paying for private daycare, housekeepers, and full-time nannies. While these mothers felt stressed, they were getting by—some just barely. What about the working moms who diverge more strongly from these political and cultural ideals? Those who don't conform to these parameters likely have a much harder time than most of the women I interviewed. Work-family conflict is magnified by intersecting inequalities of sexism, racism, classism, homophobia, and xenophobia, among others.

Central to this book are these questions: Who benefits from these policies? And at whose expense? Understanding the intersection of gender, social class, and race and migration status in shaping the daily lives of working mothers at the middle of the class structure shows how the privileges my participants enjoyed were connected to the oppression of other women and mothers. The domestic workers that women hired in Rome and Washington, DC, were primarily lower-income, racial/ethnic minority women, some of whom were immigrants with children of their own.[2] The care deficit in the Global North draws immigrants from the Global South and postcommunist countries who are seeking to escape from poverty and find better working conditions.[3] Yet the labor of these domestic workers is largely unregulated and invisible, and doesn't afford them access to social policies like paid leave, benefits the European mothers I interviewed (and many of the American mothers) received as a result of their formal employment.

So where do middle-class working mothers have it best? The most satisfied women are clearly in Sweden. I left Stockholm after the summer of 2013 feeling optimistic about the prospects for working mothers and the role that cultural attitudes and work-family policies can play in furthering a gender-egalitarian society. Mothers were most satisfied in countries with extensive work-family policies and cultural attitudes that supported the combination of parenthood and employment for women and men.

But does this mean that we can import Swedish policies to the US? This book shows how these policies are part of a larger cultural discourse about parenting, work, and gender equality. Swedish policies operate in the context of societal beliefs that child-rearing should be embraced as a collective responsibility, that both men and women can and should work for pay and care for their families, and that workplaces recognize and support employees' nonwork responsibilities and interests. These cultural beliefs are incompatible with the neoliberal ideology that is ascendant in the US.[4] In other words, work-family policies are symptomatic of larger ethical and cultural understandings of what is and isn't appropriate for mothers, and as such, they play a role in reproducing the existing social order. This book shows that mothers' stress is not of their own making, and it can't be of their own fixing.

What insights can audiences in the US glean from these stories? Much US scholarship posits work-family policy innovation as the most promising tool to promote work-family reconciliation and gender equality.[5] But realistically, the lack of consensus among competing political parties and stakeholders means that whatever policy innovations are achieved will likely be a compromise. Modest innovations are most plausible in an American context.[6] As Erik Olin Wright argues, "What we want are utopian destinations which, even if they are themselves unreachable, nevertheless have accessible waystations that help move us in the right direction."[7] The process of " 'unlearning' old policies [. . .] and learning new ones,"[8] as Germany is currently undergoing, can be a rocky road for mothers because legal changes take time to become culturally embedded.

As I discussed in chapter 4, cultural transformation tends to trail behind changes in a society's material conditions such as policy reforms.[9] So, for instance, implementing progressive, gender-egalitarian work-family policies in a society with traditional cultural attitudes where behaviors are resistant to change is likely to cause mothers stress, as women in western Germany recounted. Cultural lags may be inevitable. Nevertheless, a one-size-fits-all policy package (e.g., primarily supporting male breadwinner families, primarily supporting dual-earner families) is unlikely to suit all mothers and families, as evidenced in my interviews. Public policies need to allow people more agency in choosing the arrangements of their work and family lives. With more heterogeneity in policy offerings, we may see less rigid gender expectations in mothers' lifeworlds and more expansive cultural support for a variety of women's decisions about combining employment and motherhood. "Ultimately," community organizer and politician Alexandria

Ocasio-Cortez argues, "feminism is about women choosing the destiny that they want for themselves."[10] Indeed, feminist theories of social change suggest that structural changes to oppressive gender systems through policy may promote changes in people's everyday lives that can, over time, accrue to generate gender equality.[11]

To be clear, ridding a society of sexism is not a necessary precondition for implementing policies oriented to what I call work-family justice. Those interested in easing mothers' work-family conflict in the US—policymakers, employers, researchers, nonprofits, activists, and the like—should consider the importance of building consensus and cross-party coalitions when trying to pass new legislation in order to combat the tug of war that western German and Italian working mothers seemed to experience owing to contradictory policies and cultural attitudes. One promising illustration of this "across the aisle" consensus in the US seems to be the movement for universal pre-K, which has gained backing from progressive, conservative, and religious groups alike, as well as corporate, medical, and private sector settings in recent years. The rationale in public discourse has shifted from women's liberation toward a business case and the association of childcare with prosperity.[12]

My findings also point to the importance of implementing policies in packages—for example, implementing paid parental leave alongside greater availability of childcare for young children, so there is more comprehensive support for women's and men's work and family commitments.[13] Sociologists Joya Misra, Michelle Budig, and Irene Boeckmann argue that parental leave policy and childcare for young children can be understood as two sides of the same coin.[14] In western Germany, for instance, mothers felt stressed and conflicted when parental leave was shortened to one year but they couldn't find a place for their children to attend daycare until they were three years old. In Italy, parental leave can't exceed ten months between two parents, yet, as in western Germany, daycare facilities are still rare for kids under age three. Without complementary changes in both childcare policy and parental leave policy, mothers are likely to continue feeling conflicted.

We can't think of policies as wholly good or bad. Instead, it's important to examine a policy's assumptions, content, and practical implications in relation to the wider political, economic, and social context as work-family policies become increasingly diverse and complex.[15] We need to evaluate policy reforms in light of prevailing cultural ideals to understand their effects on mothers and how these might differ in important ways for different groups of women.[16]

I presented a series of demographic charts in the introductory chapter that painted a large-scale picture of working motherhood in the four countries. My research suggests that a demographic understanding is insufficient to appreciate the impact of work-family policy on mothers' work-family conflict cross-nationally. Interviewing working mothers about their daily lives sheds new light on the intersection of social policies with cultural ideals. For instance, maternal employment rates (see figure 1.2) in Germany (69 percent) and the United States (65 percent) are reasonably similar, which might suggest that mothers in these countries perceive similar barriers and opportunities with regard to their labor market participation. But the stories I've recounted here don't support this reading: mothers in western Germany were called "raven mothers" and "career whores" for working outside the home while their children were young, while American mothers largely reported feeling little stigma for working. In fact, many felt encouraged to aim for high-powered careers.

Mothers with children younger than three years old have similar rates of employment in Germany (51.5 percent), Italy (53.6 percent), and the US (55.8 percent) (see figure 1.4). Despite these similarities, mothers in each country have access to very different parental leave options, daycare facilities, and legal protections surrounding childbirth and parenthood. Mothers explained to me that they used different solutions for childcare. Most women in western Germany stayed home for several years after giving birth (although many wanted to return to work earlier) and then worked part time, while Italian mothers outsourced this care to grandparents and domestic caregivers. Moms in the US used a substantial portion of their incomes to secure private childcare or hired domestic helpers, and in three cases, reduced their work schedules. These employment rate statistics belie the reality that women who work do not all work the same number of hours, often for different reasons.

Italy boasts the smallest gender wage gap and the smallest wage gap between mothers and childless women (see figure 1.5). An optimistic interpretation of these minimal wage penalties might be that motherhood exacts little or no stigma in the workplace or that women and mothers are well protected under Italian labor law, since being a woman or being a mother doesn't seem to impinge upon wages. On the contrary, I found that Italian working moms felt a great deal of marginalization at work. They believed the laws rarely protected them. They faced angry bosses, unsympathetic colleagues, and employers who wouldn't allow them to use the available policies. Mothers felt pressured to live up to ideal worker norms and endured a great deal of work-family conflict. I heard similar accounts from mothers in western Germany and the United States (countries with high wage penalties for motherhood), but not from women in former East Germany or Sweden (which also has a high wage penalty for motherhood). These qualitative findings suggest the gender wage gap cannot be a sole proxy measure for gender equality cross-nationally. Instead, we should think of the gender wage gap as only one indicator of mothers' status in the labor market. Discussions with the women who help constitute these numbers paint a more complex picture of the impact of work-family policies on working mothers than statistics alone.

Researchers have pointed to the social democratic welfare states like Sweden as the most promising model for attaining gender equality. The case of Sweden suggests that a sense of shared social responsibility is needed to lessen the burdens of working mothers. This sense of shared responsibility may be tied to the country's cultural homogeneity—a sense that US women do not share given the much more extreme inequalities of race and class in this nation. Feminist welfare state scholar Ann Orloff writes:

> Historical accounts of the development of systems of social provision and regulation are increasingly highlighting the link between generous programs (such as those provided in the Nordic countries) and the existence of "we-feeling," or solidarity based on

perceived ethnic, "racial" and/or religious homogeneity. [...] This in turn has been linked to practices of social closure, until recently at the level of the nation-state.[17]

Although international movements of people, capital, and ideas have increased dramatically in recent decades owing to a hyper-accelerated era of globalization, national solidarity and this "we-feeling" still depend on a clearly delineated "we." The concept of shared social responsibility presumes that a well-defined and unified community exists, and that its members feel a sense of belonging and reciprocity.[18] A country like Sweden has long shared a sense of national solidarity, a sentiment echoed by the women I interviewed.

Conversations from my time in Stockholm suggest that Sweden's shared sense of social responsibility is tied to high levels of solidarity and a perceived sense of reciprocity between women and men, employers and employees, and citizens and the government. These are economic and social preconditions necessary for gender equality to emerge.

However, the national solidarity that undergirds Sweden's generous welfare provisions has been subject to tension since the mid-2000s as the country has struggled to contend with the rapid influx of refugees and the integration of racial and ethnic minorities, especially non-European immigrants. In some cases, these immigrant families' beliefs about parenting and employment don't necessarily align with dominant cultural ideals.[19] These changes have blurred the lines demarcating who the "we" and "other" are in Sweden, lines that have long shored up Swedes' support of extensive welfare state provisions. Orloff explains, "Gender and family practices have been part of what defines the 'we' of the West, especially in contrast with the Islamic, immigrant 'other.'" Feminists, she says, are committed to "developing a more inclusive feminist utopia, and policy institutions to support it. To say that this poses political difficulties is to put it mildly."[20] Nordic feminists are trying to amend their thinking about policy goals in the face of greater diversity, and there is not yet consensus about how social democratic welfare states can adapt to accommodate newcomers.

The Swedish working mothers I interviewed benefited a great deal from the policy endorsement of a dual earner-carer family ideal because their own families generally aligned with this model. But this is a narrow, homogenous understanding of the possibilities of family formations and women's choices about employment and motherhood. Ida, the single Swedish mother, hinted at this frustration. She reflected, "Everyone says, 'It's so good in Sweden,' but you don't have a choice." Marie, the single German mother in Stockholm did too when she said, "Please let me do whatever I want" when she picked her daughter up from childcare later than other parents did.

The expansion of choice seems central to accommodating not only single mothers like Ida and Marie (it's noteworthy that both mothers critical of the system are single parents, and one is not Swedish), but also other women who may have different goals for their work and family lives. Greater citizen "choice" and the demand for a wider array of options for combining employment and parenthood are topics of heated conversation across welfare states today, as policies that expand choice often have different gendered consequences. For instance, cash for care policies that give vouchers to stay-at-home parents tend to hamper mothers' labor force participation, especially low-income and immigrant mothers.[21]

The question arising from my research echoes one that Orloff poses: How does a society "maintain and broaden solidarity while accommodating diversity in all its guises"?[22] The Swedish women I spoke with felt supported as a result of this collective solidarity and alignment with the socially constructed ideals of Sweden's gender regime. But they are not a diverse group of women. These moms tend to win out in a social democratic welfare state with a dual earner-carer family model. But do others lose as the cost of their winning?

Some scholars say yes: welfare paradoxes and gendered trade-offs persist even in social democratic countries.[23] Others have found that Nordic welfare states simply redistribute happiness among policy-targeted demographic groups.[24] My stance follows that of other feminist scholars like Orloff: "Within the multiplicity of political and policy possibilities, feminists can and should argue for those that empower women, that give them more freedom to define their lives and to engage in the political decisions that define and support collective ends."[25]

Policy supports need to attend to the diversity of choices mothers make. To accomplish this goal, countries need a political process that provides room for women's voices to be heard and consulted in the course of policymaking and implementation. Mothers' perspectives on what they want and need should be sought out and prioritized when writing new policy. (Fathers' voices, too.) What they want and need is culturally and politically specific. Mothers' desires and expectations are also likely to differ across a range of demographics. This book sought out one swath of mothers (educated, middle-class women), but policymakers should solicit the voices of mothers across the spectrums of race, class, sexual orientation, marital status, and country of origin to ensure that the diversity of mothers' choices are fully, fairly represented.

I'm hoping that the narratives recounted here will persuade you that saving mothers from drowning in stress should be a national priority.

———

Eight years after starting this project, people sometimes ask me how I feel after so many intimate conversations with women about their families and jobs and relationships, their dreams and regrets, and their hopes for their children's futures. I feel enormous gratitude for the mothers who shared so much with me. But if I'm being honest, the truth is I mostly feel angry. I wonder whether reading the women's stories in this book makes you feel angry too.

In democratic societies like ours, the profound inequalities that combine to produce varying experiences of work-family conflict are not normal, necessary, and inevitable. "Americans," Claude Fischer and colleagues write, "have created the extent and type of inequality we have, and Americans maintain it."[26] In large part, they are "the historical result of policy choices Americans—or, at least, Americans' representatives—have made." If you close this book and recall one takeaway, I hope it's this: *Work-family conflict is not an unfortunate but inexorable part of life as a working mother in the twenty-first century.* It's just not.

When we listen to women's experiences with paid work and child-rearing across countries with completely different work-family policies and cultural attitudes about women and men, we learn quite clearly that *work-family conflict is a phenomenon that societies have created, which means that societies can change it too.* Americans can enact policies to remedy the unequal social conditions that perpetuate mothers' work-family conflict and their disproportionate burden of caregiving— as Fischer and colleagues note, to reduce and reverse our rush to a polarized society. What we're missing is the political and social will to do so.

A popular counterargument is that inequality is necessary to encourage people to work hard to get ahead, which societies need for economic growth.[27] This is empirically false. Inequality tends to hamper economic growth. More unequal countries grow less quickly than do more equal countries.[28]

Also, forget the economic argument for a moment. Inequality is wrong. The old phrase "a rising tide lifts all boats" is apt here. We all need care and support. Everyone needs a helping hand at one time or another, whether you're white, black, old, young, poor, wealthy, partnered, or not. Although it's common in the US to vilify people like welfare recipients in need of help, the reality is most people will find themselves using some form of a social safety net program at one point or another. Sociologist Mark Rank found that between the ages of twenty and seventy-five, an astounding 60 percent of Americans will experience at least a year living below the poverty line. Three-quarters of Americans will spend a year either in poverty or near it. Two-thirds of Americans ages twenty to sixty-five will wind up using a social welfare program like those we refer to as food stamps or Medicaid.[29] Everyone needs a social safety net.

Countries like Sweden, Germany, and Italy have built rescue boats for the particular waters they trawl, some better than others. The US has largely chosen to forgo the rescue boats. I learned about the consequences firsthand from mothers themselves—and as I've repeated, the middle-class moms I interviewed have it better than many other women. So I am angry. But feminist scholars and social movement researchers remind us that anger can be productive. Driven by this sentiment, my students often ask, "What now?" What do people do when they feel they have no options? When they see no plausible means of improving social conditions in the face of injustice? Anyone involved in a movement for positive social change is familiar with feelings of hopelessness, be it mobilizing against homophobia, racial domination, patriarchy, or another structural inequality.

It's time for Americans to adopt the practice of radical hope—the insistent recognition that our social world can be more just, that our lives are interdependent, and that mutual aid benefits us all.[30] To think of ourselves as a collective, Americans need to develop the "we-feeling" Ann Orloff asserts. In a welfare state centered on individual responsibility, envisioning a society defined in part by collective solidarity seems a long way off. The United States has never been more deeply divided by inequalities of race and class. In times of uncertainty, people tend to draw stricter boundaries around "us" and "them." But "Americans certainly need not feel that they must accept the high levels of inequality we currently endure in order to have a robust economy. [...] We do not need to make a morally wrenching choice between more affluence and more equality; we can have both."[31]

It's time to change the national conversation about motherhood and work. If women feel that their struggles are inevitable, precious little will exists to mobilize and challenge oppressive social conditions. It's therefore vital that women expand their understandings of the alternatives available to them—as mothers, partners, workers, and citizens. This book provides a resource to do so. We need to imagine the collective emancipatory possibilities available through transforming our system of social welfare provisioning. This is why Erik Olin Wright implores us to develop *real utopias* that can motivate a political movement for change: "The degree to which people are deeply dissatisfied with the existing conditions of life depends in part on whether they believe viable alternatives are possible."[32]

It will take a revolution in our country's laws and cultural attitudes to ease the heartache of working moms, and that's no easy feat. But it's time. Rebecca Solnit writes,

> To hope is to gamble. It's to bet on the future, on your desires that an open heart and uncertainty are better than gloom and safety. I say all this to you because hope is not like a lottery ticket you can

sit on the sofa and clutch, feeling lucky. I say it because hope is an ax you break down doors with in an emergency; because hope should shove you out the door. [. . .] To hope is to give yourself to the future, and that commitment to the future makes the present inhabitable. Anything could happen, and whether we act or not has everything to do with it.[33]

We need collective action—a social movement founded on the concept of *work-family justice* that I described in the introduction. Let's envision a society in which each person has the opportunity and power to fully participate in both paid work and family care. Social welfare policy scholars Janet Gornick and Marcia Meyers describe this real utopia as a dual earner-carer society: "One that supports equal opportunities for men and women in employment, symmetrical contributions for mothers and fathers at home and high-quality care for children provided both by parents and by well-qualified and well-compensated nonparental caregivers."[34] Nordic countries come closest to this model, but nowhere does a true gender utopia exist.

Fostering a "sense of we" might be the United States' most difficult, most important challenge yet. Let us leverage hope, in all its productive, radical, transformative potential. Our collective solidarity has to transcend the gender, race, and class divides that have defined the US since its founding. "Inequality can be shaped by policy decisions: Wittingly or unwittingly, we choose our level of inequality."[35] We need to make a different, better set of choices. Our country—its mothers, fathers, children, and families—is depending on it.

Achieving work-family justice for working mothers across Western welfare states will require (1) cultural changes in the definitions of motherhood and fatherhood, (2) the structural reorganization of work, and (3) a new public commitment to supporting all working mothers and their families. There's no doubt that these are colossal tasks. Colossal, yes, but *possible*. We can also create "accessible waystations" that move us closer, step by small step, to achieving work-family justice.

First, all mothers in my study shared one source of stress: the pressure to live up to an idealized definition of motherhood. This definition varied because the expectations of a good mother were shaped by the cultural contexts in which mothers lived, as were the work-family policies available to them. But the mothers in all five field sites had internalized the prevailing discourse that they had to dedicate intensive time and energy toward their children. The question I was left with in all the countries in which I conducted interviews was this: When did moms have any time for themselves—not as mothers or daughters or partners or friends, but alone for their own sake? The short answer was that they usually didn't. All the women I interviewed mentioned that downtime for themselves was the first thing to go once they became mothers, and the one area they usually couldn't find time for in their schedules. Reducing the pressures for mothers to enact one governing ideal of motherhood will require decoupling good mothering from all-consuming time commitment, which seemed prevalent in every city where I spent time with moms. Reducing mothers' overwhelm will also require expanding the understanding of who can and should care for children.

My findings show that work-family policies are limited in their ability to help mothers achieve advanced careers and contented home lives if, as women explained to me time and again, these policies are offered to and used disproportionately by women and not men. In other words, these policies need to be enacted in a cultural environment supportive of gender equality. Policies can be pro-mother without being pro-equality. Researchers, for instance, have documented the reality that Germany's policy goals have transformed more explicitly to stimulate changes in women's behavior, but not men's.[36] Yet previous research shows that national context can and does influence fathers' unpaid work behaviors.[37] Thus, I argue that a renewed conversation focusing on gender equality policy and policy instruments aimed at changing men's behavior must go hand in hand with work-family policy debates in order to improve the social and economic climate for working mothers.

Evidence from Sweden and Norway suggests that fathers have adapted their parenting behaviors to become more involved with the care of their children after the implementation of use-it-or-lose it "daddy months" that encourage fathers to take paid time away from work.[38] Research suggests paid paternity leave helps mothers: families with fathers who take more leave share chores and childcare more equally with mothers.[39] Men who take longer leave also report being more satisfied with parenting and are more engaged in the care of their children afterward.[40] They report having stronger bonds with their spouses and children.[41]

Second, workplaces will need to transform how and where work is completed, how productivity is assessed, and how workers are compensated and rewarded for their labor.[42] Disassociating men from the concept of the ideal worker and recognizing that all workers have nonwork interests and responsibilities that require time and attention will help achieve this goal.[43] However, reaching this objective without a concurrent transformation in our cultural understandings about gender and family will be difficult. For example, the Swedish and former East German mothers I interviewed readily used work-family policy supports like flexible schedules and reduced hours, but western German, Italian, and US mothers hesitated to use these benefits for fear that they would damage their standing at work because fathers don't use them too. This finding highlights the point that policies cannot be imported to a different cultural context with the expectation of similar results. The cultural schemas that dictate norms about gender, parenting, and employment will shape mothers' experiences with a given policy, even fueling women's marginalization.

Finally, resolving mothers' work-family conflict will require public commitment in the form of monetary and policy support and cultural recognition for the value of mothers' participation in the labor force and the value of caring labor.[44] Until countries affirm that all adults have the right to combine wage labor with caring labor, women and mothers will continue to be disadvantaged, stigmatized, and stressed when trying to navigate their work and family responsibilities. The costs of child-rearing cannot remain private and feminized if we seek to reduce the conflicts borne by working mothers today.

Appendixes

Appendix A: Notes on Methods

This project began because I was skeptical of the notion that women could have it all—not because they didn't want to, but because larger societal forces prevented them from being highly involved parents with high-flying careers. I'd read sociologist Pamela Stone's book *Opting Out? Why Women Really Quit Careers and Head Home* in my first year of graduate school.[1] The study was a response to a popular claim that the second-wave feminist movement accomplished the "gender revolution" it had spurred: American women could now be breadwinners just like men, as well as caregivers. Curiously, at the same time, highly educated middle- and upper-class women seemed to be leaving powerful careers in droves to be stay-at-home moms. Journalist Lisa Belkin dubbed this the "opt-out revolution." She asked, "Why don't women run the world? Maybe it's because they don't want to." A whole host of researchers, including Stone, were skeptical of this claim.[2] Stone interviewed educated, professional, mostly white women—bankers, lawyers, doctors, and so on—to understand mothers' decisions to opt out.

Her study debunked the myth that these women *chose* to leave their jobs. Mothers were actually pushed out of the workplace by inflexible policies, institutional barriers, and a system that punished rather than rewarded women for trying to manage their work and home lives. Stone argued that these stories didn't indicate women's renewed turn to traditionalism, but were rather a sign of deeply entrenched traditionalism in the workplace that ignored the reality of many women's lives and resisted their efforts to change it.

Reading this was a lightbulb moment for me—the kernel of a research question. My own mother had hardly chosen to quit the job she loved when I was young. She didn't see an alternative. The individualist discourse of opting out placed the blame on women themselves, as if they were unable or unwilling to manage work and family. The rhetoric that women *chose* to leave their jobs diverted attention away from the lack of support provided by work institutions and the US government.

I'd lived in Germany prior to graduate school and was intrigued by the country's maternalist policies. They seemed exceedingly generous from an American perspective. As I described in chapters 3 and 4, mothers received up to three years' maternity and parental leave, job security surrounding pregnancy, and twenty-four days of paid vacation a year. Plenty of professional jobs were available part time. It seemed like I passed a public childcare center every other block. So I wondered, what were similar women's experiences there? How did they make decisions about employment and motherhood given the extensive policy supports? I wanted to know what we would learn by turning to women in a country with the sorts of accommodations that American moms reported wanting in Stone's study. In 2011, I went back to Germany and spent three months interviewing working moms for what became my master's thesis at the University of Texas at Austin, where I also earned my PhD in sociology.

My first interview was with Julia, whose story I explored in depth in chapter 4. I began by asking, "When your children were born, did you have any concerns about what it was going to be like to balance work with family?" "A lot of them, yeah," Julia replied, nodding. My eyes widened. I hadn't expected that response. I nodded too, prompting her to continue. Within five minutes, Julia lamented the difficulty of finding a place in daycare for her young kids and the short opening hours once they were old enough to enroll. She told me about the stigma she felt for working outside the home when her kids were still toddlers. This decision earned her the painful label "raven mother" (*Rabenmutter*). Stay-at-home moms had called her selfish and a career whore. Julia explained feeling inadequate at work and at home.

Thus began an eye-opening summer of research. And another in 2012. After a couple dozen interviews, I found that although German work-family policy appeared quite generous, the policies didn't disrupt the gender hierarchy between women and men. Rather, as I've discussed at length, these policies reinforced a gender regime that was pro-mother, but not yet pro-equality. These findings led me to ask: What about mothers' experiences living somewhere with social policies that promoted both motherhood *and* equality?

Sweden always ranks at or near the top of the United Nations' Gender Equality Index. At that time, it was first. Even the official website for the Government of Sweden declared in big, bold font: A Feminist Government.[3] Fortuitously, my good friend Kate had just moved to Stockholm and offered up her sofa if I ever wanted to visit. I submitted my thesis to my advisers, Christine Williams and Jennifer Glass. Afterward, I was surprised to hear Christine announce excitedly, "Jennifer and I think you need to go to Sweden!" With their encouragement and a place to stay, I spent summer 2013 in Stockholm, funded this time by a small grant from the Swedish Excellence Endowment at UT-Austin that was just enough to cover airfare and groceries.

"It gets so personal," said Ane, "speaking about this." We met at a café bustling with the lunch rush near her office—my first interview in Sweden. I had asked Ane what it meant to her to be a good mother to her two small children. "I keep thinking that you need to be consistent." Although Ane had a flexible schedule and a supportive supervisor, colleagues, and partner, she found it tough to be as available to her children as she wanted: "I want to be in this position, I want to have fun assignments, I want to *do* this. And on the other hand, I also want to be able to have time with my kids. [. . .] You always have a bad conscience." This, again, I hadn't expected. Despite the atmosphere that promoted gender equality, moms like Ane still felt pressured to be highly involved parents.

These three summers of research laid the foundations for this book, a cross-national comparative study informed by feminist theories of gender and welfare state regimes. Back in Austin I debated over many months with my mentors and peers about other suitable field sites to round out the project. I decided to continue with interviews in the capital cities of the four archetypical welfare states. This approach would enable me to situate my findings within the existing literature on gender and work-family policy. The familialist regimes of Greece, Italy, Portugal, and Spain were in the throes of economic crises at the time, with alarming rates of unemployment. After weighing my options and considering the network of personal and professional contacts available, I decided upon Rome, Italy, as the third field site. I wanted to conduct interviews with mothers in the US, so Washington, DC, was the logical fourth location given that my sample design delineated capital cities as my field sites. And finally, to maintain consistency across welfare regimes, I returned to Germany's capital of Berlin in the summer of 2015. This last round of fieldwork afforded a useful comparison between former East and West Germany, where I'd first conducted interviews before fully conceptualizing this project to be cross-national in scope.

Methodological decisions like these are ripe for debate, as are the rest I detail below. I sought to center women's voices and paint a picture of daily life for middle-class mothers in five contexts with disparate combinations of work-family policy provisions and cultural supports for women and families. I hope this text sparks fruitful conversations about innovative approaches to studying motherhood and social policy.

In-Depth Interviews

The findings I present in this book rely primarily on in-depth interviews with working mothers. Interviewing is an ideal method to uncover the cultural frames that women use to make sense of their efforts to manage their home and work responsibilities, as well as their own perceptions of the work-family policies available to them. This method allows researchers crucial access to different levels of information about people's beliefs, motivations, meanings, feelings, and practices— information that cannot be gleaned via other methods of data collection. In particular, Allison Pugh convincingly argues that four levels of information can be accessed from an in-depth interview: the honorable, the schematic, the visceral, and the meta-feelings.[4] These four levels are evident in my research.

First, respondents conscientiously provided "honorable" information that presents them in the most favorable light. These data give the researcher a sense for what the respondent considers admirable qualities and behaviors. In my research, women highlighted the ways their attitudes and behaviors aligned with dominant cultural ideals. For example, a western German mother, Edith, who worked part time, explained that a woman can't be a successful mother if she is career-driven and works long hours, thereby aligning her career choices with German ideologies about good mothering by putting her child before her job ambitions.

Second, "schematic" information is gleaned when participants use jokes, turns of phrase, and metaphors to convey the frameworks they use to view their social world. This information may or may not be "honorable," and can operate on a semi-conscious level for a person, sometimes contradicting other explicit statements. A researcher can access these frameworks by analyzing the way people give this information, and not simply accepting it at face value—for example, by recognizing how people bend language to more richly convey their point. Asking for concrete examples is one tactic researchers use to learn not about the specific "facts" of a story, but about the frames through which the person understands his or her world. I found that the analogies, jokes, slang, anecdotes, and sometimes creative translations respondents used were at times more revealing about their frameworks than their direct responses to questions. One American interviewee, Chelsea, joked that instead of taking the popular career advice to "lean in," she was "leaning out" from her prestigious role in sales management. Yet she also explained that she worked nonstop right up until childbirth, even responding to emails on her smartphone from the hospital bed as she went into labor. I recounted earlier that Chelsea had a special name for the practice of constantly blending her work and family life: "We always talk about 'the swirl.' That's what we call it. Like when you're a working mom, there is no hard line between work and home." Chelsea's phrase "the swirl" speaks multitudes about how she views the facets of her life.

Third, "visceral" information such as verbal missteps, facial expressions, sighs, pauses, laughter, and halting syntax allow researchers to understand the emotional frameworks of desire, morality, and expectations that shape people's actions and reactions. In this research, being attentive to these forms of communication helped me understand working mothers' emotional responses both to my questions and to their answers. For example, I noted women's pauses, chuckles, sighs, crying, and raised eyebrows when I asked about experiences with their supervisors, colleagues, partners, and relatives to gain insight into their feelings about these interactions.

The emotional tenor and intensity of the interviews varied widely. In Sweden, mothers tended to be calm and reflective, getting more animated as they talked about their ideas for improving policy. American mothers, on the other hand, seemed drained. They rubbed their furrowed eyebrows or temples and cast their eyes down at times. With the exception of Sweden, some women in all countries cried during our interviews, mostly in response to one particular question: "How would you define what it is to be a good mother?" I hadn't anticipated this response before I began my fieldwork. But the power of in-depth interviews was laid bare in these instances: they revealed the emotional impact of cultural ideologies about motherhood and what was at stake for families in the debates over work-family policy. When women explained to me, in tears, that they felt they were failing their children, it became all the more obvious to me that "work-family balance" is not simply an object of academic inquiry.

Fourth, "meta feelings" are people's feelings about how they feel. This information captures the distance between how respondents feel and what they think they *should* feel. This level of information is an emotional expression of a person's relative ease with the dominant discourses around him or her. In my study, this type of data helped examine the cultural frames working mothers have internalized about their work and family responsibilities that, as Pugh says, render some emotions "more acceptable, expected, or celebrated than other emotions."[5] Samantha, an American mother, told me she was raised to believe she could "have it all," and she had worked hard to achieve this goal; yet she burst into tears during our interview when she described her own sense of guilt for not being able to attain this cultural ideal. Samantha was mad at herself for not being able to live up to a vision of motherhood that marries high-flying career advancement with involved parenting. She also apologized to me for crying.

Each type of information described above teaches us something different and important about a person's feelings, actions, and experiences. Pugh suggests that a researcher's ability to access all four types of information requires skill, training, and experience. In this way, the researcher is less like a sketch artist trying to render an exact likeness and more like a detective trained in making sense of the rich and often contradictory, paradoxical explanations given by subjects. I took Pugh's approach in my study, using working mothers' accounts as tools to uncover the emotional landscapes they inhabit and the broader social dimensions of their individual experiences.

I took detailed field notes following each interview about respondents' mannerisms, demeanor, nonverbal cues, and other notable responses to my questions. Transcriptions of interviews included notations of the respondents' laughter, crying, pauses, halting sentences, and other descriptors. During the data analysis, I coded for these four levels of information in addition to women's stated answers. I was attentive to how my participants' phrasing, tone, manner of speech, and nonverbal cues together painted a rich picture of their lived reality. Such cues extend and complicate the information researchers can access with other tools like surveys.

One simple example of the importance of both accessing and analyzing these four levels of information is the case of a western German woman, Edith, whom I interviewed in summer 2011. Edith was soft-spoken and mild-mannered through most of our meeting. But she broke into abrupt, loud laughter after I asked her halfway through the interview, "How do you and your husband divide up responsibilities around the house, like the cooking and laundry?" She tilted her head back, laughed, and then looked at me, shaking her head side to side and smiling with a slight grimace. "The division? [. . .] That's easy. I do 100 percent and he does zero." She paused for a moment, and continued, "But that's just how it is, isn't it?" Edith had a master's degree in civil engineering but was working in a part-time, flexible job far below her skill set as a university administrator in order to take care of her two small children while her husband worked long hours as a judge.

This short excerpt reveals volumes about Edith's circumstances. Her sarcasm, laughter, pauses, facial expressions, body language, and eye contact all help me understand her displeasure at her family's division of labor and perhaps the cultural frame that suggests this arrangement is normal and desirable. While Edith may be able to answer "very low" on a Likert scale–type question about her level of satisfaction with her family's division of labor, this short interview excerpt paints a richer, more nuanced portrait of Edith's work and family life in western Germany.

In-depth interviews are ideal at demonstrating the social embeddedness of an individual actor. They enable researchers to analyze the interaction among culture, emotions, and experiences. In this book, I trace the stories of women at the confluence of these intersecting forces, what I refer to as mothers' lifeworlds. I use in-depth interviews to reveal how working mothers' interests and value systems differ given the work-family policies available in their respective countries.

Research Sites and Sample

This book employs a multi-sited research design to examine mothers' experiences navigating work and family in Western welfare states with varying cultural, political, and economic contexts. I conducted fieldwork in six stages: I interviewed mothers in Stuttgart and Heilbronn, Germany (2011); in Munich, Germany (2012); in Stockholm, Sweden (2013); in Rome, Italy (2014); in Washington, DC, the United States (2015); and in Berlin, Germany (2015). I spent three months in each European field site. I spent less time in my US field site (several weeks) because I was able to rely more on my broader social networks to arrange interviews ahead of time, unlike in Europe. This study was approved by the Institutional Review Board (IRB) at the University of Texas at Austin.

During each stage of international fieldwork, I spent time as a visiting scholar at several research institutes: the Berlin Social Science Center, the Department of Political Science at Roma Tre University in Rome, the Linnaeus Center for Social Policy and Family Dynamics in Europe at Stockholm University, and the Institute for Family-Focused Research and Policy Services in Stuttgart, Germany. These positions afforded me the chance to embed myself in a community of scholars with expertise in gender inequality and work-family policy, which helped me overcome some of the difficulties inherent in conducting fieldwork as a cultural and linguistic outsider.

I established mutually beneficial relationships with my colleagues, and these temporary academic homes were vital to my success while overseas. Aside from the practical help of gaining an office, colleagues, and assistance with research and recruiting (and a new appreciation for the ritual of midmorning and midafternoon coffee and cake breaks with coworkers), it opened opportunities to begin cross-national conversations about best practices for working mothers that are ongoing today.

Before each stage of this study, I reviewed government publications outlining the current work-family policies and other legal documents to frame my understanding of the institutional context that structured mothers' lives. I also familiarized myself with the extant research on women and work-family policy in each country to better understand the historical, cultural, and political contexts.

I used my social networks and referrals to generate a snowball sample of interview respondents; these are well-established recruitment methods in qualitative research on women and work.[6] In each field site, I cast my net as far and wide as I could to find women to interview. Recruiting meant being creative and entrepreneurial since these cities were all new temporary homes to me. Prior to departing for fieldwork, I asked friends, relatives, colleagues, and neighbors whether they knew anyone, however remotely, in the cities where I would be living. I reached out to every person who was recommended to me. I posted on various social networking websites and messaged women directly, asking them to get coffee or a meal with me. I asked people to forward my call for participants to their social groups and relevant listservs.

Upon arrival in each new city, I found ways to mention my study in practically every introductory conversation I had: when anyone asked what brought me to town, I would mention my study and ask whether they knew anyone I could meet. People amazed me with their generosity and went far out of their way to help me find participants. I sometimes received emails from women offering to be interviewed, and when I looked through the email chains, I discovered there were many, many degrees of separation between us because so many people had forwarded on my plea.

Through my visiting researcher positions, I tapped into the social networks of my colleagues. They were generally eager to help me find willing subjects. So were my local roommates, who proved to be some of the best resources for finding interviewees. Americans have a reputation in Europe for being unusually friendly and chatty with strangers; I took advantage of this stereotype (one that I admittedly fit well) and struck up conversations with my local neighbors as well as shopkeepers, bus drivers, grocery store clerks, and people on public transit. I got a local cell phone in each field site and wrote the number on the back of my business cards. I kept these cards in the outer pocket of my purse so I could get to them easily, and I handed them out often. The least effective recruiting tactics were flyers posted in local daycare facilities by employees who agreed to help and pamphlets I left on local bus, train, and metro seats. After the first two stages of fieldwork, I abandoned these approaches.

Anytime I interviewed someone, I asked whether they might know anyone else interested in meeting with me. This was a productive tactic, though I limited my referral chains so as not to draw heavily on particular social networks. Some referrals occurred by happenstance. In one city, for example, a mother and I were sitting in her backyard when a neighbor stopped by and said hello over the fence. This led to an introduction, and later, an interview. In another case, a woman was giving me a tour of her office and we struck up a conversation with a colleague who suggested I interview his wife. He shared my contact information with her, and she wrote me later that week volunteering for an interview. These serendipitous meetings were common.

The decision to interview women at the middle of the class structure was partially by choice and partially a necessity. When I first began this project in 2011, I had high ambitions about the diversity of women with whom I would be able to speak. Pamela Stone's study focused on professional women. I hoped to interview mothers across the socioeconomic spectrum, including those who didn't speak English with the help of an interpreter.

During my first stages of fieldwork in Germany, I found a college student studying translation who offered to help. But we encountered three problems. The first involved recruitment. Neither of our social networks overlapped significantly with people we could consider truly low income. I interviewed a number of women whose individual salaries would place them in this category, but when combined with their partners' salaries and other contextual factors like their education and lifestyle, their families were middle class. I spent two months trying every tactic I could think of to get in touch with less economically advantaged women— through flyers, posters, local organizations, support groups, and daycare centers, among others. I reached out to advisers, experts, and my peers to discuss and troubleshoot my approaches, but none were successful.

Second, despite our best efforts at recruiting, we couldn't find German-speaking mothers willing to do an interview. Although I spoke basic German, my language barrier was indeed an obstacle, and my inability to explain myself firsthand seemed to hamper people's interest in being interviewed.

Third, this language barrier was even more complex in my efforts to access and interview low-income mothers in Germany. I quickly found that the issue wasn't that these women didn't speak English. It's that they didn't speak German either. Foreign nationals from Turkey, Poland, and Syria are overrepresented among low-income families in Germany.[7] To speak with them, I would need Turkish, Polish, and Arabic interpreters, resources that were far outside my shoestring budget. Thus, for practical reasons, I explicitly narrowed the scope of the project to middle-class mothers.

Such practical methodological decisions have important analytic consequences. My choice to interview middle-class working mothers excluded the experiences of other groups. In a world free of time and capital constraints, I would have spoken with mothers across social classes, with a broad array of racial/ethnic identities and migration backgrounds, and with more women who weren't partnered with men. Their experiences of work-family conflict are different. Women who speak English are generally more educated than non-English speakers. They may work in higher-level jobs or for international companies in roles that require the use of English to communicate with foreign colleagues or customers overseas. They may be exposed to English-language news and media, meaning that perhaps their worldviews are shaped by international sources as well as their country's news outlets. It's possible that a different approach—interviewing women solely in their native languages—would paint a clearer picture of how working mothers think and feel about their lifeworlds because they could communicate their ideas in their primary language. Perhaps they would be more country-centric in their views.

To classify a woman as middle class in each context, I considered her level of education, occupation, personal and household incomes, lifestyle, and self-reported social class. In Sweden, according to the Pew Research Center, 79 percent of the population is considered middle class, followed by Germany (72.4 percent), Italy (66.9 percent), and the US (59.2 percent).[8] The issue of selectivity—or the concern that the experiences of the women I spoke with are isolated, rare, or unique—is likely a smaller issue in Stockholm and Berlin than in Rome and Washington, DC, where interviewees represented privileged swaths of the population. None of my interviewees were poor, and all worked in professional or semi-professional contexts.

I have been explicit about the class position of my respondents so as not to generalize their views and experiences, but instead to provide insight into how rather privileged women struggle in the different policy contexts. For this project, the increased consistency in measurement was a worthwhile trade-off for excluding non-English speakers. I hope this study will inspire future research on populations that I was unable to access.

Approaches to Cross-National Interview Studies

Researchers tend to take one of two methodological approaches to cross-national interview studies. I call these methods collaborative comparative interviewing and independent comparative interviewing. They have different strengths and weaknesses.

First, *collaborative comparative interviewing* (CCI) involves studying the culture in which one was raised and comparing findings with local experts in different settings. Native scholars are well positioned to conduct this sort of research because their upbringing, language abilities, and social networks can be beneficial. Partnering with local researchers from the outset of the research design can be a productive tactic to access a wider variety of participants and address the issues described above. Sociologists Daniela Grunow and Marie Evertsson coedited a related book, *Couples' Transitions to Parenthood: Analysing Gender and Work in Europe*, that uses one version of this approach.[9] The project (called transPARENT) is a cross-national collaboration between researchers in the Czech Republic, Germany, Italy, the Netherlands, Poland, Spain, Sweden, and Switzerland. Researchers conducted 334 in-depth interviews with men and women dual-earner couples expecting their first child. Scholars from each country wrote the twelve chapters, with thirty-one contributors total. This research design has the impressive advantage of having local experts conduct the interviews and write up the findings.

As with every method, there are limitations to this approach. One is the amount of time, resources, and coordination required to undertake large-scale projects. Another drawback is the inherent closeness to the field setting. Scholars may miss seeing an important trend or pattern because, to them, it's what they know. Recall the adage that fish can't see the water they swim in: the writer David Foster Wallace explained, "the most obvious, ubiquitous, important realities are often the ones that are hardest to see and talk about." What we need, he argued, is "simple awareness; awareness of what is so real and essential, so hidden in plain sight all around us, all the time, that we have to keep reminding ourselves over and over: This is water. This is water."[10] It's much easier to see the water when one hasn't been immersed in it one's whole life.

The vantage point of an outsider was useful for me in the European cities where I interviewed women. Being a single researcher across multiple countries, I could contrast what I'd heard mothers say in one setting to what women said in another. I could also be sure that the interview questions were phrased the same way, similar probes were used to get respondents to elaborate more, and women had the same opportunities to explain themselves. I call this cross-national method *independent comparative interviewing* (ICI), in which a single researcher conducts interviews across multiple contexts or field sites. This approach allows investigators a great deal of control over the administration of interviews, consistency in the questions asked and prompts offered, and evolution of recruitment tactics. Being one researcher across sites meant I was closely attuned to the sorts of details necessary to access the four levels of information gleaned from interviews in each field site. A large team of researchers conducting single-site studies would likely find it difficult to align their observations and analyses sufficiently to make meaningful claims about these deeper levels of data. Strengths and downfalls are inherent to both these approaches, but together, they paint a rich picture of these phenomena.

My Social Location

An important consideration concerns how a researcher's positionality impacts her data collection. My own identity influenced the research experience in important ways. As a white, middle-class woman born and raised in the United States, I had access to the privileged populations that are the focus of this book. Very few English-speaking women turned me down for interviews. In some cases, I was overwhelmed by volunteers and had to make hard choices about how to delimit my sample. This happened in particular during the US stage of data collection. I asked a few contacts in Washington, DC, to disseminate the call for participants among their relevant social networks. In two days, over 175 mothers wrote asking to be interviewed. Unlike my European respondents, who volunteered or agreed with a tone of benevolence, understanding that they were doing me a favor, I noted a sense of urgency in American mothers' interest in discussing their work-family conflict—as if they yearned to discuss their struggles with a sympathetic listener.

As an American with an assumed lack of familiarity with European laws and policies, I could ask interviewees to explain these regulations in detail for me, lending important insight into their perceptions of these policies—a task potentially more difficult for a native-born researcher. In the US context, however, women likely assumed that we shared this knowledge. With regard to policy, American women would sometimes say, "You probably know this better than me. . . ." These were instances in which my education and nationality impacted my position in the US field site. Two African American respondents teased me for not knowing some of the language they used during our conversations when I asked them to clarify what they meant. In these instances, they pointed to our racial difference by laughing at my naiveté in a friendly way. American mothers also knew I wasn't from DC, so they took care to elaborate when they mentioned a certain neighborhood or school district.

I was often mistaken for a local in Germany and Sweden because of my appearance. This meant I could sit at a playground or ride near families on the metro and observe their interactions without them paying much attention to me. This was often helpful as background data for me. This wasn't the case in Italy, where people often laughed when meeting me, saying they knew straightaway before I'd spoken that I wasn't Italian.

Women occasionally asked during interviews whether I was married or had children; I told them the truth that I was unmarried and had no children. At the time of this research, I was younger than most of the interviewees. I didn't sense this was a barrier to rapport, since women shared intimate personal information with me about their struggles with issues like money, miscarriages, infertility, and infidelity. My gender may have caused women interviewees to assume some shared experiences. For example, one German woman reflected, "It's a hard time for women nowadays." She may have expected a shared understanding of how women's lives are difficult today. It was important for me, in instances like this, to probe respondents further. Women also made comments like, "Well, if you have children one day, you'll learn this yourself." Writing about his ethnographic research on the affordable housing crisis, sociologist Matt Desmond reminds us:

> Everything about you—your race and gender, where and how you were raised, your temperament and disposition—can influence whom you meet, what is confided in you, what you are shown, and how you interpret what you see. My identity opened some doors and closed others. In the end, we can only do the best we can with

who we are, paying close attention to the ways pieces of ourselves matter to the work while never losing sight of the most important questions.[11]

The same can be said of this study. I did the best I could with who I was, attending to the reality that my identity shaped what I learned from women. I tried never to lose sight of the pressing concerns that brought me to this project in the first place: how we can make life better, easier, and more enjoyable for women and their families.

Data Collection

Before beginning an interview, I gave each woman a consent form explaining my study. I asked permission to digitally record the interview. Interviews were in depth and semi-structured with a list of closed-ended demographic questions followed by specific open-ended questions. I didn't restrict myself to asking these questions in a certain order, nor to asking only these questions. Instead, I followed women's verbal and non-verbal cues to develop a dialogue and build rapport. Interviews lasted approximately one hour and were conducted in a location of the respondent's choice: in a café, restaurant, or park, or in their home or workplace. I asked mothers about their "work-family balance"; interactions with colleagues and bosses at work; previous jobs and hopes for the future; how they divide up household responsibilities with partners; thoughts on parenting; how they use and feel about a variety of work-family policies; their interpretations of their jobs, family life, wishes, and regrets; and general views about the state of life for working mothers in their country. I also gave each woman an opportunity to address issues she thought were important that we may not have covered during the interview. Appendix B contains my interview schedule.

I interviewed between twenty-five and thirty-two women in each field site (demographic snapshots are represented in tables A.1 and A.2 and figure A.1). The median age for women ranged from thirty-six in Sweden to forty-one in Italy. Salaries for women in DC tended to be higher than in other countries, which is logical given DC's extremely high cost

TABLE A.1. Snapshot of sample demographic information

	n	Median age	Median annual income range (personal)	Educational attainment				Weekly hours worked								Partner status	
				High school	Some college	Bach. degree	Adv. degree	On leave	≤19	20–24	25–29	30–34	35–39	40–44	≥45	Partnered	Single
Sweden	25	36	$60–69,999	1	4	6	14	2	1	1	0	1	5	13	2	19	6
E Germany	25	38	$32–43,000	2	0	5	18	4	0	3	4	7	2	4	1	19	6
W Germany	26	38	$21–32,000	4	0	8	14	2	3	5	4	3	1	3	5	22	4
Italy	27	41	$43–54,000	2	0	10	15	2	1	1	0	0	6	9	8	24	3
US	32	38	$90–99,999	2	1	10	19	0	0	1	2	0	4	4	21	25	7

TABLE A.2. Respondents' self-reported race or ethnicity (migration background/national origin)

Sweden (n=25)	24 white* (21 Swedish, 2 Finnish, 1 German) 1 Sri Lankan (1 Swedish)
Former East Germany (n=25)	24 white* (12 West German, 6 East German, 2 American, 1 Danish, 1 Dutch, 1 Finnish, 1 Polish) 1 Chinese (1 Chinese)
Western Germany (n=26)	26 white* (24 German, 1 French, 1 American)
Italy (n=27)	25 white* (21 Italian, 2 Italian American, 1 Swedish, 1 French) 2 Mexican (2 Mexican American) .
United States (n=32)	19 white (19 American) 6 African American (6 American) 2 Hispanic White (2 American) 1 African American Hispanic (1 American) 1 Hispanic (1 American) 1 Arab (1 American) 1 Asian (1 Canadian) 1 Lebanese (1 Lebanese)

Note: These are the respondents' race, ethnicity, and migration background or national origin as they understand it and as they reported to me. The self-report data on racial categories do not in all cases align with those that US researchers typically employ, but here I defer to women and their choice of wording.

* The white racial categories for European women were imputed because Europeans do not use the term "race" as an identity category. The more common terminology is "migration background" or "national origin."

of living—even women working as administrative assistants reported incomes over $60,000 a year, and social workers were in the $70,000 range. Race and ethnicity are understood differently in the US than in Europe, so in table A.2 I use the terms respondents provided when asked, "What is your race or migration background?" Figure A.1 shows women's working hours. It was much more common for Italian and especially US mothers to work overtime hours (more than forty-five hours weekly). Most women were partnered, and I interviewed between three and seven single mothers in each field site.

My field notes yielded crucial data for this project. Knowing that field notes are a valuable resource for preserving experiences close to when they occurred, I took lengthy notes immediately after each interview. I sought to capture and preserve a sense of the interview setting, to visualize the woman's appearance, to describe anyone I met, to recall any

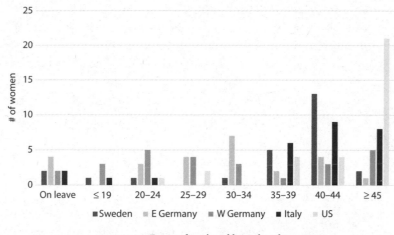

FIGURE A.1. Respondents' weekly working hours.

notable anecdotes and strong emotions like crying, and to note memorable nonverbal cues and particular insights I wanted to remember later. I took detailed notes on my initial impressions, observations of key events and incidents, my own feelings and reactions, and noteworthy reactions by respondents about what seemed significant or noteworthy to them.

Sometimes I left a woman's house, walked a block, and turned down a side street to find someplace quiet to sit, where I would park myself on a curb or bench to write as quickly as I could in a notebook immediately following the interview. If I had another interview to get to and I was some place where I could reasonably talk without being overheard, I often turned on my recorder while walking and verbally recounted my reflections and observations. I transcribed these recordings upon arriving home at the end of the day. If I was on mass transit or in a public setting and could sit down, I took handwritten notes in my notebook. If I had to stand on the bus or metro immediately following an interview, I jotted down bullet-pointed notes in my phone, fleshing them out on the computer later that day.

My goal with the field notes was to preserve memories, thoughts, scenes, and experiences that I wanted to return to while writing this book. These notes served as powerful teleportation tools—I wanted to be able to read through a field note days, months, and years after data collection and instantly visualize the woman I'd spoken with, the setting we spent time in, and the texture and feeling of our conversation. Field notes became written accounts that filtered my respondents' beliefs and experiences through me, through my perspective. The field notes therefore preserved my accounts of respondents' concerns, meanings, and experiences, which deepened my ability to reflect on and understand their perspectives.[12]

Data Analysis

All interviews were digitally recorded and transcribed.[13] I then coded and analyzed the transcripts alongside my field notes using the qualitative data analysis software ATLAS.ti. I anonymized all respondents' names and any personally identifying information, adopted pseudonyms, and altered identifying details to preserve anonymity.

I employed the qualitative analytic coding strategy developed by Robert Emerson, Rachel Fretz, and Linda Shaw.[14] I approached my data analysis as an iterative process. First, I conducted a round of line-by-line "open coding" to generate a list of analytic categories from the transcripts. I then subjected the dataset to "focused coding" using these analytic categories to hone and refine explicit theoretical propositions. This stage involved a sustained examination of themes that linked together discrete observations. As unexpected patterns emerged from comparing my data across groups, I developed new analytic themes and categories.

The final stage of analysis occurred during the process of writing up my findings, which followed the approach outlined by Emerson and colleagues. At this stage, I oriented myself to my transcripts and field notes as "texts to be analyzed, interpreted, and selected for inclusion [...] for wider audiences."[15] While writing, I sought to make observations and experiences of local scenes speak to sociological concepts and traditions. The goal here was to *represent* the particular worlds I examined for readers who aren't directly acquainted with them. This meant moving repeatedly between specific conversations and anecdotes from my interviews to more general sociological concepts, offering a scholarly analysis while maintaining the nuances of my respondents' daily lives.[16]

I constructed a series of thematically organized narratives comprised of interview excerpts and analytic commentary. With this approach, data excerpts served as "essential kernels of the story" and "building blocks" for constructing and telling the story itself, and not simply as illustrations or examples.[17] By writing in this style, I adopted Emerson, Fretz, and Shaw's approach and meant to "provide a vehicle through which the voices from the field can, in their own distinctive ways, speak; and at the same time [. . .] also speak the language of the readers, addressing their issues, theories, and concerns."[18] The final analyses occurred as I selected and organized excerpts and wove them into coherent narratives using the theoretical tools of critical feminist sociology.

Shared Stories

I benefited immensely from hearing the insights of 135 women whose footsteps I hope to follow one day in motherhood. These women welcomed me in for slices of their daily lives—not as a detached observer but as a temporary participant who chatted, reflected, laughed, wondered, cried, complained, and appreciated alongside them as they told their stories. While interviews don't capture the messy complexity of people's lives in their entirety, these extended conversations and time spent with women before, during, and after the interviews gave me a flavor for what their lives were like. In my field notes on the final day I conducted interviews, a half a decade after I'd begun, I wrote:

Today I am feeling the supreme gift and generosity of strangers who want to make the world a better place for women to work and raise a family. On my walk home on my last day here in Berlin, I passed a little band playing the sweetest song in a shady courtyard. I thanked them for their music and the banjo player said to me, "It's your music too, now that you've heard it!" For me, this also rings true about these last five years of research: Each woman's story is now a part of me. The willingness of hundreds of people to open up their social networks, spread the word, let me into their homes, meet their partners, cuddle and feed and play with their babies, explore their neighborhoods, tour their offices, eat and drink at their dining tables alongside them, and share some of their most personal, intimate beliefs and experiences makes me feel like I have the greatest job in the world.

It's my hope that the women's stories recounted here become a part of your story too. I hope that, collectively, their experiences inspire each of us to work harder, longer, and louder to improve the lives of mothers everywhere.

Appendix B: Interview Schedule

Background

Age:
Race / Migration background:
Hometown:
Highest degree / year of degree:
Occupation:
Hours worked per week:
Annual income:
Marital status:
   (If applicable)
   Years partnered/married:
   Partner's age:
   Partner's highest degree:
   Partner's occupation:
   Partner's annual income:
Number and ages of children:
Do your children attend childcare? Yes / No
   If so, how many hours a week do they spend there?
   Who picks them up and drops them off?
   What type of childcare do your children attend?

Balancing motherhood with a career

1. Where were you working when your children were born? Did you have any concerns about balancing work and family?
2. When did you tell your boss you were pregnant? What was her/ his reaction? Did you know other women with children? Did you talk to them about being a working mother?
3. How much time did you take off when your children were born?
4. How did your work life change once you became a mother? For example, did you cut back your hours or were you given different assignments?
5. What did your employer do to help you in your new role as working mother? What do you wish they had done?
6. Tell me about the benefits you get—parental leave, maternity leave, cash allowances, health insurance, sick leave, vacation days, childcare, etc.? In what ways do these things make your job as a working mother easier? In what ways could they be improved?
7. Was your mother a working mother?
8. Did you move to a different job after having children?

Dividing family care with a partner

9. Did you and your partner have a conversation about how much you would work after your children were born? What was that conversation like?
10. Did your partner take time off of work after your children were born?
11. Once your children were born, how did you and your partner divide up family responsibilities like chores? Was this different than before your child was born?
12. What are your role and your partner's role in raising and caring for your children?
13. What role do your partner and children play when you think about your decision to work full time, part time, or not at all?

14. Everyone has their own ideas about what it means to be a good parent. Can you tell me what being a good father/mother means to you?

General views on working mothers

15. Have you ever thought of stopping working altogether to take care of your children?
16. What if anything can your workplace do to make the job more attractive to mothers?
17. What are your plans for the future regarding work?
18. What advice would you or do you give to your own children about their own decisions regarding work and family as adults? What do you hope they will do?
19. What advice would you give to working women who are about to become mothers?
20. Do you think it is possible for women who are mothers to get to the top in their career? Do you think mothers can be *both* a successful mother and a successful worker?
21. Are there any other issues you would like to discuss that I haven't asked that you think are important for understanding your experience as a working mother?

Notes

Chapter 1: SOS

1. Glass 2009; Golden 2001; Gornick and Meyers 2003; Williams 2010.

2. US Bureau of Labor Statistics 2017.

3. Hochschild 1989. See also Cooper 2014; Pugh 2015; Stone 2007.

4. Bellah et al. 2007.

5. See Monica Prasad's (2012) book *The Land of Too Much* for an analysis of the United States' complex history of state governance.

6. Orloff 1993, p. 304.

7. Bogenschneider 2000.

8. Eshleman 1991. Some US states provide policy supports for families despite the lack of provisions at the federal level; see chapter 6.

9. Collins and Mayer 2010.

10. Folbre 1994, 2008.

11. Glass 2009.

12. McCrate 2005; Noonan and Glass 2012; Osterman 1995; US Bureau of Labor Statistics 2013.

13. Boston Consulting Group 2017.

14. The unequal dispersion of work-family policy is the result of America's free-market approach, which leaves the provision of assistance up to individual employers with little state interference. Jennifer Glass (2009, p. 237) writes, "The failure of the laissez-faire approach to work-family policy can be seen in the frustrations and angst of American workers in public opinion polls . . . the large 'motherhood wage gap' among American workers . . . and high rates of child poverty . . . as well as the high turnover and job churning it has produced in the service sector."

15. US Census Bureau 2012.

16. Holub 2018.

17. Reston 2018.

18. Comparative research is revealing. Leading social policy scholars Janet Gornick and Marcia Meyers (2003, p. 21) argue that "cross-national comparisons help to challenge the belief that the family-level outcomes and policy designs observed in the United States are the only ones possible, and they provide models for alternative policy designs."

19. Wolf 2012; Hegewisch and Gornick 2011, p. 133.

20. OECD 2015a.

21. Theorizing around welfare state typologies is contentious (Kremer 2007; Orloff 2009a). The last decade of the twenty-first century saw a flurry of scholarly works proposing, refuting, and refining various classification systems. At the heart of the debate was Gøsta Esping-Andersen's

(1990) preeminent "three worlds of welfare capitalism" framework. Feminist sociologists in particular have contested and clarified this model at length by drawing attention to the gendered nature of social provisions (see Lewis 1993; Orloff 1993; and Sainsbury 1997 for extended critiques). Deliberations continue around the names, nature, and number of welfare state regimes, but most typologies overlap considerably with Esping-Andersen's (Kremer 2007). Weighing in on these nuances is not the goal of this book. I draw broadly from this body of literature as a useful heuristic for identifying my cases of study, and employ a common amended version of Esping-Andersen's framework (1990) that identifies four categories of welfare regimes: social democratic, conservative, familialist, and liberal (see Bonoli 1997; Bonoli and Natali 2012). Esping-Andersen's typology lumps familialist countries into the conservative welfare category. But scholars like Mauricio Ferrera (1996), Sigrid Leitner (2003), and Manuela Naldini and Teresa Jurado (2013) argue that these countries are a distinctive cluster because familialism hasn't translated into state support for families through social policies as it has in countries like Germany, France, and Austria. I therefore use the four-category typology.

22. I am indebted to Allison Pugh for suggesting that I devise a term to capture "the specific cultural and occupational and policy environment" in which women navigate their work and family commitments. I draw on Mary Erdmans and Timothy Black (2015) in my use of the term "lifeworld." The word has its roots in German philosophy. Edmund Husserl first introduced the concept "lifeworld" (*Lebenswelt* in German) in 1936, and sociologists Alfred Schutz (1970) and Jürgen Habermas (1987) later elaborated on it. Building on these German philosophers, Björn Kraus (2017) defined a lifeworld as "a person's subjective construction of reality, which he or she forms under the condition of his or her life circumstances—their social and material environmental conditions."

23. Blair-Loy and Wharton 2002; Dilworth 2004; Gornick and Meyers 2003; Hill 2005; Hook 2006; Jacobs and Gerson 2004; Lewis 2009.

24. Glenn 2000.

25. Wright 2011, p. 37.

26. Ibid.

27. World Bank 2018.

28. Haney 2010; Hobson 1990; Orloff 1993.

29. Lewis 1993, 2009; Misra, Budig, and Moller 2007.

30. Connell 2002.

31. Sainsbury 1997.

32. European Commission 2018.

33. Berkowitz and Walker 1967; Suchman 1997; Sunstein, 1996a, 1996b.

34. Festinger 1954.

35. Albiston, Correll, Tucker, and Stevens 2012.

36. Social inequalities become established through the subtle inculcation of power relations into individuals' innermost identities— the deeply ingrained skills, habits, and dispositions that people develop through their life experiences, what Pierre Bourdieu (1987, 1990) calls *habitus*. We internalize the power and status relationships between men and women that are reflected in and reinforced by a society's public policy. They become so thoroughly embedded in our sense of selves that they feel natural and self-evident. For example, through its policies a country's

government not only shapes access to employment, public benefits, discrimination protections, and how couples divide up household responsibilities. It shapes who *seeks* access to employment, who believes they *deserve* public benefits, who feels they have *experienced* discrimination at work, and who feels *responsible* for bringing home a paycheck, keeping the home clean, and taking care of children. States create the very subjects of work-family policies, who then become carriers of the beliefs embedded in them. I think of work-family policies as gendered techniques by the state to inculcate in working mothers a habitus particular to their social circumstances that serves a political end, such as increasing a country's labor supply or fertility rate.

37. Hernes 1987; Hobson 1990; Leira 1992; Lewis 1993; Orloff 1993, 2009a; Sainsbury 1997.

38. Cooke 2011; Mandel and Semyonov 2005, 2006.

39. Budig, Misra, and Boeckmann 2012; Gornick and Meyers 2003; Hegewisch and Gornick 2011; Misra, Budig, and Boeckmann 2011; Misra, Budig, and Moller 2007; Pettit and Hook 2009; Sainsbury 1997.

40. Boeckmann, Misra, and Budig 2015; Gornick and Meyers 2003; Pettit and Hook 2009.

41. For a review, see Hegewisch and Gornick 2011.

42. Glass and Riley 1998, p. 1426.

43. Glass and Riley 1998; Mandel and Semyonov 2005; Meyersson Milgrom and Petersen 2006; Rosenfeld and Kalleberg 1990.

44. Jacobs and Gerson 2004, p. 111.

45. Kreyenfeld and Hank 2000; Pettit and Hook 2009.

46. Bergmann 2008.

47. Meyersson Milgrom and Petersen 2006; Misra, Budig, and Boeckmann 2011; Pettit and Hook 2009.

48. Mandel and Semyonov 2005.

49. Pettit and Hook 2009.

50. Acker 1990; Blair-Loy and Wharton 2002; Briscoe and Kellogg 2011; Lewin 1989.

51. Budig, Misra, and Boeckmann 2012; Charles and Grusky 2004; Gornick and Meyers 2003; Hegewisch and Gornick 2011; Korpi, Ferrarini, and Englund 2013; Mandel and Semyonov 2005, 2006; Meyersson Milgrom and Petersen 2006; Pettit and Hook 2009; Rosenfeld and Kalleberg 1990; Stier, Lewin-Epstein, and Braun 2001.

52. Acker 1990; Blair-Loy 2003; Damaske 2011a, 2011b; Gerson 1985; Hays 1996; Jacobs and Gerson 2004; Hochschild 1989, 1997; Lareau 2003; Stone 2007; Williams 2000, 2010.

53. Blair-Loy 2003.

54. Thistle 2006.

55. Dow 2016.

56. Blair-Loy 2003.

57. Lareau 2003.

58. Williams 2000.

59. Hays 1996.

60. Blair-Loy 2003.

61. Acker 1990; Williams 2000.

62. Blair-Loy 2003; Gerson 1985; Stone 2007; Williams 2000, 2010.

63. Stone 2007.

64. Blair-Loy 2003.

65. Clawson and Gerstel 2014; Collins and Mayer 2010.

66. Blair-Loy 2003.

67. Ibid.

68. Damaske 2011b.

69. Grunow and Evertsson 2016.

70. Bonoli 1997; Esping-Andersen 1990; Gornick and Meyers 2003; Siaroff 1994. Social policy theorists offer various conceptual frameworks to allow for strategic comparisons of various welfare regimes. I selected my field sites following a modified version of the most widely used typology developed by leading welfare state scholar Gøsta Esping-Andersen (Bonoli 1997). This model groups welfare states into four categories. Though scholars debate what to call these groups, how precisely various countries fit within each group, and whether and how groups are splitting and reforming over time, my intention was to select four countries whose categorizations are fairly uncontroversial. Scholars often tout Sweden, Germany, Italy, and the US as exemplary cases of the four welfare state approaches to work-family policy in the industrialized West. This allows me to situate my findings within the larger comparative theoretical and demographic literature on welfare states.

71. As I describe later in this chapter, I interviewed women in both western Germany and former East Germany. This comparison is useful because reunification brought together the West German male breadwinner gender regime and the East German dual-earner gender regime. I differentiate between Germany as a conservative welfare regime and what might be called the hybrid welfare regime of former East Germany because the latter is difficult to place in existing categories given its unique history. From 1949 to 1989, East Germany mandated full employment as a socialist welfare state. After reunification, former West Germany's conservative model was imposed on the former East. Today the entire country (both regions) has one conservative welfare regime, but former East Germany displays remnants of its socialist past: cultural attitudes and social institutions still tend to support dual-earner families (e.g., universally available childcare).

72. Lewis 2009.

73. See Althusser (1971) for more on the process of interpellation and Butler (1993) for an analysis of interpellation and gender identities.

74. I use data from the Organisation for Economic Co-operation and Development (OECD). Note that in the statistics presented here, data for Germany represent both former East and West Germany folded together. OECD data are unavailable for each region separately. However, patterns are quite distinct for mothers in each region—for instance, in former East Germany, maternal labor force participation rates are higher, mothers tend to return to work more quickly after leave, and the gender wage gap is smaller.

75. OECD 2012a.

76. A defamilialized welfare state is one in which the state takes responsibility for care work that typically falls to families, primarily mothers, thereby freeing them up to work for pay (Esping-Andersen 1999).

77. A promising direction for future research would be a comparative ethnographic study investigating what mothers *do* objectively as a matter of daily practice regarding work-family conflict.

78. Researchers commonly use extreme cases to build theoretical arguments. See, e.g., Blair-Loy 2003; Hochschild 1983; Perry-Jenkins, Repetti, and Crouter 2000; Risman 1998; Stone 2007.

79. Stone 2007, pp. 19–20.

80. Williams 2010.

81. Six of these women identified as African American and two as Hispanic white. I interviewed one Asian woman, one Arab woman, and one Lebanese woman. These are self-reported.

82. Damaske 2011b; Stone 2007; Williams 2010.

83. Gornick and Meyers 2003; Hegewisch and Gornick 2011; Jacobs and Gerson 2004; Misra, Budig, and Moller 2007.

84. Beckert 2013a, 2013b, 2016.

85. Solnit 2016, p. xx.

86. Lear 2008, p. 103.

Chapter 2: Sweden

1. Duvander 2008.

2. Gerhard, Knijn, and Weckwert 2005, p. 38.

3. Daly and Lewis 2000; Gornick and Meyers 2003; Lundqvist 2011.

4. Ferrarini and Duvander 2010.

5. Huber and Stephens 2000.

6. Ellingsæter and Leira 2006.

7. Grennes and Strazds 2016; Wiles 2016.

8. Duvander 2008; Jonung 2012.

9. Hearn et al. 2012, p. 33.

10. Numhauser-Henning 2015.

11. Duvander, Ferrarini, and Thalberg 2005.

12. Duvander 2008, p. 7.

13. Ibid.

14. The Nordic countries are generally considered leaders in recognizing same-sex relationships (Scherpe 2013), and Sweden has made strides in the last fifteen years toward ensuring legal rights for LGBT couples. But results have been mixed with regard to the right for gay and lesbian individuals to parent. Same-sex couples have been able to register for legal partnerships in Sweden since 1994, but until recently gay and lesbian couples were denied the right to parent. This law was based around children's rights rhetoric, with the assumption that children need both a mother and a father as role models—a line of reasoning that privileges heterosexual couples (Friðriksdóttir 2016). Substantial reforms in the past decade have begun granting more rights to same-sex couples as parents. For instance, gay and lesbian couples gained adoption rights in 2003, and single women and lesbian couples gained the right to receive insemination assistance in 2005 (Friðriksdóttir 2016). Sweden was the seventh country in the world to legalize same-sex marriage in 2009. Today, with changing attitudes toward gender, the work-family policies available no longer privilege heterosexual couples as the only (or ideal) family form in which to raise children.

15. Swedish Institute 2013.

16. Berggren 2004.

17. Roughly half of all employed mothers reduce their working hours to part time at some point, while less than one-tenth of fathers do so (Duvander 2008).

18. Ferrarini and Duvander 2010.

19. Svensk författningssamling 2016. This bonus paid up to 3,000 Swedish kronor (US$460) per month. After a review of the efficacy of the gender equality bonus conducted by the Swedish Social Insurance Agency, the federal government decided to end the benefit because it didn't have a noticeable impact on couples' division of paid leave.

20. Duvander 2006.

21. OECD 2014a. Children of parents with low education or an immigrant background are underrepresented in Swedish childcare services (Ellingsæter 2012). Studies have found that immigrant mothers use parental leave and cash for care benefits more intensively than Swedish-born mothers, but this difference diminishes when controlling for labor market status (Mussino and Duvander 2016).

22. Ferrarini and Duvander 2010.

23. Ellingsæter 2012.

24. Duvander and Ellingsæter 2016.

25. Duvander, Ferrarini, and Thalberg 2005; Ferrarini and Forssén 2005; Oláh and Bernhardt 2008. Although some policies, like health care, are a universal right for all residents in Sweden, other financial supports are available to assist specific types of families with diverse needs. For instance, low-income individuals and families are eligible for a housing allowance (*bostadsbidrag*) if they lack the means to afford housing without governmental assistance (referred to as means-tested support). The main recipients are single mothers, and the benefit is considered vital in raising the incomes of one-parent households. Other policies apply to families when parents separate. If noncustodial parents fail to pay child support, maintenance support is available through social insurance. This assistance guarantees that custodial parents receive their support payments on time each month. Liable parents then accumulate a debt to the state. Currently, social insurance pays maintenance support for 13 percent of all children in Sweden.

26. Ferrarini and Duvander 2010. And in 2017, the #MeToo campaign, which calls out harassment by men in positions of power, also caught on in Sweden (Edwards 2017), Italy (Horowitz 2017), and Germany (Kirschbaum 2018), reaffirming that sexual violence is still very much on the public agenda. Reactions to and media exposure of the campaign vary between the nations.

27. International Social Survey Program (ISSP) 2012.

28. World Values Survey 2011.

29. Dribe and Lundh 2011; Duvander 2001.

30. Hearn et al. 2012.

31. Björklund 2007.

32. Florin and Nilsson 1999; Hedlin 2013.

33. ISSP 2012.

34. The Social Democratic Party in Sweden held power alone or in coalition for almost the entire twentieth century.

35. World Values Survey 2011.

36. Stone 2007.

37. It's difficult for scholars to glean new insights in the field and from their data if they hold onto preconceived ideas about the social phenomenon in which they're interested. Bourdieu

(1996) calls the process of separating from one's personal experiences an epistemic break from what we take for granted—a vital step for qualitative researchers entering unfamiliar social worlds.

38. ISSP 2012.

39. Pugh 2015.

40. Pomerleau 2015.

41. Overtime is regulated by collective agreement, and employees are typically entitled to overtime pay (*övertidsersättning*) or compensatory leave time (*kompledighet*) if they are asked to work overtime.

42. International Monetary Fund 2018.

43. The share of national income collected by the US government is proportionately less than that collected in Sweden, but Americans also receive less for their money. In order to enjoy the same level of benefits as Swedes receive through their socialized welfare system, people in the US have to pay much more out of pocket in addition to their annual income taxes, in the form of fees, surcharges, insurance premiums, co-payments, costly school tuition, childcare, elder-care, and more. Many cannot afford these benefits. Some question whether these services can really be considered discretionary, or whether they are fundamental to living healthy, productive lives (Hill 2013).

44. OECD 2015b.

45. Thorsén and Brunk 2009; OECD 2016d.

46. Kalleberg 2011; Pugh 2013.

47. Rosenfeld 2014.

48. Törnkvist 2013.

49. Because Sofia and her colleagues had only just begun contacting their unions to complain when we met, I don't know whether the unions eventually intervened on their behalf. Unions in Sweden are revered for their strength and considered a backbone of the Swedish economy. Whether the clash between Sweden's social democratic labor policy and the very un-Swedish neoliberal workplace culture Sofia described reaches a crescendo remains to be seen. Sweden has worked hard to opens its doors to more international companies in recent years—the official website of Sweden, Sweden.se, has English-language articles on its homepage titled, "How to Start a Business in Sweden" and "Taking Care of Business in Sweden." The impact of this move on Swedish workers is a worthy direction for future research.

50. ISSP 2012.

51. Collins 2018.

52. I follow bell hooks's (2000, p. 1) formulation of feminism: "A movement to end sexism, sexist exploitation, and sexist oppression."

53. World Values Survey 2011.

54. Averett 2015.

55. ISSP 2012.

56. This page has fifty articles. Other titles include: "7 Examples of Sustainability in Sweden," "Gender Equality in Sweden," "Openness Shapes Swedish Society," "Sweden and Human Rights," "Why Swedes Are Okay with Paying Taxes," "Working for a Gay-Friendly Sweden," "Elderly Care in Sweden," "Sweden—From Ice Age to IT Age," and "Sweden's Disability Policy," among others. It has its own page for migration (https://sweden.se/migration).

57. England and Folbre 2002.

58. Duvander 2008. Study after study shows that children enrolled in high-quality early childhood education and care do better over the course of their lives than similar peers who do not attend such programs. Put simply, high-quality care for young children sets them up for a lifetime of success (Heckmann 2006). In Sweden, all children receive this strong foundation.

59. Duvander 2008.

60. Hays 1996.

61. Bennhold 2010.

62. ISSP 2012.

63. Bennhold 2010.

64. Ibid.

65. In 2017 95 percent of Swedes had access to the Internet, and 85 percent use the Internet via their smartphones (https://sweden.se/society/openness-shapes-swedish-society/).

66. Internet access isn't reserved to just the wealthy in Sweden, meaning that programs like these are widely accessible. The country has a higher proportion of residents who are Internet users than any other EU nation: 81 percent of Swedes had smartphones in 2016, and 92 percent had computers (Mjömark 2016).

67. Work-family policies seem to have instilled in my interviewees a value system that aligned with state-level political goals—tactics that sociologists might call *gendered techniques of the welfare state*. The working mothers I spoke with governed themselves in ways that were compatible with the dual earner-carer welfare state—a model that encouraged the development of a homogenous gendered subject.

68. Brady and Burroway 2012.

69. ISSP 2012.

70. Ellingsæter 2012; Mussino and Duvander 2016.

71. Mussino and Duvander 2016; Wente 2015.

Chapter 3: Former East Germany

1. Kreyenfeld 2004.

2. Ostner 2010.

3. Kreyenfeld 2004.

4. Adler and Brayfield 2006; Fleckenstein and Lee 2014; Ostner 2010; Ziefle and Gangl 2014.

5. Lewis 1993; Ostner 2010; Pfau-Effinger and Smidt 2010.

6. Adler and Brayfield 1997; Hummelsheim and Hirschle 2010; Pfau-Effinger and Smidt 2010.

7. Matthews 2014.

8. Hagemann 2006; Kreyenfeld 2004; Ostner et al. 2003; Szydlik 2002; Trappe and Rosenfeld 1998.

9. Kreyenfeld 2004.

10. Struffolino, Studer, and Fasang 2015.

11. Kreyenfeld 2004.

12. Gangl and Ziefle 2015; Kolinsky 2003; Rosenfeld, Trappe, and Gornick 2004; Schenk 2003.

13. Jarausch 1999.

14. Ibid.

15. Rosenfeld, Trappe, and Gornick 2004.

16. Rudd 2000.

17. Ferree 2012.

18. Many of my respondents gave birth to their children when they were still legally entitled to take a total of three years of leave.

19. Ziefle and Gangl 2014.

20. Bundesministerium für Familie 2013; *Spiegel* 2011; Ziefle and Gangl 2014.

21. Breitenbach 2016.

22. Eurostat 2014b.

23. Gangl and Ziefle 2009.

24. Ostner 2010; Ziefle and Gangl 2014.

25. Lewis et al. 2008, p. 270.

26. Ibid.

27. *Spiegel* 2013.

28. Engstler and Menning 2003.

29. Rosenfeld, Trappe, and Gornick 2004; Hanel and Riphahn 2012.

30. Braun, Scott, and Alwin 1994; Lee, Alwin, and Tufiş 2007.

31. Lee, Alwin, and Tufiş 2007, p. 494.

32. Federal State of Berlin 2014; Segarra 2015.

33. Kroehnert, Medicus, and Klingholz 2006; *Spiegel* 2015.

34. Some mothers chose to hire a *Tagesmutter* or "childminder" to care for their children prior to enrolling them in the *Kita* (daycare). These caregivers are registered with the city and take on a small number of children in their own homes. They are covered by all labor and social legislation and pay taxes and social security contributions. The few *Tagesmütter* (in the plural form of the word, *u* changes to *ü*) my interviewees hired were all native-born German women. I couldn't find any data on the sorts of workers employed as *Tagesmütter* in Berlin or in Germany in general.

35. Schober and Stahl 2014. The calculations, based on data from the International Social Survey Programme and computed by the German Institute for Economic Research (Deutsches Institut für Wirtschaftsforschung), do not specify how the eastern and western portions of Berlin are accounted for.

36. Rosenfeld, Trappe, and Gornick 2004.

37. Kreyenfeld 2004.

38. Several mothers who felt healthy throughout their pregnancies and up until childbirth mentioned with admiration that women could work up until giving birth in the US. They didn't realize that mothers didn't have a choice until I explained it to them after our interviews had ended. Their faces registered looks of surprise and dismay upon learning about the lack of paid time off before and after childbirth. Most European women I talked to had a vague sense that policies were less supportive in the US, but they seemed shocked to learn the specifics.

39. Webber and Williams 2008.

40. Gangl and Ziefle 2009.

41. Blair-Loy 2003; Epstein et al. 1999; Risman 1998; Webber and Williams 2008.

42. Pfau-Effinger 2005.

43. Risman 1998; Webber and Williams 2008.

44. Presser 1989, 1994; Webber and Williams 2008.

45. People's views of equality are subjective. They are bound up not only in how people act but also in how they *feel* about their roles and those of others. Michael Walzer (1983) and others call this "complex equality." See Armstrong 2002.

46. Schober and Stahl 2014.

47. Gornick and Meyers 2003; Stone 2007.

48. In March 2015, the German parliament decreed that 30 percent of supervisory board seats at roughly one hundred of Germany's most well-known companies be allocated to women starting in 2016 (following Norway, Spain, France, and Iceland, which have 40 percent quotas; Italy with a one-third quota; and Belgium with a 30 percent quota). Currently 18.6 percent of supervisory board members in Germany are women (Smale and Cain Miller 2015).

49. Holst and Wieber 2014.

50. Rank 2011.

51. World Values Survey 2011.

52. ISSP 2012.

53. Holst and Wieber 2014.

54. International Labour Organization 2014.

Chapter 4: Western Germany

1. Mahon 2006, p. 179.

2. Adler and Brayfield 2006; Esping-Andersen 1990, 2009; Lewis 2009; Ostner 2010.

3. Korpi, Ferrarini, and Englund 2013; Ostner 2010; Rürup and Gruescu 2003.

4. Ostner 2010.

5. Esping-Andersen 2002; Ostner 2010.

6. Eurostat 2016.

7. Ostner et al. 2003.

8. Damaske 2011a; Glass 2009; Gornick and Meyers 2003, 2004; Hochschild 1989, 1997; Jacobs and Gerson 2004; Pedulla and Thébaud 2015; Pettit and Hook 2009; Williams 2000.

9. Landler 2006. In the plural form of the word, *u* changes to *ü*.

10. Pascoe 2007.

11. I use *ambivalence* in the colloquial sense of the term, not in reference to "sociological ambivalence" (i.e., Merton and Barber 1963). See Poulson 2016 for a discussion of these two uses.

12. Adler and Brayfield 2006; Lee, Alwin, and Tufiş 2007.

13. Ogburn 1957; Swidler 1986.

14. Hochschild 1997.

15. Edin and Kefalas 2005, p. 172.

16. Ibid.

17. Ferree 1976, 1980; Hochschild 1997.

18. Hawley 2012.

19. *Economist* 2012.

20. Rønsen 2009.

21. OECD 2004.

22. Correll, Benard, and Paik 2007.

23. Hebl et al. 2007; Masser, Grass, and Nesic 2007.

24. As I explained previously, besides the maternity leave available solely to mothers, parental leave (*Elternzeit*) is available to mothers and fathers in Germany. Payments for this time (*Elterngeld*) are funded by the federal government through general taxation, so employers are unlikely to feel the same frustration about this part of the leave scheme.

25. Acker 1990; Blair-Loy 2003.

26. Webber and Williams 2007, 2008.

27. Although the middle-class working mothers I interviewed told me they felt a great deal of guilt, other groups of women with children are likely to have different experiences. For instance, immigrant mothers have much lower levels of employment than native-born German mothers, so it's possible that they experience less guilt than the moms I spoke to. This is an open empirical question. Whether immigrant mothers in western Germany have knowledge of or feel pressured by German norms about work and family is a topic worthy of further exploration. Another important area for future research concerns the perceptions of women in Germany without children. Across the socioeconomic spectrum and regardless of migration background, it's likely they experience stigma because they aren't mothers. As in all my field sites, men in western Germany stand to benefit from the current welfare state work-family model, policies, and cultural expectations.

Chapter 5: Italy

1. Naldini 2003. See Ferrera (1996) for a discussion of the familialist welfare regime in Italy, Spain, Portugal, and Greece, also called the "Southern European welfare model" or "Mediterranean model."

2. Esping-Andersen 1999.

3. Naldini (2003) suggests that a series of distinctive cultural, ideological, and socioeconomic developments in Italian society meant that a true male breadwinner family model never materialized. Instead, the Italian welfare state "stretched" the male breadwinner family model to include not just a wife and children as dependent family members for the purposes of social protection benefits (employment protection and income maintenance), but also unmarried adult children, children's new families, elderly parents, and other relatives. These benefits cover only core workers with standard employment contracts.

4. For more on the consequences of labor market flexibilization and segmentation for Italy, see Barbieri and Scherer (2009).

5. Naldini and Jurado 2013.

6. The state implemented these protective labor policies as industrial sector employment expanded quickly in Italy after World War II and into the mid-1970s (see Cooke 2009). For more on the historical influence of unions on labor markets across capitalist democratic countries, see Thelen (2014); Western (1999).

7. Simonazzi et al. 2009.

8. Naldini (2003) examines the reasons why Italy and Spain show weak economic support for families with children while other nations with similarly strong Catholic influences like France and Belgium developed robust public supports for families with children.

9. Naldini and Jurado (2013, p. 44) explain: "In the family/kinship solidarity model the gender division of work is asymmetrical and women's care work is essential for the provision of welfare within kinship. As a matter of fact, the State provides few care services and poor family subsidies."

10. OECD Online Database, http://stats.oecd.org.

11. Jessoula 2012.

12. As in many countries, the baby boomer cohort is aging at the same time life expectancy has increased, leaving Italy with a significantly older population (Mazzola et al. 2016.)

13. Eurostat 2016. Explaining this low fertility rate is a topic of heated debate among demographers. See Cavalli and Rosina (2011) for a discussion of changing fertility ideals in Italy and Goldstein, Lutz, and Testa (2003) for a discussion of the broader European context.

14. Kohler, Billari, and Ortega 2002.

15. OECD 2016d.

16. One telling example is that in 2016, the unemployment rate in northwest Italy was 8.7 percent compared to 7.3 percent in the northeast, 10.5 percent in central Italy, and 19 percent in the south. The EU average was 8.6 percent that same year (Eurostat 2017).

17. Saraceno 2003.

18. Da Roit and Sabatinelli 2013; Saraceno 2003.

19. Cooke 2009, p. 127.

20. Da Roit and Sabatinelli (2013) argue that, as elsewhere in southern Europe, the Italian government has not only condoned but enabled the growth of the country's sizeable informal care market by establishing very few regulations. Cultural and political attitudes tend to be accepting of informal labor in general. These factors have helped attract undocumented workers to Italy in large numbers, particularly in the field of eldercare. See Caponio and Graziano (2011), Da Roit (2010), and Reyneri (2001) for more discussion of care migration flows in the case of Italy.

21. Da Roit and Sabatinelli 2013.

22. Caldwell 1978.

23. Unlike in Germany, Sweden, and the United States, there has been a notable lack of women's activism independent from the Italian political parties over the last half-century. Women's political representation, a factor associated with the development of social policies, has long been weak in Italy (Da Roit and Sabatinelli 2013; Misra 2003).

24. Torrisi 2017.

25. Bonoli 1997; Da Roit and Sabatinelli 2013.

26. Da Roit and Sabatinelli 2013; Martin and Palier 2007.

27. European Commission 2018.

28. Culhane 2016.

29. International Labour Organization 2014.

30. Ibid.

31. Masselot, di Torella, and Burri 2012.

32. Del Boca and Vuri 2007; Del Boca 2015. Seventy-one percent of Italian dual-earner couples with small children both work full time (Cooke 2009). Cross-national survey studies have documented a high correlation between the proportion of part-time jobs and women's labor force participation rates—especially married women with children (Meulders, Plasman, and Plasman

1994). Del Boca and Vuri (2007, p. 5) write that Italy's "low proportion of part-time workers seems mainly to be induced by characteristics of the demand side of the labor market."

33. Del Boca, Locatelli, and Vuri 2005.

34. Oliver and Mätzke 2014.

35. Cooke 2009; Del Boca 2015; Naldini and Saraceno 2008.

36. This high education level among my Italian sample is likely the result of my need to interview women in English.

37. OECD 2017.

38. Eurobarometer 2014.

39. Rates of unemployment are considerably higher for young people in Italy than elsewhere. While the average unemployment rate among people fifteen to twenty-four years old across the EU was 18.7 percent in 2016, that figure was 37.8 percent in Italy. What's more, the unemployment rate varied dramatically by region: 20.4 percent of people ages fifteen to twenty-four were unemployed in northeast Italy in 2016, compared to a staggering 49.2 percent of young people in the south (Eurostat 2017).

40. It stands to reason that anyone would prefer to be financially stable before having kids. But people's abilities to act on or plan according to this preference vary dramatically. My Italian respondents' comments were voiced from a position of considerable class privilege. Sociologists Kathryn Edin and Maria Kefalas (2005) interviewed low-income mothers in the US who echoed the sentiments of the middle-class Italian moms I spent time with. However, the women in Edin and Kefalas's study thought it made little sense to postpone motherhood in the interest of a solid financial future that might never be realized. A similar study with low-income moms in Italy would be a fruitful point for comparison.

41. Modena and Sabatini 2012.

42. Figari and Narazani 2017. I asked Giordana whether her two children attended daycare when they were young: "Yes. They started—the eldest one at eight months and the youngest . . . at thirteen months." I clarified, "Was it a public or private one?" Giordana replied, "It's a public but we pay a part." For a family with one child in Italy, the average monthly cost varies from €221 (US$270) in southern Italy to €364 (US$446) in the north. The cost per child decreases incrementally for families with multiple children. Compare these figures to the US, where the average daycare cost for one child age birth to four years is $800 a month. The cost also varies by region; in Arkansas, the average monthly cost is $477, and in Massachusetts it's $1,100. In DC, that figure is $1,321 a month (Schulte and Durana 2016).

43. Eurobarometer 2014.

44. Riva 2016.

45. ISSP 2012.

46. Blair-Loy 2003, p. 116.

47. This is similar to what Joan Acker (1990), Mary Blair-Loy (2003), and Joan Williams (2000) found for women in US workplaces.

48. Lo Scalzo et al. 2009.

49. Bansak, Hainmueller, and Hangartner 2016.

50. Magaraggia 2012; Ruspini 2009.

51. Ibid.

52. Bergmann 2008.

53. Billari et al. 2008.

54. Da Roit and Sabatinelli 2013.

55. Williams, Blair-Loy, and Berdahl 2013.

56. Rather than enter nursing facilities, parents expect their children to care for them in old age. The majority of Italians report being willing to provide long-term care for the elderly. The supply of formal public care services for the elderly is quite limited: fewer than 3 percent of the elderly live in a residential care facility. Families therefore rely heavily on relatives throughout the life course, especially those who can't afford private care (Naldini and Jurado 2013).

57. León and Migliavacca 2013; Naldini and Jurado 2013.

58. Arber and Timonen 2012.

59. Jappens and van Bavel 2012.

60. Eurostat 2016.

61. Crocetti and Meeus 2014.

62. Albertini and Kohli 2013.

63. Barzi, Menon, and Perali 2011; Bertolini 2011.

64. Naldini and Jurado 2013.

65. Kvist 2014.

66. L'Istituto Nazionale della Previdenza Sociale 2017.

67. Arpino, Pronzato, and Tavares 2012.

68. Naldini and Saraceno 2008.

69. Da Roit and Sabatinelli 2013; Morgan 2005.

70. Naldini and Saraceno 2008.

71. Da Roit and Sabatinelli 2013; Parreñas 2008.

72. Parreñas 2008.

73. Caponio and Graziano 2011; Damiani 2010.

74. IRES-CGIL 2009.

75. Parreñas 2001.

Chapter 6: The United States

1. FMLA only mandates that a person be "restored to the same job or to an 'equivalent job,'" but not the actual job held prior to the leave.

2. Glass 2009; Gornick and Meyers 2003; Williams 2000.

3. Glass 2009.

4. Collins and Mayer 2010, p. 112.

5. Collins and Mayer (2010, p. 14) write: "New theories of welfare contractualism are premised on the trading of civil rights for aid. By accepting assistance from the state, poor women are asked to relinquish a range of rights and liberties, from the freedom to decide whether to stay home with their children and to maintain ties to the fathers of their children, to the right to choose when and where to work and at what kind of job, to basic labor rights and protections while working at that job."

6. P.H. Collins 1998, 2001, 2004.

7. Gornick and Meyers 2003.

8. National Partnership for Women and Families 2018a.

9. Georgetown University Law Center 2010.

10. Boston Consulting Group 2017.

11. Ho 2015.

12. Schulte 2013; Story, Kaphingst, and French 2006.

13. Story, Kaphingst, and French 2006.

14. Heckman 2006.

15. McCrate 2005; Noonan and Glass 2012; Osterman 1995.

16. McCrate 2002.

17. Glass and Noonan 2016.

18. Blair-Loy 2003; Damaske 2011b; Glass 2009; Gornick and Meyers 2003; Hochschild 1989, 1997; Jacobs and Gerson 2004; Orloff 1993; Pettit and Hook 2009; Sainsbury 1997.

19. Gornick and Meyers 2003; Jacobs and Gerson 2004; Lambert 2008; Schlosser 2001; Thistle 2006.

20. Glass, Simon, and Andersson 2016.

21. Glass 2009.

22. Gerson 2010.

23. It's interesting that Tiana longed to be a nurse. In their study of four health care sector jobs, sociologists Dan Clawson and Naomi Gerstel (2014) find that doctors and nurses in the US both have considerable control over their schedules (unlike their working-class counterparts, emergency medical technicians and nursing assistants), but they use it in gendered ways. Doctors, who are primarily men, use the time to work even longer hours, leaving the upkeep of the domestic sphere to their spouses. Nurses, who are primarily women, use their schedule flexibility to accommodate the needs of their spouses and children—exactly the kind of flexibility Tiana reported wanting to care for her two kids. So although a job in nursing may give moms like Tiana more scheduling control associated with their social class advantage at work, Clawson and Gerstel show that that same workplace benefit is likely to perpetuate traditional gender norms within households.

24. Hays 1996; Villalobos 2014.

25. For more on the process of inculcation into systems of power, see Bourdieu 1977.

26. Blair-Loy 2003.

27. Griffin 2012; June 2016; Luberecki 2017.

28. Hertz 2008.

29. Pugh 2015.

30. Blair-Loy 2003.

31. Ibid., p. 141.

32. See Viviana Zelizer's book (1985) *Pricing the Priceless Child* for a fascinating discussion of the changing social value of children in the US.

33. ISSP 2012.

34. Deutsch 2004.

35. Hochschild 1989.

36. Without more robust work-family policy supports, lower-income mothers are also often forced to leave work, typically with more deleterious consequences for their families than moms with higher incomes experience. This churning and employee turnover at the bottom of the low-wage labor market is a central feature of the US welfare state (Collins and Mayer 2010).

37. Barston 2012; Jung 2015; Wall 2001.

38. Hochschild 1989.

39. Acker 1990; Williams, Muller, and Kilanski 2012.

40. US Department of Labor 2015.

41. OECD 2006; Swedish Institute 2018.

42. Stein 2015. Washington, DC's minimum wage rate at the time of my interviews was far higher than the federal minimum wage of $7.25. And as of 2018, DC's is the highest in the nation, at $13.25 (DePietro 2018).

43. Lichter 1997.

44. See also Clawson and Gerstel 2014.

45. Heymann et al. 2009.

46. National Partnership for Women and Families 2018b.

47. Ray, Sanes, and Schmitt 2013.

48. Blair-Loy 2003, p. 184.

49. Webber and Williams 2008.

50. Jacobs and Gerson 2004.

51. Edin and Lein 1997.

52. Cooper 2014. Sociologist Ana Villalobos (2014) similarly found in interviews with a diverse group of American mothers that in the face of rising economic inequality and volatility, women enact intensive mothering as a security strategy: they see a close mother-child bond as one way to feel secure in an increasingly insecure world. Unfortunately, she learned, this security strategy backfires for mothers because it's a "one-relationship solution to society-sized insecurities" (p. 3).

53. Collins and Mayer 2010.

54. Hays 1996; Lareau 2003; Martin 2005.

55. Avishai 2007.

56. Ibid., p. 136.

57. Annette Lareau (2003) calls this intensive parenting approach "concerted cultivation," a model common in middle-class families across racial groups.

58. Collins and Mayer 2010; Stone 2007.

59. Folbre 2001.

Chapter 7: Politicizing Women's Work-Family Conflict

1. Blair-Loy 2003; Damaske 2011b; Gornick and Meyers 2003; Jacobs and Gerson 2004; Stone 2007; Williams 2000.

2. Hondagneu-Sotelo 2001; Parreñas 2001, 2005.

3. Ehrenreich and Hochschild 2003.

4. We can understand neoliberalism as "a form of governance that seeks to inject marketized principles of competition into all aspects of society and culture" (Gane 2014, p. 1092). Neoliberal ideology is the belief that "open, competitive, and unregulated markets, liberated from all forms of state interference, represent the optimal mechanism for economic development" (Brenner and Theodore 2002, p. 350). See also Harvey 2007; Kalleberg 2009.

5. Albiston et al. 2012.

6. For example, several feminist advocacy groups want to see the US federal government implement one paid year of family leave for women and men. They know that chances are slim to none that this proposal will become law anytime soon. More feasible will be to pass *any* nationwide paid family leave legislation, of even a short duration. Passing *any* paid family leave at a federal level would signal that the public has a role to play in supporting families and caregiving.

7. Wright 2011, p. 37.

8. Mahon 2006, p. 179.

9. Ogburn 1957; Swidler 1986.

10. Colucci 2017, n.p.

11. Chafetz 1990; Deutsch 2007; Ridgeway and Correll 2000.

12. Prentice 2009. These shifts are in fact associated with a *de*-politicization of issues surrounding care. In other words, the shift toward an economic case for supporting care isn't simply a neutral tactic to "bridge the aisle" but in fact serves to reduce the likelihood of mobilization around the topic.

13. Gornick and Meyers 2008.

14. Misra, Budig, and Boeckmann 2011.

15. Ellingsæter 2003; Misra, Budig, and Boeckmann 2011; Pfau-Effinger 1998, 2010.

16. Mandel and Shalev 2009a, 2009b; Misra, Budig, and Boeckmann 2011.

17. Orloff 2009b, p. 141.

18. Ibid. For other examples of research on the relationship between social identities, social policy, and the state, see Jensen (2017) for an ethnography of the asylum process that determines who qualifies for refugee status in Brazil and Liebermann (2003) for a discussion about how beliefs about race and racial categories shape attitudes regarding progressive taxation in Brazil and South Africa.

19. Orloff 2009b.

20. Ibid., p. 144.

21. Ellingsæter 2012; Orloff 2009b.

22. Orloff 2009b, p. 245.

23. Mandel and Semyonov 2005, 2006; Pettit and Hook 2009.

24. Ono and Lee 2013.

25. Orloff 2009b, p. 150.

26. Fischer et al. 1996, p. 20.

27. Ibid., pp. 23–24.

28. Ibid.

29. Rank 2011.

30. Lear 2008; Díaz 2016.

31. Fischer et al. 1996, p. 23.

32. Wright (2011, p. 37) argues, "Exploring real utopias implies developing a sociology of the *possible*, not just the *actual*."

33. Solnit 2016, p. 5.

34. Gornick and Meyers 2003.

35. Fischer et al. 1996, p. 23.

36. Lewis et al. 2008.

37. Hook 2006.

38. Duvander and Johansson 2012.

39. Kotsadam and Finseraas 2011; Patnaik 2016.

40. Huerta et al. 2013.

41. Doucet 2006; Rehel 2014; Seward et al. 2006.

42. Blair-Loy 2003.

43. Williams 2000.

44. England and Folbre 1999a, 1999b; Glass 2000; Gornick and Meyers 2003.

Appendix A

1. Stone 2007.

2. Graff 2007; Williams, Manvell, and Bornstein 2006.

3. Here is how the Government Offices of Sweden (2018) define a feminist government on their website: "Sweden has the first feminist government in the world. This means that gender equality is central to the Government's priorities—in decision-making and resource allocation. A feminist government ensures that a gender equality perspective is brought into policy-making on a broad front, both nationally and internationally. Women and men must have the same power to shape society and their own lives. This is a human right and a matter of democracy and justice. Gender equality is also part of the solution to society's challenges and a matter of course in a modern welfare state—for justice and economic development."

4. Pugh 2013. Allison Pugh's article responds to critiques about the ability of interviews to elicit adequate data pertaining to culture. For more on interviewing, also see Lamont and Swidler 2014; Vaisey 2014; Weiss 1994.

5. Pugh 2013, p. 52.

6. E.g., Blair-Loy 2003; Stone 2007; Williams 1995.

7. Statistisches Bundesamt 2016.

8. Kochlar 2017; see also Vaughan-Whitehead 2016.

9. Grunow and Evertsson 2016.

10. Wallace 2005, n.p.

11. Desmond 2016, pp. 325–26.

12. Emerson, Fretz, and Shaw 2011.

13. I transcribed a portion of the interviews myself and hired three transcriptionists to help with other portions. One was a man, and the other two were women who explained that this topic was of interest because they were mothers themselves. Both had started transcription businesses to improve their work-family balance. Both women reached out to me afterward to tell me how deeply they had been impacted by the experience of working with these interview data. One wrote, "Your transcripts really made me take a step back to think about what I'm doing as a mom. I'm not sure that I'll be doing much transcription work this new year. I've spent a lot of long nights and time away from my daughter that I think is unnecessary. It's something I'm going to have to step back and evaluate, so I really appreciate this project. It has put some things in focus for me." The other wrote, "I was a working mother. I listened to so many mothers in your interviews talk about what it means to be a good parent, the hopes they had for their children, their wish to keep them safe. In the end, I was almost all the way across the country [...] the

night my son was murdered [...] just two weeks after his twenty-sixth birthday. I kept wanting to tell the women you talked to—and you—to cherish every single moment with their children, because it might just happen from one day to the next they'll be gone." Attached to her email was a photograph of her son, another of his headstone, a copy of her eulogy, and a local news article about his murder. Both of these emails signaled how deeply rooted the topic of motherhood is for contemporary women. As Mary Blair-Loy (2003) argued, work-family conflict may appear to be a personal problem for mothers, but it gets to the heart of shared beliefs of what it means to be a good worker and a good mother.

14. Emerson, Fretz, and Shaw 2011.

15. Ibid., p. 169.

16. Ibid., pp. 169–70.

17. Ibid., p. 171.

18. Ibid.

References

Acker, Joan. 1990. "Hierarchies, Jobs, Bodies: A Theory of Gendered Organizations." *Gender & Society* 4:139–58.

Adler, Marina, and April Brayfield. 2006. "Gender Regimes and Cultures of Care." *Marriage and Family Review* 39:229–53.

———. 1997. "Women's Work Values in Unified Germany: Regional Differences as Remnants of the Past." *Work and Occupations* 24(2):245–66.

Albertini, Marco, and Martin Kohli. 2013. "The Generational Contract in the Family: An Analysis of Transfer Regimes in Europe." *European Sociological Review* 29(4):828–40.

Albiston, Catherine R., Shelley J. Correll, Traci Tucker, and Christina Stevens. 2012. "Laws, Norms, and the Caretaker Penalty." Presented at the European Group for Organizational Studies, Helsinki, Finland, July 2–7.

Althusser, Louis. 1971. "Ideology and Ideological State Apparatuses." Pp. 127–86 in *Lenin and Philosophy and Other Essays*, translated by Ben Brewster. New York: Monthly Review Press.

Arber, Sara, and Virpi Timonen. 2012. *Contemporary Grandparenting: Changing Family Relationships in Global Contexts*. Bristol, UK: Policy Press.

Armstrong, Chris. 2002. "Complex Equality: Beyond Equality and Difference." *Feminist Theory* 3(1):67–82.

Arpino, Bruno, Chiara D. Pronzato, and Lara P. Tavares. 2012. "Mothers' Labour Market Participation: Do Grandparents Make It Easier?" Discussion Paper Series No. 7065, Institute for the Study of Labor.

Averett, Kate Henley. 2015. "The Gender Buffet: LGBTQ Parents Resisting Heteronormativity." *Gender & Society* 30(2):189–212.

Avishai, Orit. 2007. "Managing the Lactating Body: The Breast-Feeding Project and Privileged Motherhood." *Qualitative Sociology* 30:125–52.

Bansak, Kirk, Jens Hainmueller, and Dominik Hangartner. 2016. "How Economic, Humanitarian, and Religious Concerns Shape European Attitudes toward Asylum Seekers." *Science* 354(6309):217–22.

Barbieri, Paolo, and Stefani Scherer. 2009. "Labour Market Flexibilization and Its Consequences in Italy." *European Sociological Review* 25(6):677–92.

Barston, Suzanne. 2012. *Bottled Up: How the Way We Feed Babies Has Come to Define Motherhood, and Why It Shouldn't*. Berkeley: University of California Press.

Barzi, Federica, Martina Menon, and Federica Perali. 2011. "Youth Aspirations to Economic Independence." Paper presented at the Espanet Conference Innovare il Welfare, Percorsi di Trasformazione in Italia e in Europa, Milan, September 29–October 1.

Beckert, Jens. 2016. *Imagined Futures: Fictional Expectations and Capitalist Dynamics*. Cambridge, MA: Harvard University Press.

Beckert, Jens. 2013a. "Capitalism as a System of Expectations: Toward a Sociological Micro-foundation of Political Economy." *Politics & Society* 41(3):323–50.

———. 2013b. "Imagined Futures: Fictional Expectations in the Economy." *Theory and Society* 42(3):219–40.

Bellah, Robert N., Richard Madsen, William M. Sullivan, Ann Swidler, and Steven M. Tipton. 2007. *Habits of the Heart: Individualism and Commitment in American Life.* Berkeley: University of California Press.

Bennhold, Katrin. 2010. "The Stigma of Being a Housewife." *New York Times*, July 20. https://www.nytimes.com/2010/07/21/world/europe/21iht-LETTER.html.

Berggren, Stina 2004. "Flexibel föräldrapenning—Hur mammor och pappor använder föräl-draförsäkrin- gen och hur länge de är föräldralediga". RFV Analyserar 14. Stockholm: National Social Insurance Board.

Bergmann, Barbara. R. 2008. "Long Leaves, Child Well-Being, and Gender Equality." *Politics and Society* 36:350–59.

Berkowitz, Leonard, and Nigel Walker. 1967. "Laws and Moral Judgments." *Sociometry* 30(4):410–22.

Bertolini, Sonia. 2011. "The Heterogeneity of the Impact of Labour Market Flexibilization on the Transition to Adult Life in Italy: When Do Young People Leave the Nest?" Pp. 163–87 in *Youth on Globalised Labour Markets: Rising Uncertainty and Its Effects on Early Employment and Family Lives in Europe*, edited by Hans-Peter Blossfeld and Dirk Hofäcker. Opladen, Germany: Budrich.

Billari, Francesco C., Alessandro Rosina, Rita Ranaldi, and Clelia Romano. 2008. "Young Adults Living Apart and Together (LAT) with Parents: A Three Level Analysis of the Italian Case." *Regional Studies* 42(5):625–39.

Björklund, Erika. 2007. "Issue Histories Sweden: Series of Timelines of Policy Debates." QUING Project, Vienna: Institute for Human Sciences (IWM). http://www.quing.eu/ files/results /ih_sweden.pdf.

Blair-Loy, Mary. 2003. *Competing Devotions: Career and Family among Women Executives.* Cambridge, MA: Harvard University Press.

Blair-Loy, Mary, and Amy S. Wharton. 2002. "Employees' Use of Work-Family Policies and the Workplace Social Context." *Social Forces* 80(3):813–45.

Boeckmann, Irene, Joya Misra, and Michelle Budig. 2015. "Mothers' Employment in Wealthy Countries: How Do Cultural and Institutional Factors Shape the Motherhood Employment and Working Hours Gap?" *Social Forces* 94(3):1301–33.

Bogenschneider, Karen. 2000. "Has Family Policy Come of Age? A Decade Review of the State of US Family Policy in the 1990s." *Journal of Marriage and Family* 62:1136–59.

Bonoli, Giuliano. 1997. "Classifying Welfare States: A Two-Dimension Approach." *Journal of Social Policy* 26(3):351–72.

Bonoli, Giuliano and David Natali. 2012. *The Politics of the New Welfare State.* Oxford, UK: Oxford University Press.

Boston Consulting Group. 2017. "Why Paid Family Leave Is Good Business." http://media-publications.bcg.com/BCG-Why-Paid-Family-Leave-Is-Good-Business-Feb-2017.pdf.

Bourdieu, Pierre. 1996. "Understanding." *Theory, Culture & Society* 13(2):17–37.

———. 1990. *The Logic of Practice.* Cambridge, UK: Polity Press.

————. 1987. "What Makes a Social Class? On the Theoretical and Practical Existence of Groups." *Berkeley Journal of Sociology* 32:1–17.

————. 1977. *Outline of a Theory of Practice*, vol. 16. Translated by Richard Nice. Cambridge, UK: Cambridge University Press.

Brady, David, and Rebekah Burroway. 2012. "Targeting, Universalism, and Single-Mother Poverty: A Multilevel Analysis across 18 Affluent Democracies." *Demography* 49:719–46.

Braun, Michael, Jacqueline Scott, and Duane F. Alwin. 1994. "Economic Necessity or Self-Actualization? Attitudes toward Women's Labour-Force Participation in East and West Germany." *European Sociological Review* 10:29–47.

Brenner, Neil, and Nik Theodore. 2002. "Cities and the Geographies of 'Actually Existing Neoliberalism.'" *Antipode* 34(3):349–79.

Breitenbach, Dagmar. 2016. "How Parents in Germany Rate All-Day Schools." *Deusche Welle,* September 19. https://www.dw.com/en/how-parents-in-germany-rate-all-day-schools/a -19561983.

Briscoe, Forrest, and Katherine Kellogg. 2011. "The Initial Assignment Effect: Local Employer Practices and Positive Career Outcomes for Work-Family Program Users." *American Sociological Review* 76:291–319.

Budig, Michelle J., Joya Misra, and Irene Boeckmann. 2012. "The Motherhood Penalty in Cross-National Perspective: The Importance of Work-Family Policies and Cultural Attitudes." *Social Politics* 19(2):163–93.

Bundesministerium für Familie, Senioren, Frauen und Jugend. 2013. *Vierter Zwischenbericht zur Evaluation des Kinderförderungsgesetzes.* Berlin: BMFSFJ.

Butler, Judith. 1993. *Bodies That Matter: On the Discursive Limits of "Sex."* New York: Routledge.

Caldwell, Lesley. 1978. "Church, State, and Family: The Women's Movement in Italy." Pp. 68–95 in *Feminism and Materialism: Women and Modes of Production,* edited by Annette Kuhn and AnnMarie Wolpe. London: Routledge.

Caponio, Tiziana, and Paolo R. Graziano. 2011. "Towards a Security-Oriented Migration Policy Model? Evidence from the Italian Case." Pp. 105–20 in *Migration and Welfare in the New Europe: Social Protection and the Challenges of Integration,* edited by Emma Carmel, Alfio Cerami, and Theodoros Papadopoulos. Bristol, UK: Policy Press.

Cavalli, Laura, and Alessandro Rosina. 2011. "An Analysis of Reproductive Intentions of Italian Couples." *Population Review* 50(1):21–39.

Chafetz, Janet Saltzman. 1990. *Gender Equity: An Integrated Theory of Stability and Change.* Newbury Park, CA: Sage.

Charles, Maria, and David B. Grusky. 2004. *Occupational Ghettos: The Worldwide Segregation of Women and Men.* Stanford, CA: Stanford University Press.

Clawson, Dan, and Naomi Gerstel. 2014. *Unequal Time: Gender, Class, and Family in Employment Schedules.* New York: Russell Sage.

Collins, Caitlyn. 2018. "Americans Love Seeing Swedish Dads out with Their Children. This Is a Problem." *Slate,* April 11. https://slate.com/human-interest/2018/04/americans-love-these -swedish-dads-out-and-about-with-their-kids-thats-exactly-the-problem.html.

Collins, Jane L., and Victoria Mayer. 2010. *Both Hands Tied: Welfare Reform and the Race to the Bottom of the Low-Wage Labor Market.* Chicago: University of Chicago Press.

Collins, Patricia Hill. 2004. *Black Sexual Politics: African Americans, Gender, and the New Racism*. New York: Routledge.

———. 2001. *Black Feminist Thought: Knowledge, Consciousness, and the Politics of Empowerment*. New York: Routledge.

———. 1998. *Fighting Words: Black Women and the Search for Justice*. Minneapolis: University of Minnesota Press.

Colucci, Crystelle. 2017. "Interview with Alexandria Ocasio-Cortez." *Cooties Zine*, July 23.

Connell, Raewyn. W. 2002. *Gender*. Cambridge, UK: Polity Press.

Cooke, Lynn Prince. 2011. *Gender-Class Equality in Political Economies*. New York: Routledge.

———. 2009. "Gender Equity and Fertility in Italy and Spain." *Social Politics* 38(1):123–40.

Cooper, Marianne. 2014. *Cut Adrift: Families in Insecure Times*. Berkeley: University of California Press.

Correll, Shelley J., Stephen Benard, and In Paik. 2007. "Getting a Job: Is There a Motherhood Penalty?" *American Journal of Sociology* 112(5):1297–338.

Crocetti, Elisabetta, and Wim Meeus. 2014. " 'Family Comes First!' Relationships with Family and Friends in Italian Emerging Adults." *Journal of Adolescence* 37(8):1463–73.

Culhane, John. 2016. "In Italy, a Narrow Definition of Family Means Same-Sex Couples Still Can't Adopt." *Slate*, May 12. http://www.slate.com/blogs/outward/2016/05/12/italy_now_has_same_sex_civil_unions_but_gays_still_can_t_adopt.html.

Daly, Mary, and Jane Lewis. 2000. "The Concept of Social Care and the Analysis of Contemporary Welfare States." *British Journal of Sociology* 51(2):281–98.

Damaske, Sarah. 2011a. " 'A Major Career Woman?': How Women Develop Early Expectations about Work." *Gender & Society* 25:409–30.

———. 2011b. *For the Family? How Class and Gender Shape Women's Work*. New York: Oxford University Press.

Damiani, Mirella. 2010. "Labour Regulation, Corporate Governance and Varieties of Capitalism." Quaderni Dipartimento di Economia, Finanza e Statistica, no. 76, Università di Perugia.

Da Roit, Barbara. 2010. *Strategies of Care: Changing Care Policies and Practices in Italy and the Netherlands*. Amsterdam: Amsterdam University Press.

Da Roit, Barbara, and Stefania Sabatinelli. 2013. "Nothing on the Move or Just Going Private? Understanding the Freeze on Child- and Eldercare Policies and the Development of Care Markets in Italy." *Social Politics* 20(3):430–53.

Del Boca, Daniela. 2015. "Child Care Arrangements and Labor Supply." IDB Working Paper Series No. IDB-WP-569, Inter-American Development Bank.

Del Boca, Daniela, and Daniela Vuri. 2007. "The Mismatch between Employment and Child Care in Italy: The Impact of Rationing." *Journal of Population Economics* 20(4):805–32.

Del Boca, Daniela, Marilena Locatelli, and Daniela Vuri. 2005. "Child-Care Choices by Working Mothers: The Case of Italy." *Review of Economics of the Household* 3:453–77.

DePietro, Andrew. 2018. "The Best Cities to Be a Minimum Wage Worker." *Forbes*, August 24. https://www.forbes.com/sites/andrewdepietro/2018/08/24/best-cities-minimum-wage-earner/

Desmond, Matthew. 2016. *Evicted: Poverty and Profit in the American City*. New York: Broadway Books.

Deutsch, Francine M. 2007. "Undoing Gender." *Gender & Society* 21(1):106–27.

————. 2004. "Strategies Men Use to Reist." Pp. 469–75 in *Men's Lives*, 6th ed., edited by Michael S. Kimmel and Michael A. Messner. Boston: Allyn and Bacon.

Díaz, Junot. 2016. "Radical Hope." *New Yorker*, February 21. https://www.newyorker.com/magazine/2016/11/21/aftermath-sixteen-writers-on-trumps-america#anchor-diaz.

Dilworth, Jennie E. Long. 2004. "Predictors of Negative Spillover from Family to Work." *Journal of Family Issues* 25:241–61.

Doucet, Andrea. 2006. "'Estrogen-Filled Worlds': Fathers as Primary Caregivers and Embodiment." *Sociological Review* 54(4):696–716.

Dow, Dawn Marie. 2016. "Integrated Motherhood: Beyond Hegemonic Ideologies of Motherhood." *Journal of Marriage and Family* 78(1):180–96.

Dribe, Martin, and Christer Lundh. 2011. "Cultural Dissimilarity and Intermarriage: A Longitudinal Study of Immigrants in Sweden 1990–2005." *International Migration Review* 45(2):297–324.

Duvander, Ann-Zofie. 2008. "Family Policy in Sweden 2008." *Social Insurance Report 2008*, 15 Socialförsäkringsrapport.

————. 2006. "När är det dags för dagis? En studie om vid vilken ålder barn börjar förskola och föräldrars åsikt om detta" [Time for daycare? A study on when children start daycare and parents' opinions]. Institute for Future Studies Working Paper.

————. 2001. "Do Country-Specific Skills Lead to Improved Labor Market Positions?" *Work and Occupations* 28(2):210–33.

Duvander, Ann-Zofie, and Anne Lise Ellingsæter. 2016. "Cash for Childcare Schemes in the Nordic Welfare States: Diverse Paths, Diverse Outcomes." *European Societies* 18(1): 70–90.

Duvander, Ann-Zofie, and Mats Johansson. 2012. "What Are the Effects of Reforms Promoting Fathers' Parental Leave Use?" *Journal of European Social Policy* 22(3):319–30.

Duvander, Ann-Zofie, Tommy Ferrarini, and Sara Thalberg. 2005. "Swedish Parental Leave and Gender Equality." Institute for Futures Studies Working Paper.

Economist. 2012. "German Family Policy: Pay to Stay at Home." May 5. https://www.economist.com/europe/2012/05/05/pay-to-stay-at-home.

Edin, Kathryn, and Maria Kefalas. 2005. *Promises I Can Keep: Why Poor Women Put Motherhood before Marriage*. Berkeley: University of California Press.

Edin, Kathryn, and Laura Lein. 1997. *Making Ends Meet: How Single Mothers Survive Welfare and Low-Wage Work*. New York: Russell Sage.

Edwards, Catherine. 2017. "What Does the #MeToo Campaign Reveal about Swedish Feminism?" *Local*, November 24. https://www.thelocal.se/20171124/what-does-the-metoo-campaign-tell-us-about-swedish-feminism.

Ehrenreich, Barbara, and Arlie Russell Hochschild, eds. 2003. *Global Woman: Nannies, Maids, and Sex Workers in the New Economy*. New York: Metropolitan Books.

Ellingsæter, Anna Lise. 2012. "Cash for Childcare: Experiences from Finland, Norway, and Sweden." Report for Friedrich-Ebert-Stiftung.

————. 2003. "The Complexity of Family Policy Reform: The Case of Norway." *European Societies* 5(4):419–43.

Ellingsæter, Anna Lise, and Arnlaug Leira, eds. 2006. *Politicising Parenthood in Scandinavia: Gender Relations in Welfare States*. Bristol, UK: Policy Press.

Emerson, Robert M., Rachel I. Fretz, and Linda L. Shaw. 2011. *Writing Ethnographic Fieldnotes*. Chicago: University of Chicago Press.

England, Paula, and Nancy Folbre. 2002. "Wages of Virtue: The Relative Pay of Care Work." *Social Problems* 49(4):455–73.

———. 1999a. "The Cost of Caring." *Annals* 561:39–51.

———. 1999b. "Who Should Pay for the Kids?" *Annals* 563:194–207.

Engstler, Heribert, and Sonja Menning. 2003. "Die Familie im Spiegel der amtlichen Statistik." Berlin: Bundesministerium für Familie, Senioren, Frauen und Jugend.

Epstein, Cynthia Fuchs, Carroll Seron, Bonnie Oglensky, and Robert Saute. 1999. *The Part-Time Paradox*. New York: Routledge.

Erdmans, Mary, and Timothy Black. 2015. *On Becoming a Teen Mom: Life before Pregnancy*. Berkeley: University of California Press.

Eshleman, J. Ross. 1991. *The Family: An Introduction*. Boston: Allyn and Bacon.

Esping-Andersen, Gøsta. 2009. *Incomplete Revolution: Adapting Welfare States to Women's New Roles*. Cambridge, UK: Polity Press.

———. 2002. "A Child-Centred Social Investment Strategy." Pp. 26–67 in *Why We Need a New Welfare State*, edited by Gøsta Esping-Andersen. Oxford: Oxford University Press.

———. 1999. *Social Foundations of Postindustrial Economics*. Oxford: Oxford University Press.

———. 1990. *The Three Worlds of Welfare Capitalism*. Cambridge, UK: Blackwell.

Eurobarometer. 2014. ZA5923 (81.2 March): Europeans in 2014: Financial and Economic Crisis, European Citizenship, and European Values.

European Commission. 2018. "Italy: Maternity and Paternity Leave Allowance." http://ec.europa .eu/social/main.jsp?catId=1116&intPageId=4618&langId=en.

Eurostat. 2017. "Unemployment in the EU Regions in 2016." Eurostat News Release, April 27. http://ec.europa.eu/eurostat/documents/2995521/8008016/1-27042017-AP-EN.pdf /6617d81f-e62f-4063-9393-a74703badad4.

———. 2016. "Fertility Statistics." http://ec.europa.eu/eurostat/statistics-explained/index. php/Fertility_statistics/.

———. 2014a. "Labour Market and Labour Force Survey [LFS] Statistics Explained." http:// ec.europa.eu/eurostat/statistics-explained/index.php/Labour_market_ and_Labour _force_survey_(LFS)_statistics.

———. 2014b. "Unemployment Statistics." http://ec.europa.eu/eurostat/statistics-explained/ index.php/Unemployment_statistics.

Federal State of Berlin. 2014. "25 Years after the Fall of the Wall. Berlin: A Success Story." Press and Information Office of the Federal State of Berlin.

Ferrarini, Tommy, and Ann-Zofie Duvander. 2010. "Earner-Carer Model at the Crossroads: Reforms and Outcomes of Sweden's Family Policy in Comparative Perspective." *International Journal of Health Services* 40(3):373–98.

Ferrarini, Tommy, and Katja Forssén. 2005. "Family Policy and Cross-National Patterns of Poverty." Pp. 118–46 in *Social Policy and Economic Development in the Nordic Countries*, edited by Olli Kangas and Joakim Palme. New York: Palgrave Macmillan.

Ferree, Myra Marx. 2012. *Varieties of Feminism: German Gender Politics in Global Perspective*. Stanford, CA: Stanford University Press.

―――. 1980. "Working Class Feminism: A Consideration of the Consequences of Employment." *Sociological Quarterly* 21(2):173–84.

―――. 1976. "Working-Class Jobs: Housework and Paid Work as Sources of Satisfaction." *Social Problems* 23(4):431–41.

Ferrera, Maurizio. 1996. "The 'Southern Model' of Welfare in Social Europe." *Journal of European Social Policy* 6(1):17–37.

Festinger, Leon. 1954. "A Theory of Social Comparison Processes." *Human Relations* 7(2):117–40.

Figari, Francesco, and Edlira Narazani. 2017. "Female Labour Supply and Childcare in Italy." JRC Working Papers on Taxation and Structural Reforms No. 02/2017.

Fischer, Claude S., Michael Hout, Martín Sánchez Jankowski, Samuel R. Lucas, Ann Swidler, and Kim Voss. 1996. "Inequality by Design." Pp. 20–24 in *The Inequality Reader: Contemporary and Foundational Readings in Race, Class, and Gender*, edited by David B. Grusky and Szonja Szelényi. New York: Routledge.

Fleckenstein, Timo, and Soohyun Christine Lee. 2014. "The Politics of Postindustrial Social Policy: Family Policy Reforms in Britain, Germany, South Korea, and Sweden." *Comparative Political Studies* 47(4):601–30.

Florin, Christina, and Bengt Nilsson. 1999. "'Something in the Nature of a Bloodless Revolution . . .'" How New Gender Relations Became Gender Equality Policy in Sweden in the 1960s and 1970s." Pp. 11–77 in *State Policy and Gender System in the Two German States and Sweden 1945–1989*, edited by Rolf Torstendahl. Uppsala, Sweden: Uppsala Universitet.

Folbre, Nancy. 2008. *Valuing Children: Rethinking the Economics of the Family*. Cambridge, MA: Harvard University Press.

―――. 2001. "Accounting for Care in the United States." Pp. 175–92 in *Care Work: The Quest for Security*, edited by Mary Daly. Geneva: International Labour Office.

―――. 1994. *Who Pays for the Kids? Gender and the Structures of Constraint*. London: Routledge.

Friðriksdóttir, Hrefna. 2016. "Nordic Family Law: New Framework—New Fatherhoods." Pp. 53–78 in *Fatherhood in the Nordic Welfare States: Comparing Care Policies and Practice*, edited by Guðný Björk Eydal and Tine Rostgaard. Bristol, UK: Policy Press.

Gane, Nicholas. 2014. "Sociology and Neoliberalism: A Missing History." *Sociology* 48(6):1092–106.

Gangl, Markus, and Andrea Ziefle. 2015. "The Making of a Good Woman: Extended Parental Leave Entitlements and Mothers' Work Commitment in Germany." *American Journal of Sociology* 121(2):511–63.

―――. 2009. "Motherhood, Labor Force Behavior, and Women's Careers: An Empirical Assessment of the Wage Penalty for Motherhood in Britain, Germany, and the United States." *Demography* 46(2):341–69.

Georgetown University Law Center. 2010. "Family and Medical Leave: Selective Background Information." http://scholarship.law.georgetown.edu/legal/31.

Gerhard, Uta, Trudie Knijn, and Anja Weckwert, eds. 2005. *Working Mothers in Europe: A Comparison of Policies and Practices*. Cheltenham, UK: Edward Elgar.

Gerson, Kathleen. 2010. *The Unfinished Revolution: How a New Generation Is Reshaping Family, Work, and Gender in America*. New York: Oxford University Press.

———. 1985. *Hard Choices: How Women Decide about Work, Career, and Motherhood*. Berkeley: University of California Press.

Glass, Jennifer L. 2009. "Work-Life Policies: Directions for Future Research." Pp. 231–50 in *Work-Life Policies That Make a Difference*, edited by Alan Booth and Nan Crouter. New York: Sage.

———. 2000. "Envisioning the Integration of Family and Work: Toward a Kinder, Gentler Workplace." *Contemporary Sociology* 29(1):129–43.

Glass, Jennifer L., and Mary C. Noonan. 2016. "Telecommuting and Earnings Trajectories among American Women and Men 1989–2008." *Social Forces* 95(1):217–50.

Glass, Jennifer L., and Lisa Riley. 1998. "Family Responsive Policies and Employee Retention Following Childbirth." *Social Forces* 76(4):1401–35.

Glass, Jennifer L., Robin W. Simon, and Matthew A. Andersson. 2016. "Parenthood and Happiness: Effects of Work-Family Reconciliation Policies in 22 OECD Countries." *American Journal of Sociology* 122(3):886–929.

Glenn, Evelyn Nakano. 2000. "Creating a Caring Society." *Contemporary Sociology* 29(1):84–94.

Golden, Lonnie. 2001. "Flexible Work Schedules: Which Workers Get Them?" *American Behavioral Scientist* 44:1157–78.

Goldstein, Joshua, Wolfgang Lutz, and Maria Rita Testa. 2003. "The Emergence of Sub-Replacement Family Size Ideals in Europe." *Population Research and Policy Review* 22(5-6):479–96.

Gornick, Janet C., and Marcia K. Meyers. 2008. "Creating Gender Egalitarian Societies: An Agenda for Reform." *Politics and Society* 36(3):313–49.

———. 2004. "More Alike Than Different: Revisiting the Long-Term Prospects for Developing 'European-Style' Work/Family Policies in the United States." *Journal of Comparative Policy Analysis* 6:251–73.

———. 2003. *Families That Work: Policies for Reconciling Parenthood and Employment*. New York: Russell Sage.

Government Offices of Sweden. 2018. "A Feminist Government." https://www.government.se/government-policy/a-feminist-government/.

Graff, E. J. 2007. "The Opt-Out Myth." *Columbia Journalism Review*, April. https://archives.cjr.org/essay/the_optout_myth.php.

Grennes, Thomas, and Andris Strazds. 2016. "What Can the U.S. Learn from Big Government in Sweden and Denmark?" *Economonitor*, February 15. http://archive.economonitor.com/blog/2016/02/what-can-the-u-s-learn-from-big-government-in-sweden-and-denmark/.

Griffin, Kat. 2012. "Pregnancy and the Office: When to Tell and When to Wait." *Forbes*, September 4. https://www.forbes.com/sites/work-in-progress/2012/09/04/pregnancy-and-the-office-when-to-tell/#25259c3a2341.

Grunow, Daniela, and Marie Evertsson. 2016. *Couples' Transitions to Parenthood: Analysing Gender and Work in Europe*. Cheltenham, UK: Edward Elgar.

Habermas, Jürgen. 1987. *The Theory of Communicative Action. Lifeworld and System: A Critique of Functionalist Reason*, 2nd ed. Boston: Beacon Press.

Hagemann, Karen. 2006. "Between Ideology and Economy: The 'Time Politics' of Child Care and Public Education in the Two Germanys." *Social Politics: International Studies in Gender, State and Society* 13(2):217–60. '

Hanel, Barbara, and Regina T. Riphahn. 2012. "The Employment of Mothers: Recent Developments and Their Determinants in East and West Germany." *Jahrbücher für Nationalökonomie und Statistik* 232:146–76.

Haney, Lynne. 2010. *Offending Women: Power, Punishment, and the Regulation of Desire.* Berkeley: University of California Press.

Harvey, David. 2007. *A Brief History of Neoliberalism.* Oxford, UK: Oxford University Press.

Hawley, Charles. 2012. "Childcare Draft Law Fuels Feminism Debate in Germany." *Spiegel,* May 14. http://www.spiegel.de/international/germany/childcare-allowance-proposal-splits -germany-a-838663.html.

Hays, Sharon. 1996. *The Cultural Contradictions of Motherhood.* New Haven, CT: Yale University Press.

Hearn, Jeff, Marie Nordberg, Kherstin Andersson, Dag Balkmar, Lucas Gottzén, Roiger Klinth, Keith Pringle, and Linn Sandberg. 2012. "Hegemonic Masculinity and Beyond: 40 Years of Research in Sweden." *Men and Masculinities* 15(1):31–55.

Hebl, Michelle R., Eden B. King, Peter Glick, Sarah L. Singletary, and Stephanie Kazama. 2007. "Hostile and Benevolent Reactions toward Pregnant Women: Complementary Interpersonal Punishments and Rewards that Maintain Traditional Roles." *Journal of Applied Psychology* 92(6):1499–511.

Heckman, James. 2006. "Skill Formation and the Economics of Investing in Disadvantaged Children." *Science* 312:1900–1902.

Hedlin, Maria. 2013. "Swedish Schools and Gender Equality in the 1970s." *International Education Studies* 6(3):76–87.

Hegewisch, Ariane, and Janet C. Gornick. 2011. "The Impact of Work-Family Policies on Women's Employment: A Review of Research from OECD Countries." *Community, Work and Family* 14(2):119–38.

Hernes, Helga M. 1987. *Welfare State and Woman Power: Essays in State Feminism.* Oslo: Norwegian University Press.

Hertz, Rosanna. 2008. *Single by Chance, Mothers by Choice: How Women Are Choosing Parenthood without Marriage and Creating the New American Family.* Oxford: Oxford University Press.

Heymann, Jody, Hye Jin Rho, John Schmitt, and Alison Earle. 2009. "Contagion Nation: A Comparison of Paid Sick Day Policies in 22 Countries." Center for Economic and Policy Research.

Hill, E. Jeffrey. 2005. "Work-Family Facilitation and Conflict, Working Fathers and Mothers, Work-Family Stressors and Support." *Journal of Family Issues* 26(6):793–819.

Hill, Steven. 2013. "The Myth of Low-Tax America: Why Americans Aren't Getting Their Money's Worth." *Atlantic,* April 15. https://www.theatlantic.com/business/archive/2013/04/the -myth-of-low-tax-america-why-americans-arent-getting-their-moneys-worth/274945/.

Ho, Christine. 2015. "Welfare-to-Work Reform and Intergenerational Support: Grandmothers' Response to the 1996 PRWORA." *Journal of Marriage and Family* 77(2):407–23.

Hobson, Barbara. 1990. "No Exit, No Voice: Women's Economic Dependency and the Welfare State." *Acta Sociologica* 33:235–50.

Hochschild, Arlie Russell. 1997. *The Time Bind: When Work Becomes Home and Home Becomes Work.* New York: Metropolitan Books.

———. 1989. *The Second Shift: Working Parents and the Revolution at Home.* New York: Viking.

Hochschild, Arlie Russell. 1983. *The Managed Heart: Commercialization of Human Feeling.* Berkeley: University of California Press.

Holst, Elke, and Anna Wieber. 2014. "Eastern Germany Ahead in Employment of Women." *DIW Economic Bulletin* 11. https://www.diw.de/documents/ publikationen/73/diw_01.c.491960 .de/diw_econ_bull_2014–11–5.pdf.

Holub, Christian. 2018. "Ellen DeGeneres Asks Kamala Harris about 2020 Presidential Aspirations." *Entertainment Weekly,* April 5. https://ew.com/tv/2018/04/05/kamala-harris-ellen -degeneres/.

Hondagneu-Sotelo, Pierrette. 2001. *Doméstica: Immigrant Workers Cleaning and Caring in the Shadows of Affluence.* Berkeley: University of California Press.

Hook, Jennifer L. 2006. "Care in Context: Men's Unpaid Work in 20 Countries, 1965–2003." *American Sociological Review* 71(4):639–60.

hooks, bell. 2000. *Feminism Is for Everybody.* London: Pluto Press.

Horowitz, Jason. 2017. "In Italy, #MeToo Is More Like 'Meh.'" *New York Times,* December 16. https://www.nytimes.com/2017/12/16/world/europe/italy-sexual-harassment.html.

Huber, Evelyn, and John D. Stephens. 2000. "Partisan Governance, Women's Employment, and the Social Democratic Service State." *American Sociological Review* 65(3):323–42.

Huerta, María del Carmen, Willem Adema, Jennifer Baxter, Wen-Jui Han, Mette Lausten, RaeHyuck Lee, and Jane Waldfogel. 2013. "Fathers' Leave, Fathers' Involvement and Child Development: Are They Related? Evidence from Four OECD Countries." OECD Social, Employment and Migration Working Papers No. 140.

Hummelsheim, Dina, and Jochen Hirschle. 2010. "Mothers' Employment: Cultural Imprint or Institutional Governance? Belgium, West and East Germany in Comparison." *European Societies* 12(3):339–66.

International Labour Organization. 2014. *Maternity and Paternity at Work: Law and Practice across the World.* Geneva: International Labour Organization.

International Monetary Fund. 2018. "IMF DataMapper: World Economic Outlook, GDP Per Capita, Current Prices." http://www.imf.org/external/datamapper/PPPPC@WEO/ OEMDC/ADVEC/WEOWORLD.

International Social Survey Program (ISSP). 2012. "Family and Changing Gender Roles." Module of the International Social Survey Program. http://zacat.gesis.org/.

IRES-CGIL. 2009. "Il Lavoro Domestico e di Cura: Scenario, Condizioni di Lavoro e Discriminazioni." Rome: IRES.

Jacobs, Jerry A., and Kathleen Gerson. 2004. *The Time Divide: Work, Family, and Gender Inequality.* Cambridge, MA: Harvard University Press.

Jappens, Maaike, and Jan Van Bavel. 2012. "Regional Family Norms and Child Care by Grandparents in Europe." *Demographic Research* 27:85–120.

Jarausch, Konrad H. 1999. *Dictatorship as Experience: Towards a Socio-Cultural History of the GDR.* New York: Berghahn.

Jensen, Katherine. 2017. "The Epistemic Logic of Asylum Screening: (Dis)embodiment and the Production of Asylum Knowledge in Brazil." *Ethnic and Racial Studies* 41(15):2615–33

Jessoula, Matteo. 2012. "A Risky Combination in Italy: 'Selective Flexibility' and Defined Contributions Pensions." Pp. 62–92 in *Labour Market Flexibility and Pension Reforms: Flexible Today, Secure Tomorrow?,* edited by Karl Hinrichs and Matteo Jessoula. New York: Palgrave Macmillan.

Jonung, Lars. 2012. "The 2012 Report of the Swedish Fiscal Policy Council." Paper presented at the conference on Gouvernance budgétaire en Europe. Paris, France. October 9.

June, Laura. 2016. "How to Tell Your Boss You're Pregnant." *New York Magazine*, March 9. https://www.thecut.com/2016/03/how-to-tell-your-boss-youre-pregnant.html.

Jung, Courtney. 2015. *Lactivism: How Feminists and Fundamentalists, Hippies and Yuppies, and Physicians and Politicians Made Breastfeeding Big Business and Bad Policy*. New York: Basic Books.

Kalleberg, Arne L. 2011. *Good Jobs, Bad Jobs: The Rise of Polarized and Precarious Employment Systems in the United States, 1970s–2000s*. New York: Russell Sage.

———. 2009. "Precarious Work, Insecure Workers: Employment Relations in Transition." *American Sociological Review* 74(1):1–22.

Kirschbaum, Erik. 2018. "Germany Had Seemed Immune to the #MeToo Movement. Then a Prominent Director Was Accused." *Los Angeles Times*, January 31. http://www.latimes.com/world/europe/la-fg-germany-sexual-harassment-20180130-story.html.

Kochhar, Rakesh. 2017. "Middle Class Fortunes in Western Europe." Pew Research Center, April 24. http://www.pewglobal.org/2017/04/24/middle-class-fortunes-in-western-europe/.

Kohler, Hans-Peter, Francesco C. Billari, and José Antonio Ortega. 2002. "The Emergence of Lowest-Low Fertility in Europe during the 1990s." *Population and Development Review* 28(4):641–80.

Kolinsky, Eva. 2003. "Gender and the Limits of Equality in East Germany." Pp. 100–27 in *Reinventing Gender: Women in Eastern Germany since Unification*, edited by Eva Kolinsky and Hildegard Maria Nickel. London: Frank Cass.

Korpi, Walter, Tommy Ferrarini, and Stefan Englund. 2013. "Women's Opportunities under Different Family Policy Constellations: Gender, Class, and Inequality Tradeoffs in Western Countries Re-Examined." *Social Politics* 20(1):1–40.

Kotsadam, Andreas, and Henning Finseraas. 2011. "The State Intervenes in the Battle of the Sexes: Causal Effects of Paternity Leave." *Social Science Research* 40(6):1611–22.

Kraus, Björn. 2017. "Plädoyer für den Relationalen Konstruktivismus und eine Relationale Soziale Arbeit." *Forum Sozial* 1:29–35. http://www.ssoar.info/ssoar/handle/document/51948.

Kremer, Monique. 2007. *How Welfare States Care: Culture, Gender and Parenting in Europe*. Amsterdam: Amsterdam University Press.

Kreyenfeld, Michaela. 2004. "Fertility Decisions in the FRG and GDR: An Analysis with Data from the German Fertility and Family Survey." *Demographic Research* 3:275–318.

Kreyenfeld, Michaela, and Karsten Hank. 2000. "Does the Availability of Child Care Influence the Employment of Mothers? Findings from Western Germany." *Population Research and Policy Review* 19(4):317–37.

Kroehnert, Steffen, Franziska Medicus, and Reiner Klingholz. 2006. "The Demographic State of the Nation: How Sustainable are Germany's Regions?" Berlin: Institute for Population and Development.

Kvist, John. 2014. "A Framework for Social Investment Strategies: Integrating Generational, Life Course and Gender Perspectives in the EU Social Investment Strategy." *Comparative European Politics* 13(1):1–19.

Lambert, Susan J. 2008. "Passing the Buck: Labor Flexibility Practices That Transfer Risk onto Hourly Workers." *Human Relations* 61(9):1203–27.

Lamont, Michèle and Ann Swidler. 2014. "Methodological Pluralism and the Possibilities and Limits of Interviewing." *Qualitative Sociology* 37(2):153–71.

Landler, Mark. 2006. "Quoth the Raven: I Bake Cookies, Too." *New York Times*, April 23. https://www.nytimes.com/2006/04/23/weekinreview/quoth-the-raven-i-bake-cookies-too.html.

Lareau, Annette. 2003. *Unequal Childhoods: Class, Race and Family Life.* Berkeley: University of California Press.

Lear, Jonathan. 2008. *Radical Hope: Ethics in the Face of Cultural Devastation.* Cambridge, MA: Harvard University Press.

Lee, Kristen S., Duane F. Alwin, and Paula A. Tufiş. 2007. "Beliefs about Women's Labour in the Reunified Germany, 1991–2004." *European Sociological Review* 23:487–503.

Leira, Amlaug. 1992. *Welfare States and Working Mothers: The Scandinavian Experience.* Cambridge, UK: Cambridge University Press.

Leitner, Sigrid. 2003. "Varieties of Familialism: The Caring Function of the Family in Comparative Perspective." *European Societies* 5(4):353–75.

León, Margarita, and Mauro Migliavacca. 2013. "Italy and Spain: Still the Case of Familistic Welfare Models?" *Population Review* 52(1):25–42.

Lewin, Tamar. 1989. "'Mommy Career Track' Sets Off a Furor." *New York Times*, May 8. https://www.nytimes.com/1989/03/08/us/mommy-career-track-sets-off-a-furor.html.

Lewis, Jane. 2009. *Work-Family Balance, Gender, and Policy.* Cheltenham, UK: Edward Elgar.

———. 1993. *Women and Social Policies in Europe: Work, Family and the State.* Cheltenham, UK: Edward Elgar.

Lewis, Jane, Trudie Knijn, Claude Martin, and Ilona Ostner. 2008. "Patterns of Development in Work/Family Reconciliation Policies for Parents in France, Germany, the Netherlands, and the UK in the 2000s." *Social Politics* 15(3):261–86.

Lichter, Dan. 1997. "Poverty and Inequality among Children." *Annual Review of Sociology* 23:121–45.

Liebermann, Evan. 2003. *Race and Regionalism in the Politics of Taxation in Brazil and South Africa.* Cambridge, UK: Cambridge University Press.

L'Istituto Nazionale della Previdenza Sociale (National Institute of Social Security, INPS). 2017. "Pensione di vecchiaia per gli iscritti all'Assicurazione Generale Obbligatoria AGO (Fondo Pensioni Lavoratori Dipendenti FPLD e gestioni speciali dei lavoratori autonomi) e alla Gestione Separata." https://www.inps.it/nuovoportaleinps/default.aspx?sPathID=%3b0%3b49467%3b&lastMenu=49467&iMenu=1&itemDir=50736.

Lo Scalzo, Alessandra, Andrea Donatini, Letizia Orzella, Americo Cicchetti, Silvia Profili, and Anna Maresso. 2009. "Italy: Health System Review." *Health Systems in Transition* 11(6). European Observatory on Health Systems and Policies.

Luberecki, Beth. 2017. "So You're Pregnant. How Do You Tell Your Boss?" *Washington Post*, November 14. https://www.washingtonpost.com/express/wp/2017/11/14/so-youre-pregnant-how-do-you-tell-your-boss/?noredirect=on&utm_term=.c63787528b27.

Lundqvist, Åsa. 2011. *Family Policy Paradoxes: Gender Equality and Labour Market Regulation in Sweden, 1930–2010.* Bristol, UK: Policy Press.

Magaraggia, Sveva. 2012. "Tensions between Fatherhood and the Social Construction of Masculinity in Italy." *Current Sociology* 61(1):76–92.

Mahon, Rianne. 2006. "The OECD and the Work/Family Reconciliation Agenda: Competing Frames." Pp. 173–97 in *Children, Changing Families, and Welfare States*, edited by Jane Lewis. Cheltenham, UK: Edward Elgar.

Mandel, Hadas, and Moshe Semyonov. 2006. "A Welfare State Paradox: State Interventions and Women's Employment Opportunities in 22 Countries." *American Journal of Sociology* 111:1910–49.

———. 2005. "Family Policies, Wage Structures, and Gender Gaps: Sources of Earnings Inequality in 20 Countries." *American Sociological Review* 70:949–67.

Mandel, Hadas, and Michael Shalev. 2009a. "Gender, Class, and Varieties of Capitalism." *Social Politics* 16(2):161–81.

———. 2009b. "How Welfare States Shape the Gender Pay Gap: A Theoretical and Comparative Analysis." *Social Forces* 87(4): 1873–911.

Martin, Claude, and Bruno Palier. 2007. "Editorial Introduction. From 'A Frozen Landscape' to Structural Reforms: The Sequential Transformation of Bismarckian Welfare Systems." *Social Policy & Administration* 41(6):535–54.

Martin, Karin A. 2005. "William Wants a Doll. Can He Have One? Feminists, Child Care Advisors, and Gender-Neutral Child Rearing." *Gender & Society* 19(4):456–79.

Masselot, Annick, Eugenia Caracciolo di Torella, and Susanne Burri. 2012. "Fighting Discrimination on the Grounds of Pregnancy, Maternity and Parenthood—The Application of EU and National Law in Practice in 33 European Countries." Thematic Report of the European Network of Legal Experts in the Field of Gender Equality. Brussels: European Commission.

Masser, Barbara, Kirsten Grass, and Michelle Nesic. 2007. " 'We Like You, but We Don't Want You': The Impact of Pregnancy in the Workplace." *Sex Roles* 57(9–10): 703–12.

Matthews, Chris. 2014. "Poor Germany: Why the East Will Never Catch Up to the West." *Fortune*, November 9. http://fortune.com/2014/11/09/germany-east-west-economy/.

Mazzola, Paolo, Stefania Maria Lorenza Rimoldi, Paolo Rossi, Marianna Noale, Federico Rea, Carla Facchini, Stefania Maggi, Giovanni Corrao, and Giorgio Annoni. 2016. "Aging in Italy: The Need for New Welfare Strategies in an Old Country." *Gerontologist* 56(3):383–90.

McCrate, Elaine. 2005. "Flexible Hours, Workplace Authority, and Compensating Wage Differentials in the US." *Feminist Economics* 11(1):11–39.

———. 2002. "Working Mothers in a Double Bind: Working Moms, Minorities Have the Most Rigid Schedules, and Are Paid Less for the Sacrifice." Briefing Paper #124 for the Economic Policy Institute.

Merton, Robert, and Elinor Barber. 1963. "Sociological Ambivalence." Pp. 91–120 in *Sociological Theory, Values, and Sociocultural Change*, edited by Edward A. Tiryakian. New York: Free Press of Glencoe.

Meulders, Danièle, Olivier Plasman, and Robert Plasman. 1994. "Atypical Employment in the European Community." Working Paper No. 2013/13464. Universite Libre de Bruxelles.

Meyersson Milgrom, Eva M., and Trond Petersen. 2006. "The Glass Ceiling in the United States and Sweden: Lessons from the Family-Friendly Corner of the World, 1970 to 1990." Pp. 156–211 in *The Declining Significance of Gender?*, edited by Francine D. Blau, Mary C. Brinton, and David B. Grusky. New York: Russell Sage.

Misra, Joya. 2003. "Women as Agents in Welfare State Development: A Cross-National Analysis of Family Allowance Adoption." *Socio-Economic Review* 1(2):185–214.

Misra, Joya, Michelle J. Budig, and Irene Boeckmann. 2011. "Work-Family Policies and the Effects of Children on Women's Employment Hours and Wages." *Community, Work and Family* 14(2):139–57.

Misra, Joya, Michelle J. Budig, and Stephanie Moller. 2007. "Reconciliation Policies and the Effects of Motherhood on Employment, Earnings, and Poverty." *Journal of Comparative Policy Analysis: Research and Practice* 9(2):135–55.

Mjömark, Per-Ola. 2016. "The Swedes and the Internet." Internet Foundation in Sweden. https://www.iis.se/english/blog/the-swedes-and-the-internet-2016/.

Modena, Francesca, and Fabio Sabatini. 2012. "I Would If I Could: Precarious Employment and Childbearing Intentions in Italy." *Review of Economics of the Household* 10(1):77–97.

Morgan, Kimberly J. 2005. "The 'Production' of Child Care: How Labor Markets Shape Social Policy and Vice Versa." *Social Politics* 12:243–63.

Mussino, Eleonora, and Ann-Zofie Duvander. 2016. "Use It or Save It? Migration Background and Parental Leave Uptake in Sweden." *European Journal of Population* 32(2):189–210.

Naldini, Manuela. 2003. *The Family in the Mediterranean Welfare States*. London: Routledge.

Naldini, Manuela, and Teresa Jurado. 2013. "Family and Welfare State Reorientation in Spain and Inertia in Italy from a European Perspective." *Population Review* 52(1):43–61.

Naldini, Manuela, and Chiara Saraceno. 2008. "Social and Family Policies in Italy: Not Frozen but Far from Structural Reforms." *Social Policy and Administration* 42(7):733–48.

National Partnership for Women and Families. 2018a. "State Paid Family Leave Insurance Laws." http://www.nationalpartnership.org/research-library/work-family/paid leave/state-paid -family-leave-laws.pdf.

———. 2018b. "Paid Sick Days: State and District Statutes." http://www.nationalpartnership .org/research-library/work-family/psd/paid-sick-days-statutes.pdf.

Noonan, Mary C., and Jennifer L. Glass. 2012. "The Hard Truth about Telecommuting." *Monthly Labor Review* 135:38–45.

Numhauser-Henning, Ann. 2015. "The Policy on Gender Equality in Sweden." European Parliament.

Organisation for Economic Co-operation and Development (OECD). 2017. "CO3.1: Educational Attainment by Gender and Expected Years in Full-Time Education." https://www .oecd.org/els/family/CO3_1_Educational_attainment_by_gender.pdf.

———. 2016a. "LMF 1.2: Maternal Employment Rates." OECD Family Database. http:// www.oecd.org/els/family/LMF_1_2_Maternal_Employment.pdf.

———. 2016b. "LMF 1.3: Maternal Employment by Partnership Status." OECD Family Database. http://www.oecd.org/els/soc/LMF_1_3_Maternal_employment_by_partnership_status.pdf.

———. 2016c. "LMF: 2.2: Patterns of Employment and the Distribution of Working Hours for Couples with Children." OECD Family Database. http://www.oecd.org/els/family/LMF-2-2-Distribution-working-hours-couple-households.pdf.

———. 2016d. "OECD Better Life Index: Work-Family Balance in Detail by Country: Sweden." http://www.oecdbetterlifeindex.org/topics/work-life-balance/.

———. 2015a. "LMF1.2 Maternal Employment Rates". https://www.oecd.org/els/family /LMF_1_2_Maternal_Employment.pdf.

————. 2015b. "OECD Income Inequality Data Update: Sweden." https://www.oecd.org/els/soc/OECD-Income-Inequality-Sweden.pdf.

————. 2014a. PF3.2: Enrollment in Childcare and Pre-School. https://www.oecd.org/els/soc/PF3_2_Enrolment_childcare_preschool.pdf.

————. 2014b. "Social Expenditure Database." www.oecd.org/social/expenditure. htm.

————. 2012a. "Closing the Gender Gap: Act Now." Italia. http://www.oecd.org/gender/closing thegap.htm.

————. 2012b. "The High Price of Motherhood." http://www.activecharts.org/share/58860e3 83bd40245e2dd3c714910916f.

————. 2006. "Starting Strong II: Early Childhood Education and Care." Paris: OECD Publishing. http://www.oecd.org/education/school/startingstrongiiearlychildhoodeducationand care.htm.

————. 2004. Female Labour Force Participation: Past Trends and Main Determinants in OECD Countries. Paris: OECD.

Ogburn, William F. 1957. "Cultural Lag as Theory." Sociology and Social Research 41(3):167–74.

Oláh, Livia Sz., and Eva M. Bernhardt. 2008. "Sweden: Combining Childbearing and Gender Equality." Demographic Research 19(28):1106–44.

Oliver, Rebecca J., and Margitta Mätzke. 2014. "Childcare Expansion in Conservative Welfare States: Policy Legacies and the Politics of Decentralized Implementation in Germany and Italy." Social Politics 21(2):167–93.

Ono, Hiroshi, and Kristen Schultz Lee. 2013. "Welfare States and the Redistribution of Happiness." Social Forces 92:789–814.

Orloff, Ann Shola. 2009a. "Gendering the Comparative Analysis of Welfare States: An Unfinished Agenda." Sociological Theory 27(3):317–43.

————. 2009b. "Should Feminists Aim for Gender Symmetry? Why a Dual-Earner/Dual-Caregiver Society Is Not Every Feminist's Utopia." Pp. 129–57 in Institutions for Gender Equality: Transforming Family Divisions of Labor, edited by Janet Gornick and Marcia Meyers. New York: Verso.

————. 1993. "Gender and the Social Rights of Citizenship: The Comparative Analysis of Gender Relations and Welfare States." American Sociological Review 58(3):308–23.

Osterman, Paul. 1995. "Work/Family Programs and the Employment Relationship." Administrative Science Quarterly 40(4):681–700.

Ostner, Ilona. 2010. "Farewell to the Family as We Know It: Family Policy Change in Germany. German Policy Studies 6:211–44.

Ostner, Ilona, Michael Reif, Hannu Turba, and Christoph Schmitt. 2003. "Family Policies in Germany." Third Report for the Project: Welfare Policy and Employment in the Context of Family Change. York, UK: Social Policy Research Unit.

Parreñas, Rhacel Salazar. 2008. "Perpetually Foreign: Filipina Migrant Domestic Workers in Rome." Pp. 99–112 in Migration and Domestic Work: A European Perspective on a Global Theme, edited by Helma Lutz. New York: Routledge.

————. 2005. Children of Global Migration: Transnational Families and Gendered Woes. Stanford, CA: Stanford University Press.

————. 2001. Servants of Globalization: Women, Migration, and Domestic Work. Stanford, CA: Stanford University Press.

Pascoe, C. J. 2007. *Dude, You're a Fag: Masculinity and Sexuality in High School*. Berkeley: University of California Press.

Patnaik, Ankita. 2016. "Reserving Time for Daddy: The Short and Long-Run Consequences of Fathers' Quotas." Social Science Research Network working paper.

Pedulla, David, and Sarah Thébaud. 2015. "Can We Finish the Revolution? Gender, Work-Family Ideals, and Institutional Constraint." *American Sociological Review* 80(1):116–39.

Perry-Jenkins, Maureen, Rena L. Repetti, and Ann C. Crouter. 2000. "Work and Family in the 1990s." *Journal of Marriage and Family* 62(4):981–98.

Pettit, Becky, and Jennifer L. Hook. 2009. *Gendered Tradeoffs: Family, Social Policy, and Inequality in Twenty-One Countries*. New York: Russell Sage.

Pfau-Effinger, Birgit. 2010. "Cultural and Institutional Contexts." Pp. 125–46 in *Dividing the Domestic: Men, Women, and Household Work in Cross-National Perspective*, edited by Judith Treas and Sonja Drobnič. Stanford, CA: Stanford University Press.

———. 2005. "Welfare State Policies and the Development of Care Arrangements." *European Societies* 7(2):321–47.

———. 1998. "Change of Family Policies in the Socio-Cultural Context of European Studies." *Comparative Social Research* 18:135–59.

Pfau-Effinger, Birgit, and Maike Smidt. 2010. "Differences in Women's Employment Patterns and Family Policies: Eastern and Western Germany." *Community, Work and Family* 14:217–32.

Pomerleau, Kyle. 2015. "How Scandinavian Countries Pay for Their Government Spending. *Tax Foundation*, June 10. https://taxfoundation.org/how-scandinavian-countries-pay-their -government-spending/.

Poulson, Stephen. 2016. "Sociological Ambivalence." *Stephen Poulson Blog*, December 9. https://stephen-poulson.blog/2016/12/09/sociological-ambivalence-2/.

Prasad, Monica. 2012. *The Land of Too Much: American Abundance and the Paradox of Poverty*. Cambridge, MA: Harvard University Press.

Prentice, Susan. 2009. "High Stakes: The 'Investable' Child and the Economic Reframing of Childcare." *Signs* 34(3):687–710.

Presser, Harriet B. 1994. "Employment Schedules among Dual-Earner Spouses and the Division of Household Labor." *American Sociological Review* 5:348–64.

———. 1989. "Can We Make Time for Children? The Economy, Work Schedules, and Child Care." *Demography* 26:523–43.

Pugh, Allison J. 2015. *The Tumbleweed Society: Working and Caring in an Age of Insecurity*. Oxford: Oxford University Press.

———. 2013. "What Good Are Interviews for Thinking about Culture? Demystifying Interpretive Analysis." *American Journal of Cultural Sociology* 1(1):42–68.

Rank, Mark R. 2011. "Rethinking American Poverty." *Contexts* 10:16–21.

Ray, Rebecca, Milla Sanes, and John Schmitt. 2013. "No-Vacation Nation Revisited." Center for Economic and Policy Research.

Rehel, Erin M. 2014. "When Dad Stays Home Too: Paternity Leave, Gender, and Parenting." *Gender & Society* 28(1):110–32.

Reston, Maeve. 2018. "Kamala Harris Urges Activists in Nevada to 'Go in Fighting.' " *CNN Politics*, March 11. https://www.cnn.com/2018/03/11/politics/harris-in-nevada/index.html.

Reyneri, Emilio. 2001. "Migrants in Irregular Employment in the Mediterranean Countries of the European Union." *International Migration Papers*, 41 (December). Geneva: ILO.

Ridgeway, Cecilia L. and Shelley J. Correll. 2000. "Limiting Inequality through Interaction: The End(s) of Gender." *Contemporary Sociology* 29(1):110–20.

Risman, Barbara. 1998. *Gender Vertigo: American Families in Transition*. New Haven, CT: Yale University Press.

Riva, Egidio. 2016. "Familialism Reoriented: Continuity and Change in Work-Family Policy in Italy." *Community, Work and Family* 19(1):21–42.

Rønsen, Marit. 2009. "Long-Term Effects of Cash for Childcare on Mothers' Labour Supply." *Labour* 23(3):507–33.

Rosenfeld, Jake. 2014. *What Unions No Longer Do*. Cambridge, MA: Harvard University Press.

Rosenfeld, Rachel A., and Arne L. Kalleberg. 1990. "A Cross-National Comparison of the Gender Gap in Income." *American Journal of Sociology* 96:69–106.

Rosenfeld, Rachel A., Heike Trappe, and Janet C. Gornick. 2004. "Gender and Work in Germany: Before and after Reunification." *Annual Review of Sociology* 30:103–24.

Rudd, Elizabeth C. 2000. "Reconceptualizing Gender in Postsocialist Transformation." *Gender & Society* 14(4):517–39.

Rürup, Bert, and Sandra Gruescu. 2003. "Familienpolitik im Interesse einer Aktiven Bevölkerungsentwicklung." Gutachten. Berlin: BMfFSFJ.

Ruspini, Elisabetta. 2009. "Italian Forms of Masculinity between Familism and Social Change." *Culture, Society and Masculinity* 1(2):121–36.

Sainsbury, Diane. 1997. *Gender, Equality, and Welfare States*. Cambridge, UK: Cambridge University Press.

Sandberg, Sheryl. 2013. *Lean In: Women, Work, and the Will to Lead*. New York: Knopf.

Saraceno, Chiara. 2011. "Childcare Needs and Childcare Policies: A Multidimensional Issue." *Current Sociology* 59(1):78–96.

Schenk, Sabine. 2003. "Employment Opportunities and Labour Market Exclusion: Towards a New Pattern of Gender Stratification?" Pp. 53–77 in *Reinventing Gender: Women in Eastern Germany since Unification*, edited by Eva Kolinsky and Hildegard Maria Nickel. London: Frank Cass.

Scherpe, Jens M. 2013. "The Legal Recognition of Same-Sex Couples in Europe and the Role of the European Court of Human Rights." *Equal Rights Review* 10:83–96.

Schlosser, Eric. 2001. *Fast Food Nation: The Dark Side of the All-American Meal*. New York: Houghton Mifflin.

Schober, Pia Sophia, and Juliane F. Stahl. 2014. "Childcare Trends in Germany: Increasing Socio-Economic Disparities in East and West." *DIW Economic Bulletin* 4(11):51–58.

Schulte, Brigid. 2013. "Parents Miss Work, Lose Jobs Trying to Get Childcare Subsidy." *Washington Post*, May 15. https://www.washingtonpost.com/local/parents-miss-work-lose-jobs-trying -to-get-child-care-subsidy/2013/05/15/3031ac2c-ba59-11e2-b94c-b684dda07add_story.html ?noredirect=on&utm_term=.da509ab0b2bd.

Schulte, Brigid, and Alieza Durana. 2016. "The New America Care Report." https://www .newamerica.org/better-life-lab/policy-papers/new-america-care-report/.

Schutz, Alfred. 1970. *Alfred Schutz on Phenomenology and Social Relations*. Chicago: University of Chicago Press.

Segarra, Marielle. 2015. "How Berlin Is Helping Immigrants and Trying to Get Residents to Think Differently about National Identity." *Newsworks*, June 29. https://whyy.org/articles/how-berlin-is-helping-immigrants-and-trying-to-get-residents-to-think-differently-about-national-identity/.

Seward, Rudy Raw, Dale E. Yeatts, Lisa K. Zotarelli, and Ryan G. Fletcher. 2006. "Fathers Taking Parental Leave and Their Involvement with Children." *Community, Work and Family* 9(1):1–9.

Siaroff, Alan. 1994. "Work, Welfare, and Gender Equality: A New Typology." Pp. 82–100 in *Gendering Welfare States*, edited by Diane Sainsbury. London: Sage.

Simonazzi, Annamaria, Paola Villa, Federico Lucidi, and Paolo Naticchioni. 2009. "Continuity and Change in the Italian Model: Italy's Laborious Convergence towards the European Social Model." Pp. 201–22 in *European Employment Models in Flux*, edited by Gerhard Bosch, Steffen Lehndorff, and Jill Rubery. London: Palgrave Macmillan.

Smale, Alison, and Claire Cain Miller. 2015. "Germany Sets Gender Quota in Boardrooms." *New York Times*, March 6. https://www.nytimes.com/2015/03/07/world/europe/german-law-requires-more-women-on-corporate-boards.html.

Solnit, Rebecca. 2016. *Hope in the Dark: Untold Histories, Wild Possibilities*. Chicago: Haymarket Books.

Spiegel. 2015. "Dark Germany, Bright Germany: Which Side Will Prevail under Strain of Refugees?" August 31. http://www.spiegel.de/international/germany/spiegel-cover-story-the-new-germany-a-1050406.html.

———. 2013. "A 200-Billion-Euro Waste: Why Germany Is Failing to Boost Its Birth Rate." February 5. http://www.spiegel.de/international/germany/study-shows-germany-wasting-billions-on-failed-family-policy-a-881637.html.

———. 2011. "A Land without Children: Why Won't Germans Have More Babies?" August 12. http://www.spiegel.de/international/germany/a-land-without-children-why-won-t-germans-have-more-babies-a-779741.html.

Statistisches Bundesamt. 2016. "Migration and Integration." https://www.destatis.de/EN/FactsFigures/SocietyState/Population/MigrationIntegration/MigrationIntegration.html.

Statistics Sweden. 2014. "Labor Force Surveys (LFS)." http://www.statistikdatabasen.scb.se.

Stein, Perry. 2015. "Starting Today, the D.C. Minimum Wage Jumps to $10.50." *Washington Post*, July 1. https://www.washingtonpost.com/news/local/wp/2015/07/01/starting-today-the-d-c-minimum-wage-jumps-to-10-50/?utm_term=.af88a4521943.

Stier, Haya, Noah Lewin-Epstein, and Michael Braun. 2001. "Welfare Regimes, Family-Supportive Policies, and Women's Employment along the Life-Course." *American Journal of Sociology* 106:1731–60.

Stone, Pamela. 2007. *Opting Out? Why Women Really Quit Careers and Head Home*. Berkeley: University of California Press.

Story, Mary, Karen M. Kaphingst, and Simone French. 2006. "The Role of Child Care Settings in Obesity Prevention." *Future of Children* 16(1):143–68.

Struffolino, Emanuela, Matthias Studer, and Annette Eva Fasang. 2015. "Gender, Education, and the Family Life Courses in East and West Germany: Insights from New Sequence Analysis Techniques." *Advances in Life Course Research* 29:66–79.

Suchman, Mark C. 1997. "On beyond Interest: Rational, Normative and Cognitive Perspectives in the Social Scientific Study of Law." *Wisconsin Law Review* 475–77.

Sunstein, Cass R. 1996a. "Social Norms and Social Roles." *Columbia Law Review* 96(4):903–68.

Sunstein, Cass. R. 1996b. "On the Expressive Function of Law." *University of Pennsylvania Law Review* 144(5):2021–53.

Svensk författningssamling. 2016. "Lag om upphävande av lagen (2008:313) om jämställdhets-bonus." December 20. http://www.notisum.se/rnp/sls/sfs/20161295.pdf.

Swedish Institute. 2018. "Preschool–A Place to Grow." https://sweden.se/society/play-is-key -in-preschool/.

———. 2013. "Facts about Sweden. Gender Equality: The Swedish Approach to Fairness." October. https://www.sweden.se/wp-content/uploads/2013/11/Gender-equality-high-res.pdf.

Swidler, Ann. 1986. "Culture in Action: Symbols and Strategies." *American Sociological Review* 1:273–86.

Szydlik, Marc. 2002. "Vocational Education and Labour Markets in Deregulated, Flexibly Co-ordinated and Planned Societies." *European Societies* 4(1):79–105.

Thelen, Kathleen. 2014. *Varieties of Liberalization and the New Politics of Social Solidarity*. Cambridge, UK: Cambridge University Press.

Thistle, Susan. 2006. *From Marriage to the Market: The Transformation of Women's Lives and Work*. Berkeley: University of California Press.

Thorsén, Yvonne, and Thomas Brunk. 2009. "Working Time in the European Union: Sweden." European Observatory of Working Life. https://www.eurofound.europa.eu/publications /report/2009/working-time-in-the-european-union-sweden.

Törnkvist, Ann. 2013. "Is the Swedish Model the Fairest of Them All?" *Local*, November 12. https:// www.thelocal.se/20131112/is-the-swedish-model-the-fairest-of-them-all-labour-employment.

Torrisi, Claudia. 2017. "Non Una di Meno Protests for Women's Rights: 'Enough Is Enough.'" *Open Democracy*, October 3. https://www.opendemocracy.net/protest/non-una-di-meno.

Trappe, Heike, and Rachel A. Rosenfeld. 1998. "A Comparison of Job-Shifting Patterns in the Former East Germany and the Former West Germany." *European Sociological Review* 14(4):343–68.

US Bureau of Labor Statistics. 2017. "Employment Characteristics of Families—2017." https:// www.bls.gov/news.release/pdf/famee.pdf.

———. 2013. "Employee Benefits Survey. Leave Benefits: Access." http://www.bls.gov/ncs/ ebs/benefits/2013/ownership/private/table21a.htm.

US Census Bureau. 2012. "Facts for Features. Mother's Day: May 13, 2012." https://www.census .gov/newsroom/releases/archives/facts_for_features_special_editions/cb12-ff08.html.

US Department of Labor. 2015. "Paternity Leave: Why Parental Leave for Fathers Is So Important for Working Families." DOL Policy Brief.

Vaisey, Stephen. 2014. "Is Interviewing Compatible with the Dual-Process Model of Culture?" *American Journal of Cultural Sociology* 2(1):150–58.

Vaughan-Whitehead, Daniel, ed. 2016. *Europe's Disappearing Middle Class? Evidence from the World of Work*. Cheltenham, UK: Edward Elgar.

Villalobos, Ana. 2014. *Motherload: Making It All Better in Insecure Times*. Berkeley: University of California Press.

Wall, Glenda. 2001. "Moral Constructions of Motherhood in Breastfeeding Discourse." *Gender & Society* 15(4):592–610.

Wallace, David Foster. 2005. "This Is Water." Kenyon College Commencement Address May 21. https://genius.com/David-foster-wallace-this-is-water-kenyon-college-commencement-address-2005-annotated.

Walzer, Michael. 1983. *Spheres of Justice: A Defense of Pluralism and Equality*. New York: Basic Books.

Webber, Gretchen, and Christine L. Williams. 2008. "Part-Time Work and the Gender Division of Labor." *Qualitative Sociology* 31:15–36.

———. 2007. "Mothers in 'Good' and 'Bad' Part-Time Jobs: Different Problems, Same Results." *Gender & Society* 22(6):752–77.

Weiss, Robert. 1994. *Learning from Strangers: The Art and Method of Qualitative Interview Studies*. New York: Free Press.

Wente, Margaret. 2015. "Sweden's Ugly Immigration Problem." *Globe and Mail*, September 11.

Western, Bruce. 1999. *Between Class and Market: Postwar Unionization in the Capitalist Democracies*. Princeton, NJ: Princeton University Press.

Wiles, David. 2016. "Why Swedes Are Okay with Paying Taxes." https://sweden.se/society/why-swedes-are-okay-with-paying-taxes/.

Williams, Christine L. 1995. *Still a Man's World: Men Who Do Women's Work*. Berkeley: University of California Press.

Williams, Christine L., Chandra Muller, and Kristine Kilanski. 2012. "Gendered Organizations in the New Economy." *Gender & Society* 26(4):549–73.

Williams, Joan C. 2010. *Reshaping the Work-Family Debate: Why Men and Class Matter*. Cambridge, MA: Harvard University Press.

———. 2000. *Unbending Gender: Why Family and Work Conflict and What to Do about It*. Oxford, UK: Oxford University Press.

Williams, Joan C., Mary Blair-Loy, and Jennifer L. Berdahl. 2013. "Cultural Schemas, Social Class, and the Flexibility Stigma." *Journal of Social Issues* 69(2):209–34.

Williams, Joan C., Jessica Manvell, and Stephanie Bornstein. 2006. " 'Opt Out' or Pushed Out? How the Press Covers Work/Family Conflict." San Francisco: UC Hastings College of Law Center for Work-Life Law.

Wolf, Naomi. 2012. "Why Women Still Can't Ask the Right Questions." *Project Syndicate*, June 30. http://www.project-syndicate.org/commentary/why-women-still-can-t-ask-the-right-questions.

World Bank. 2018. *Women, Business and the Law 2018*. https://openknowledge.worldbank.org/bitstream/handle/10986/29498/9781464812521.pdf.

World Values Survey. 2011. "Online Data Analysis." http://www.worldvaluessurvey.org/WVS Online.jsp.

Wright, Erik Olin. 2011. "Real Utopias." *Contexts* 10(2):36–42.

Zelizer, Viviana A. 1985. *Pricing the Priceless Child: The Changing Social Value of Children*. Princeton, NJ: Princeton University Press.

Ziefle, Andrea, and Markus Gangl. 2014. "Do Women Respond to Changes in Family Policy? A Quasi-Experimental Study of the Duration of Mothers' Employment Interruptions in Germany." *European Sociological Review* 30:562–81.

Index

NOTE: Page numbers followed by *f* indicate a figure.

Discussion Questions

1. Caitlyn Collins notes that "women's work-family conflict is a national crisis." Do you agree or disagree and why?

2. In 2013, the UN and the World Economic Forum ranked Sweden as the most gender-egalitarian nation in the world and first for women's economic opportunities. Its policies are often looked to as a model for others. As you read the details of Sweden's work-family policy, did anything surprise you? Discuss some of the advantages of the policies, both inside and outside the home.

3. The Swedish welfare system and society generally expect all adults, including mothers, to engage in paid work. Are there any unintended consequences of this system?

4. The German case is particularly useful in illuminating the ways in which policy alone cannot change things for women. How were the experiences of women in East Germany different from those in the West?

5. How does the cultural trope of the *mammoni* ("mama's boys") in Italy come into play in discussions about the division of household labor?

6. Collins notes that Italian women were unique in "working the system" to try to resolve their work-family conflict. Did you feel sympathetic toward this strategy? Why or why not?

7. What was the most striking difference in how American women experienced work-family conflict and stress in comparison with the women from Sweden, Germany, and Italy?

8. Throughout the book, many of Collins's respondents talk about what it means to be a "good mother." Discuss the similarities and differences in each country.

9. Compare and contrast the practicality and experience of part-time work in Sweden, Germany, Italy, and the United States.

10. If you were to advise an American politician about which policies might improve the situation in the United States, what would you suggest and why?